Living Space in Fact and Fiction

The Dairy at Blaise

Living Space
in
Fact and Fiction

Philippa Tristram

ROUTLEDGE
London and New York

First published in 1989 by
Routledge
11 New Fetter Lane, London EC4P 4EE
29 West 35th Street, New York NY 10001

© 1989 Philippa Tristram

Printed in Great Britain by
T.J. Press (Padstow) Ltd, Cornwall

Typeset by Columns of Reading

British Library Cataloguing in Publication Data
Tristram, Philippa, 1934–
Living space in fact and fiction.
Fiction in English, 1740–
1914. Special themes.
Great Britain. Residences.
Critical studies.
I. Title
307′.336

Library of Congress Cataloging in Publication Data
Tristram. Philippa.
Living space in fact and fiction / Philippa Tristram.
p. cm.
Bibliography: p.
Includes index.
1. English fiction—History and criticism. 2. Setting
(Literature) 3. Dwellings in literature. 4. Architecture,
Domestic, in literature. 5. Domestic fiction, English—History and
criticism. 6. Family in literature. 7. Dwellings—Great Britain.
8. Architecture, Domestic—Great Britain. 9. Family—Great
Britain—History. I. Title.
PR830.S48T75 1989
823′.009′355—dc19   89–15801

ISBN 0–415–01279–1

To Philip

Contents

Illustrations

Acknowledgements

The illustrations specified are reproduced by kind permission of the following: Ashmolean Museum, 91; Bridgeman Art Library, 75; Bristol City Museum and Art Gallery, 24, 55, 99; British Architectural Library, RIBA, London, cover illustration and frontispiece; British Library, 7a, 7b, 18, 20, 80; Mary Castell, 45; James Chambers, 2; Joan and John Clerk, sketch by Geoffrey A. Walker, 100; Gregg International Publishing Ltd, 4, 6, 8a, 8b, 8c, 14, 17, 25, 27a, 27b, 64, 65, 77, 78, 96a; Guildhall Museum, Rochester, 12b; Charles G. Harper, *The Hardy Country* 1904, published by A. & C. Black, 46, 47, 85; Harris Museum and Art Gallery, Preston, 93; Professor John Hunt, 3a, 48; Kunsthistorisches Museum, Vienna, 81; Kupferstichkabinett, West Berlin, 82; Victorian Library Editions, Leicester University Press, 9, 19, 29, 30, 31, 33, 34a, 34c, 35, 40, 60, 73; Manchester Public Libraries, 95; Oxfordshire Museum Services, drawing by D. Aylwin, 43; Arthur Raistrick, 59; Lady Sempill, 90; Tate Gallery, 92, 97, 98; Victoria and Albert Museum, 5; Vicky Wheeler, 1, 61a. The author and publisher have made every effort to obtain permission to reproduce copyright material throughout this book. If any proper acknowledgement has not been made, or permission not received, we would invite any copyright holder to inform us of this oversight.

I am deeply indebted to Mary Castell, Anne Smith, and Annys Wilson for their enduring enthusiasm and interest; to Jacques Berthoud and Philip Brockbank for their constructive criticisms of the text; to Derek Linstrum and Richard Verdi for their generous professional advice; to Corinne and Keith Bennett who tell me houses like stories; to Keith Parker, librarian of the Architecture Collection at the University of York, for his inexhaustible helpfulness and patience; to Gordon Smith and David Whiteley, photographers for the University of York, who have taken so many excellent photographs for me; to Andrew Wheatcroft for his incisive editorial encouragement; and finally to Hugo Tristram for all the times he didn't interrupt.

1

The Dairy House at Blaise
Facts and fictions

The drawing that forms the frontispiece to this book is poised on the borderline between fact and fiction. It could illustrate that symbolic episode, common to fairy-tales and Gothic novels, in which the heroine, lost in a dark wood, comes suddenly upon a sunlit clearing. The cottage at its centre is all that such a refuge from a cruel world should be: modest, but not mean; quaint, but not peculiar; 'antiqued', but perfectly comfortable and convenient. Heroines like Mrs Radcliffe's Emily in *The Mysteries of Udolpho* (1794)* are used to living in much grander houses; but this little building is designed to reassure even the most genteel with a sense of arrival, so that the wanderer feels instantly 'at home'.

The drawing does not, however, illustrate a fiction. It is an actual design, almost contemporary with *Udolpho*, by the great Regency architect, John Nash, sketched by John Adey Repton (son of Humphry) in his brother's notebook. The building itself exists, although it is rather more prosaic in its material than in its imagined form; it is close to the mansion and the brooding trees are gone. Nevertheless, in a different sense, it remains a fiction, for appearances – as such stories themselves sometimes remind us – can deceive. It is not the poor man's shelter it pretends to be, but a rich man's plaything, related to that larger Dairy House which Richardson's heroine, Clarissa, inherits half a century earlier from her grandfather. Throughout her long seduction in city streets, Clarissa's mind returns continually to her Dairy House, both as an image of what might still be, but also of what was – her virginal nature.

Like the 'graceful habit' that Clarissa assumes to play the milkmaid's part,[1] the Dairy House at Blaise is fancy-dress, but it serves to emphasize the fictional nature of more serious buildings. Every new-built house or freshly furnished room is a fiction of the life intended to be lived there. Every inhabited building or interior tells a different story, of how life is or was: 'The joyous shot at how things ought to be/Long fallen wide'.[2] Moreover, a house, like a novel, is a small world defined against, but also reflecting, a larger one. The plan and appearance of houses, the way they are

*Date of publication is given in the text or a note when a primary source is first mentioned. Dates are also given in the index.

1

furnished, mirror the social values of their time; but the best define themselves against those values, inheriting the past, receiving the present, but shaping the future. The same can of course be said of a great novel, for if houses are like stories, stories are also like houses. It is no accident that many of the terms used in critical discourse – 'structure', 'aspect', 'outlook', even 'character' – are related to domestic architecture; or that the titles of so many great nineteenth-century novels were taken from the houses at their centre – *Mansfield Park*, *Wuthering Heights*, *Bleak House*, *The Mill on the Floss*. Most of life, after all, is spent within four walls, and the space they define, the objects that fill them, the prospects on which they open, inevitably influence and express our consciousness. Victorian writers often present themselves as speaking from their fireside to those of their readers, while the stories they tell, like those of Dickens's narrator, Master Humphrey, may be prompted by the objects that surround them. Because the novel is invincibly domestic, it can tell us much about the space we live in; equally, designs for houses and their furnishings can reveal hidden aspects of the novelist's art.

From the beginning the house and the novel are interconnected, for the eighteenth century, which saw the rise of the novel, was also the great age of the English house. 'Every Man Now, be his fortune what it will, is to be *doing something at his Place*, as the fashionable Phrase is,' writes an enthusiast in 1739;[3] 'and you hardly meet with any Body, who, after the first Compliments, does not inform you, that he is *in Mortar* and *moving of Earth*; the modest terms for Building and Gardening'. Mr B, the hero of Richardson's *Pamela*, which began publication in the following year, is a man of his time. Having failed to seduce his late mother's maid, he marries her, thus freeing his mind for more important matters. He sets to work at once, restoring the chapel at his place in Lincolnshire, then moves rapidly on from his main house in Bedfordshire (already improved) to a third estate in Kent which needs attention. There he is into the moving of earth as well as mortar: having repaired the house, he constructs a vista culminating in a 'pretty alcove' of his own design,[4] thus providing a prospect to view through the large panes of glass he has let into his lattices (he disapproves of the new fashion for sash-windows). Mr B's altered appetite – for improvements as distinct from ladies' maids – is proof of his moral reformation, for the villainy of Lovelace in *Clarissa* (1748–9) is signified by his neglect of his country seat; while the excellence of Sir Charles Grandison, Richardson's pattern hero, is indicated by his obsession with mortar, creating a little heaven on the earth of his estate. On the smaller scale of his country villa, Richardson himself was equally active, earning the admiration of Miss Talbot who visited him there in 1756:

> His Villa is fitted up in the same Style his Books are writ. Every Minute detail attended to, yet every one with a view to its being useful or pleasing. Not an inch in his Garden unimproved or unadorned, his very Poultry made happy by fifty little neat Contrivances.[5]

Richardson is not of course the first great English novelist, but he is the first to be interested in houses, for the characters created by his predecessor, Defoe, and his contemporary, Fielding, are too often on the move to develop much awareness of their living space. In the first half of the eighteenth century the roads of England improved immeasurably, thanks to 400 separate Acts of Parliament,[6] and travel became a popular pursuit with gentlemen. Throughout the Georgian period, novels – in part as a consequence – tend to divide between those who travel in order to broaden the mind, and those who choose to do so by staying at home. The travels of Sir Charles Grandison are censured by his Harriet with the remark that the sight of ruins on the Tour, which most gentlemen (including himself) then made of Europe, is actually less instructive than the knowledge of them to be gained from books.[7] She has obviously learnt from her creator, who amended Defoe's actual *Tour through the Whole Island of Great Britain* (1724–6), by introducing with the aid of books further description of historic buildings,[8] without venturing further into the country than his garden. Although the eighteenth-century house was essentially public with its absence of corridors and its interconnecting rooms, expressing what Henry Wotton had described in 1624 as 'the fond Ambition of displaying to a Stranger all our Furniture at one Sight',[9] it nevertheless made generous provision for those who wished to make their journeys privately, within the mind. Even a relatively small

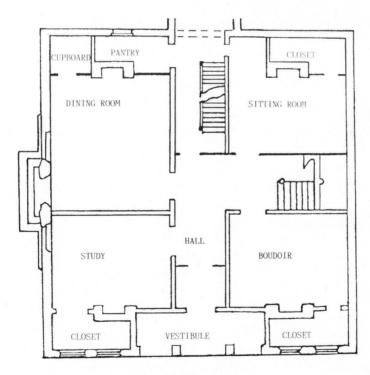

1 Planning for privacy

2 Blenheim Palace

building, like Fenton House in Hampstead (Fig. 1), is liberally provided with rooms of retreat, while Richardson himself rejoiced at having closets on each of the three floors of his house at Fulham. The mid-century architect Robert Morris makes the case for them with fervour: 'the *Geographer* can travel from one Country to another, through various Climates, over Sea and Land . . . and yet be only retir'd to his Closet'.[10] He even recommends their equivalent, like Mr B's alcove, in the garden: 'Such Retreats would give unspeakable Raptures to a Soul capable to pursue a Tract of Thought in Infinity of Space.'[11] Improvements and self-improvement are interrelated.

As that implies, Palladian architecture, which changed the face of England in the eighteenth century, is from one point of view a moral movement. Pope's Fourth Moral Essay, addressed in 1731 to its great advocate, Lord Burlington, makes this clear in its subject title, 'The Use of Riches'. The new taste rejected Baroque extravagances such as Vanbrugh's Blenheim (Fig. 2) celebrating Marlborough's great victory in 1704, where architecture expresses pomp and circumstance, in favour of good sense, proportion, use, the harmony of a building with its site (Fig. 92). It may seem strange that Vitruvius, a Roman architect in the first century BC, interpreted by Palladio, an Italian in the sixteenth century, should have made such a mark upon Georgian England, but the values of Augustan Rome and Renaissance Italy have much in common with those of the Enlightenment.[12] More specifically, Palladio's clients were in search of the same satisfactions as many eighteenth-century aristocrats, who also wished, when called from town to their estates, to combine the life of a gentleman farmer with that of a cultivated humanist. Palladian houses were not new in England – Coleshill in Berkshire, designed by Roger Pratt in 1650, already had many of their characteristics – but it was the publication of two books in 1715 that established the style as the dominant, even exclusive, taste. One was the first volume of *Vitruvius Britannicus* with an introduction by Colen Campbell in which he attacked Baroque and called for a return to antique simplicity; the other a translation of the *Quattro Libri* of Palladio, to whose publication the mother of Lord Burlington subscribed. At Chiswick Burlington built himself a villa, modelled on the Villa Rotonda of Palladio, but Pope at Twickenham had a villa too which was also expressive of Palladian principles (Figs 3a, 3b).

The eighteenth-century novel is concerned with much the same social range as the designs of architects. Moreover, when its characters stay at home, the walls of their houses, though rarely described in any detail, reflect the values and aspirations of Palladian architecture. That absence of detail is, however, most surprising, given this sensitivity to living space, for there are almost none of those sustained descriptions that become almost routine in Victorian fiction. John Cornforth notes a similar discrepancy in painting,[13] where the outsides of houses, particularly in relation to their setting, are frequently recorded, their interiors rarely so. His explanation – that the emphasis falls on portraiture without the contextual detail of Dutch painting – is almost as insufficient as the literary critic's – that this 'technique' was not yet included in the novelist's repertoire. In relation to literature at least, two other explanations suggest themselves. Throughout the eighteenth century and into the Regency, houses were – to a modern eye – extremely bare (Fig. 7a). Unless in use, both tables and chairs were ranged against the wall, where some heavier items might belong to a fixed position, forming a part of the mural decoration, while the rest were designed to be portable. As Adam Smith remarks in 1759: 'When a person comes into his chamber, and finds the chairs all standing in the middle of the room, he is angry with his servant, and rather than see them continue in that disorder, perhaps takes the trouble himself to set them all in their places with their backs to the wall.'[14] The room, in consequence, is dominated not by its furniture but by its structural features – walls, floor, and ceiling; windows, doors, and fireplace. As a result, the novelist tends to sense, rather than see, domestic environments, registering the definition of space and not its detail. A second explanation may lie in what is often called the 'Rule of Taste'. Just as a gentleman was defined by his likeness to other gentlemen, so a house should resemble other houses of a similar standing; it would therefore be redundant to describe what every courteous author must assume was already known to his readers. When Goldsmith writes in *The Vicar of Wakefield* (1766) of 'an elegant house, situate in a fine country, and a good neighbourhood', or remarks of a room in an unusually magnificent mansion merely that it was 'perfectly elegant and modern',[15] he clearly feels that he has said enough, since every reader can gloss those adjectives himself. It is the *inappropriate* context

3(a) Pope's villa

3(b) Pope's grotto

that needs description, like the room in which Clarissa is imprisoned for debt.[16] In all the many pages of that novel, it is the sole interior to be described at any length, and in such detail that Richardson even mentions the rusty heads of tacks retaining scraps of a former wallpaper.

Even beyond the middle of the century, when Palladian architecture acquires some rivals, the description of houses does not become more frequent. Those who travelled went further still and discovered Greece, but it too is 'classical' and altered the decoration of Palladian houses rather than their design. The Gothic, a more formidable opponent, might have been expected to have had a greater impact on the depiction of fictional living space. In the first place, it is the antithesis of the classical: its inspiration is indigenous, not foreign; Christian, not pagan; medieval or even Tudor, not antique. Its structures, moreover, are irregular, supposedly answering to the needs of those within, not dictated from without by the demands of symmetry; their emphasis is vertical, aspiring heavenwards (as the Victorians frequently remarked), where that of the classical house is horizontal, connecting with the values of this earth. One style directs itself to individualism; the other seeks harmony with a social whole. Second, the affection for medievalism is literary before it is architectural, and architects themselves invariably refer it back to the same lines from Milton's *Il Penseroso* (c. 1631):

> But let my due feet never fail,
> To walk the studious Cloysters pale,
> And love the high embowed Roof,
> With antick pillars massy proof,
> And storied Windows richly dight
> Casting a dimm religious light.[17]

Throughout the social and satiric age of Augustan reason, poets continued to walk that way from time to time, indulging their anti-rational and unsociable propensities for solitude, melancholy, and intense emotion. Pope's confidently discursive *Essay on Man* (1733–4) co-exists with his anguished Gothic soliloquy, *Eloisa to Abelard* (1717); while his Palladian villa at Twickenham with its open, balanced façade (Fig. 3a) concealed a subterranean grotto (Fig. 3b) connecting with his sombre garden across the road. Horace Walpole describes the effect of walking through the grotto into the garden in language that both recalls *Eloisa to Abelard* and anticipates descriptions in the Gothic novel: 'The passing through the gloom from the grotto to opening day; the retiring and again assembling shades; the dusky groves, the larger lawn, and the solemnity of the termination at the cypresses that led up to his mother's tomb, are managed with exquisite judgement.'[18]

The Gothic, as can be seen, invites description, but in terms that are generalized and atmospheric rather than particular and domestic. This may relate to its revival in the garden, where the style, as architecture, first secured a footing. At the beginning of the century it is still a term of abuse, equivalent to 'Hun' or 'Vandal', denoting 'barbaric' as its Renaissance originators intended: 'Ah, rustic, ruder than Gothic!'

Millamant accuses Sir Wilfull Witwoud in Congreve's *Way of the World* (1700).[19] But the taste for landscape gardening encouraged buildings as the focus for a vista, and these were not always (as Mr B's alcove probably was) classical in style. Batty Langley, whose pattern books did so much to disseminate Palladianism, suggests in 1728 that 'such Walks, whose Views cannot be extended, [should] terminate in Woods, Forests, mishapen Rocks, strange Precipices, Mountains, old Ruins, grand Buildings, &c.'.[20] For those whose grounds are not naturally endowed with these facilities, Paul Decker provides, in 1759, 'Gothic Architecture Decorated, Consisting of a Large Collection of Temples, Banqueting, Summer and Green Houses; Gazebo's, Alcoves; Faced, Garden and Umbrello'd Seats; Terminari's, and Rustic Garden Seats; Rout Houses, and Hermitages for Summer and Winter; Obelisks, Pyramids, &c.'.[21] In 1755 Rousseau's discovery of the noble savage[22] had made some men think twice before dismissing the barbaric out of hand, and Milton's 'arched walks of twilight groves' were thought to resemble the aspiring arches of the Gothic church. The word began to mean 'natural' rather than 'barbaric', and the style, in some circles at least, became respectable. Horace Walpole also had a villa at Twickenham, Strawberry Hill; but he seems to have been inspired less by the Palladian principles of his neighbour's house than by Pope's grotto and the sensations of his garden. He began to redesign and embellish Strawberry Hill on Gothic lines in the 1750s. In 1764 he wrote there the first Gothic novel, *The Castle of Otranto*, which, in his *Description of Strawberry Hill*, he connects directly with the house: 'A very proper habitation of, as it was the scene that inspired, the author.'[23]

Neither the novel nor the house, however, treat Gothic as more than a superficial application to values that remain essentially Palladian. The Castle of Otranto is as unspecific (and discomforting) as Walpole's description of Pope's grotto: 'An awful silence reigned throughout these subterraneous regions, except now and then some blasts of wind that shook the doors she had passed, and which grating on the rusty hinges were re-echoed through that long labyrinth of darkness.'[24] The prose seems about to burgeon into satire on the very taste that it advances – reminding one that its author was himself convinced that all true poetry had died with Pope. Strawberry Hill itself, like the Dairy at Blaise, is only superficially irregular, for the disposition of the house remains symmetrical. The Gothic decoration of its rooms expresses a variety of moods, but in some instances, as in the library (Fig. 4), qualifies for the adjectives of the Gothic novel. More importantly, the emphasis still falls on structural features, not on furnishing, inviting Sir John Soane's criticism of the Adam (classical) house – that its interior was too architectural, and insufficiently distinguished from the exterior.[25]

William Beckford, Walpole's successor as both Gothic novelist and builder, carried his imaginings too far to have had as much effect on either fact or fiction. In 1796 he began to replace his father's classical mansion, which he detested, with a grandiose creation, Fonthill Abbey (Fig. 5), whose tower was intended to rival his neighbour, Salisbury Cathedral. Like the palace in his exotic novel, *Vathek* (1786), Fonthill Abbey both resembled Babel and suffered the same fate. Beckford was as

4 The library, Strawberry Hill

5 Fonthill Abbey

impatient as Vathek to complete his building, but did not have a magical assistant; the tower twice collapsed, for the last time in 1825, and Beckford's contractor confessed upon his death-bed that he had not provided it with foundations, although they had been specified and paid for. Nothing today remains of Fonthill Abbey, though Strawberry Hill is still more or less intact. Like its predecessor, Fonthill Abbey is said to have been a symmetrical building in Gothic disguise, while *Vathek* provides even less domestic detail than *Otranto* – the adjective, indeed, scarcely applies. The excesses of Vathek do have some emulators – in Matthew Lewis's *The Monk* (1796), and even in the Victorian novels of Sheridan Le Fanu – but it is the polite feeling of *Otranto* that flourishes in the hugely popular Gothic novels of the Regency. Fonthill Abbey, however, was not a success that anyone would (or could)

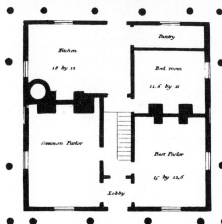

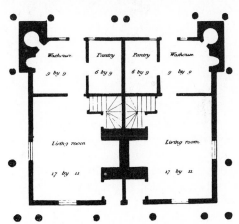

Plan as a Single Cottage   *Plan as a Double Cottage*

6 Single or double cottage *ornée*

have chosen to emulate, where the playfulness of Strawberry Hill was infectious, and moreover suited to much humbler houses.

By the beginning of the nineteenth century, encouraged by the new taste for the Picturesque,[26] Gothic had established its domestic footing, at least in a decorative sense, and had even imported with it other exotica – Chinese and Egyptian, Arabic and Indian. It was, moreover, widely disseminated by a profusion of pattern books which concentrated upon smaller houses. These were sometimes intended, as in the eighteenth century, both to provide an event in the garden and house a labourer; but they were also directed to those of the middle class who might want a retreat in the country or a retirement home. The second type of house was described as a 'cottage *ornée*', 'a new species of building', according to one designer, 'not the habitation of the laborious, but of the affluent, of the man of study, of science, or of leisure'.[27] Occasionally the same design could serve both purposes, as can be seen in Figure 6 where the single version is intended for a retired couple, the double for two families of labourers. Its external appearance, 'of a grotesque Gothic character . . . and pointed Gothic arches',[28] with those sharp contrasts of light and shade recommended by the Picturesque, is applied to the standard plan of a four-square Georgian house. Most superior buildings also sustained their Palladian principles, but they became less formal: for example, the central salon, the grand reception room of the Palladian house (Fig. 14), lost some of its ceremonial identity and might even be occupied by a billiard table; women were no longer debarred from the library, as they had been for much of the previous century. 'The Comfort of the Billiard Table here is very great,' Jane Austen writes from her brother's house at Godmersham (Fig. 16).[29] 'It draws all the Gentlemen to it whenever they are within, especially after Dinner, so that my B^r Fanny & I have the Library to ourselves in delightful quiet.' Private rooms became almost a thing of the past, for closets went out of fashion; bedrooms, which had formerly existed on all floors, went upstairs, but, although their dressing-rooms were often furnished as boudoirs, these were out-of- bounds from after breakfast, except in times of illness. When her mother is convalescing, the novelty of spending her days in a dressing-room appeals to Jane Austen: 'I always feel so much more elegant in it than in the parlour.'[30]

To the novelist, that alteration in domestic mores seems at first sight to have had more significance than the increasing diversity of styles. Where Richardson wrote his novels, and his heroines their letters, in little closets removed from the public eye, Jane Austen and her heroines spend their time in parlours which are anything but private. The apprehension of the house thus alters from the personal to the social: his drama is the inward one of conscience; hers, the outward trial by social ordeal. 'I should hardly like to live with her ladies and gentlemen in their elegant but confined houses,' Charlotte Brontë writes in 1848,[31] reporting the sensations of a reader rather than commenting upon description, for Jane Austen's contexts are, like Richardson's, still sensed rather than seen. The definition of living space continues to be of more importance than its detail, and even Gothic novelists, who are fond of adjectives and often describe the landscape at some length, elaborate very little on interiors.

The model remains the great house, not the small one, and great houses still try to be like other great houses. Even *Hermsprong* (1796), one of the first political novels, whose eponymous hero models himself on the noble savage, confines itself to great houses or to those that emulate them, while the savage himself, in true romance tradition, turns out to be an aristocrat, and the rightful heir to his wicked uncle's estate.

On the other hand, if one reads between the lines, or simply attends with care to domestic allusions, signs of incipient change are numerous. It is not perhaps surprising that Sir Walter Scott, with his antiquarian interest, should have had a sharp eye for architectural difference, or even for interior detail, provided it could claim to be antique. But even writers who have no historical sense, like Mrs Radcliffe (who provides Emily in 1584 with what is clearly a cottage *ornée*, complete with greenhouse, 'two excellent sitting rooms' and a rustic hall),[32] are much more observant than their predecessors of different types of houses in the landscape. Jane Austen is less descriptive than either the Gothic novelists or Scott, for although her letters are full of domestic detail and she enjoins her sister, Cassandra, to omit nothing in her account of a house – 'For one's own dear self, one ascertains & remembers everything'[33] – novels are not written for 'one's own dear self', and she was not one to inflict what she did not enjoy – 'your descriptions are often more minute than will be liked',[34] she warns her niece, Anna Austen, an aspiring writer. Nevertheless, her sparing detail is invariably more fully indicative of social change than that of her more prolix contemporaries.[35] The village of Uppercross in *Persuasion* (1818), for example, 'had been completely in the old English style', two houses only showing themselves to be superior to the dwellings of yeomen and labourers: the squire's mansion with its high walls and great gates, and 'the compact, tight parsonage, enclosed in its own neat garden'.[36] That traditional patriarchy, two classes walled off from each other yet co-existent, is disturbed by the elevation of a farmhouse into a cottage *ornée* 'with its viranda, French windows, and other prettinesses', for this contends with the great house for the traveller's eye. Those new French windows are favoured by Sir John Soane, the Regency architect, because they provide a cheerful effect,[37] although he also complains that windows generally have become preposterously large.[38] A similar ambivalence can be sensed in Uppercross Cottage: on the one hand, its windows can relieve a social occasion by allowing those under stress to admire the view and recover their composure; on the other, the tendency of the younger generation to appear at those windows unannounced, and even to come in by them, suggests a social life that has become altogether too informal and erratic. Even in the squire's mansion, a similar transition is in progress:

> To the Great House accordingly they went, to sit the full half hour in the old-fashioned square parlour, with a small carpet and a shining floor, to which the present daughters of the house were gradually giving the proper air of confusion by a grand piano forte and a harp, flower-stands and little tables placed in every direction. Oh! could the originals of the portraits against the wainscot, could the

7(a) Old-fashioned cedar parlour

7(b) Modern living-room (c. 1816)

gentlemen in brown velvet and the ladies in blue satin have seen what was going on, have been conscious of such an overthrow of all order and neatness! The portraits themselves seemed to be staring in astonishment.[39]

The formal circle of the old regime is represented in Repton's cedar parlour (Fig. 7a), where the servants have evidently not yet got round to setting the chairs back against the wall. The new look, illustrated in his modern living room (Fig. 7b), is what the squire's parlour is becoming, and what the drawing-room at Netherfield in *Pride and Prejudice* (1813) has already become, for activities there include letter-writing, reading, needlework, piquet, loo, singing, piano-playing, and strolling, as well as conversation.[40]

'The Musgroves, like their houses', Jane Austen remarks of the family in *Persuasion*, 'were in a state of alteration, perhaps of improvement.'[41] She is sharply aware of changing social patterns, but neither resents them, like the portraits on the wall, nor approves them with an automatic word like 'progress'. The domestic style of 1816 was partly owed to the Argand lamp, invented in 1783, popularized and improved during the Regency.[42] It was ten to twenty times more powerful than a candle, and thus encouraged the furniture into the room away from the fire, which had often served as supplementary lighting. The old-fashioned objected that it was dangerous to eyesight, and that those who read by candlelight did not need spectacles, but one cannot imagine that Jane Austen was among them. It is Catherine Morland, not her creator, who is disappointed when she discovers that the great fireplace in the common sitting-room at Northanger Abbey has been 'contracted to a Rumford',[43] a more efficient way of producing heat that could be introduced into existing openings, invented by the American, Count Rumford, in 1796. She rarely seems resistant to change as such, but scrutinizes its social and moral effects, deciding each case according to its merits. Where, in *Persuasion*, the younger Musgroves' search for novelty gets them into trouble, other new ventures meet with approval, like Emma's introduction into Hartfield of a large modern circular table, as in Fig. 7b, in place of the smaller portable Pembroke (Fig. 41a) on to which her father's tea and supper have been crowded for the previous forty years.[44] This innovation alarms poor Mr Woodhouse, who would much prefer his guests – for medical, not mercenary, reasons – to confine themselves to gruel; but his daughter's hospitable instinct is prophetic, for that circular table becomes a standard piece of drawing-room furniture for the rest of the century. Around it, people do their work and linger to chat as well as eat: 'Tea passed pleasantly' for Emma's guests, 'and nobody seemed in a hurry to move'.[45]

In Jane Austen's writing allusions of this kind are so succinct, and so well integrated with dramatized events, that they can easily pass the reader by. But her novels are not nearly so remote from the realities of her time as is often claimed. To explore Regency England in her company is much like taking *Rural Rides* with Cobbett a decade later, not least because they both detect in the details of domestic building and furnishing indications of much more comprehensive change.[46] But where he spells out (sometimes in capitals or in italics) the implications of his observation, she leaves her readers to make their own deductions. The fine brush strokes on her 'little bit (two Inches wide) of Ivory'[47] require sharp eyesight, but repay minute attention.

By the mid-century, the novelist's art has entirely changed in this respect: extensive description of living space is no longer the rare exception but the rule. When Charles Kingsley discovers in chapter 6 of *Alton Locke* (1850) that he has not yet described the home, entered in chapter 2, of his eccentric bookseller, Sandy Mackaye, he is quick to repair the omission which he regards as 'unpardonable, in these days of Dutch painting and Boz'. Dickens published *Sketches by Boz* in 1836–7, just twenty years after Jane Austen's death, and it is not difficult to discover, by a comparison, why Kingsley should have regarded that book as a watershed in the depiction of fictional living space.

Mrs Tibbs's boarding house in the first of the tales is characteristic, although it is not Dickens at his later best:

> Mrs Tibbs was, beyond all dispute, the most tidy, fidgety, thrifty little personage that ever inhaled the smoke of London: and the house of Mrs Tibbs was, decidedly, the neatest in all Great Coram Street. The area and the area steps, and the street-door and the street-door steps, and the brass handle, and the door-plate, and the knocker, and the fanlight, were all as clean and bright as indefatigable whitewashing, and hearthstoning, and scrubbing and rubbing could make them. The wonder was, that the brass door-plate, with the interesting inscription 'MRS TIBBS', had never caught fire from constant friction, so perseveringly was it polished. There were meat-safe-looking blinds in the parlour windows, blue and gold curtains in the drawing-room, and spring-roller blinds, such as Mrs Tibbs was wont in the pride of her heart to boast, 'all the way up'. The bell-lamp in the passage looked as clear as a soap-bubble; you could see yourself in all the tables, and French-polish yourself on any one of the chairs. The banisters were bees'-waxed; and the very stair-wires made your eyes wink, they were so glittering.[48]

This description is not only more extended and specific than any one would find in Jane Austen's novels; it conceives of a house in a totally different way, as the foreground, not the background, of a fiction. We are told much less of Mrs Tibbs's appearance – only, indeed, that she is 'somewhat short in stature' – while the opening sentence, which describes her personality, is comparatively so brief that she seems to reflect the house, not vice versa. The process by which, in Dickens's later writing, objects become more animate than human beings is already under way. An aggressive verbal life, which sets the visitor back, inheres in them; paint and woodwork, glass and metal, even stone, dazzle his eyes and threaten conflagration; the blinds appear to snap, the chairs French-polish him.

Like all great writers, but even more than most, Dickens's vision is idiosyncratic. Where lesser imaginations, like that of Charlotte M. Yonge, can be adequately described as 'products of their time' (because, like mirrors, they reflect back to their world merely the domestic images they took from it), a vision as peculiar as Dickens's not only transforms the actuality, but subtly alters the reader's perception of it. A book concerned with the influence of fiction upon taste in architecture and furnishing would properly concern itself with those lesser imaginations, because they popularize what they reflect. But the major writer, where his imagination is responsive to environments, has an influence that is both less obvious and more profound, since it transforms awareness of the significance of domestic contexts. In the person of Master Humphrey, Dickens acknowledges in *The Old Curiosity Shop* (1840–1) that it was external objects, rather than people, that first captured his attention as a writer.[49] Little Nell, perceived in a commonplace context, would have had no purchase on his imagination. It is the 'heaps of fantastic things' in the old curiosity shop which, by making her exist in a kind of allegory, suggest her story to him, 'holding her solitary way among a crowd of wild grotesque companions'. When people begin to owe their significance to objects, or objects themselves begin to upstage people, not only the house, but the world of which it forms a part, has altered.

It would, however, be equally misleading, as that last sentence implies, to suggest that Dickens's extraordinary image of living space was achieved in total independence of its actual transformation in his time. Twenty years earlier, he could not have seen it in quite the way he does, for even in Repton's modern living room (Fig. 7b) the structural features of a room, together with the figures of its occupants, still dominate the furnishings; these are sparse, and still tend to have their backs against the wall. Twenty years later, the emphasis has changed. In those intervening years, handmade furniture was gradually displaced, first by the products of wood-working machinery, then by mechanical production methods.[50] Upholstery became a separate trade, and seating began to put on weight in consequence. Furniture not only became cheaper and more plentiful: many more objects could be presented to the eye and dispersed about the room as the Argand lamp was succeeded by gas lighting.[51] By 1823 Sir Walter Scott had already installed it in Abbotsford, his Neo-Gothic house (Fig. 53), and by the mid-century it had become quite common in urban houses of the middle classes. A Victorian room, in contrast with both Georgian and Regency, is much more lavishly carpeted, festooned, upholstered, while most of the floor-space is occupied by 'things' (Figs 96, 97).

It has been claimed that the confused clutter of furnishings and knick-knacks commonly associated with the Victorians became fashionable only after the 1870s;[52] but that impression, if only by contrast with the Regency, is certainly made upon novelists at an earlier date. In Thackeray's *Pendennis* (1848–50), for example, Lady Clavering, whose London house has been made over to the interior decorators, is put out of countenance by the result.[53] The dining-room has been fitted up (but she 'couldn't for goodness gracious tell why') in the 'middle-aged style', and the drawing-room, supposedly her province, has become a kind of Bedlam which assaults both eye and ear:

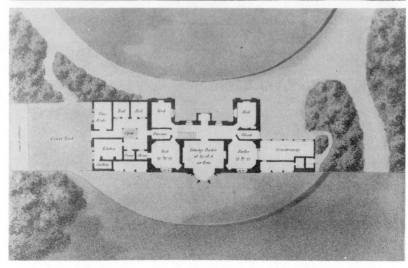

8(a)(b)(c) Classic and Gothic compromise

about the room were high chairs and low chairs, bandy-legged chairs, chairs so attenuated that it was a wonder any but a sylph could sit upon them, marqueterie tables covered with marvellous gimcracks, china ornaments of all ages and countries, bronzes, gilt daggers, Books of Beauty, yataghans, Turkish papooshes and boxes of Parisian bonbons. . . . There were muslin curtains and brocade curtains, gilt cages with parroquets and love-birds, two squealing cockatoos, each out-squealing and out-chattering the other; a clock singing tunes on a console-table, and another booming the hours like Great Tom, on the mantelpiece.

Not only has the furniture occupied the room, but the 'Rule of Taste' has been utterly confounded by eclecticism. It is no accident that the ingenuous and unpretentious Lady Clavering should have left to professionals the task of deciding what is, and what is not, good taste. It was a problem (to be discussed below in chapter 5) which was to perplex not only the wealthy but every level of the middle classes for the remainder of the century.

That problem, moreover, related not only to furnishing but to architecture, where the Rule of Taste was in similar disarray. In the early years of the nineteenth century, the classical had sustained its peaceful co-existence with the Gothic and a variety of other styles, largely because each house remained at heart Palladian, assuming alternatives merely as decoration. John Plaw's design in 1800 for a gentleman's country retreat on the Isle of Wight engagingly illustrates this co-existence: the south-east front (Fig. 8a) – to be seen against the harbour, a view that is socialized by boats and buildings – is Grecian in style and covered in stucco; while the north-west front (Fig. 8b), against a natural background, is 'of Monastic character' and built in local stone. The plan of the family part of the house (Fig. 8c), from either point of view, remains symmetrical, although it has acquired a conservatory to one side, and a range of offices to the other. But in the years between Jane Austen's death and the publication of *Boz*, the growth of interest in the actual past, promoted partly by the novels of Scott, began to disturb this peaceful co-existence by taking Gothic style more seriously – an alteration in attitude which can be illustrated by the difference between a Gothic novel like *Udolpho*, where ancient buildings are impressionistic, and an historical novel like *Ivanhoe* (1819), rooted in fact and actual place. In 1836 war was declared upon the pagan styles by Augustus Welby Northmore Pugin, whose father, Augustus Charles, had been a devoted student of genuine Gothic architecture in the 1820s. His impassioned *Contrasts* (1836) is a manifesto, both visual and verbal, for the Gothic, for it contrasts a town in 1440 with the same town in 1840 (Fig. 30), a comparison in which 1840 fails in every respect.

Contrasts, however, is more than a manifesto for the Gothic: it is, implicitly, a diagnosis of the social and cultural evils of the time, and a proposal for political and social change. More will be said of its proposals in the next chapter on the houses of the great,[54] but, as a sample of Pugin's diagnosis, the small print of his satiric illustration, 'dedicated, without permission, to THE TRADE', repays examination

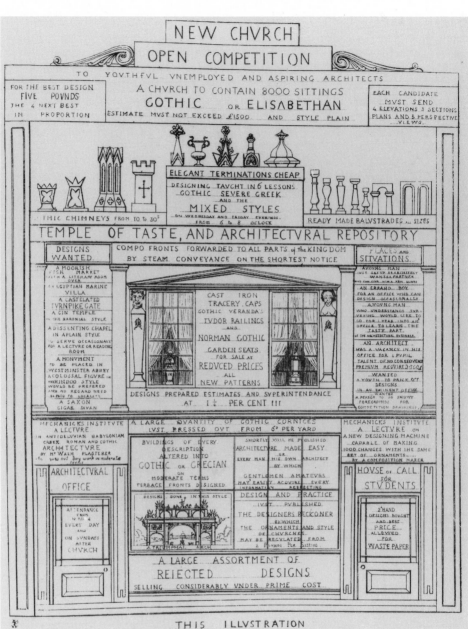

9 Victorian eclecticism

(Fig. 9). Its image of rampant eclecticism outside the house is quite as vivid as that offered by Lady Clavering's London interior. Exotic models are not only Greek and Roman, but Moorish, Egyptian, Hindoo, and 'Antideluvian'. Indigenous styles are quite as shamelessly exploited, for they are not confined to Gothic but include Saxon, Norman, Tudor, Elizabethan, and Baronial. The increasing professionalism of the architect, which culminated in the foundation of their Institute in 1834, only confirmed the divorce, already apparent in the Regency, between the style of a building and its function.[55] The architect who advertises for a pupil ('talent no consideration' but a premium of £100 required) might be Dickens's fictitious Mr Pecksniff, who has never himself designed or built anything real, and trains his pupils on similar lines, 'constructing in the air a vast quantity of Castles, Houses of Parliament, and other Public Buildings',[56] a divorce between the idea and the actuality noted by Joe Gargery in the expressive phrase, 'drawd too architectooralooral'.[57] At the root of this divide, as Pugin and Dickens both perceive, lie mechanical production and the profit motive, both of which are reflected in many details of the drawing, and are summed up in the subject of the lecture, advertised by the 'Mechanicks Institute', 'on a new designing machine capable of making 1000 changes with the same set of ornaments'.

The Industrial Revolution had, of course, begun some twenty years before Jane Austen's birth, at a time when the Rule of Taste had established an unquestioned supremacy; but it was in the twenty years following her death in 1817 that it really began to change the face of England. It was not only that, by 1837, the structure and contents of houses had begun to change as a result of early mass production, but that society itself had undergone a (technically) peaceful revolution, incidentally undermining the consensus that the middle-class house was a scaling down of the houses of the great. In 1817 England was still, as it had been for centuries, an agricultural nation, only 20 per cent of the population living in towns. In the world of fiction from the time of Richardson 'home' is, in consequence, almost invariably located in the countryside, where the great house of the locality is the model for the lesser houses of other gentlefolk. Even an apparently new fortune like Sir Lewis de Bourgh's, displayed by his dictatorial widow Lady Catherine in *Pride and Prejudice*, enables Rosings to set the standard for Hunsford. 'Home' in Victorian fiction, corresponding to the actual shift in population, is mainly in the city or its suburbs, where there are no great houses to set the standard; and even when characters do live in the country, great houses no longer dominate rural communities in the same way. Too many new ones, based on fresh industrial fortunes, had no connection with the land around them; too many old ones, succumbing to the profit motive, had abandoned responsibility and thus forfeited respect. Their history will be traced in the next chapter.

With the gradual eclipse of the great house, however, many smaller ones came into focus. No novelist writing earlier than Dickens would, for example, have concentrated on a boarding house – not that fictional characters don't stay in them occasionally, but they are not seen from the landlady's (or boarding house's) point of view. In 1833 J. C. Loudon, who has been described as the first architectural journalist, announced that the 'great object' of his *Encyclopaedia of Cottage, Farm and Villa Architecture* was 'to show how the dwellings of the whole mass of society may be equalized in point of all essential comforts, conveniences and beauties'.[58] The basis was no longer to be the palace scaled down, but the cottage extended: 'In this view of a villa, the dwelling is to be considered as only an amplification of the cottage.'[59] It is a point of view that very few, at the time of Jane Austen's death, would have comprehended. Below a certain level of affluence, as Loudon himself points out, the word 'architecture' had had no application; at their best, the houses of the poor were the work of country builders, finding traditional solutions to simple needs. It is true that the taste for the Picturesque which had developed at the end of the eighteenth century had led the educated to take a visual pleasure in the exteriors of vernacular buildings (Jane Austen pokes fun at the taste on more than one occasion).[60] It is also true that, in the later eighteenth century, many landowners had begun to build cottages for their labourers, and even to erect whole villages; but these were usually designed for the owner from the outside (not from the inside, for the occupant) as the focus for a prospect (Fig. 25) or, in the case of a village, as the approach to his park (Fig. 23c).[61] Until the time of Dickens, novelists likewise rarely entered houses below the 'architectural' levels of society; only misfortune, compassion or the pursuit of vice could take their characters into humbler buildings. Much more will be said of the houses of the poor in chapter 3, but the basic contrast can be readily tested – one has only to compare the range of interiors in the novels of Richardson or Jane Austen with the range in almost any one of Dickens's novels. With a few exceptions dictated by compassion, Jane Austen's visiting list extends no lower than 'the smallest habitation which could rank as genteel',[62] while Richardson's, misfortune apart, is even more exclusive.

The fictional houses of Dickens are, moreover, not only of all types, but of all ages. Eighteenth-century novelists, generally speaking, were no more interested than architects in the buildings that survived from earlier periods; some, indeed, were actively contemptuous of them.[63] When they are included, it is usually for the *frisson* connected with them as omens of mortality and transience, as in the poetry of melancholy: Clarissa, for example, is frequently threatened by her family with imprisonment in the moated house of her Uncle Anthony, if she does not agree to marriage with the odious Mr Solmes. Even in the Regency, when Gothic had grown popular in architecture and literature alike, ancient houses are unspecific, atmospheric settings for the heroines of Gothic novels, inducing a depression of the spirits, if not worse. Scott himself, at least in the view of Ruskin,[64] is guilty of this sentimental vagueness, sensing his buildings rather than perceiving them. It is of course very difficult for the eye to register detail when it is not trained to look for it; it is only when true students of the Gothic, like the elder Pugin, begin to distinguish the styles of different periods, that the buildings of the past really come into focus in the novel. More will be said below of their history in fiction (chapter 4); for the present it is enough to notice that in this case, too, *Sketches by Boz* appears to mark a divide. When Dickens's narrator is left alone in a panelled and smoke-darkened parlour, he acknowledges the influence of the Gothic novel in remarking that he should have 'followed the established precedent' and 'fallen into a fit of musing without delay'.[65] But the type of musing he entertains has a significant difference, for it is not, as that precedent would suggest, either moralistic or subjective. Instead, objects start into life and tell their stories. The convention, so familiar in the Victorian novel, that ancient things themselves have histories to relate, allows to long-inhabited places and well-used objects an individual being of their own.

Not only the last, but also those other alterations in attitude to domestic environment mentioned earlier, which seem to occur between 1817 and 1837, combine to give a building and its contents a quite different claim upon the imagination from their significance in Jane Austen's time. For most historians of architecture and décor this transition is regrettable, since it is marked by the collapse of taste; but for the novelist it opens up many new territories for exploration. It is not only that the social range of fiction becomes much more inclusive, allowing the writer to explore interiors that make no claim to architecture, but that living space itself develops individual character. It has been said, for example, that Victorian interiors are not reflections of taste, they are memorials to personality.[66] But it is only from an aesthetic point of view that they merit, in consequence, much less attention; in the novelist's eyes they become, on the contrary, more revealing. Great wealth can no longer disguise an absence of true values: the mirrors in Mr Dombey's ice-palace reflect the chilling image of a marriage based on purchase;[67] the roses on his wallpaper and carpets are set about with thorns. Conversely, vulgarity, if innocent, does not prevent the meanest of houses from becoming a home. The illuminated castle and black velvet kittens on the mantelpiece of the Toodles' home in Staggs's Gardens do not detract from it, but rather add to its sense of welcome.[68]

If the eighteenth century is often described by architectural historians as the great age of the English house, the Victorian period might equally well be called the great age of the English home. Neither good taste nor wealth, as its novelists keep telling us, can transform a house into a home, for a home does not consist in the quality of its architecture or décor, but in the quality of the lives that it expresses. The Victorian obsession with comfort has some relation to this conviction, for the first – and even the final – test of a home is whether it makes the visitor feel at ease. In an article written in the mid-century, 'Home is Home, be it never so homely',[69] Henry Mayhew argues that 'if the idea of ease be essentially connected with the English notion of home, certainly that of comfort forms a special part of it'. He goes on to point out that words like 'comfort' and 'home' are peculiar to the English language, so that the benighted French are driven to borrow *confortable*, since *à la maison* and *chez nous* relate merely to eating and sleeping places. Because these qualities have no relation to aesthetics, a true home, in the eyes of the novelists, is not defined by its likeness to other houses of similar or superior social standing, but rather by its individuality expressed in unpretentious honesty; its contents, that is, are determined by the affections, not by conformity to an agreed standard of 'taste'. Although it

10 Farmhouse fireplace

seems so fanciful, Wemmick's cottage *ornée* at Walworth in *Great Expectations* (1860–1), surrounded by a moat complete with drawbridge to 'cut off the communication',[70] is the quintessence of the Victorian home: entirely true to its owner, radiant with contented domesticity, though without the slightest claim to taste or wealth. With his pig and his vegetable patch, Wemmick even aims at self-sufficiency as though the domestic affections were under siege. His little castle is not part of a larger world, but exists in spite of it and is defined against it.

In fact as well as fiction the Victorian house had become more private than its Regency predecessors; one might even claim that it had developed distinct symptoms of Wemmick's siege mentality. Country house visiting, which had been common in the eighteenth century and Regency when everyone liked to have their taste admired, became infrequent as even the greatest houses closed their gates to visitors, persuaded that the sanctities of 'home' were not for exhibition to the public eye.[71] Moreover, as will emerge in later chapters, segregation became the order of the day, not only in relation to the world outside the house, but in the arrangement of its internal plan.[72] So far as possible, the upper and lower orders of society were made invisible to one another by the separation, in towns of the prosperous from the indigent, in houses of the servants from their masters. Private rooms and permission to retreat to them returned to fashion. In *The Young Stepmother* (1861) Charlotte M. Yonge represents Mr Kendal as a positive recluse within his study; and even when his lively second wife contrives to drive him out of it into her morning-room, she has to prevent him from turning that room too into a 'literal boudoir', by which she seems to mean 'a place to sulk in'.[73]

It is often claimed, both by the Victorians themselves and by subsequent historians of design, that the impetus towards the formulation of new standards of taste in the latter half of the century was provided by the negative example of the Great Exhibition of 1851. Although intended to demonstrate to all the world what the Industrial Revolution had achieved in England, the Exhibition seemed to the discriminating evidence rather of what it had destroyed. Certainly many of the objects in its Catalogue (Figs 68d–e, 70, 74b) appear to be designed for purchasers like Dickens's Mr Podsnap, whom William Morris later took as a personification of the problem;[74] for 'Podsnappery' had only one criterion: solid worth – in the financial, not the moral, sense. It is possible, however, that the search which then began for communal standards was prompted not only by this evident nadir of design, but by a wish to re-establish contact between the house and the community. As in the case of Pugin's *Contrasts*, new departures in design are also prescriptions for a new society. Even Charlotte M. Yonge, who is not the most perceptive of Victorian novelists, is well aware that Mr Kendal's retreat into his study is part of the reason why certain areas of Bayham have degenerated into slums. Within two pages of his translation to the morning-room, he sallies forth to raze Tibbs's Alley to the ground, and reconstruct it from the sewers upwards.[75] Such missionary zeal does not, however, pause to question the validity of those middle-class standards that it seeks to impose upon the poor. More perceptive writers were not as certain that their own

11 *The Money Changer and his Wife*

houses were in order, and, in their search for some contrasting model, they turned, as designers did themselves, to those vernacular buildings which the Rule of Taste had once despised. Here, if anywhere, was a domestic order that expressed community, a model for life as well as a model for art.

In his influential *Hints on Household Taste* (1868), Charles Eastlake, whose name is also linked with the Arts and Crafts Movement inspired by William Morris, describes the eagerness with which 'many of us have peeped inside the threshold of a Welsh Cottage or Devonshire farmhouse, and longed to sketch its ample hearth'.[76] He succumbs to the temptation (Fig. 10), in order to illustrate the superiority of rural interiors to those in cities, a difference which, he claims, did not formerly exist. The finest novelists contemporary with him, particularly George Eliot and Hardy, are drawn to describe similar interiors for related, although slightly different, reasons. Eastlake, in common with the Arts and Crafts Movement, preferred the simpler articles of household furniture – dressers, for example, as distinct from the sideboards of the middle classes – because they were made in traditional ways. For George Eliot, the charm of similar objects inheres in the evidence they give of use:

> Dorcas had led the way into the best kitchen, as charming a room as best kitchens used to be in farmhouses which had no parlours – the fire reflected in a bright row of pewter plates and dishes; the sand-scoured deal tables so clean you longed to stroke them; the salt-coffer in one chimney-corner, and a three-cornered chair in the other, the walls being handsomely tapestried with flitches of bacon, and the ceiling ornamented with pendent hams.[77]

If 'things', proclaiming merely material values, were unduly obtrusive in middle-class parlours, their display in such kitchens was sanctified by domestic labour and domestic pleasure.

Not surprisingly, George Eliot shared in the Victorian enthusiasm for Dutch interior painting, which dwells in a similar way upon the potency of objects, eliciting from the contemplation of such things the expression of useful lives (Fig. 81),[78] almost in the manner of medieval Flemish painters for whom such details are invariably symbolic of spiritual states. Even bourgeois rooms may come to express values other than the merely material, as in Figure 11, a seventeenth-century Dutch copy of the famous painting by Quentin Massys, *The Money Changer and his Wife* (1514), which in its turn may be based upon a lost original by the fifteenth-century Flemish artist, Jan van Eyck.[79] It is a painting which requires the eye to interpret objects, each of which is discrete, distinct, with its own meaning. In the seventeenth century itself the well-worn books, the half-burnt candle, were emblems of the transience of life; while in the paintings of van Eyck similar motifs – candlestick, basin, perfect fruit, and carafe of clear glass – are used to indicate unfallen nature.[80] A balance between the things of this world and those of the next is represented in the scales to which the eyes are directed, an interpretation that was once confirmed by a quotation from Leviticus 19:36 inscribed on the frame: 'Let the balance be just and the weights equal'. Victorians like George Eliot did not need to be expert in iconography (the reading of this painting is still disputed) in order to sense in such interiors a spiritual meaning in material things. Although the viewer's eye is won from a consideration of material possessions to the contemplation of transcendent values, it is 'things' themselves which, properly understood, call his attention to this higher truth. Dutch painting thus suggests a vision of interiors more revelatory by far than that of 'taste'. To use the words of Henry James: 'in the light, strange and coloured, like that of a painted picture, which fixed the impression for her, objects took on values not hitherto so fully shown'.[81]

It must surely have been that quality, suggestive of significance, which drew so many writers and designers to vernacular styles, in both the later Victorian and the Edwardian periods. In houses built from local materials, furnished in traditional ways by country craftsmen, the imagination sought to rediscover a way of life in harmony with the human community that produced it: 'In these English farms, if anywhere,' E. M. Forster writes in *Howards End* (1910), 'one might see life steadily and see it whole . . . connect without bitterness until all men are brothers.'[82] That division in sensibility, which still haunts the English middle classes, between the unsatisfactory domestic environments of cities, and the idyll of a cottage in the country, will be the subject of a later chapter.[83] It is noted here because it indicates the increasing dissatisfaction of many Edwardian novelists with the high Victorian ideal of the exclusive 'home', despite (or because of) the fact that in that period, as Walter Crane observed, 'the beautifying of houses, to those to whom it is possible, has become in some cases almost a religion'.[84]

With the outbreak of the First World War, this dissatisfaction was to develop into a kind of domestic agnosticism. In Lawrence's *Women in Love*, completed in 1916, Birkin contemplates the purchase of a 'clear, beautiful chair' which expresses for him the living thoughts of 'England, even Jane Austen's England', before these were destroyed by 'sordid and foul mechanicalness'.[85] Ursula is angered by his characteristic preference for the past, and, though he does not deny the preference, he does reject the chair, along with the 'hateful' thought of a home: 'a horrible tyranny of a fixed milieu, where each piece of furniture is a commandment stone'. Instead, he proposes a new domestic freedom: 'You must leave your surroundings sketchy, unfinished, so that you are never contained, never confined, never dominated from the outside!' *Women in Love*, as Lawrence himself says,[86] is a war book, and that conflict itself helped to induce this conviction. When Christopher Tietjens, the hero of Ford Madox Ford's *Parade's End*, returns from the trenches to his eighteenth-century London house, he inhabits a single room which he furnishes like an army tent.[87] The bitterness of war put an end to the beautifying of houses – for a time. But even in time the unfinished and the sketchy, an impermanence of setting that does not contain or define, became the characteristics of a new domestic agnosticism. In 1958, fifty years after *A Room with a View* was first published, Forster added an appendix to it in which he described the fate of his characters after the First World War was ended:

> The George Emersons now had two girls and a boy and were beginning to want a real home – somewhere in the country where they could take root and unobtrusively found a dynasty. But civilization was not moving that way. The characters in my other novels were experiencing similar troubles. *Howards End* is a hunt for a home. India is a passage for Indians as well as English. No resting-place.[88]

Beyond the Second World War, though the View remains, they find that they have lost the Room for good. The First World War thus marks a real divide in the conception of fictional living space, a truth which perhaps is rather less evident in the history of architecture and interior design. It is for this reason that I have confined myself to novels concerned with the period before 1914. Interiors do not of course cease thereafter to be important to the writer – but their nature has changed, partly in the way that Lawrence predicted.

It would be mistaken, however, as much in fact as in fiction, to assume that our sense of living space alters exclusively in response to events in the outer world, although their influence is considerable, as has been suggested. In the seventy-seven years that divide the publication of *Pamela* from the death of Jane Austen, houses have a homogeneous being for the novelist. If they receive much less description in fiction, it is because they are sensed rather than seen. Certainly the Industrial Revolution, with its multiplication of domestic objects, reverses that emphasis between 1817 and 1837. In the seventy-seven subsequent years that divide the publication of *Sketches by Boz* and the accession of Queen Victoria from the outbreak of the First World War, fictional houses are seen rather than sensed, until the burden of acquisition, despite attempts to redeem it, becomes a tyranny which ultimately destroys the Victorian notion of 'home'.

But, as novelists are well aware, it is true, as I hope to show in the final chapter, that houses have an autonomous being of their own: 'I've no control over the saucy things,' Margaret Schlegel complains in *Howards End*, 'Houses are alive.'[89] This autonomy is particularly apparent in older buildings, because they outlast generations of occupants: 'It always seems strange to me,' Fay Weldon remarks, 'how different families serve shifts in the same house; as if the house owned them, sucked them dry, spat them out and tried again – and not the family that controlled the house at all.'[90] But even a new house, as freshly conceived as the Dairy at Blaise, in response to a fiction of how life ought to be, has a wayward personality of its own, produced by the subconscious, both individual and collective, of its makers. To that extent, as novelists rather than designers are aware, the house has the upper hand from the beginning.

2

Aspects of Chesney Wold
The houses of the great

The houses of the great in England had for centuries served as the model for the aspiring middle classes. The lives of the great had been the main subject of their stories, in romance, in drama, and subsequently in the novel. Into the nineteenth century, as I have mentioned,[1] middle-class houses were regarded as a scaling down of the houses of the great, while a majority of novels still referred themselves to the dominant mansion at their centre.[2] Between the death of Jane Austen and the appearance of *Sketches by Boz* the emphasis does however begin to shift from the greatest houses to those below them. Writers on architecture such as J. C. Loudon in the 1830s and George Godwin in the 1840s,[3] interest themselves in the houses of the poor; while in the latter decade not only Dickens but many other novelists are concerned with a variety of living spaces for which the middle-class home, rather than the aristocrat's, sets the standard. But the dream of the great house endures well beyond its actual supremacy. Into our own time, many architectural historians confine themselves to that subject; it has moreover continued to have a nostalgic appeal to novelists. *Brideshead Revisited* (1945) is a prime example, and, although Waugh wrote it in a spirit of retrospection, he also added in a preface of 1959, 'It was impossible to foresee, in the Spring of 1944, the present cult of the English country house.'

If one looks for the perfect image of a great country seat in the Victorian novel, it is hard to better this one, seen by middle-class eyes which have no place in the picture they present to the reader:

It was a picturesque old house, in a fine park richly wooded. Among the trees, and not far from the residence, he pointed out the spire of the little church of which he had spoken. Oh, the solemn woods over which the light and shadow travelled swiftly, as if Heavenly wings were sweeping on benignant errands through the summer air; the smooth green slopes, the glittering water, the garden where the flowers were so sympathetically arranged in clusters of the richest colours, how beautiful they looked! The house, with gable and chimney, and tower, and turret, and dark doorway, and broad terrace-walk, twining among the balustrades of which, and lying heaped upon the vases, there was one great flush of roses, seemed scarcely real in its light solidity, and in the serene and peaceful hush that rested on all around it. . . . On everything, house, garden, terrace, green slopes, water, old oaks, fern, moss, woods again, and far away across the openings in the prospect, to the distance lying wide before us with a purple bloom upon it, there seemed to be such undisturbed repose.[4]

Out of context, even readers devoted to the Victorian novel may have difficulty in identifying that house, for they take from the novel that contains it a very different impression, one that has less to do with idyllic life than with decay and death. It is Chesney Wold in *Bleak House*, Sir Leicester Dedlock's place in Lincolnshire where it is almost always raining.

Chesney Wold is supposedly based upon Rockingham Castle (Fig. 12a), a mainly Elizabethan house within its Norman walls, where Dickens had spent some pleasant periods of his life when staying with his friends, the Watsons. But it is also reminiscent of Cobham Park (Fig. 12b), which had been his first glimpse as a child of the distant houses of the great.[5] Sir Leicester Dedlock retains many of the characteristics of a great eighteenth-century landowner. He assumes that his family is not only as old as the hills, but rather more structural, and that nature, although on the whole a good idea – 'a little low, perhaps, when not enclosed with a park-fence' – is none the less 'dependent for its execution on your great county families'.[6] He is a gentleman of complete integrity, 'disdainful of all littleness and meanness',[7] to whom honour has more importance than life itself. When Harold Skimpole declares to him that 'The owners of such places as Chesney Wold . . . are public benefactors . . . good enough to maintain a number of delightful objects for the admiration and pleasure of us poor men', Sir Leicester receives the compliment as no more than his due.[8]

Behind Sir Leicester's back, however, Skimpole is not so complimentary. He derides particularly the Dedlock family portraits: 'The whole race he represented as having evidently been, in life, what he called "stuffed people", – a large collection, glassy eyed, set up in the most approved manner on their various twigs and perches, very correct, perfectly free from animation, and always in glass cases.'[9] The dream-like house that Ada and Esther see, 'scarcely real in its light solidity', is, in many senses, a mirage. As the view from its windows alters at sunset 'into a distant phantom', so too will the house, 'not the first or the last of beautiful things that look so near and will so change'.[10] The serenity and peace that pervade Esther's first impression of Chesney Wold is not the living rest she takes it to be; as the reader already knows, it is the repose of death. Those portraits, and the chill damp of the ominously vacant house that contains them, have already been so vividly impressed on us by Dickens that, for many readers, this remains their dominant, and perhaps exclusive, impression. The long drawing-room at sunset, illustrated by Phiz (Fig. 13), is a place from which life has suddenly departed. Although, in the novel, the house awaits the return of Sir Leicester and Lady Dedlock, in the picture it

12(a) Rockingham Castle

12(b) Cobham Park

appears as if they have that moment left, abandoning their ordinary occupations. As in the novel, the figures carved above the fireplace, the portraits on the wall, assume a macabre life of their own as the setting sun streams in through the windows. If the dead live, the living are as dead as the focal statue of the mother and child, for Sir Leicester has no children, and the domestic affections, so prized by the Victorians, have departed from his house.

The destruction of Chesney Wold may be traced back, in more senses than one, to the family ghost, for it is haunted by one who represents the cause of commonwealth and people, as opposed to monarchy and the pride of privilege. When, in the nineteenth century, Chesney Wold finally dies, it is not destroyed by demotic jealousy; it is simply displaced by the increasing power of the middle class. Sir Leicester may think it appropriate to keep Mr Rouncewell waiting, 'opposing his repose and that of Chesney Wold to the restless flight of ironmasters',[11] but it is his housekeeper's son who now wields the moral authority, for he has come to remove his future daughter-in-law, the lady's maid Rosa, from Lady Dedlock's charge because he thinks that position is unsuitable. True repose is not to be found in that great house, and the flag that proclaims it a 'happy home' lies to 'the lightsome air'.[12] The days of the aristocracy are past, and it is Sir Leicester's middle-class enemy, Lawrence Boythorn, who enjoys within the orderly limits of his modest neighbouring house a true 'stillness and composure'.[13] The novel is not named from its great house (as are *Mansfield Park* and *Northanger Abbey*), but from the comfortable home, no longer bleak, where John Jarndyce exercises his abundant hospitality. When the orphans of the Chancery case find their way to Bleak House, they are guided by its 'light sparkling on the top of a hill'.[14] When Sir Leicester and Lady Dedlock reach Chesney Wold, although 'fires gleam warmly through some of the windows', they are too few 'to give an inhabited expression to the darkening mass of front'.[15] The aristocratic house has become a mausoleum of sad secrets. At the end of the novel it is closed to the public, and most of its stately rooms are shut up: 'the light of the drawing-room seems gradually contracting and dwindling until it shall be no more'.[16] In contrast, the middle-class Bleak House admits the light and air of day through its open windows, and is so fertile in its humanity that it even gives birth to another, the 'rustic cottage of doll's rooms' which shares its name, prepared for Esther by Mr Jarndyce on her marriage to Alan Woodcourt.[17]

Bleak House was first published in 1852–3, when the transference of power from the aristocracy to the upper middle class was already under way. The idea of the great house as a pattern for everyone is already an anachronism in the mind of Sir Leicester. Yet the radiant aspect of Chesney Wold as Esther first sees it had only just begun to lose its fascination for the English as the ideal that humbler men might emulate in a reduced form. The different aspects of Chesney Wold thus seem to be deliberately contrasted, in order to dramatize Dickens's insight into the incipient decline of the great house. The first signs of its waning authority can certainly be perceived (with hindsight) in earlier novels, particularly Jane Austen's; but novelists before Dickens do not write as though they are aware that the failures they criticize

13 Sunset in the long drawing-room at Chesney Wold

are irreversible. The origin of those failures may be traced even further back, in the altering plan and exclusive position of the eighteenth-century house, but neither creative writers nor architects elicit their portentous implications.[18]

In the eighteenth century the possession of land was still, as it had been for centuries, the only firm basis of influence and power.[19] In country as in town,[20] the aristocrat accepted – in theory at least – that wealth and position were indivisible from a commitment to the social good. Although Richardson regarded himself as writing with a new realism, his novels gravitate towards the houses of the great as much as did the wealthier middle-class houses of his time. It may be true, as Lord Chesterfield claimed, that 'whenever he goes . . . into high life, he grossly mistakes the modes',[21] or, as Walpole did, that his are 'pictures of high life as conceived by a book-seller',[22] but Sir Charles Grandison on his country estate nevertheless represents the middle-class idealization of the aristocracy. He does not only improve himself and his estate, but his servants too, as Harriet remarks:

> We went thro' all the Offices, the lowest not excepted. The very servants live in paradise. There is room for every thing to be in order: Every-thing *is* in order. The Offices so distinct, yet so conveniently communicating – Charmingly contrived! – The low servants, men and women, have Laws, which at their own request, were drawn up, by Mrs. Curzon, for the observance of the minutest of their respective duties; with little mulcts, that at first *only* there was occasion to exact. It is a house of harmony to my hand. Dear madam! What do good people leave to good people to do?[23]

The housekeeper's room even contains a servants' library with books in three categories: 'One of books of *divinity* and *morality*: Another for *housewifry*: A third of *history*, true adventures, voyages and innocent amusement'[24] – the last, one notes, does not seem to include the novel. Sir Charles also operates a miniature health service, employing a salaried apothecary who 'dispenses physic to all his tenants, who are not able to pay for advice; nor are the poor who are not his tenants, refused',[25] provided they are recommended by the clergyman. He houses an eminent surgeon rent-free for similar services, paying him handsomely for cures, but by the hour when the patient dies. Richardson even defines the failings of his bachelor Mr B (who is not a pattern as a husband either), partly by comparison with an ideal of an English landowner. During the lifetime of Mr B's mother, his great house has represented for Pamela, as a servant, the opportunity for an education in the morals, skills, and tastes of a true lady. Morally speaking, it has raised her not only to Mr B's level, but above it. In seeking to seduce her, he betrays those notions of responsibility that his mother had observed so fully.

Few who lived when the aristocratic rule of taste prevailed would have questioned Sir Henry Wotton's definition in the previous century of 'Every Man's proper Mansion House and Home' as 'the Theatre of his Hospitality, the Seat of Self-Fruition, the comfortablest Part of his own Life, the noblest of his Son's Inheritance, a kind of private Princedom; nay, to the Possessors thereof, an Epitomy of the whole World',[26] although, on occasions, this was not of course the reality. Fielding's novels contain plenty of barbarous squires, who would as soon hunt down a parson as a fox, and whose houses are too muddy and unruly to be in any sense comfortable, much less seats of self-fruition. Nevertheless, even for Fielding, Mr Allworthy in his Gothic mansion is an ideal as his name implies, a man whose estate epitomizes the whole world.[27] Because such houses set the standard, those who write upon architecture in the eighteenth century and Regency invariably regard houses of moderate size for more limited means as a scaling down of the houses of the great. This applies not only to the independent middle-class dwelling, but to the working class too when part of a great estate. The poor man at the gate, as in Harewood village, might inhabit a version of the rich man's house (Fig. 23c). The persistent conviction that one should model one's house on houses superior to it is further emphasized by the popular practice of country house visiting. Sir Charles takes his Harriet off to view 'fine houses' as an appropriate pastime for the newly wed.[28] Fanny Burney's heroine, Camilla, makes one of a similar party to Knowle.[29] Smollett even conducts the reader into his own house, 'a plain yet decent habitation . . . kept in excellent order', in the company of Matthew Bramble's party.[30] The practice persists into the Regency, for Jane Austen's heroines are frequently entertained with such expeditions, though sometimes with embarrassing consequences, as in the case of Elizabeth Bennett's visit to Pemberley, her future home,[31] an early indication, confirmed in *Bleak House*, that this activity could be intrusive.

It may be significant, however, that Mr Allworthy's house *is* Gothic, and thus belongs to an older pattern of society and architecture with a rather different idea of human community. Where great houses, from the middle ages into the seventeenth century, had been built to contain a single household in an ordered hierarchy beneath one roof, their classical counterparts in the eighteenth century and Regency became increasingly an expression of stratification into two quite distinct classes, though as yet on nothing like the scale of the grand Victorian house. John Plaw's plan for a mansion house in 1802 (Fig. 14) might be Mr Palmer's 'spacious, modern-built house', Cleveland, in *Sense and Sensibility* (1811).[32] In many ways it is transitional between the eighteenth century and the Regency: there is still the odd closet, a bedroom and dressing-room are still downstairs, and the house itself perches on its semi-basement. It is a cultivated house with a large library; it is a hospitable house, with spacious dining-room and emphatic portico; it is devised, like Adam's town houses, for 'an elaborate social parade, a parade which was felt to be the necessary accompaniment of active and responsible living'.[33] But the servants have no place in a house like this, which is designed to make them as inconspicuous as possible down their passage to the offices. Mr Palmer plants out his offices, with a 'thick screen' of fir, mountain ash, acacia, and Lombardy poplar; Plaw effaces them completely. They appear from his plan to be attached to the house by a passage on the viewer's right, but there is no sign of them at all in his elevation.

The segregation of servants from the family had already begun at Coleshill, the

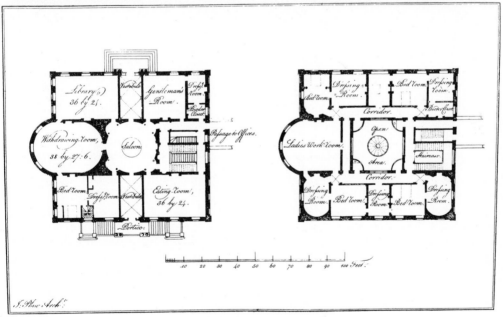

14 Regency mansion

ancestor of the Palladian houses of the eighteenth century, where Roger Pratt, who believed that a house should be 'so contrived . . . that the ordinary servants may never publicly appear in passing to and from for their occasions there',[34] had given them separate rooms, adjacent to their masters, so that they no longer slept at his door or at the foot of his bed. During the eighteenth century they were further removed, elevated to the attic, sunk in the basement, and, in the Regency, planted out in wings. Family privacy was also increased by the provision of back stairs, so that the master of the house on his main stairway might not meet his 'last night's faeces coming down them'.[35] On the main floors, where the family circulated freely from room to room, corridors could be made in the thickness of the inner wall, communicating with the back stairs at either end. The house was thus one structure for the family, horizontal and open in its plan; to the servants it was quite another, vertical and confined from attic to basement. Pamela, the maid, is constantly beating a breathless retreat up and down back stairs, or pressing her back to walls to let the gentry pass; her ascendancy to wife is dramatized by her spacious and easy progress from room to room.

Nevertheless, the presence – and even the personality – of servants is a conspicuous aspect of Richardson's fictional world, where in Jane Austen's they are chiefly remarkable by their absence. In properly regulated households they are invisible, as though the house were a magical place, ministered to by disembodied presences. It is at Portsmouth, where Fanny constantly collides with the unsatisfactory Rebecca and Sally (not least so, perhaps, in the fact that they have names, which Jane Austen's servants normally do not, though Richardson's do), that her heroine discovers the true virtues of Mansfield Park:

> At Mansfield, no sounds of contention, no raised voice, no abrupt bursts, no tread of violence was ever heard. . . . Here, every body was noisy, every voice was loud. . . . Whatever was wanted, was halloo'd for, and the servants halloo'd out their excuses from the kitchen.[36]

Along with the servants has gone much of Sir Charles's sense of responsibility to a local community larger than the household. While Mr Knightley in *Emma* displays one of his many virtues in his preoccupation with the land round Donwell Abbey, and, although he would not invite William Larkin and Robert Martin into his drawing-room, appears to enjoy their conversation more than that around his tea-table, that community is one of interest; it does not extend to the cure of souls. Where Pamela eagerly restores the chapel in the house in Lincolnshire, the one at Sotherton in *Mansfield Park* signifies an age that is past and irrecoverable. Household prayers, both morning and evening, as conducted by Sir Charles Grandison, are regarded even by Fanny as a practice which, though desirable, is obsolete: 'It was a valuable part of former times.'[37] In Jane Austen's novels a community is defined by a village, rather than its great house, where it is proper that the parson should assume responsibility for the cure of souls.

Like Jane Austen's houses, John Plaw's mansion house (Fig. 14) is no longer

15 Proximity at Chawton

designed as 'an Epitomy of the whole World'. Its site, significantly, is visualized as private; there are no buildings to be seen in the long perspective to the viewer's right. Chesney Wold, as an older house, is close to the village church; but this proximity to one's neighbours came to be regarded as undesirable by the fashionable in the eighteenth century and Regency, due largely to the fashion for 'emparkment' which will be discussed in the next chapter. It is these large-scale 'improvements' of the countryside that later lead Sir Leicester to assume that nature is dependent for its execution on great county families. Thus William Gilpin remarks in 1791 that Petworth House is badly situated because it does not lie at the centre of its park, but at an extremity, where it is elbowed by the churchyard;[38] Repton, whom Mr Rushworth thinks of employing at Sotherton,[39] explains that proximity to a village may lessen dignity.[40] In this case, however, Jane Austen does not assume that past values are irrecoverable. It is Maria Bertram, whose moral sense is dubious, who rejoices that the church at Sotherton 'is not so close to the Great House as often happens in old places'[41] (it is a full mile away), while the admirable Colonel Brandon's Delaford in *Sense and Sensibility* 'is close to the church, and only a quarter of a mile from the turnpike-road, so 'tis never dull. . . . A butcher hard by in the village, and the parsonage-house within a stone's throw'.[42] Jane Austen's brother's secondary and older house at Chawton (Fig. 15), unlike his primary eighteenth-century residence (Fig. 16), also lies close to the church, and in such instances her views on the relation of the great house to its village are evidently conservative. For the same reason, Cobbett warmly commends Mr Evelyn's house in *Rural Rides*; dating from the Restoration and 'by no means magnificent' it 'stands on a little flat by the side of the parish church'.[43] Jane Austen, one feels, would not have been surprised to hear that Mr Evelyn both employed and reformed offenders among the poor.

The association between a great house and its local community was undermined because their traditional connection with the land was severed when, towards the end of the eighteenth century, houses based on new fortunes began to be built. Beckford's Fonthill (Fig. 5) was one of these and, like many Victorian country houses, it was an individual's dream imposed upon the land, not an outward and visible sign of commitment to it. As Summerson remarks of London, the Reform Bill of 1832 marked the final end of that tradition, and thereafter 'social responsibility was gradually shaken out of the aristocracy without being shaken into the bourgeoisie'.[44] This change during the Regency may be noted even in the detail of interiors. Furniture becomes more intimate and domestic, adapted to family life, not public display. The aristocrat's furniture was an elaboration of the middle class's, where once the middle-class interior had been a reduction of the aristocrat's.[45]

Despite his elevation of Pamela from maid to lady, a solecism that Jane Austen would never have committed, Richardson makes a much clearer distinction than she does between the genuine landed family and aspirants to that status from the middle class. The vices of Lovelace are, for example, those of the traditionally aristocratic variety, where Clarissa's family, which aims at elevation, has developed the rabidly acquisitive instincts peculiar to their aspiring breed. 'Everybody knows Harlowe Place,' Lovelace comments dismissively, 'for, like Versailles, it is sprung up from a dunghill, within every elderly person's remembrance.'[46] Jane Austen makes no such marked distinction in her novels between the old family and the new, with a new 'place'. Mansfield Park, for example, is no less a great house because it has recently arrived, or because the income that supports it is drawn from the West Indies and not from its own land. Even the exacting Mary Crawford sees it as a desirable prize, 'a park, a real park five miles round, a spacious modern-built house, so well placed and well screened as to deserve to be in any collection of engravings of gentlemen's seats in the kingdom';[47] the absence of family portraits does not deter her. Where the new Lady Grandison exclaims, with an effusiveness Sir Leicester would have approved – 'What pleasure had I in hearing the history of this antient family, from this unbroken series of the pictures of it, for so many generations past!'[48] – family portraits are rather put in their place by Jane Austen. At Pemberley the 'many family portraits . . . could have little to fix the attention of a stranger';[49] at Sotherton they are 'no longer any thing to any body but Mrs Rushworth, who had been at great pains to learn all that the housekeeper could teach'.[50]

Although in many ways conservative, Jane Austen tolerates and even welcomes change. At the least, as in the case of her new families, she keeps an open mind and

16 Exclusiveness at Godmersham

judges each case according to its merits. Nevertheless, in a final analysis, her older houses have an edge over the new, or relatively new. The furnishings at Pemberley, 'neither gaudy nor uselessly fine', have 'less of splendour, and more real elegance, than the furniture of Rosings', which has been recently erected.[51] Pemberley's fine library is 'the work of many generations', and the house itself, as Bingley acknowledges, cannot be imitated; it can only be bought.[52] Despite its absence of prospect and its irregularity, Donwell Abbey, rather than Mansfield Park, is Jane Austen's ideal of an English country house. Seen from the outside, the Abbey is in Emma's eyes: 'a sweet view – sweet to the eye and the mind, English verdure, English culture, English comfort.'[53]

Jane Austen had of course much more first-hand experience of 'high life' than Richardson, on her brother's estate at Godmersham (Fig. 16) and elsewhere.[54] Her view must in consequence be truer than his to the actualities of her time. It is certainly less idealized, and less given to black-and-white distinctions. If, for example, she sometimes finds the superfluities of Godmersham amusing – 'At this present time I have five Tables, Eight & twenty Chairs & two fires all to myself'[55] – she none the less savours the 'luxurious sensation' of sitting 'in idleness over a good fire in a well-proportioned room'.[56] Even where they are not, her great houses should always ideally be theatres of hospitality, seats of self-fruition, and the comfortablest part of life. She strongly approves of her brother's attention to his second great house at Chawton, because he is 'proving & strengthening his attachment to the place by making it better',[57] even down to a 'solicitude' for the inadequate dimensions of a pantry door; for an attention to domestic minutiae, if normally unstated, indicates a concern for other people, at least at one's own level of society. Elizabeth attends most closely to the furniture at Pemberley where it suggests Mr Darcy's affection for his sister.

It is, however, obvious in her novels that the centre of gravity has shifted from the great house into the middle-class home. Although the great house remains the focus of her village society of two or three families, their pervasive flaw is a pride and ceremony that detracts from comfort – that middle-class word which was to be so crucial for the Victorians. This unease is intensely felt on Sir Thomas's return to Mansfield Park from the West Indies, a flaw in him which is finally accountable for Julia's errors and for Maria's exclusion from polite society. Mr Knightley's defective sociability, Mr Darcy's pride, and the absurd arrogance of Sir Walter Elliot mark different degrees of frost on the same scale. It is those rather less well-born – Elizabeth, Emma, and particularly Fanny – whose livelier feelings will make Pemberley, Donwell Abbey, and Mansfield Park not merely great houses, but comfortable homes. Sir Walter Elliot is beyond redemption, more atrophied even than Sir Leicester Deadlock. That Kellynch Hall must be let, 'a beloved home made over to others',[58] is deeply felt; but, within a few weeks of the Crofts' arrival as tenants, Anne 'could not but in conscience feel that they were gone who deserved not to stay, and that Kellynch-hall had passed into better hands than its owners.'[59] Admiral Croft, who has made his fortune at sea, makes few alterations at Kellynch (minutiae apart, like an inconvenient laundry door). It is the couple's happy capacity to make a home anywhere, due to the fact that sea-going men have no 'place' of their own, that alters Kellynch. Their contribution to the great house is to restore to it its appropriate character, as a hospitable (but undeniably middle-class) home.

Jane Austen makes no sweeping judgements of her changing society. She does not, like Repton, attribute 'the increase of novel or fantastic edifices' simply to the increase of new fortunes and a corresponding decay in the old families.[60] But a sense of social change is pervasive in her novels. As I have said,[61] to look in them around the countryside is much like taking rural rides with Cobbett. They both express the same, slightly ironic, delight in the munificence of old houses: Cobbett, when walking through the Duke of Buckingham's park, remarks in a manner that anticipates Harold Skimpole's: 'I, like POPE'S cock in the farm-yard, could not help *thanking* the DUKE and DUCHESS for having generously made such ample provision *for our pleasure.*'[62] Both admire the cultivation and beauty of many country houses, old and new, modest and fine, but always in harmony with their surroundings and with themselves. Both note the signs of alteration and transition – old houses for sale or to let, new ones being built – and both are aware of the encroaching tide of middle-class building. It is no accident that Jane Austen's last, unfinished, novel, *Sanditon*, should take its name from a new resort of speculative buildings, and that the leading speculator should have abandoned his contented old house, with its English verdure, comfort, and lack of prospect, for a new eminence and exposure in a villa *ornée* on a cliff-top, with an up-to-the-minute name, Trafalgar House.

Changes more radical were still to come. In the 1830s, as we have seen, Loudon reversed the traditional orientation of architects, and in doing so turned society, by implication, upside-down. His *Encyclopaedia*, though devoted to the cottage, farm, and villa, is nevertheless intended to contain 'all that is essentially requisite for health, comfort and convenience, to even the most luxurious of mankind'.[63] Indeed, he states quite unequivocally, 'in such dwellings every labourer ought to live, and any nobleman might live'.[64] In the following decade, Pugin also enquires why the middle-class dwelling should be regarded as a scaling down of the houses of the great, for 'the smaller detached houses which the present state of society has generated, should possess a peculiar character: they are only objectionable when made to appear diminutive representations of larger structures'.[65] In other words, the greatest houses no longer set the pattern for the nation.

Great houses did not of course cease to be built; on the contrary, almost as many were erected in the nineteenth century as a whole as in the three centuries that preceded it put together.[66] In 1835–9 the ratio of old to new families was three to one; by 1885–9 the new outnumbered the old by two to one.[67] The relationship of old and new was intricate. On the one hand, the new owners of great country houses accepted the life of the landed gentleman, even where they had little land. Severing their connection with the world of trade, they adopted the style of Arnold's barbarian – hunting, shooting, and fishing, rather than reading.[68] On the other hand, as Jane Austen's novels had already foreseen, aristocratic families adopted the morality of Arnold's philistines, the middle class, in cultivating the sanctity of home. It is in making this adjustment that the last generation of the Dedlocks particularly fails:

> My Lady Dedlock (who is childless), looking out in the early twilight from her boudoir at a keeper's lodge, and seeing the light of a fire upon the latticed panes, and smoke rising from the chimney, and a child, chased by a woman, running out into the rain to meet the shining figure of a wrapped-up man coming through the gate, has been put quite out of temper. My Lady Dedlock says she has been 'bored to death'.[69]

Lady Dedlock, lacking the life of the affections, is not bored but frozen to death; the Victorian angel of domestic happiness has gone to shelter beneath a humbler roof. Her view of the keeper's cottage is at once prophetic and anachronistic. The lodge itself is still a feature in the landscape, possibly built in the style of the great house as those latticed panes would suggest; but the family within it is to displace with its architecture the great houses of the Victorians, whether old or new. Writers on its history have sometimes seen the century from 1780 to 1880 as a protracted interlude between the aristocratic rule of taste and the modern uniformity of the masses,[70] for, with the agricultural slump in the 1880s, the great houses of the past lost their confidence in land and often their fortunes too. Thereafter their path lay increasingly downwards.

Their displacement was not however immediately perceptible even to a writer like Disraeli, who was critically interested both in the architecture and in the social function of great houses. When in 1831 he published his second novel, *The Young Duke*, the faults of the aristocracy lacked their social dimension. The young Duke squanders his enormous fortune in commissioning Sir Carte Blanche to remodel his palace in town and his genuinely Gothic castle. He also commissions M. Bijou de Millecolonnes, who despises the ancients, and whose 'lightness, gaiety, and originality' are the antipodes of the 'solidity, solemnity and correctness' of Sir Carte Blanche, to build in a 'wild sequestered spot' in Regent's Park a pavilion reminiscent of Nash's at Brighton, which gives rise to a rumour 'that the Zoological Society intended to keep a Bengal tiger *au naturel*, and that they were contriving a residence which would amply compensate him for his native jungle'.[71] But Disraeli was later to criticize his own novel for its affectation, and in the following decade, when his trilogy (*Coningsby*, *Sybil*, and *Tancred*) was published, his account of great houses had acquired a newly serious dimension. If the aristocracy alone could heal the rift between the two nations,[72] the rich and the poor, into which England had divided, they must, as a first step, quite literally put their own houses in order. The quickest way to revive the principle that privilege was indivisible from responsibility was to build a Gothic house designed for a single household, not, like Palladian houses, for two separate communities. Although it is doubtful that throughout the middle ages masters and servants ate at the same table, above and below the salt, as the Victorians supposed,[73] the Gothic hall, entered directly from the outside world and accommodating every social rank, symbolized their ideal of social integration.

Jane Austen, whose attitude to the Gothic will shortly be discussed, would certainly have thought Disraeli's proposal ludicrous as a means of restoring authority to great houses; but the notion has its actual antecedents in certain aspects of eighteenth-century Gothic taste. There is for Fielding, as we have seen, a felt connection between the humane attitudes of Mr Allworthy and the genuine Gothic of his house whose 'air of grandeur . . . struck you with awe, and rivalled the beauties of the best Grecian architecture'.[74] Moreover, although the Gothic novel was largely escapist, its plebeian characters tended to be much more conspicuous than Jane Austen's servants, and to have a distinct character of their own. In his preface to *The Castle of Otranto*, Walpole states that Shakespeare is the model for his domestics, and that, although their simplicity may excite smiles, it is drawn from nature. Because they do not have the sublime sensations of princes, they do not express their passions in the same dignified tone; but that contrast, in itself, should make more truly pathetic the fate of their superiors. Mrs Radcliffe too shows more interest than Jane Austen in her peasants and their dwellings: mirth may co-exist with poverty and ignorance in hovels without chimneys or windows where men and beasts shelter together, while her more fortunate poor live in cottages so arcadian that her wandering gentlefolk may even stay in them overnight.[75]

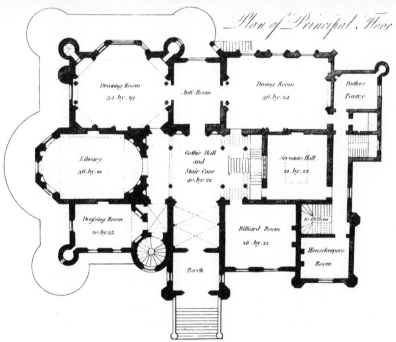

Plan of Principal Floor

Drawing Room
34. by. 29

Anti-Room

Dining Room
36. by. 24

Butlers
Pantry

Library
36. by. 22

Gothic Hall
and
Stair Case
40. by. 22

Servants Hall
22. by. 22

Dressing Room
20. by. 15

Billiard Room
26. by. 21

to Offices

Porch

Housekeepers
Room

17 Mansion in the castle style

Nevertheless, when one examines the actual design of a Regency Gothic house, like Pocock's 'Mansion in the Castle Style' (Fig. 17), one can see how very little relation it has to Disraeli's aspirations. Just as Robert Morris in 1736 recommended that the classical orders of architecture should be matched to the situation of a house (Doric for open country, Ionic for the 'cheerful vale', etc.),[76] so Pocock matches the Gothic style to the wildness of woods, water, and hills. His Gothic hall is, moreover, no more than a salon rechristened; there is a separate dining-room and the servants are kept firmly at a distance by the staircase. Pocock does, however, strive to make his building irregular, and it was primarily this feature of the Gothic that Jane Austen disliked. Although in her writing this objection is expressed in literary, not architectural, terms, it chimes exactly with Sir John Soane's criticism of Neo-Gothic: 'Irregularity is . . . too generally admitted.'[77] Her own novels are structured like the classical house, either contained within a single place (under one roof), or, if wings are added by excursions elsewhere, the harmony of the whole – as in her brother's house at Godmersham (Fig. 16) – is sustained by symmetry and consistency of style. In 1816 she satirizes the rambling, retrospective structure of the Gothic novel, producing a satiric plan for one such story, where the scene constantly shifts from one set of people to another, and the greater part of the first volume is taken up with a narration, by the heroine's father, of past events in his various life.[78] Moreover, the word 'irregularity' has moral connotations, and Gothic novels are often concerned with disreputable doings. The heroine in her scenario is, for example, 'often carried away by the anti-hero, but rescued either by her Father or the Hero – often reduced to support herself & her Father by her Talents & work for her Bread; – continually cheated & defrauded of her hire, worn down to a Skeleton, & now & then starved to death'. Jane Austen was an avid reader of Gothic novels as her letters show, and eagerly awaited the arrival of the most recent productions at the circulating library. A protestation like John Thorpe's, 'I never read novels' (he does except *The Monk*),[79] is smartly dismissed as 'common cant'.[80] Nevertheless, such fictions are not meant to be taken literally, for it can be dangerous to indulge the Gothic imagination in ordinary life, as Catherine learns to her cost at Northanger Abbey. Mrs Radcliffe may have charm, but is not a trustworthy guide to human nature in the midland counties of England. It is no accident that two of Jane Austen's titles – *Sense and Sensibility* and *Pride and Prejudice* – should express symmetry and invoke proportion; while two others – *Mansfield Park* and *Northanger Abbey* – should not only be taken from houses, but can be read, respectively, as an apologia for Palladianism and a satire on the Gothic taste.

Thirty years, of course, divide the publication of Jane Austen's novels from the appearance of Disraeli's trilogy, and much had happened in the interim to make the Gothic house grow serious. Scott's novels had created a view of the remoter British past as a time of high romance and chivalry. Pugin's advocacy of the Gothic as a Christian, not pagan, architecture, had given it moral overtones. The foundation of the Camden Society in 1839 had promoted a much more careful study of medieval architecture. Disraeli's fascination with the Gothic has, however, very little relationship to scholarship of any kind; it is a curious mixture of Scott's romanticism with Pugin's social passion. His notion of what (or even when) the middle ages were remains extremely vague; his conviction that the values they embodied could provide an answer to the Condition of England question was correspondingly intense.

Lord Marney, whose younger brother Egremont is the hero of *Sybil*, represents, in the context of his house, the irresponsible, self-interested aristocracy who have divided England into two nations. He is not, in the first place, a 'real' aristocrat, but is descended from 'a confidential domestic of one of the favourites of Henry VIII' who thus acquired the lands of Marney (or Fountains) Abbey. There, in the reign of James I, the family house (or Fountains Hall) was built. The new Marney Abbey had the appropriate symbolism, for 'the portal opened to a hall, such as is now rarely found; with the dais, the screen, the gallery, and buttery-hatch all perfect, and all of carved black oak'.[81] But the reader is mistaken if he assumes that the humble eat below the salt in that great hall, or that the poor come to the buttery-hatch for alms. The 'lay abbots' of Marney recognize only one responsibility – promotion to the ducal strawberry leaves. As to the poor, Lord Marney's solutions are simple: emigration on a large scale and the destruction of as many cottages as possible so that the population of his parishes is not increased.[82] In this respect Lord Marney is even worse than his far more newly arrived neighbour, Lord Mowbray, whose father was a waiter and whose Gothic castle has been recently built. The latter's daughter, Lady Joan, is certainly interested in 'the Condition of England Question', and his guests include the principled, High-Church, and well-born clergyman, St Lys, who retorts to Lord Marney that war on the cottage does not *at first* seem so startling a cry as war on the castle.

As Disraeli had already made clear in *Coningsby*, it was possible to do still better: to build a new great house from a great fortune, in order to recreate the historic role of the paternalistic landowner. Mr Lyle, a Catholic and a commoner, has built St Geneviève, 'a pile of modern building in the finest style of Christian architecture'.[83] It has of course a 'baronial' hall (in addition to, not instead of, a salon), complete with 'its rich roof, its gallery and screen', not to mention its buttery-hatch which is, moreover, put to its proper use. At Christmas Mr Lyle 'holds his revel' in that hall with his 'beauteous bride' and their guests, from her noble parents to his faithful tenants, so that 'all classes are mingled in the joyous equality that becomes the season, at once sacred and merry'.[84] The buttery-hatch is open from dawn to dusk for the entire week; everyone may eat as much as he can, and take off in a basket as much as he can carry, including clothing, 'for a Christian gentleman of high degree was Eustace Lyle'.

Not everyone can attempt reform on this scale, but established houses can also bridge the gap by showing themselves, like others, to be human, transforming their ceremony where 'everything is as stiff, formal, and tedious, as if your host were a Spanish grandee in the days of the Inquisition'[85] – Chesney Wold, in effect – into something like the easy welcome of a middle-class home. Mr Lyle's neighbours at Beaumanoir contrive, despite its size, to make it seem intimate and domestic by

18 The 'lived-in look' at Cassiobury Park

creating the 'lived-in look' (which Jane Austen appears to be describing with some scepticism in *Persuasion*):[86]

> Such a profusion of flowers! Such a multitude of books! Such a various prodigality of writing materials! So many easy chairs too, of so many shapes; each in itself a comfortable home; yet nothing crowded. . . . And the ladies' work! How graceful they look bending over their embroidery frames, consulting over the arrangement of a group, or the colour of a flower. The panniers and fanciful baskets, overflowing with variegated worsted, are gay and full of pleasure to the eye, and give an air of elegant business that is vivifying. Even the sight of employment interests.[87]

The scene is not dissimilar from the aquatint of the Great Library at Cassiobury Park (Fig. 18), based on a drawing by Pugin and published in 1838. Disraeli's message is plain: the aristocracy is not only human, but even its women have their work to do.

It is clear, however, that in Disraeli's view, the middle classes take their key from the aristocrats, not vice versa. His two mill owners, Mr Millbank in *Coningsby* and Mr Trafford in *Sybil*, conduct their enterprises on lines that are similarly feudal, but acknowledge the difference in their status by building themselves houses that are classical, not baronial. Mr Lyle, although a commoner, has a very distinguished genealogy, for where the aristocracy are concerned, the further back they go, the better they get. Pre-Conquest families have a special immunity to the contagion of capitalism, defined by Disraeli as the bankers who came into England with 'Dutch William'. Lord Valentine, who possesses a suit of armour which 'stood by Simon de Montfort on the field of Evesham', is one such.[88] He is able to talk man to man with the Chartist delegates, in the confidence that his family has worked through many generations for the common good – building churches and bridges, making roads, digging mines, planting trees, and draining marshland. The working-class delegates are not left to kick their heels in an anteroom, but are ushered into the salon (it is a London house) which Lord Valentine evidently occupies. There, among plashing fountains, brilliant mirrors, richly painted ceiling, walls hung with blue satin, rich furniture, and priceless folios, they settle down to discuss the Chartist demands. Like Mr Lyle at St Geneviève, Lord Valentine clearly wishes the people 'constantly and visibly to comprehend that Property is their protector and their friend'.[89] Such aristocrats are the antithesis of the Lord Marneys, who 'mortgage industry to protect property'.[90]

It is, however, noticeable that Disraeli models his new feudalism less on the great houses than on the monasteries of the past. It is not the Jacobean Marney Abbey but the actual abbey from whose stones it was built which should become the model for the great houses of Victorian England, because the original abbey – in Disraeli's view – held its property for the common good. Mr Lyle is modestly explicit on this point: ' "I have revived the monastic customs at St Geneviève," said the young man, blushing. 'There is an almsgiving twice a-week." '[91] Gerard in *Sybil* explains the advantages of the monastery as landowner to Lord Marney's troubled younger

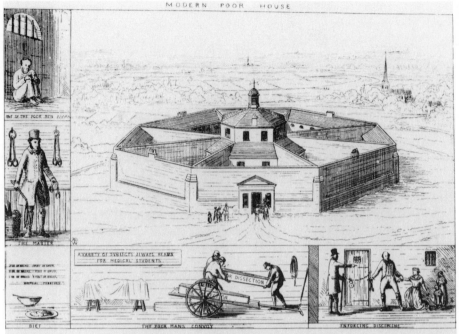

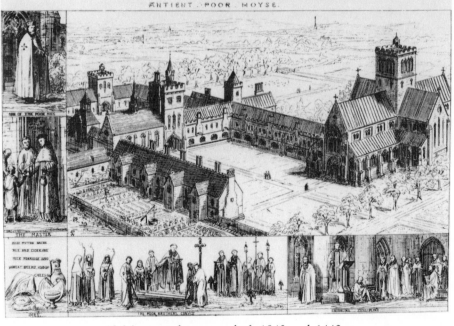

19 Measures for poor relief, 1840 and 1440

brother, Egremont.[92] It had no private property, could save nothing and bequeath nothing; as a result, revenues were expended for the common good. It was moreover 'a proprietor that never died and never wasted', so that property was on the people's side. This is identical with the view expressed in Pugin's *Contrasts* nine years before, where the Utilitarian measures for poor relief – of which, as Pugin depicts them, Lord Marney would certainly have approved – are juxtaposed with the supposedly benign regime of the medieval monastery as Gerard describes it (Fig. 19).

One might think that the distance from the monastery to the great house was considerable, but Gerard, continuing, takes it in his stride: 'How proud we are still in England of an old family, though, God knows, 'tis rare to see one now.' He must have sensed the connection in his bones, for Gerard, the man of the people and one of the Chartist delegates, turns out to be a descendant of the last Abbot of Marney, and the rightful heir to Mowbray Castle, a claim that defies all legal and moral description. The parallel between the monastery and the revival of feudal paternalism does not have to be quite so ingenious. Carlyle's *Past and Present* (1843) verbally juxtaposes modern capitalism with medieval monasticism, just as Pugin's 'Contrasted Residences for the Poor' do visually. Even Marx and Engels in the *Communist Manifesto* (1848) entertain the same idealized image of the medieval past:

> The bourgeoisie, wherever it has got the upper hand, has put an end to all feudal, patriarchal, idyllic relations. It has pitilessly torn asunder the motley feudal ties that bound man to his 'natural superiors', and has left remaining no other nexus between man and man than naked self-interest, than callous 'cash payment'.[93]

That diagnosis is not far distant from Disraeli's own; it is in their prescriptions for the future that they differ. Gerard appears to be Disraeli's spokesman: 'Try to imagine the effect of thirty or forty Chatsworths in this country, the proprietors of which were never absent.'[94] It was easier to imagine the future as Marx and Engels foresaw it.

It is evident, nevertheless, that Disraeli's comments on architecture in the trilogy, as distinct from *The Young Duke*, become evaluations of the society that produced such buildings; and his comments on that society become, in their turn, a manifesto for his own time. Moreover, improbable as such ideas of benevolent paternalism and renascent feudalism may appear, they were sometimes translated into bricks and mortar. Canford Manor in Dorset, built by Sir Charles Barry in 1848–52, is not unlike St Geneviève, 'a gathering as it seemed of galleries, halls, and chapels, mullioned windows, portals of clustered columns, and groups of airy pinnacles and fretwork spires'.[95] Like many others, it too had its great hall in which the classes did sometimes mingle for such festivities as Mr Lyle's Christmas celebration.[96]

Mr Lyle had his critics, who realized – as seems evident to us – that his prescription would not resolve the problems of industrial England. His views are taken to task by Lancelot, the hero of Kingsley's *Yeast* (1848): 'It may suit the Mr Lyles of this age . . . to make the people constantly and visibly comprehend that property is their protector and their friend, but I question whether it will suit the people themselves, unless they can make property understand that it owes them something more definite than protection.'[97] Kingsley has some sympathy with Lord Vieuxbois, his representative of Disraeli's group, the Young Englanders, but he also has sympathy with Lord Minchampstead, whose views resemble those of Mrs Gaskell's industrialist, Robert Thornton, in *North and South* (1855). Lord Vieuxbois is paternalistic and feudalistic; he improves his estates on principles that are, like Mr Lyle's, ultimately religious. He lives among 'high art and painted glass, spade farms, and model smell-traps, rubricalities and sanitary reforms, and all inventions, possible and impossible, for "stretching the old formula to meet the new fact" '.[98] His principles, those of an old title, are contrasted with Lord Minchampstead's, those of a new one; the latter are economic, not religious, and are rooted in self-interest rather than charity. Lord Minchampstead installs new steam-engines on his farms, enforces the new Poor Law to the letter, and will not give a farthing away in alms. He does, however, set up a first-rate industrial school, give every man a pig and a garden, and rebuild his cottages. Before the cholera outbreak in *Two Years Ago* (1857), where he makes a second appearance, he alone among the landowners takes the doctor's advice and sees that the pig keeps its distance from the cottage, and that the cottages themselves are thoroughly scoured.[99] As Kingsley says, 'England has need of him as a transition-stage between feudalism and ****, for many a day to come.'[100] He approaches the ideal of a landowner more nearly than all, save Lord Vieuxbois, who 'has much to learn; and a little to unlearn':

> He has to learn that God is a living God now, as well as in the middle ages; to learn to trust not in antique precedents, but in eternal laws: to learn that his tenants, just because they are children of God, are not to be kept children, but developed and educated into sons.[101]

Kingsley does not tell his readers what **** will be, but it is evident that he does not have the welfare state in mind. One way of achieving **** lies through the marriage of the old and new, for Lord Vieuxbois marries Lord Minchampstead's daughter, thus symbolizing a synthesis of their different attitudes to the responsibilities of a great estate.

No one, least of all Disraeli when he came to power, really believed in Gerard's prescription for the future; but that connection between the former abbey and the great house adjacent to it, often actually constructed from its stones, continued to haunt the Victorian imagination, perhaps with a sense of unrealized possibilities. Jane Austen has her abbeys too, but she values them for rather different reasons. When she comes to Henry VIII in her *History of England*, she observes that 'nothing can be said in his vindication, but that his abolishing Religious Houses & leaving them to the ruinous depradations of time has been of infinite use to the landscape of England in general'.[102] Her comment reflects the taste of the eighteenth century, in which the abbey is a highly desirable asset to the landscape gardener. Fountains Abbey, which, as Christopher Hussey remarks, has since 1768 'provided the culmination of John Aislabie's elysium',[103] is a prime example. Two of the great houses in Jane Austen's novels, Donwell and Northanger, have their origin in abbeys; but they acquire no spiritual dimension in consequence, as they would do in the Victorian novel, where the proportion of great houses grown from abbeys must surely exceed the proportion of those that, like Fountains Hall, actually did so in fact. Northanger Abbey is only tolerable because it has been modernized; like Sir John Soane, Jane Austen clearly feels that survivals of medieval ecclesiastical architecture are 'little calculated for the common habits of life'.[104] Donwell Abbey remains her ideal of an English country house, but Emma's view of it recalls the landscape gardener's perspective.[105]

Among Victorian novelists the abbey has a spiritual significance much closer to that with which Pugin, Carlyle, and Disraeli himself invested it, as an admonitory contrast with modern values. But that contrast in later writers is retrospective; it is not a proposal for great houses in the future. Perhaps the most striking example is Monk's Topping in *Daniel Deronda* (1874–6), acquired by the Mallinger family in the reign of Henry VIII: the 'place was one of the finest in England, at once historical, romantic and homelike: a picturesque architectural outgrowth from an old abbey, which had still remnants of the old monastic trunk'.[106] To some extent it is still a feature in the landscape, for Deronda takes Gwendolen to admire it from a special window, round which 'a sort of bower had been made . . . turning it into a recess'.[107] But it is in sight of that abbey, 'the calm light and shadow, the ancient steadfast forms', that Gwendolen makes her confession to Deronda.[108] Sir Hugo Mallinger, in life as in architecture, does not want to reproduce the old, but his house is specifically contrasted with Grandcourt's Diplow, 'a comparatively landless place which had come into the family from a rich lawyer on the female side who wore the perruque of the Restoration'.[109] Diplow too is a beautiful house – 'the old green turf on the lawn; the soft, purplish colouring of the park beyond'[110] – but it is not 'homelike' as Monk's Topping is. When we see Grandcourt at breakfast there with Mr Lush, the scene is suggestively rendered as a 'still-life', artfully composed but with no vital principle, the room 'seeming the stiller for its sober antiquated elegance, as if it kept a conscious, well-bred silence'.[111] Grandcourt is Sir Hugo Mallinger's nephew and his heir, but they are ethically as distant from each other as Disraeli's Lord Marney is from his Mr Lyle. Sir Hugo Mallinger, to a limited extent, uses his property for the common good, not least in raising Daniel Deronda; Grandcourt regards his inheritance as the means by which he can indulge his vices.

Even Trollope has his abbey, although he despised both Disraeli's challenge to Young England and his novels: 'To me they have all had the same flavour of paint and unreality . . . a feeling of stage properties . . . and that pricking of the conscience which must be the general accompaniment of paste diamonds.'[112] Trollope does not suffer much himself from prickings of conscience (though whether his diamonds are real or paste is another matter). But he does, on the middle-class and moral grounds to be described in chapter 5, condemn the ostentation of Gatherum Castle belonging to the Duke of Omnium,[113] and favour the older, humbler Matching with its adjacent priory, where the Duke's heir, Plantagenet Palliser, lives. Gatherum Castle is of immense size and quite new, having been built by the Duke for a quarter of a million pounds. It is 'very cold, very handsome, and very dull': 'Who'd live in such a great, overgrown place as this,' Lady Glencora asks, 'if they could get a comfortable house like Matching?'[114] In the cloisters at Matching Priory, Lady Glencora, like Gwendolen, makes her confession – and nearly catches her death of cold.[115] The house itself – 'not a palace, nor a castle, nor was it hardly to be called a mansion'[116] – is 'pretty' (Trollope's highest term of praise), unpretentious, and comfortable. Although an older house, it moves with its time in that is expresses the highest values of the middle classes in words such as 'home-like' and 'comfortable', those used to describe Monk's Topping as well as Matching.

Both Monk's Topping and Matching are 'improving' – that is, they refine the spiritual states of the upper class. But, even though Sir Hugo Mallinger holds parties for his tenants in the gallery he has built above his cloisters, the social dimension that Disraeli liked to imagine is not a conspicuous aspect of such houses as it is of St Geneviève. Pugin had complained that Victorian Gothic was considered suitable only for some purposes, 'MELANCHOLY, and therefore fit for religious build-ings!!!'[117] But even where it was extended from churches to houses, a spiritual asceticism seems to be its distinguishing characteristic. In retrospect, George Eliot even discerns this quality in eighteenth-century Gothic, which seems to us now comparatively playful and exuberant. Cheverel Manor, in one of her *Scenes of Clerical Life*, has been transformed in 1788 by Sir Christopher Cheverel, from a plain brick family mansion into a Gothic manor house,[118] thus anticipating (in George Eliot's view) 'that general reaction from the insipid imitation of the Palladian style'.[119] Inspired by his study of Milan Cathedral, his models are not domestic but ecclesiastical – 'pretty near like the churches, you know,' as one character remarks[120] – and his transformation, like Walpole's, seems to consist less in an alteration of domestic concept than in a face-lift to its exterior and interior. Despite its casing of stone, its castellations, and its mullioned windows with their many-shaped panes, George Eliot comments on the 'too formal symmetry' of the front,[121] while the effect of its dining-room (no communal hall, one notes) is formidably decorative, not unlike that of Eaton Hall (Fig. 20), where similar alterations began in 1803. George Eliot clearly admires the one at Cheverel Manor, 'which was so bare of furniture that it impressed one with its architectural beauty like a cathedral'.[122] She delights particularly in this dominance of architecture over furnishing, 'a piece of space enclosed simply for the sake of beautiful outline', so that the small dining-table appears as 'an odd and insignificant accident'. To Victorian eyes, any interior from that earlier period might have seemed underfurnished; but the construction that George Eliot puts on the dominance of walls and ceiling is decisively Victorian in its moral emphasis: 'in walking through these rooms with their splendid ceilings and their meagre furniture, which tell how all the spare money had been absorbed before personal comfort was thought of, I have felt that there dwelt in this old English baronet some of that sublime spirit which distinguishes art from luxury, and worships beauty apart from self-indulgence'.[123] As at Matching and Monk's Topping, one is

20 Eaton Hall dining-room

struck by the personal nature of the virtue expressed by the house. It completely lacks the social dimension that Pugin and Disraeli both intended.

The many Victorian great houses had developed in the contrary direction, separating themselves progressively from the 'other nation' on whose labours they depended. During Queen Victoria's reign, many that had been formerly open to the public closed their gates, preferring to cultivate the sanctity of 'home'.[124] It is an indication of the anachronism of Chesney Wold that, until the final pages of the novel, it is accessible to casual visitors – sometimes very casual, for they seem to form a category much less exclusive than Jane Austen's. Dickens regards the behaviour of Mr Guppy as 'usual' in people who go over houses: 'They straggle about in wrong places, look at wrong things, don't care for the right things, gape when more rooms are opened, exhibit profound depression of the spirits, and are clearly knocked up.'[125] The respect to which Sir Leicester undoubtedly feels that his house is entitled is evidently waning; Mr Guppy is in fact intruding on his privacy, for his interest lies in Sir Leicester's family secrets, not in his house. Furthermore, the separation of the great house from its neighbours, which had developed in Jane Austen's lifetime, became the rule in Queen Victoria's reign: 'A solitude in the centre of a wide park is now the only site that can be recognized as eligible.'[126] Loudon,[127] as one might expect, and Trollope,[128] as one might not, both comment on it adversely.

But the separation of the two nations from each other is most evident of all in the internal plan of the great Victorian house. As the architect, Robert Kerr, states unequivocally: 'The family constitutes one community: the servants another.'[129] His plan for Bearwood (Fig. 21), executed in 1865–74 for John Walter, chief proprietor of *The Times*, and included in *The Gentleman's House*, is an expression of what Mark Girouard describes as the Victorian 'genius for analysis and definition',[130] a genius which led them to classify everything from insects through households to societies. As a beginning, it illustrates the division, acceptable to Kerr, of England into two nations, both in its external appearance, where the servants' quarters are reduced in size and in ornament, and in the detail of its plan:

> Primarily the House of an English gentleman is divisible into two departments; namely, that of THE FAMILY, and that of THE SERVANTS. . . . As the importance of the family increases the distinction is widened – each department becoming more and more amplified and elaborated in a direction contrary to that of the other.[131]

Bearwood is so designed that the ladies get no closer to the offices than the door between the transverse and the butler's corridor. Gentlemen may venture as far as the gun room, but the door at the end of the housekeeper's corridor prevents an encounter with any but upper servants of their own sex. What passes on either side of the boundary 'shall', Kerr declares, 'be both invisible and inaudible on the other';[132] even encounters in passages are to be avoided.

Divisions do not, however, end with the green baize door; on either side of it the

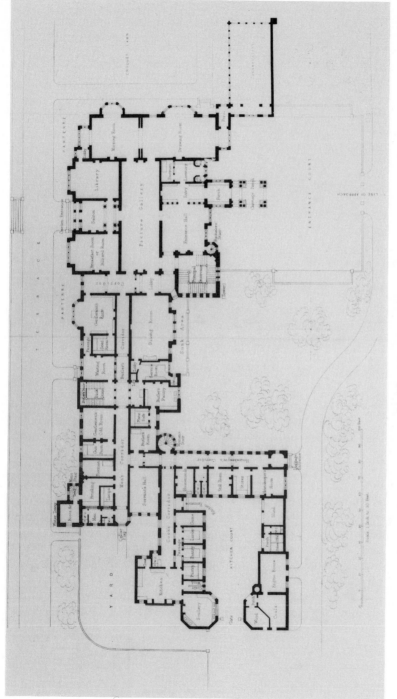

21 The Victorian plan

sexes are strictly segregated. Bachelors have their staircase at the front of the house off the entrance hall; young ladies theirs from the mistress's boudoir on the first floor to their bedrooms above it. Particular rooms are appropriated to the different sexes. The library doubles as a gentleman's room, or, failing that (for Kerr remarks elsewhere that 'the ladies are not exactly excluded' from it),[133] they are sure to have the billiard-room to themselves, while the young of the sex may 'do as they like' in the odd room.[134] Conversely, the morning-room was generally a female preserve. Disraeli comments favourably on an exception to this rule at Beaumanoir: 'How delightful was the morning room . . . from which gentlemen were not excluded with that assumed suspicion that they can never enter it but for felonious purposes.'[135] In the other nation, the sexes are as strictly segregated. The women have their own staircase to the first-floor bedrooms, where they sleep under the housekeeper's eye; male servants have a staircase and rooms at the back, off the brushing room. Divisions are drawn by function as well as by sex: 'There are thus *three chief Departments* among the Offices, namely, that of the *Butler* and the men on one side, that of the *Cook* and the Back-Offices in a manner central, and that of the *Housekeeper* (including the Women's-room) on the other side.'[136] There is a fourth division, of grooms and gardeners, which is literally off the map; it is above the stables where, Kerr advises, smells should be prevented, although the men themselves will be indifferent to them.

Not only this, but the servants have a rigid class structure of their own. At the very top are those superior employees – librarian, tutor, governess, lady's companion – who not only work but live on the family side of the house, and may sometimes even eat at the family table. Inferior to these, and lodged behind the green baize door, are the upper servants. The butler and housekeeper have their own rooms, but these must be open (by invitation) to visiting partners of the same rank, 'not including, however, any persons of the lower grade, which is thus very clearly marked'.[137] The lower servants, if male, are to congregate in the servants' hall; if female, in the women's workroom. Outside workers, the lowest of the low, are to have their own 'mess room' over the stables, though head gardeners and grooms may use the servants' hall. One might have thought that these divisions would at least cease to operate in church, but there too Kerr advocates a rigid hierarchy: 'The best of all systems of arrangement is to place the family and their guests in front, strangers of position next behind them, and the upper and lower servants, together with strangers of their classes respectively, in successive order.'[138] One notes, however, that family chapels, neglected in the Regency, have returned to fashion, though 'Private Chantries, stalls, and so on, are all affectation.'

Bearwood is built in the Elizabethan style and has a hall with screen, but it is no expression of community; rather, like other houses of its type, it is a microcosm of Victorian society. Its various divisions – by function, class, and sex – correspond to the analysis of that society as Marx and Engels presented it. The house, moreover, has its relation to the industrial town as Engels describes it, which is also planned so that the paths of the separate nations need never cross.[139] The gradation of its rooms in terms of area, aspect, and ornament, relates closely to the various types of housing in towns. Kerr includes a table of estimates in which it is clear that the ceilings of servants will be several feet lower, the cost of their rooms a mere quarter, and their floor space – despite their larger numbers – less than two-thirds of that allowed to the family.[140] Aspect and prospect will be 'makeshift at the best'; 'Elegance, Importance, and Ornament, it would be quite out of place to notice'; but '*Cheerfulness*, so far as this quality can be conferred upon the offices, will still be desirable'.[141]

The plan of houses like Bearwood also has its relation to the structure of many Victorian novels, which are as rambling and intricate in their connections, as Jane Austen's, like the houses of her time, are frankly open and proportioned. In the great Victorian house, lives are inevitably connected because they are passed beneath a single roof, depend on the same resources, and cannot but have an effect on one another; yet the planning of the great house does all it can to obliterate these connections. Girouard mentions that the Duke of Portland sacked any housemaid he met with in the corridors, and that a certain Lord M in Wiltshire never spoke to a servant unless to give an order.[142] Such cases may have been exceptional, but a great many servants seem to have passed their lives in households where their employers knew them by their functions, not their names. In a similar way, the lives of all in a novel like *Bleak House* – from Sir Leicester and Lady Dedlock, through the whole gamut of society, down to the outcast Jo of Tom-all-Alone's – are intimately connected, yet are unaware of that connection. Social analysts and novelists alike seem determined to make these connections visible – hence the detective element in many Victorian novels. But the great Victorian house, like the cities of the period,[143] is built in defiance of these connections, and resolutely refuses to acknowledge them.

In the English house privacy is a major preoccupation in the period. Rooms did not interconnect or have folding doors, as they did on the Continent; they had a single door that could be shut.[144] But where privacy in the little closets of the eighteenth-century house is the individual's privilege, for the Victorians the emphasis falls much more upon exclusion. There are numbers of rooms that an individual cannot enter at all, or only at certain times, for reasons of status, sex, or even age. Those that are open to him are usually devoted to a purpose, not appropriated to a person: ladies congregate in the morning-room or mistress's boudoir; men in the odd room, billiard-room, or library. Only the master of the house has a room that can be described as a personal sanctum, because he alone (it would seem) has to spend his mornings 'more or less . . . in practical affairs'.[145] Rooms bear the mark of those who spend most time in them. 'Woman alone can organize a drawing-room; man succeeds sometimes in a library,' Disraeli declares.[146] While the dining-room, according to Kerr, should have an air of 'masculine importance', the drawing-room should be 'entirely *ladylike*'.[147]

The new-built mansions of Victorian England were undoubtedly much closer to Gatherum than to St Geneviève or even Beaumanoir, exhibiting the principles of

Lord Minchampstead, not Lord Vieuxbois, in their disposition. 'What foolish rabbit-warrens our well-to-do houses are obliged to be,' William Morris complained in 1884; 'instead of being planned in the rational ancient way . . . a big hall, to wit, with a few chambers tacked on to it for sleeping or sulking in.'[148] Why, he asks, can this 'mean and shabby custom' not be changed? But he answers the question himself:

> Because we cannot: because our servants wouldn't have it, knowing, as we know, that both parties would be made miserable by it. The civilization of the nineteenth century forbids us to share the refinement of a household among its members!

The living quarters of servants undoubtedly improved. A pride in the quality of one's offices is already perceptible in General Tilney of Northanger Abbey. Thirty years later even the sceptical Thackeray remarks the improvement, contrasting it with Clavering Park, a Jacobean house with a Georgian face-lift:

> I do not know any more cheering mark of the increased philanthropy of our own times, than to contrast our domestic architecture with that of our ancestors, and to see how much better servants and poor are cared for at present.[149]

Yet this 'philanthropy' has in it a considerable element of Minchampstead self-interest. As Cobbett had noted in 1822: 'Society is in a *queer* state when the rich think, that they must *educate* the poor in order to insure their *own safety*.'[150] Part of that safety lay in accommodating them well – at a safe distance. In the great house, where relationships with servants are mentioned – Lady Dedlock and Rosa, Mrs Transome and Jenner in *Felix Holt* are examples – they signify a perilous moral isolation. It is in the middle-class home that a sense of genuine community is created – by the Hales in relation to Dixon in *North and South*, by Esther with Charlie in *Bleak House*, or Maggie and the Jakins in *The Mill on the Floss*. Kerr deplores the invasion of privacy in small houses, where visitors rub shoulders with the tradespeople, where the sounds of the scullery can be heard in the dining-room, where the kitchen can hear what goes on in the drawing-room, and the dresser or cooking-range may be seen in the kitchen.[151] But these 'evils', as he calls them, are seen by many novelists to have their advantages.

Although a number of minor Victorian novelists continue to weave romances round great houses (the popular *Heir of Redclyffe* [1853] by Charlotte M. Yonge is one example), in the view of the major Victorian writers, Disraeli excepted, the great house had had its day. Where it is clear from Jane Austen's novels that those of humbler birth, if they had something to teach them, also had something to learn from them – Fanny, William, and Susan are all improved by their contact with Mansfield Park – in the reign of Victoria even Mrs Gaskell, who was certainly gifted with what Charlotte Bronte described as 'the organ of veneration', is less inclined to revere great houses than to laugh at them. When Molly Gibson in *Wives and Daughters* (1866) has been to visit the Towers, her father declares that he had expected to find her so 'polite and ceremonious' that he read a few chapters of *Sir*

Charles Grandison in order to bring himself up to concert pitch.[152] But his daughter proves to have been very properly ill-at-ease among its dazzling lights, long corridors, great staircases and phalanxes of ladies' maids; that his second wife should revel in them is an indication of her moral inferiority. When Mrs Gaskell herself went to stay with a duke, her daughter, Meta, suggested that they should dress themselves up in the bed curtains 'of thick white satin stamped with little rosebuds'.[153]

Few, however, go quite as far as Dickens, who is apt to burn great houses down. Although Sir John Chester (who lives in sumptuous lodgings in London) is his prototype of the cold-hearted aristocrat in *Barnaby Rudge* (1841), while the brother he persecutes is both principled and humane, the family house the latter inhabits (significantly named 'The Warren') is ripe for destruction, 'the very ghost of a house, haunting the old spot in its old outward form, and that was all'.[154] It is not irrelevant that *Barnaby Rudge* is concerned with the Gordon Riots of 1780, although The Warren is not consumed with quite the virulence that destroys the chateau of Monseigneur in *A Tale of Two Cities* (1859) during the French Revolution:

> In the roaring and raging of the conflagration, a red-hot wind, driving straight from the infernal regions, seemed to be blowing the edifice away. With the rising and falling of the blaze, the stone faces showed as if they were in torment. When great masses of stone and timber fell, the face with the two dints in the nose became obscured: anon struggled out of the smoke again, as if it were the face of the cruel Marquis, burning at the stake and contending with the fire.[155]

The English aristocracy have, it seems, rather less to answer for than the French; they are merely as redundant as the dinosaur. Their salvation lies in the adoption of middle-class values; it is even possible that the heir of Monseigneur can find his – in a quiet, modest, comfortable English home.

If other Victorian novelists do not set fire to their great houses with as much frequency as Dickens,[156] they tend in other ways to undermine them, suggesting that they too perceive them, not merely as fabrics, but as expressions of an outmoded system. Although the Gothic novel and the Gothic taste helped to give such houses a new lease of imaginative life, they also assisted in their demolition. The connection between ancient houses and mysteries of a shameful kind has its origin in Gothic romance. Although Trollope once remarked that 'when we have once learnt what was that picture before which was hung Mrs Ratcliffe's solemn curtain, we feel no further interest about either the frame or the veil',[157] his remark is valid only for her species of the Gothic. In the Victorian novel such mysteries have their social value, whose interest endures – as in the case of Chesney Wold – well beyond their solution. Their Gothic origin is, for example, apparent in the novels of the Brontë sisters: the mystery of its tenant makes Wildfell Hall both an appropriate setting and intrinsically interesting; the segregated upper storey of Thornfield Hall shadows the radiance of the fairy palace below, for all the light of its candles, fires, and lamps, reflected in mirrors or gleaming brass or polished wood. But when the veil is removed, the interest of its necessity remains, for in both cases it has covered the inadmissible aspects of that social institution, marriage.

Such well-kept secrets more frequently relate to legal disputes about possession, and it often turns out that the estate in question does not belong to the family that lives there, but to a claimant of undistinguished origin. Wuthering Heights and Thrushcross Grange do not belong (ultimately) to the Earnshaws and Lintons, but to Heathcliff, originally a waif from the city slums. Transome Court in *Felix Holt* (1866) does not belong to Harold Transome, but to the tramp, Tommy Trounsem, who dies in a ditch. Restored by Harold's money,

> the home looked like an eminently desirable one. The white frost lay on the broad lawn, on the many-formed leaves of the evergreens, and on the giant trees at a distance. Logs of dry oak blazed on the hearth; the carpet was like warm moss under his feet.[158]

It has become 'such a home as many women would covet', but Esther has good reason to be oppressed by its 'well-lit solitude', for Transome Court is built on the sands of extortion and duplicity, and at the price of many lives; she is felt to do well in electing to marry poverty along with Felix Holt. In *Daniel Deronda*, Gwendolen's enjoyment of 'her own furlong of corridors' at Ryelands, with its 'rich glow of light and colour' in numerous rooms,[159] is destroyed by her awareness that, although each detail is superficially right, the whole is profoundly wrong, for this house too rests upon the ruin of other lives, those of Grandcourt's mistress and her unacknowledged children. Secrets are not confined to the great houses of antiquity: Mr Merdle in *Little Dorrit* has his own new secrets, and is uneasy beneath the eye of his butler in his new London palace: 'He would have clasped himself by the wrists in that constabulary manner of his, and have paced up and down the hearth-rug, or gone creeping about among the rich objects of furniture, if his oppressive retainer had appeared in the room at that very moment.'[160] This recurrent unease within the houses of the great suggests a dissatisfaction, wider than each particular case, with the social order that they represent.

The only form in which the great house seems acceptable to the imagination of the novelists is in a state of decay. The very shabbiness of Hamley Hall in *Wives and Daughters* endears it to the reader; its neglected beauty makes it a home as the grand and prosperous Towers is not. But it is not merely that shabbiness makes the great house seem less daunting: in its decay, it becomes acceptable as part of English history. Such houses, Trollope wrote, 'explain more fully, more truly than any written history can do, how Englishmen have become what they are'.[161] This is not because of their magnificence – Grex Castle in Yorkshire, built in the reign of James I, although very wild and very uncomfortable,[162] is compared favourably by the Duke of Omnium himself with Gatherum – it is because of the social traditions that they represent. Trollope thus praises Mr Thorne for continuing to inhabit the great hall at Ullathorne Court (there is no dining-room), with no more concession to modernity than a modern grate, although it is now only the socially acceptable, not the humble, who come to the great front door that opens into it.[163] Similarly, he celebrates the great house at Allington, which is early Stuart and built next to the road, with the comment: 'To be near the village, so as in some way to afford comfort, protection, and patronage, and perhaps also with a view to the pleasantness of neighbourhood for its own inmates, seemed to be the object of a gentleman when building his house in the old days.'[164] Trollope evidently shares Jane Austen's preference for past community to present isolation; but where she felt those sites to be alternatives, he knows that the first is a part of history.

The imaginative response to historical houses, as the expression of an order that is past, thus has none of Disraeli's optimism, for it is persistently pervaded by the sense of an order passed quite beyond recall. It seems ironic that where, in the eighteenth century, novelists and architects alike look out of their elegant windows on to the cottages of the poor as pleasing little features in the landscape, the Victorians, for whom the dwellings of the middle class tended increasingly to set the standard, should view the great house itself from that perspective – from the outside, as the focus for a landscape, much as the eighteenth-century painters had done (Fig. 24). George Eliot, although hard on the picturesque view of decaying farmhouses,[165] sees her great houses to best advantage in that perspective, much as Esther does when viewing Chesney Wold. Jane Austen also approaches her great houses from the outside, but, as I have said, they are sparingly described; more importantly, there is nothing to suggest that their façades do not accord with their interiors. For George Eliot, as for Dickens in the case of Chesney Wold, to stand outside and look in is to perceive a perfect picture; to stand within and look out is to experience a moral chill. Brackenshaw Park in *Daniel Deronda* forms a picturesque background for an archery contest: 'The castle, which stood on the highest platform of the clustered hills, was built of a rough-hewn limestone, full of lights and shadows made by the dark dust of lichens and the washings of the rain.'[166] But in its softly lit ballroom, scented by the adjacent conservatory, Grandcourt's lethal contest with Gwendolen is begun. Diplow Hall, with 'its fine elms and beeches, its lilied pond and grassy acres specked with deer',[167] is another idyll – until the reader sits down with Grandcourt at his breakfast table. Gwendolen's first glimpse of Ryelands is also a picture – a 'white house . . . with a hanging wood for a background, and the rising and sinking balustrade of a terrace in front'[168] – but this graceful place, despite the warmth and light inside it, is the context in which she faces the chilling implications of 'getting her choice'.

Where George Eliot tends simply to employ terms from painting in the description of her great houses, Henry James, for whom they have retreated a stage further, actually presents them in the two dimensions of paint. Medley is 'everywhere infinitely a picture';[169] Lockleigh, 'as they saw it from the gardens, a stout grey pile, of the softest, deepest, most weather-fretted hue, rising from a broad, still moat . . . a castle in legend', is another 'noble picture'.[170] Lord Mark's house is the centre of 'an almost extravagantly grand Watteau-composition, a tone as of old gold kept "down" by the quality of the air, summer full-flushed but attuned to the general perfect taste'.[171] One could name many more. But James's great houses are rarely inhabited by ancestral families: Lord Mark is an exception, and Lord Warburton offers to move from Lockleigh if Isabel (however mistakenly) argues damp from its moat;[172] in any event, his family's hold on the house is so frail that his sisters seem no more than faded chintz figures among the faded chintz of their drawing-room. Many of James's houses have been rented: Medley and Fawns are both examples;[173] while no one even knows whom Mertle belongs to, from which Mr Longden argues that society has grown vulgar.[174] Sometimes, like Gardencourt and possibly Poynton,[175] they have been bought up by those who admire their antiquity, but have no connection with their land or history. For Henry James the great house is a presence by itself, 'a serenity of success, an accumulation of dignity and honour';[176] 'the spectacle of long duration unassociated with some sordid infirmity or poverty';[177] 'a place of which the beauty would have had a sweet odour' even in the absence of 'flowers in rare vases';[178] 'the ache of antiquity';[179] 'the sign of *appointed* felicity'.[180]

In the three decades before the First World War, the great house appears more and more often as a picture, with a dream-like, self-sufficient existence of its own. It is surely significant that the enchanting country houses designed by Edwin Lutyens at this period should often be described as 'dream houses'. They are not the high expression of a society and its order; they seem intended, though newly built, to be what older houses had become – a nostalgic, retrospective vision, a painting in brick or stone. Ivy Compton-Burnett, who wrote beyond the First World War of ancestral houses in the 1890s, the setting of her own childhood, once declared that 'when an age is finished you see it as it is'.[181] What she saw in retrospect, with the eyes of an insider, was a nightmare rather than a dream. Her houses, too, have taken on a life of their own. In *A Heritage and its History* (1959), Julia, the mistress of the house, acknowledges its traditional sanctities: 'It is the one house I know where the present has not ousted the past. Everything is as it has been and will be.'[182] The younger generation is more sceptical: 'We have known the place and served it. We have seen it regarded as something it could not be. As a force in the background, with human lives helpless in the fore.'[183] Her houses, too, are dogged by destructive secrets: murder and worse are done to secure inheritance. In its growth, the ancestral house had meant more than property. The ideal is splendidly expressed in the seventeenth century by Ben Jonson in his poem 'To Penshurst':

> And though thy walls be of the countrey stone,
>   They'are rear'd with no mans ruine, no mans grone,
> There's none, that dwell about them, wish them downe;
>   But all come in, the farmer, and the clowne.[184]

But in its decline, as Ivy Compton-Burnett depicts it, the ancestral house becomes a mere rapacity for lost estate. The absence of description in her novels is functional, for it denies her houses any intrinsic claim on the imagination.

The external view of the great house, seen with middle-class eyes, continues, however, to be more sparing. Both Groby[185] and Branshaw Teleragh,[186] in the novels of Ford Madox Ford, are nostalgically conceived, for they express the passing of the possibility of that kind of order that Disraeli had hoped to see revived in them. Even before Branshaw is let to an American, to whom his tenants do not raise their hats in the same way, the house has already begun to alter:

> The whole of that familiar, great hall had a changed aspect. The andirons with the brass flowers at the ends appeared unreal; the burning logs were just logs that were burning and not the comfortable symbols of an indestructible mode of life. The flame fluttered before the high fireback; the St Bernard sighed in his sleep. Outside the winter rain fell and fell.[187]

That fire, like the light in the drawing-room at Chesney Wold, also 'seems gradually contracting and fading until it shall be no more'. When families like those in the novels of Ivy Compton-Burnett hold on to their houses at all costs, it is only to discover that their houses hold on to them. When they are deserted, like Branshaw, and Breadalby in *Women in Love*, though 'silent and forsaken' they are 'unchanged and unchanging'.[188] They become history and art, 'sunny and small like an English drawing of the old school, on the brow of the green hill, against the trees,' as Lawrence describes Breadalby; complete and final 'as an old aquatint'. But Gudrun's admiration for Breadalby is grudging, perhaps because it is still in private hands: 'she spoke with some resentment in her voice, as if she were captivated unwillingly, as if she must admire against her will'. When the great house becomes the possession of a nation, it can more easily be accepted as 'a noble picture', 'a history in stone', preserving in art, if not in life, that radiant aspect of Chesney Wold as Esther first sees it, that remembered notion of human community which has gone for good.

3

Dorothea's cottages
The houses of the poor

In the novels of the eighteenth century and Regency, the great houses of England occupy the foreground, while its cottages, when seen at all, are merely glimpsed as details in the scenery. In the novels of Queen Victoria's reign the converse comes to be true: the cottage begins to assume centrality, while the great house dwindles in an ever lengthening perspective. If Disraeli failed to persuade the aristocracy of England to provide every county with forty St Genevièves, each with its Mr Lyle, he with others (many of them novelists) did much, especially in the 1840s, to draw the attention of those more privileged to the destitute houses of the poor. It is ironic both that the new architecture of the masses should eventually have ended the dominance of great houses, and that more ordinary men and women should have become protagonists in the novel, for these were not the developments, either in life or in art, that Disraeli had in mind. Nevertheless, they were ones he helped to foster.

The difference between Regency attitudes and those of the mid-Victorians to the houses of the poor can be focused in George Eliot's *Middlemarch*, first published in 1871–2, but set in 1829–32. When its heroine, Dorothea, first entertains the illusion that marriage to Mr Casaubon will confer upon the everyday the aspect of great things, she makes one exception to the frustration of her efforts as a single woman to lead a significant life in that period in England: 'I don't feel sure about doing good in any way now; everything seems like going on a mission to a people whose language I don't know; – unless it were building good cottages – there can be no doubt about that.'[1] Modern readers of *Middlemarch* sometimes find it perplexing that significant social action, even for a woman in a provincial town in 1829, should be precluded, and that the single exception – the building of cottages – should be so inadequately dramatized within the novel. The explanation of these apparent omissions seems to lie in the forty years that separate the story, which extends to include the first Reform Bill in 1832, from the date of its publication shortly after the passing of the second Reform Bill in 1867. Both Dorothea's discomforting sense of an almost impassable gulf dividing rich and poor and her peculiar confidence in the building of cottages are slight anachronisms in the early 1830s; by the 1870s they are pervasive assumptions, indicating that, in the forty intervening years, attitudes to the poor and their houses had undergone a radical change.

Privileged characters in eighteenth-century fiction do not share Dorothea's discomforting sense that the poor are another species, as remote from their experience, as incomprehensible, as an African tribe. Servants are sometimes actually protagonists, and even in subordinate roles they are represented as men and even brothers. For Smollett they have as much to say as their masters, if less well spelt, while one even gives his name to the title, *Humphry Clinker*. In Sterne's Shandy Hall the similarity of its servants Obadiah and Susannah to the rest of that eccentric household might almost be described as a family likeness. The case is quite altered by the Regency. As I have mentioned, servants are normally invisible for Jane Austen, who identifies ministering hands only when, as at Portsmouth in *Mansfield Park*, they bang the doors and clatter the cutlery.[2] But it is not until the 1840s that an awareness, not only of the gulf between rich and poor, but of its dangerous significance in the lurid light of revolution, comes into being. By the close of that decade even writers like Thackeray, who are content to believe that all is well in the other nation, are none the less keenly aware of the divide – though he sees no reason to cross it – between a gentleman and his servants, 'who live with us all our days and are strangers to us: so strong custom is, and so pitiless the distinction between class and class'.[3]

Dorothea's distress at her distance from that other nation is thus in advance of her time, but the absence of scenes in *Middlemarch* showing her within the houses of the poor is quite appropriate to the period in which it is set. George Eliot's restraint in this respect is the more striking, for she delights elsewhere in describing simple interiors. In fact and in fiction, not only in the Regency but in the eighteenth century as well, the upper classes seem rarely to have ventured beneath an impoverished roof, much less imagined what it would be like to live beneath one. A novelist like Fielding, who is on familiar terms with the other nation (he married his deceased wife's maid and friend, Mary Daniel), may sometimes take his gentlemen into such rooms, but not for moral reasons: Molly Seagrim's narrow garret, shaped like the great delta of the Greeks, is a setting for sexual comedy, not social concern.[4] The philanthropist Albany in Fanny Burney's *Cecilia* (1782) is regarded even by his creator as 'partially deranged',[5] and in any case spends less time with the authentic poor than with the middle-class Belfield, fallen on evil days. In the Regency, Emma and Harriet certainly visit the poor, but Jane Austen keeps the reader in the roadway, to observe no more than 'the outward wretchedness' of poverty, and 'recal the still greater within'.[6] Even in the case of Harriet's visit to Robert Martin's pleasant farm with its two parlours, the reader waits with Emma at the gate.[7]

The novels of the 1840s are in this respect a total contrast. It is part of their purpose to open the eyes of their readership to the true conditions of working-class life, and many scenes are set in impoverished interiors. The importance of this (literal) step is emphasized rhetorically by Dickens in *Hard Times* (1854):

> For the first time in her life, Louisa had come into one of the dwellings of the Coketown Hands; for the first time in her life, she was face to face with anything like individuality in connection with them. She knew of their existence by hundreds and by thousands. She knew what results in work a given number of them would produce in a given space of time. She knew them in crowds passing to and from their nests, like ants or beetles. But she knew, from her reading, infinitely more of the ways of toiling insects than of these toiling men and women.[8]

To enter such houses, to know at first hand such interiors, was to give a face to the masses, mitigating on the one hand the terror of revolution, satisfying on the other the promptings of Christian conscience.

Dorothea's confidence that the gulf can best be bridged by the building of cottages, although again somewhat anachronistic, is not eccentric. To the first readers of *Middlemarch*, however, an elaboration of her plans might have seemed redundant, for if her ambitions were unusual in her own time, they were routine responsibilities by the 1870s. The days when Disraeli's Lord Marney was not afraid to admit that he built no cottages, but, on the contrary, pulled down as many as possible, were by then well over. Trollope's witty Duchess of Omnium, Glencora, is led by the collapse of her husband's ministry to lament: 'Then everything is over for me. I shall settle down in the country and build cottages, and mix draughts.'[9] No doubt the Duchess, like George Eliot's readers, would have possessed her own copy of Dorothea's sourcebook: 'I have been examining all the plans for cottages in Loudon's book, and picked out what seem the best things,' she tells Sir James.[10] One of his plans, of two cottages for country labourers, that Dorothea might have chosen, is shown in Figure 22. Each has an entrance lobby (a), a kitchen (b), back kitchen (c), parlour or best bedroom (d), dairy (f), fuel-store (g), cow-house (h), privy (i), and pigsty (k), not to mention two upstairs bedrooms. With their conveniences and their pleasant façades, the two cottages justify her affirmation, which exactly echoes Loudon's own conviction, that 'Life in cottages might be happier than ours, if they were real houses fit for human beings from whom we expect duties and affections.'[11]

Although Loudon's *Encyclopaedia of Cottage, Farm, and Villa Architecture* first appeared in 1833, its presence in Dorothea's hands in 1829 probably went unnoticed by George Eliot's early readers, so firmly was it then established as a household classic and indispensable sourcebook. Loudon's avowed objective, 'the amelioration of the great mass of society in all countries',[12] may appear to a modern reader grandiose, but to the Victorian reformer a bloodless revolution in housing seemed the best way of avoiding the carnage already witnessed on the European mainland. Under the guidance of Loudon, Disraeli's reformist landowners and manufacturers could find their way from fiction into fact, as Jane Loudon suggests by this incident, recounted in her biographical note upon her husband:

> These hints were followed up by many gentlemen: and I think I never saw Mr Loudon more pleased than when a highly respectable gardener once told him that

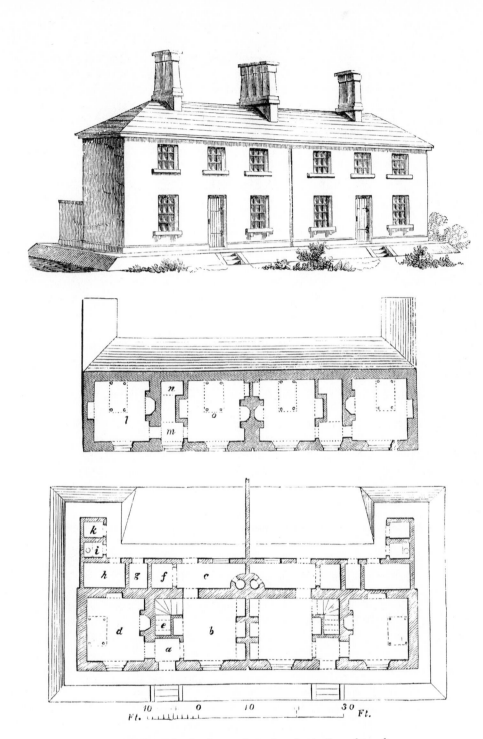

22 Dorothea's choice from Loudon's *Encyclopaedia*

he was living in a new and most comfortable cottage, which his master had built for him; a noble marquess, who said that he should never have thought of it, but for the observations in Mr Loudon's *Gardener's Magazine*, as they made him consider whether the cottage was comfortable or not, and that, as soon as he did so, he perceived its deficiencies.[13]

The way in which the privileged were eventually led, not only by writers like Loudon but also by some of the greatest Victorian novelists, to consider whether the houses of the poor were comfortable or not, together with the consequences of their interest, will be the theme of this chapter.

Even in country areas, and in provincial towns like Middlemarch, largely untroubled by the growth of industry and the independent proletariat it generated, there are obvious reasons why the gulf between the two nations should have begun to open during the Regency. As was explained in the previous chapter, the architecture of upper-class housing itself became increasingly divisive. Servants no longer slept within earshot of their masters, but were banished to garret or basement, and subsequently planted out in separate wings. The invention of back stairs and corridors rendered the family rooms increasingly private, since they now needed to be entered only for specific purposes, and no longer functioned as thoroughfares. The introduction of bell-hanging in the late eighteenth century made it possible to station servants quite out of earshot, behind the green baize door.

The poor man was also banished from the grounds of the house to take up his station either at the gate or beyond it. The fashion for 'emparkment', which started at the beginning of the eighteenth century, involved the transplantation of entire communities which were then rehoused outside the park in new-built villages. 'Why may not a whole estate be thrown into a kind of garden?' asked Joseph Addison in 1712.[14] Goldsmith, having seen the results, explains why not in 1770:

> The man of wealth and pride
> Takes up the space that many poor supplied;
>
> . . .
>
> His seat, where solitary spots are seen,
> Indignant spurns the cottage from the green.[15]

But in the following year William Whitehead, a poet laureate, defends the village of Nuneham Courtenay (possibly one origin of Goldsmith's Auburn),[16] built in the previous decade to replace the old, which stood much too close to Lord Harcourt's new Palladian mansion:

> The careful matrons of the plain
> Had left their cots without a sigh
> Well pleased to house their little train
> In happier mansions, warm and dry.[17]

'Mansions' seems a slight exaggeration, since the cottages, two-up, two-down, were small by later standards, and the 'little train' would need to be minute. Nevertheless, given the one-roomed hovels many lived in at that period, there may indeed have been a real improvement. The objection made to such settlements was more usually to their artificiality. They did not express community, clustered around the green and church, in the adventitious manner of the true village; they were drawn up in parallel lines to each side of the road. Uvedale Price objects in 1810 to villages like Nuneham Courtenay (Fig. 23a) on aesthetic grounds, as might be expected from an advocate of the picturesque: 'Such a methodical arrangement saves all further thought and invention; but it is hardly necessary to say that nothing can be more formal and insipid.'[18] Moreover, although such villages were often described as 'model', they were evidently built more for the lord than for the labourer. The one at Harewood (Fig. 23c), erected by Carr in 1760 for the first earl,[19] is designed to form an appropriate approach to the great gate (Fig. 23b) of the new Palladian house. As Loudon later comments, cottages built like this in a continuous row often had many of the inconveniences and nuisances of impoverished back streets in a country town.[20] Like Jane Austen,[21] he is also well aware of the social divide that had been created by such villages, for he observes that 'the possessors of extensive parks abhorred the appearance of a human habitation, however humble or however distant; and the first object of a new settler, of the rank of a gentleman, was, generally, to purchase everything around him; and to seclude himself in a sort of artificial forest, for his own exclusive enjoyment and that of his friends'.[22] This practice, he adds, is not at all understood by landowners in other countries. He favours instead proximity to the village, not only for the improvement of the villagers, but because it will remove for the proprietor 'that unpleasant feeling of cheerless solitude'.[23] Similarly, when Dorothea exclaims, 'Instead of Lazarus at the gate, we should put the pig-sty cottages outside',[24] she seems to be planning to build her model ones within the grounds of the complaisant Sir James.

The majority of the rural population did not, however, live either in the parks of the landowners, or just outside them; and if estate housing did begin to improve, the situation elsewhere was far otherwise. As the enclosure movement gained impetus towards the end of the eighteenth century, many of the poor could not afford the fences necessary to confirm their claim to the land, and therefore sold it to the wealthy; those who could were often unable to raise a living on the poor land they acquired, and sold it too; those who were squatters had no right to land at all and none to sell. A class of landless labourers developed, wages fell, and from 1795 many parishes adopted the Speenhamland system, which relieved the congestion of the workhouse by supplementing the income of the able-bodied when wages fell below the level of subsistence.

In the 1820s William Cobbett passes some beautiful parks with principled owners on his rural rides; but these are the exceptions, for he adds, '*The labouring classes* . . . God knows, have very few friends amongst the rich.'[25] Throughout the rides, he comes everywhere on evidence quite contrary:

23(a) Nuneham Courtenay:
'an unbroken line'

(b) Main entrance to
Harewood House

(c) Harewood village:
the approach to greatness

In all the really agricultural villages and parts of the kingdom, there is a *shocking decay*; a great dilapidation and constant pulling down or falling down of houses. The farmhouses are not so many as they were forty years ago by three fourths. . . . The labourers' houses disappear also. And all the *useful* people become less numerous.[26]

Cobbett can himself recall the days when labourers ate bread and meat, not potatoes; when they drank their home-brewed beer by their own fireside; when young people could purchase decent furniture for a house when they married, without appealing to the parish for a miserable nest. In his delightful account of a Methodist preacher, 'talking very loud about *houses! houses! houses!*',[27] Cobbett indicates that, at least in Kent, the working class was not yet reconciled to exchanging a cottage on earth for a mansion in heaven: 'they appeared to me to be thinking much more about getting houses for themselves *in this world first*: just to *see a little* before they entered, or endeavoured to enter, or even thought much about, those *"houses"* of which the parson was speaking; *houses* with pig-styes and little snug gardens attached to them, together with all the other domestic and conjugal circumstances.' The preacher's enquiry, 'Do you KNOW. . . do you KNOW, that you have ready for you houses, houses I say; I say do you KNOW; do you KNOW that you have houses in the heavens not made with hands?' falls on ears preoccupied with earthly buildings and builders. Such sermons, Cobbett concludes, have power only over the minds of the many miserable.

Ironically, it was just as such images of contentment began to vanish that the taste for the picturesque caused the upper classes to fall in love with the idea of the cottage.[28] The difference between Cobbett's perspective and theirs, one often reflected in idealized contemporary painting, is indicated by the contrast between the direct, unmannered prose of *Rural Rides*, and James Malton's distanced, florid sentences in his *Essay on British Cottage Architecture* in 1798:

> The greatly affluent in sumptuous equipage, as they pass the chearful dwelling of the careless rustic . . . involuntarily sigh as they behold the modest care-excluding mansion of the lowly contented; and often from the belief that solid comfort can be found only in retirement, forsake their noisy abodes, to unload their oppressing inquietudes in the tranquil retreat of the rural shelter. Often has the aching brow of royalty resigned its crown, to be decked with the soothing chaplet of the shepherd swain.[29]

The picturesque taste invariably distances and romanticizes, viewing the cottage from the outside, not the inside; regarding it as a feature in the landscape, not as a place to live in. This is particularly marked in *The Mysteries of Udolpho*, for when Mrs Radcliffe describes the cottage in which her heroine has taken shelter,[30] she writes of this 'bower of sweets' as though the reader stood outside it, although Emily, whose view he shares, is indoors, at her bedroom window: 'The cottage, which was shaded by the woods from the intenser rays of the sun, and was open only to his evening

24 Repton's view from Blaise Castle House

light, was covered entirely with vines, fig-trees, and jessamine whose flowers surpassed in size and fragrance any that Emily had seen.' Richard Payne Knight, in his *Analytical Inquiry into the Principles of Taste* (1805), observes that the 'objects and circumstances called *picturesque*' can 'afford no pleasure, but to persons conversant with the art of painting'.[31] When Dorothea cannot admire the sort of painting her uncle likes to praise – 'They are a language I do not understand'[32] – Mr Brooke attributes her inability to defective education. Her indifference to art lies rather in her sensitivity – unusual in that period – to the reality of poverty. 'I should like to make life beautiful – I mean everybody's life,' she later remarks.[33] 'And then all this immense expense of art, that seems somehow to lie outside life and make it no better for the world, pains one.' Prompted by this wish, Dorothea approaches her cottages from the inside, beginning with the plan; but the enthusiasts of the eighteenth century and Regency began with the elevation, and often effectively ended there as well. They were not seeking, as she was, to improve the living conditions of the labourer; they were concerned with the visual beauty of an estate. The many enchanting designs from that period are almost wholly devoted to external appearance, to cottages as features in the landscape. They function as a diversion to the eye, a focus for a view, a foretaste of grandeurs to come at the entrance to a park. Their role as accommodation is strictly secondary.

In his 'Red Book' for Blaise Castle (1795–6), Humphry Repton describes the

creation of one such picture.[34] Although he feels that the view from the dining-room of the new house will be relatively unimportant, he takes great pains to render it interesting, if not allegoric (Fig. 24). Beneath the castle he proposes to open a bay in the woods and build there a cottage that 'will give an air of cheerfulness and inhabitancy to the scene which would without it be too sombre, because the castle tho' perfectly in character with the solemn dignity of the surrounding woods, increases rather than relieves the apparent solitude'. The smoke from the cottage chimney will lend a 'vapoury repose' and motion to the scene which a painter himself might strive in vain to capture, making the valley seem larger than it really is. The cottage itself must seem to belong to the owner of the mansion and the castle, but without imitating the character of either, exciting notions rather of '*la Simplicité soignée*'. Raising his eyes from his mutton, the owner may see inscribed upon his own horizon the acceptable difference between the rich and the poor.

One did not, moreover, have to be very rich to cultivate such an outlook. John Plaw's design in 1800 for a cottage or small farmhouse, 'Intended for a Gentleman in the New Forest . . . as an object to be seen from his Mansion' (Fig. 25),[35] has a much less extensive landscape than that of Blaise Castle in mind, but it is typical of many at about the turn of the century. It makes an enchanting picture, formed from those features that the pastoral poetry of the period had established as the attractions of rural life: thatched roof, ascending smoke, mimic antiquity in Gothic window and

25 Cottage as feature in view

26 The gentry encounter peasant life

drip-course, contented swains and kine, over-arching trees. It only lacks the overgrowth, which refuses to be mimicked, that delights both Emily in *The Mysteries of Udolpho* and Richard Payne Knight in his poem, *The Landscape* (1794):

> Nor yet unenvy'd, to whose humbler lot
> Falls the retired and antiquated cot; –
> Its roof with weeds and mosses cover'd o'er,
> And honeysuckles climbing round the door;
> While mantling vines along its walls are spread,
> And clustering ivy decks the chimney's head.[36]

No plan for the upper floor is given, and the ground floor plan is very simple, with none of those carefully considered amenities that Dorothea might have looked for in Loudon's *Encyclopaedia*.

The picturesque taste certainly had its satirists: William Combe's poem *The Tour of Doctor Syntax in Search of the Picturesque* (1809) is one example. It is illustrated by Rowlandson who takes evident delight in depicting the encounter of the gentry with peasant life (Fig. 26). Neither writers nor architects were wholly unaware that these were to be houses for human beings to live in. In *Sense and Sensibility* Jane Austen's sensible Edward much prefers a 'snug farmhouse' to 'ruined, tattered cottages', a preference which amazes Marianne, who cultivates her sensibilities.[37] Repton himself comments in his *Enquiry* that 'the "*antiquated cot*", whose chimney is choked with ivy, may perhaps yield a residence for squalid misery and want';[38] and an awareness develops that cottages do not have to be ruinous to be picturesque. John Papworth, for example, remarks that their genuine adornments are neatness and cleanliness, for these suggest industry and cheerfulness, whereas 'the broken casement, the patched wall, the sunken roof, the hatch unhinged, the withered shrub, are corresponding testimonies of the husbandman's relaxed energies and broken spirit'.[39]

When it came to planning, however, very little seemed to follow from these observations. Joseph Gandy, who claims in 1805 that his designs originate 'in the humane desire of increasing the comforts and improving the condition of the Labouring Poor',[40] makes little provision for them. The family he proposed to house within a single room (Fig. 27a) could scarcely have cultivated the 'habit of neatness, and attention to cleanliness' which, he suggests, should do much to form 'the dispositions of the Labouring Class'.[41] His priority remains external appearance, for 'the advancement of Public Taste requires more than this – that we should combine convenience of arrangement with elegance in external appearance; a point of much consequence to the general aspect of the country'.[42] As a result, the labourer has no view down the vista of which, from his master's point of view, he forms the conclusion, his windows being so arranged that he cannot overlook it. William Shenstone, writing forty years earlier, explains in more realistic terms that the privileged interest themselves in the cottage 'partly on account of the variety it may introduce; on account of the tranquillity that seems to reign there; and perhaps, (I am somewhat afraid) on account of the pride of human nature'.[43]

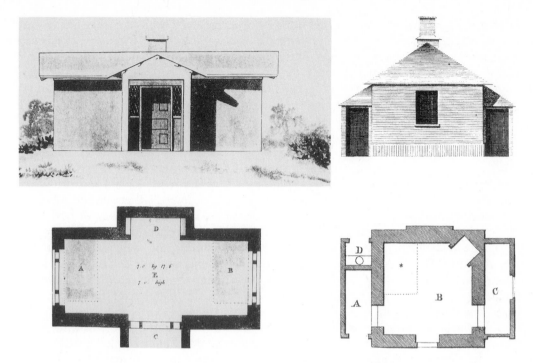

27 One-roomed cottages (a) J. Gandy: 1805 (b) J. Wood: 1781

Even the most conscientious writers did not find it easy to part with the picturesque view. Jane Austen may seem in *Sense and Sensibility* to join with Edward in preferring cottages in good repair, even at the cost of the picturesque;[44] but on another occasion, in *Northanger Abbey*, she appears to side with Catherine, who is so delighted by the view of 'a sweet little cottage' among apple trees which she sees from the windows of the parsonage at Woodston that her enthusiasm even saves it from demolition.[45] Loudon himself, though anxious to 'discard those fanciful comfortless dwellings which are often erected as ornamental cottages', admits that he would 'scarcely have courage to pull down a fine old specimen of a picturesque cottage, unless in a case of extreme necessity'.[46] Even the socially conscious Victorians allow their principles to waver on this question. Mrs Gaskell, who knew much better than Jane Austen how the poor really lived, and saw that her readers knew it too by taking them inside (at least in towns), nevertheless allows her heroine, Margaret, to take pleasure in sketching the exterior of a squatter cottage which is due for demolition in the New Forest.[47] When Margaret returns once more to Helstone, educated in reality by the industrial north, she is still grieved to find that it has disappeared and that a new one, tidy and respectable, has been built in its place.[48] Dickens's Will Fern, with first-hand knowledge of life inside one, complains of this female tendency: 'It looks well in a picter, I've heerd say; but there an't weather in picters, and maybe 'tis fitter for that than for a place to live in.'[49] One might add, however, that there is generally very little weather in most of Dickens's country cottages either, although one finds a good deal of it in his towns. George Eliot too is not without sympathy for the picturesque, and admits that 'the stray hovel, its old, old thatch full of mossy hills and valleys with wondrous modulations of light and shadow', is an element of joy in landscape to her midland-bred soul;[50] yet her attack on the picturesque view of the decaying farm, owned by Mr Brooke and ironically known as 'Freeman's End', shows her to be substantially in sympathy with Dorothea. The place has all the appropriate externals, chimneys choked with ivy, windows with jasmine, worm-eaten shutters, mossy thatch, all of which 'under the quiet light of a sky marbled with high clouds would have made a sort of picture which we have all passed over as a "charming bit", touching other sensibilities than those which are stirred by the depression of the agricultural interest, with the sad lack of farming capital, as seen constantly in the newspapers of that time'.[51] The impoverished tenant farmer, Dagley, with his pitchfork and milking hat, cuts an appropriate figure in such a setting; but his sentiments are not those of 'the lowly contented', and his house is anything but a 'care-excluding mansion'. His exchange with the negligent Mr Brooke is abrasive, and the price paid for upper-class ignorance in human misery – the worn wife, the thieving child, the drunkenness – throws into unsparing relief his landlord's enthusiasm for the fine arts and social reform. He wonders at Mr Brooke's advocacy of the first Reform Bill, for in Dagley's view its purpose is 'to send you an' your likes a-scuttlin'; an' wi' pretty strong-smellin' things too'.

With the passage of the Poor Law Amendment Act in 1834 the condition of labourers deteriorated still further. Outdoor relief was removed, and the indigent were consigned to workhouses which were designed to be punitively unattractive. In 1839, the year of the Chartist petition to Parliament (itself precipitated by the Act), Disraeli's delinquent Lord Marney is pulling down as many of his cottages as possible so that the poor do not become a charge upon his parish.[52] He regards eight shillings a week for those in work as quite sufficient, even for a family with eight children, for after all people who work in the open air, a healthy life, do not require as much food as those in manufacturing districts. Nevertheless, even beyond the 1840s, when the novel had begun to venture into the houses of the poor, rural interiors are almost invariably pleasant; it is those in towns that more often reveal indigence and misery. The picturesque view, which envisages life as art, took a long time to die.

An increasing number of architects had, however, begun to explore the distance between poetry and fact. The process had already begun in 1775 when Nathaniel Kent wrote:

> The shattered hovels which half the poor in this kingdom are obliged to put up with, is truly affecting to a heart fraught with humanity. Those who condescend to visit these miserable tenements can testify that neither health nor decency can be preserved in them.[53]

Whatever the poets might say, no children could 'run to lisp their sire's return'[54] and climb his knee in a hovel, measuring 7 feet by 12 feet, housing five people, the bed's end within a foot of the fire and the floor no better than the pavement of a street.[55] Edmund Bartell, who describes the realities in his *Picturesque Improvements* of 1804, is fond of quoting from Thompson and Cowper, in order to illustrate the discrepancy between the actuality and their poetic view of rural life. Some years earlier, John Wood tries 'however quaint the thought may appear . . . to feel as the cottager himself; and for that end to visit him; to enquire after the conveniences he wanted, and into the inconveniences he laboured under'.[56] His account of the 'shattered, dirty, inconvenient, miserable hovels' that he entered has little relation to the picturesque idyll. He lists the 'inconveniences' he found to be most common, some of which are directly attributable to picturesque design. The dwellings were often damp as a result of their situation; not only was this chosen to please the owner's eye, but the cottage was sometimes actually sunk in the earth, in order to preserve a humble outline. Rooms were too few and stairs too narrow; ceilings were too low or, on the upper floor, did not exist, so that sleepers stifled in summer and froze in winter. They tended to face north and west when they should have faced south and east, because they were there to be looked at, not to be looked from, and the windows of the mansion faced in the contrary direction. Since entrances were not screened and materials were poor – many of them one brick thick or built in *pisé*, a version of mud

28 Cottage interior

– they were cold and cheerless, with rain actually driving in through the walls. The frailty of such buildings is indicated in William Godwin's novel, *Caleb Williams* (1794), for Mr Falkland seems to be able to demolish a cottage with little more than his bare hands in order to prevent a fire from spreading.[57] This was the actuality of the pretty designs so liberally provided by the cottage enthusiasts of the time.

Wood's principles are those of Loudon more than three decades later: 'a palace is nothing more than a cottage IMPROVED', he wrote.[58] Both consider that house design should be based upon the cottage scaled up, not the palace scaled down. Conditions were, however, slow to improve. If one-roomed cottages were rarely built in the nineteenth century, those with two were common, though very few survive today. A reporter in the *Morning Chronicle*, 24 October 1849, describes one vividly: the mud outside, the low doorway, the dark and chill interior, the sparse and derelict furniture. A similar room is sketched by John Brown in 1854 for George Godwin's *London Shadows* (Fig. 28). But the writer in the *Morning Chronicle*, although a punctilious recorder, only alludes in his final sentence to the worst feature of such dwellings: 'And yet you fancy you could put up with everything but the close earthy smell, which you endeavour in vain to escape by breathing short and quickly.'

That earthy smell, though keenly sensed, is euphemistic. It is not until the 1860s or even later that details of plumbing are really considered, even by architects. Henry Roberts, an important reformer, is statistically most precise in his *Dwellings of the Labouring Classes* (1850), but is entirely unspecific in his discussion of defective drainage. Novelists writing for a 'polite' audience are even more evasive: Dickens, for example, and even Mrs Gaskell, tend to avoid smells and do not define the nature of the 'stickiness' they sometimes mention underfoot. Kingsley is almost alone in saying what he means in this respect. As his Colonel Bracebridge remarks to the hero of *Yeast*:

> What a yet unspoken poetry there is in that very sanitary reform! It is the great fact of the age. We shall have men arise and write epics on it, when they have learnt that 'to the pure all things are pure', and that science and usefulness contain a divine element, even in their lowest appliances. . . .

> Smells and the Man I sing

> There's a beginning at once. Why don't *you* rather, with your practical power, turn sanitary reformer – the only true soldier – and conquer those real devils and 'natural enemies' of Englishmen, carbonic acid and sulphuretted hydrogen?[59]

River, meadow, and woodland may lead the spectator to predict 'Arcadia among fertility, loveliness, industry and wealth',[60] but the illusion can be sustained only by those who keep their distance, for such 'picturesque villages are generally the perennial hotbeds of fever and ague, of squalid penury, sottish profligacy, dull discontent too stale for words'. The contrast between the remoter, romantic view and the actuality when seen close up is illustrated by George Godwin in *Town Swamps and Social Bridges*, published in 1859 (Fig. 29), a decade after *Yeast*. As

29 Arcadia and actuality

Kingsley's hero comments: 'No wonder you have typhus here . . . with this filthy open drain running right before the door.'[61] But when he asks why it is not cleaned out, he is told that the man of the house is in no humour for it, after the fourteen hours of his day's labour, and that there is in any case no water for the purpose since the poor must pay to fetch it up the hill.

It was not until the second half of the nineteenth century that houses for the rural working class really began to improve. Even the reforming Wood designs a one-roomed cottage (Fig. 27b), intended to accommodate a family with one or two children in a space of only 13 feet square. When his plan is compared with Gandy's (Fig. 27a), the main difference lies in the care he has taken to consider what it might be like to live inside. There is a privy (D) separated from the rest of the cottage and reached from the outside – a necessity with an earth closet. There is a separate pantry (C), and a porch (A) which both screens the front door and acts as a fuel store. Both fireplace and bed are placed beyond the reach of draughts. His ceilings are a generous 8 feet high (not 7 feet); the walls are almost three times the normal thickness (not 6 but 16 inches, if made of stone), and the building, far from being sunk in the ground, is raised 15–18 inches above it to avoid damp. But where available floor space and amenities are concerned, there is no comparison between his design and the one that Dorothea might have chosen (Fig. 22). Wood indeed advocates three bedrooms, but it is clear from the majority of his designs that he does not expect his labourers to achieve them. Beyond the mid-century standards improved considerably. The three-bedroomed cottage was certainly rare in Dorothea's time, but by the close of Queen Victoria's reign the majority of those new-built were of this type. The impetus for change was to come, however, less from acknowledging the true condition of rural cottages, than from discovering what working-class housing in towns was really like.

As a single woman living with her uncle, the negligent landlord Mr Brooke, Dorothea has good reason to concern herself with cottages, although she intends them for the estate of the obliging Sir James, having presumably abandoned her uncle as a hopeless case. Marriage to Mr Casaubon is, in many senses, another matter. The double cottages under his care in Lowick, with their low rents, their livestock, their back gardens, and gilliflowers, make Dorothea ashamed of her desire to live in a parish with a greater share of the world's misery. Because the 1830s marked the translation of much of the rural population – and with it the problem of housing the poor – from the country into the cities, Dorothea's second, more satisfactory marriage to Will Ladislaw seems symbolic: she turns her attention, one assumes, from rural to urban housing, as he does his from pictures to politics. In 1801 the population of London had been 900,000; by 1831, at 1,654,994, it had nearly doubled. During the decade 1831–41, the number of those living in industrial towns increased by over 40 per cent, and the population of England was, for the first time, dominantly urban. 1832 was, moreover, not only the year of the first Reform Bill, but of a major epidemic of cholera. The condition of the urban poor could no longer be ignored.

The context of Milton's 'glittering spires and pinnacles', over which Uvedale Price had enthused at the close of the eighteenth century as the desirable outline of a Gothic city,[62] was at last identified as Pandemonium, the creation of the 'dark satanic mills'. The true Gothic city, as Pugin indicates in his contrasting townscapes of 1440 and 1840 (Fig. 30), was a thing of the past, not only because its architecture had largely been destroyed, but even more because the spirit that had animated it had been wholly lost. Where the skyline of the town in 1440 is composed of spires, expressive of religious aspiration, the vertical accent in 1840 is provided by factory chimneys, whose smoke ascends as incense to the new God of Mammon. Where the town in 1440 has 13 churches, in 1840 it has 7, all new-built, for in nineteenth-century England more churches were erected than in any other century since the middle ages. But these have fragmented into seven different denominations, and are no longer – like Grey Friars or St Maries Abbey – sanctuaries for the indigent and outcast, who are consigned instead to the lunatic asylum and new jail, both expressions of Utilitarianism. Where in the old town education was the province of the church, and even the mercantile ethic assumed a religious form in the Guildhall, in the new one secular and technological structures dominate: gas works and iron works, new town hall and socialist hall of science. Humanitarian ideals have totally vanished.

Rural housing had been the first to receive attention because it could be regarded as the responsibility of each landowner; but the housing in towns was literally nobody's business and could pass unnoticed, just as factory hands could be laid off in a recession, as farming labourers with tied cottages could not. For Robert Thornton, Mrs Gaskell's honourable industrialist, this indifference is almost a matter of principle: 'The masters would be trenching on the independence of their hands, in a way that I, for one, would not feel justified in doing, if we interfered too much with the life they lead out of the mills.'[63] Margaret, who comes from a rural background, and whose sympathies have much in common with Dorothea's, objects to this as 'an

THE SAME TOWN IN 1840

1. St Michael's Tower, rebuilt in 1750.   2. New Parsonage House & Pleasure Grounds.   3. The New Jail.   4. Gas Works.   5. Lunatic Asylum.   6. Iron Works & Ruins of St Maries Abbey.   7. Mr Evans Chapel.   8. Baptist Chapel.   9. Unitarian Chapel.   10. New Church.   11. New Town Hall & Concert Room.   12. Westleyan Centenary Chapel.   13. New Christian Society.   14. Quakers Meeting.   15. Socialist Hall of Science.

Catholic town in 1440.

1. St Michaels on the Hill.   2. Queens Cro∫s.   3. St Thomas's Chapel.   4. St Maries Abbey.   5. All Saints.   6. St Johns.   7. St Peters.   8. St Alkmunds.   9. St Maries.   10. St Edmunds.   11. Grey Friars.   12. St Cuthberts.   13. Guild hall.   14. Trinity.   15. St Olaves.   16. St Botolphs.

30 Pugin's contrasting townscapes

unchristian and isolated position'. So, too, thought many others, especially Disraeli, who in *Sybil* and *Coningsby* constantly urges the point that property, in land and the means of production alike, is indivisible from responsibility. Mr Thornton's position may be more sympathetically received today, when 'paternalism' has become a dirty word; but if, as a later critic was to claim,[64] such philanthropists as Dorothea wished only to fulfil their own personal sentiment of pity and justice, and could not escape the disability of their arbitrary self-appointment, they undoubtedly had a great deal to contribute in the absence of state measures to fill the gap. In his *London Shadows* Godwin even finds a function for the voyeurs who made it fashionable to tour the slums 'and wonder at the peculiarities of that strange land',[65] because 'it was partly owing to these visits that some improvements were carried into effect'. By the 1840s the influence of the philanthropists was considerable. 1842 saw the Poor Law Board's *Report on the Sanitary Conditions of the Labouring Population*, and also the foundation of the magazine, *The Builder*, edited by George Godwin and devoted to housing and sanitary reform. In 1843 the Government set up a Royal Commission on the Health of Towns; in 1844 the Health of Towns Association was founded, whose central committee included Disraeli and Lord John Manners, the other moving spirit in the Young England Movement, characterized as Lord Henry Sydney in *Coningsby*. Whatever their political persuasions, it was the early work of such reformers and philanthropists which created a climate of opinion that began to see the housing of the very poor as part of the social purpose of the state.

It was far easier than might now be supposed to remain ignorant of the deplorable housing in English cities, even where it affected the great majority, as in the London of *Little Dorrit*, with its 10,000 responsible houses and 50,000 lairs, 'where people lived so unwholesomely, that fair water put into their crowded rooms on Saturday night, would be corrupt on Sunday morning'.[66] The responsible houses, 'frowning heavily on the streets they composed', could remain irresponsibly ignorant of the 50,000 lairs. As was pointed out in the previous chapter, the plan of the Victorian house and the Victorian city have this in common: that both are so designed that the few who live on the privileged side of the divide need know nothing of the many who are crowded beyond it into a fraction of the space. 'In many instances,' writes Godwin, 'these hotbeds fever and vice are so effectually hidden by goodly houses that the inhabitants of the latter are scarcely aware of the poverty and disease which exist within a stone's throw from their own doors.'[67] Mrs Gaskell, when living in Manchester, need never have set foot (had she so chosen) in the slums of Miles Platting and Ancoats with their crowded courts. As Engels wrote in 1845:

> The town itself is peculiarly built, so that a person may live in it for years, and go in and out daily without coming into contact with a working-people's quarter or even with workers, that is, so long as he confines himself to his business or pleasure walks. This arises chiefly from the fact, that by unconscious tacit agreement, as well as with outspoken conscious determination, the working-people's quarters are sharply separated from the sections of the city reserved for the

middle-class. . . . And the finest part of the arrangement is this, that the members of this money aristocracy can take the shortest road through the middle of all the labouring districts to their places of business without ever seeing that they are in the midst of the grimy misery that lurks to the right and the left.[68]

On a less generalized scale, these contrasts are part of the experience of *Mary Barton*, where, for example, the workman, unemployed because times are bad, observes the manufacturers in their carriages visiting shops that contain expensive luxuries;[69] or where Jem Wilson leaves the destitution of the Davenport cellar to seek an infirmary order from Mr Carson in his luxurious library, at his well-spread breakfast table.[70] The only feature of the city shared by rich and poor alike was the atmosphere, and as time went on the manufacturers stopped living next to their mills, as Robert Thornton does, and retreated further and further into the suburbs.

In part the slums of Manchester were created, as slums so often are, by this departure of the prosperous to modern houses of improved design in healthier areas. Engels vividly describes the decay of the old town, its once spacious houses crammed with tenements, 'dirty, old, and tumbledown, and the construction of the side streets utterly horrible'.[71] But a great deal of new building was also needed to accommodate the influx from the country – Ancoats itself was developed in the nineteenth century – and this could be equally substandard before it was well up. Much of it was erected by small speculators with limited means, who came themselves from the working class. Engels quotes from a description of one such development, produced by the co-operation of a carpenter and bricklayer, in which a whole street followed the course of a ditch to save the cost of excavating cellars in which people were to live.[72] As a result, not a house in that street escaped the cholera. Conditions elsewhere, with dung-hills in the middle of unpaved streets, were little better. The artisan Wodgate in *Sybil*,[73] one 'vast squalid suburb', its alleys 'seldom above a yard wide, and streaming with filth', is evidently no exaggeration; many such 'gutters of abomination, and piles of foulness, and stagnant pools of filth' existed. Godwin describes a similar street in London, Paradise Row, behind the new-built Paddington station, where the heaps of refuse before the pitiful buildings were a cause of wonder to all visitors.[74]

It would be mistaken to assume, however, that developments on a larger scale, financed by more prosperous contractors, were necessarily an improvement. With their broader streets and freshly painted houses they might appear to be so, but, as Engels remarked, those streets were often unpaved and lacked a sewer, the paint was bound to fade within a decade, and their apparent solidity of build would then be revealed as no more than that of bricks laid end to end. In the novels of Dickens, slum housing invariably goes upon crutches, but that does not necessarily mean that it is advanced in years.

Whether old or new, these undesirable buildings were always overcrowded, housing not only people, but animals as well. 'London cows', as Godwin observes, 'are, in many cases, kept in places where the poor brutes are not only destroyed

31(a) A London cow-byre (b) A London sheep-fold

themselves, but are made the cause of destruction to those living around.'[75] (Fig. 31a) The sheep in his other illustration (Fig. 31b) seem equally reluctant to enter one of the cellar-dwellings already referred to, which could prove uninhabitable by both animals and human beings. The Davenports' second cellar in *Mary Barton*, though described as a 'back apartment', and making a difference in the rent of threepence, is fit for neither with its floor of evil-smelling mud and its grating through which drop 'the moisture from pigsties, and worse abominations'.[76] Two rooms to a family of five would indeed be a luxury. In his *London Shadows*, Godwin removes the façade from a house (Fig. 32a–d), so that the reader may see for himself how many people are crammed in behind it. The room on the second floor houses fifteen people, and the other three little less, all at the same rent of 2*s*. 3*d*. per week. Conditions like these were not exceptional. Both Roberts and Engels, for example, make specific mention of the aristocratic parish of St George's, Hanover Square. According to Engels, two-thirds of its working people possess no more than a single room per family,[77] and Roberts's figures are even more specific: 929 families have only one room, 623 only one bed.[78] In St Giles he visits a room, 22 feet by 16 feet, which houses 40 to 60 people, not to mention cats and dogs. Sometimes conditions could be even worse: Godwin, for example, describes a London court where 'the basement story of nearly all the houses was filled with foetid refuse, of which it had been the receptacle for years',[79] and one water barrel of 50 to 60 gallons is intended to serve two houses, containing between them at least a hundred people.

In such conditions the inadequacies of rubbish disposal, water supply, sewage, and drainage became insuperable problems on a scale unknown in country villages. What are possibly the rubbish heaps of *Our Mutual Friend* loomed even larger in fact than they do in fiction. They are illustrated by Godwin (Fig. 33) with the caption given. This suburban mountain, the parkland of the poor, was composed not only of soot, ashes, and household detritus, but possibly of excrement as well.[80] Water supplies,

(a) attic

(b) second floor

(c) first floor

(d) ground floor

32 Overcrowding

33 Nova Scotia Gardens, and what grew there

invariably inadequate, were often polluted. Godwin illustrates on a small scale the proximity of cesspool and pump (Fig. 34a) which an investigator in the town of Stafford in 1866 found to be a more general rule: 'The water supply of the whole town is obtained from wells, many of them in close proximity to receptacles of filth; and I am in the habit of saying, partly in joke, but principally in earnest, that the persons living at No. 6 drink the water that is *made* at No. 7.'[81] Moreover, when Dickens alludes in *Bleak House* to 'a hemmed-in churchyard, pestiferous and obscene, whence malignant diseases are communicated to the bodies of our dear brothers and sisters who have not departed',[82] he is not being metaphorical. Godwin illustrates the crowded and shallow graves of St Pancras's churchyard (Fig. 34b) with the comment, 'The retention of burial-places in the midst of the living is a costly wickedness and a national disgrace.'[83]

The disposal of sewage was, of course, a related problem of equal magnitude, which the invention of the water-closet exacerbated rather than solved, because the available sewers could not accommodate the increased volume. A smell from the

(a) Proximity of
pump and cesspool

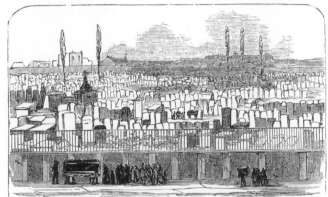

(b) Churchyard

(c) Miasma

34 Hazards to health

35 Life in a cesspool

drains preoccupied even the most prosperous, due to the consequent backing up, but conditions among the poor were infinitely worse. In his discussion of *The Legal Aspects of Sanitary Reform*, Edward Jenkins includes an account of newly built cottages in the East End of London in the 1860s, where the contents of an adjacent cesspool were actually being used to make mortar for further dwellings, crammed into the back gardens of the first.[84] In *Alton Locke* Kingsley takes the reader into a house like the ones depicted by Godwin with the caption given (Fig. 35), where the rush-light picks up reflections through the broad chinks in the floorboards of the sewer below.[85] That sewer, with its 'phosphorescent scraps of rotten fish . . . bubbles of poisonous gas, and bloated carcases of dogs, and lumps of offal, floating on the stagnant olive-green hell-broth', is also the occupants' water-supply.

Accounts as overt as Kingsley's are, as I have said, most unusual in Victorian novels. The pitiful rooms of the labouring poor are more often detailed, though real destitution like that of the Davenports is rare. It is the domestic courage and creativity of the poor in the most adverse circumstances that is usually emphasized. Although the Hexams' Thames-side tenement, a former mill, in *Our Mutual Friend*, is in itself atrocious – 'roof, and walls, and floor . . . alike had a look of decomposition'[86] – it is the effort to make the place a home – 'a small dresser, making a spare show of the commonest articles of crockery and cooking vessels' – that is drawn to the reader's attention. In the same vein, Mrs Gaskell commends the order and arrangement of Alice Wilson's cellar dwelling in *Mary Barton*, the check curtain at the modest bedhead, the 'little bit of crockery-ware . . . ranged on the mantelpiece, where also stood her candlestick and box of matches'.[87] Godwin describes a similar room, measuring only 7 feet by 6 feet, containing no food but a small crust on a shelf beside the teapot.[88] But above the fireplace are several framed prints that offer happier perspectives: a middle-aged couple in a richly furnished room; two lovers walking on a terrace, overlooking trees and gardens bright in the light of a clear sky. 'Poor as this place is,' Godwin concludes, 'it is *still a home.*'

But, as Godwin comments, the room he describes is not an example of the direst stage of London poverty, for it contains various objects that could be sold. Nevertheless, in fact as well as in fiction, even those almost totally indigent retained their pride. In his formidable survey of 1849–50, *London Labour and the London Poor*, Mayhew describes a room in the poorest of his three classes of costermonger.[89] The roof, which is stripped of tiles, provides the water-supply; the chimney smokes so thickly that the opposite wall is barely visible; the few remaining window-panes are stained and the majority are stuffed with rags and paper. There is very little furniture: a mattress on the floor; three chairs, of which the best has no back and only half its stuffing; and three or four old mats to stop objects dropping through the cracks in the floor on to the donkeys below. Yet even here the fireplace is carefully 'dressed', with an earthenware sugar-basin in the centre, and a cracked teacup and saucer to each side. But it too is a home, which some might starve to death rather than leave:

> Deceased died on Saturday morning. The family never had enough to eat. – Coroner: 'It seems to me deplorable that you did not go into the workhouse.' – Witness: 'We wanted the comforts of our little home.' A juror asked what the comforts were, for he only saw a little straw in the corner of the room, the windows of which were broken. The witness began to cry, and said they had a quilt and other little things. The deceased said he never would go into the workhouse.[90]

This is no fiction, but a report from the *Daily Telegraph* of 1864 which so impressed itself upon Ruskin that he reprinted it in red type in *Sesame and Lilies*: 'Be sure, the facts themselves are written in that colour, in a book which we shall all of us, literate or illiterate, have to read our page of, some day.'

An assault on the conscience as direct as Ruskin's may prove to be a two-edged weapon, eliciting self-justification rather than remorse. The reformers were normally more circumspect. It is difficult, with twentieth-century hindsight, to appreciate just how many obstacles stood in their way. No one, for example, was quite certain how diseases were disseminated. At the mid-century there were three conflicting theories – by germs, by spontaneous production, by atmospheric (miasmic) generation (Fig. 34c).[91] The last (held by Florence Nightingale and Charles Kingsley, to name only two) was for a time more popular than the first; and although to some extent the preventive measures suggested by each did overlap, their priorities were somewhat different. The vagueness of novelists is sometimes due to these uncertainties, but they can capitalize imaginatively upon them. When Charles Kingsley writes in his description of the sewer of 'the slow sullen rows of oily ripple . . . sending up . . . hot breaths of miasma',[92] he is being quite specific; but in Dickens's *Little Dorrit* the word is virtually symbolic of confusion, as the pervasive fog is in *Bleak House*. A sense of diffused uncertainty, of groping in the dark for remedies, associates itself with the theory even where it is accepted. Charlotte M. Yonge, one such believer and a literal writer, associates the miasma from a pond with a hysterical state of neurotic dread in *The Young Stepmother*. This uncertainty might, on the one hand, encourage social commentators in the attitude expressed by a writer in *The Economist* in 1848: 'In our condition suffering and evil are nature's admonitions; they cannot be got rid of; and the impatient attempts of benevolence to banish them from the world by legislation, before benevolence has learnt their object and their end, have always been productive of more evil than good.'[93] On the other hand, the mysterious passage of disease can be made in fiction to serve God's judgement on the rich. In Kingsley's social novels particularly, the diseases of the poor have a way of transmitting themselves to the other nation by way of their omissions – neglected ponds or the products of tailors' sweat-shops.

If, in the Victorian novel, a disproportionate number of working-class interiors are attractive, it is partly because the theorists of infection were all agreed that cleanliness was the first step towards prevention. Moreover, many writers took the opportunity to stress that the other nation was quite capable of home-making, the root of all goodness in that period. 'Oh! if those who rule the destinies of nations would but remember . . . how hard it is for the very poor to have engendered in their hearts that love of home from which all domestic virtues spring, when they live in dense and squalid masses where social decency is lost, or rather never found,' Dickens exclaims in *The Old Curiosity Shop*.[94] Environmental determinists are also numerous among the social commentators of the period: 'Wretched houses make wretched homes; and while immoral or slatternly habits convert fine dwellings into styes, it is almost as true that dirty and unhealthy habitations transfer a taint to the character and habits of the persons who occupy them.'[95] For a nation of monetarists, however, more than this was required. Others therefore argued that improved housing would bring financial benefits by lessening the number of the 'dangerous classes' and allowing the rest 'to play their proper part in increasing the sum of general wealth and general happiness'.[96] Even rewards such as these were a shade oblique for those who expected a direct return upon money invested. Just as the poor could not expect to get something for nothing, so the rich did not expect to get nothing for something. The most powerful argument of all, which, despite its futility in a large proportion of cases, was advanced repeatedly from 1840 to 1880, was that working-class housing could be made to pay. Henry Roberts, who has been described as the motivating force behind housing improvements, makes this the first of his contentions; his second is health, and his third moral improvement.[97] When one considers that the rents for the poorest housing were often as high, per square foot, as those of the wealthy middle class, his argument may seem less unconvincing; but of course, the area per person regarded as model involved a greater number of square feet. Where such projects did produce their 'fair return' (a minimum of 5 per cent), their tenants were drawn from the relatively prosperous upper working class of artisans, and not from the truly indigent for whom they were intended.

The second might be found in greater numbers among the inhabitants of lodging houses in great cities. Mayhew describes a spectrum of these, some quite appalling, with 6 or 7 to a single verminous bed, a few others almost home-like. The model lodging houses were, he found, neater and more sanitary but much stricter; indeed, they seem sometimes to have been not too far distant from the workhouse, scarcely calculated to engender the love of home. Mrs Gaskell, writing to an American friend in 1860, certainly thought that those in Streatham Street were not designed to be so: 'There is but *one* sink &c for every *floor*; the fireplaces were the poorest kind of parlour grate, over or by which there was not the least [hope] of cooking; there was not a peg, a shelf, or a cupboard, or even a recess in which one might be *cheaply* made.'[98] Moreover, she states quite emphatically that 'they *don't* pay as an investment', despite a rent of 6s. for two bare though good-sized rooms. Thanksgiving Buildings (Fig. 36), which Roberts designed himself, so named because they were built with money given in thanksgiving for the removal of the cholera, were less expensive, 1s. per person in a double room. They were not, however, fully tenanted, perhaps because the 'stringent regulations as to the hours of closing and constant supervision' discouraged the single women for whom they were intended.[99] The first of the Peabody buildings, financed by a trust founded by an American philanthropist in 1862, charged 2s. 6d. per week for a room for a single person; while tenements for families, some of 2 rooms each, some of 3, cost a maximum of 5s. The rents seem low, but when one considers that Mayhew's seller of songs with a dependent wife earned less than 10s. a week and sometimes less than 5s., it is easy to see why he might cling to his far from model room, where he has his own 'bits and sticks', even at an exorbitant rent of 2s. 3d. Despite its lack of amenities, he might in any case have preferred it to Peabody accommodation, with its ban upon wallpaper and its walls bare of plaster to prevent vermin.

When in 1857 something new began to grow in Nova Scotia Gardens, financed by Angela Burdett-Coutts at the prompting of Dickens, the residents protested so vehemently that they had to be pacified by the architect and restrained by the law. Not only was their dustheap to be removed, but much of the slum building that surrounded it. Columbia Square was built on principles similar to the Thanksgiving and Peabody buildings; but it did allow for a club room and a covered area where

36 Thanksgiving model buildings

children might play on wet days, where Roberts had avoided communal amenities, questioning whether the working class would have time to enjoy them. Dickens, who was always convinced like his Mr Sleary that people must be amused, certainly took an active interest in its planning. In this role he was more specifically practical than his novels might suggest, advising Angela Burdett-Coutts to consult with the Board of Health, rather than simply trusting to her architect, in order to 'get good sanitary arrangements on the most efficient and simple terms'.[100] But, although it was well designed and firmly built, Columbia Square was also grim. It was followed by the much more extravagant and fanciful Columbia Market, but this overawed potential vendors, who were not allowed to do too many things (like sticking bills on the columns inside), while potential buyers of the poorer classes did not dare to put a foot inside it. It became successively a fish market, a cheap restaurant, and finally a store for the London County Council.[101]

Buildings designed to accommodate families as independent units were more individual and less institutionalized. Although almost all working-class housing in the novel is of that type, since it can better be represented as a 'home', it was for that very reason much too expensive for the very poor. The little terraced houses, with gardens front and back, that Loudon advocates[102] have now doubtless been

MODEL HOUSES FOR FOUR FAMILIES,

ERECTED BY COMMAND OF

HIS ROYAL HIGHNESS PRINCE ALBERT, K.G.,

AT THE EXPOSITION OF THE WORKS OF INDUSTRY OF ALL NATIONS, 1851,

And subsequently rebuilt in Kennington New Park, Surrey.

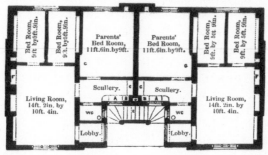

A Sink, with Coal Box under.	E Staircase of Slate, with Dust Place under.
B Plate Rack over entrance to Dust Shaft, D.	F Cupboard warmed from back of Fireplace.
C Meat Safe, ventilated through hollow bricks.	G Linen Closet in this recess if required.

Scale of ⸻⸻⸻⸻⸻ feet.

37 Prince Albert's model houses

demolished as substandard, for each floor could measure as little as 12 feet by 12 feet; but they were not only a great advance on the slum housing in industrial towns; they provided interiors that could give the domestic virtues at least a chance of growth. Even they, however, were intended for mechanics, the upper level of the working class. Prince Albert, who did much to promote a concern for working-class housing, not least by dying himself from typhoid, gave his name to a model building for four families which, although again intended for artisans, had been rejected as too ambitious by the organizers of the Great Exhibition (Fig. 37). The dimensions of the flats are almost as modest as Loudon's, but they make the maximum use of the space provided, as the key to the plan suggests. The three bedrooms cater 'for that separation which, with a family, is so essential to morality and decency';[103] moreover, 'the children's bedrooms . . . opening out of the living-room, an opportunity is afforded for the exercise of parental watchfulness'. With so much vigilance about, it is surprising how human and mature the working classes appear to be in many novels. The façade of the building at least escaped from rigour.

Designs for artisans did not in any case reach to the root of the problem – the housing of the poorest. In the 1850s Godwin wrote: 'The problem how capitalists are to provide such accommodation as will be liked, with a pecuniary return, is not solved yet';[104] it never was. As he noted at the time, new houses intended for single families were subdivided into tenements on their first letting, for the very poor simply could not afford to pay their landlords a realistic return on their investment. Slum clearance was no answer, since the indigent were simply displaced from the centre of cities to make slums of the suburbs; it was useless, and moreover dangerous, to destroy the housing of the poor without replacing it, as Godwin again remarked, with his eye on Paris. In an effort to find a solution to the problem in its widest sense, realism began to replace the idealism of the 1840s. Robert Kerr caused outrage in the mid-1860s by suggesting that the doctrine of three bedrooms (stipulated in the 1840s when the blue books revealed a high incidence of incest) should be abandoned; but, though the moral problems did not of course vanish, his view came to be increasingly shared.[105] Where Roberts had commended Prince Albert's provision of three bedrooms because the use of the living-room as sleeping quarters led to unwholesome crowding, the realists began to point out that the crowding occurred in any case, since even those who could afford to rent the extra rooms, could not afford to furnish them. All in all, it was better to have a tolerable tenement than the ideal which no one could afford.

A more plausible alternative was the renovation of existing buildings, some of which had originally been solid structures. A group of such houses, Wild Court in Lincoln's Inn, is described in the 1850s in *Household Words*, the weekly run by Dickens, in which a number of Mrs Gaskell's novels first appeared.[106] Built 200 years before as legal chambers, they still bore traces of their former grandeur: beams, joists, and bearing timbers of sound oak; wainscoting and lofty rooms. Thirteen of them were purchased by the Society for Improving the Condition of the Labouring Classes, chaired by Lord Shaftesbury. When first visited, their condition was nauseating:

'there were open troughs of ordure passing through the upper rooms into a half-stagnant open sewer in the parapet, immediately below the uppermost windows . . . the cellars were full of refuse filth . . . the open stairs were the night haunt of the filthy, and the back yards of a morning deep in all abomination'.[107] It was calculated that, after their 'return to Christianity', they would yield no less than 15 per cent profit, as against the maximum of 6 per cent for model lodging houses. During renovation that figure dropped to 12 per cent, because 150 cartloads were necessary to remove sewage from the 16 cesspools, 350 to clear the 'accumulated filth, animal and vegetable, collected in the basements and elsewhere, including vermin', and a ton of bugs.[108] At the end of the process, the 13 houses, once inhabited by 200 families, their numbers swollen to 1,000 people by transients who made their way in and slept on the stairways at night, were reduced to lodging 300 or 400 people in 108 rooms, only a quarter of whom were the original tenants, although the rents apparently had not been raised. One wonders what became of the dispossessed.

Such schemes had advantages other than the 12 per cent. If they did not reach the very poorest, they went further down the scale than most model buildings, and provided the sort of accommodation the poor were used to, despite the introduction of a guardian and a gate to keep the transients at bay and the tenants up to scratch. In 1865 Octavia Hill gave the realists further impetus when, with Ruskin's help, she bought slum dwellings at Paradise Place to which she acted as manager, visiting the tenants frequently, in part to collect the rents which she spent on improvements.[109] Like the Society, she intended to help the poor to help themselves. Her experiment was successful because she exacted high standards of cleanliness and co-operation; but it also involved her exceptional degree of commitment, and although her success was often cited and sometimes emulated, it could no more serve as a general prescription than the 5 per cent philanthropy of Peabody and others. In any case, it was concerned only with slum housing which eventually had to be cleared.

Although it set a standard, model housing of any description could only touch the fringes of the problem; the vast majority of the poor continued to live in houses far from model. The Code of Building, introduced by the Public Health Act of 1875, set higher general standards of construction, for it specified a minimum width of street, adequate drainage, and sufficient light and ventilation to the rear. Nevertheless, in 1883 Andrew Mearns's *Bitter Cry of Outcast London* described conditions all too similar to those that outraged Engels in the 1840s and Godwin in the 1850s. Neither philanthropists nor speculators could solve the problem of the very poor; there were too few philanthropists, and no speculator could make housing for the poorest pay. As Sir Patrick Geddes, an early sociologist, commented in 1904: 'Whether, under favourable circumstances and the rare public spirit of private owners, much can be done, or to any wide extent, so long as absolute individual ownership in land and ground values is allowed, seems to me very doubtful.'[110] The responsibility lay ultimately with the local councils and the government. Others continued to argue, as they had done before, and as they do today, that the indigent could never be adequately housed because they did not know how to live with cleanliness and decency.

This account of urban housing in the reign of Queen Victoria has been protracted for three reasons. In the first place, by juxtaposing novelists with social commentators, it becomes evident that fictional accounts are not exaggerated, but often the reverse. Secondly, a comparison indicates the centrality of housing to the political thinking of the time, and the extent to which some novelists, notably Dickens and Disraeli, became actively involved in practical measures. Finally, this background provides an explanation of the idealization and occasional vagueness of which some writers, like Dickens and Mrs Gaskell, are sometimes accused. Due to a multiplicity of problems, the 'proper course of action' was not as evident as it might seem to be in retrospect. There was really only one ground on which the reformers could agree, in fiction as in fact: that cleanliness, above all, was the answer, and that the working class could achieve it in conditions where it was possible to make a genuine home.

It is for this reason that in Victorian novels the description of working-class interiors, as I have mentioned, invariably emphasizes their hard-won decency. There are of course some deliberately emphasized exceptions: destitution, like that depicted in *Alton Locke* and *Mary Barton*, precludes decency; moral turpitude may have the same effect, as in the case of Mrs Brown in *Dombey and Son* – 'In an ugly and dark room, an old woman, ugly and dark too'.[111] Generally speaking, however, novelists are much more likely to celebrate the domestic virtues that, given half a chance, the working class can be expected to display; and, in order to produce that image, a certain amount of cleaning-up goes on. It is revealing, for example, to compare Engels' description of Manchester courts close to the Irk, 'from the depths of which bubbles of miasmatic gas constantly arise and give forth a stench unendurable',[112] with Mrs Gaskell's account of a Manchester court in *Mary Barton*.[113] Engels' emphasis is primarily upon 'the piles of *débris*, the refuse, filth and offal from the courts', coupled with derelict, overcrowded conditions, each house 'packed close behind its neighbour . . . all black, smoky, crumbling, ancient, with broken panes and window-frames'. Mrs Gaskell's account is comparatively anodyne: 'a little paved court having the backs of the houses at the end opposite to the opening, and a gutter running through the middle to carry off household slops, washing suds, &c.' She does not define '&c.', or mention crowding, though this, in the reports of the time, was the main objection to such courts; her emphasis falls instead on neighbourliness, cleanliness, and laundry.

In town and country alike, working-class interiors in fiction are curiously uniform in consequence. In *The Old Curiosity Shop* little Nell tentatively asks if she and her grandfather may rest in one of a 'cluster of labourers' huts', a good five miles from the nearest town or village.[114] They are instantly welcomed inside (Fig. 39), and Nell's grandfather is invited to sit in the elbow chair while the child looks around her:

> The furniture of the room was very homely, of course – a few rough chairs and a table, a corner cupboard with their little stock of crockery and delf, a gaudy tea-tray, representing a lady in bright red, walking out with a very blue parasol, a few

common, coloured Scripture subjects in frames upon the wall and chimney, an old
dwarf clothes-press and an eight-day clock, with a few bright saucepans and a
kettle, comprised the whole. But everything was clean and neat . . . [with] a
tranquil air of comfort and content.

If one compares this relatively brief account with Mrs Gaskell's much more detailed
one of the Barton lodgings off that court in Manchester, the eye picks up very similar
detail.[115] The 'houseplace' is entered directly from the court, and is in almost total
darkness, 'except one bright spot . . . a red-hot fire'. When John Barton stirs it into
life, 'the effect instantly produced was warm and glowing light in every corner of the
room'. Since they have visitors, Mrs Barton supplements it with a dip in a tin
candlestick, although its light is lost in the glow of the fire, before pausing to look
about her:

The room was tolerably large and possessed many conveniences. On the right of
the door, as you entered, was a longish window, with a broad ledge. On each side
of this, hung blue-and-white check curtains, which were now drawn, to shut in
the friends met to enjoy themselves. Two geraniums, unpruned and leafy, which
stood on the sill, formed a further defence from out-door pryers. In the corner
between the window and the fireside was a cupboard, apparently full of plates and
dishes, cups and saucers, and some more nondescript articles, for which one would
have fancied their possessors could find no use – such as triangular pieces of glass
to save carving knives and forks from dirtying tablecloths. However, it was
evident Mrs. Barton was proud of her crockery and glass, for she left her cupboard
door open, with a glance round of satisfaction and pleasure. On the opposite side
to the door and window was the staircase, and two doors; one of which (the
nearest to the fire) led into a sort of little back kitchen, where dirty work, such as
washing up dishes, might be done, and whose shelves served as larder, and pantry,
and store-room, and all. The other door, which was considerably lower, opened
into the coal-hole – the slanting closet under the stairs; from which, to the
fireplace, there was a gay-coloured piece of oil-cloth laid. The place seemed
almost crammed with furniture (sure sign of good times among the mills). Beneath
the window was a dresser, with three deep drawers. Opposite the fire-place was a
table, which I should call a Pembroke, only that it was made of deal, and I cannot
tell how far such a name may be applied to such humble material. On it, resting
against the wall, was a bright green japanned tea-tray; having a couple of scarlet
lovers embracing in the middle. The fire-light danced merrily on this, and really
(setting all taste but that of a child's aside) it gave a richness of colouring to that
side of the room. It was in some measure propped up by a crimson tea-caddy, also
of japan ware. A round table on one branching leg, really for use, stood in the
corresponding corner to the cupboard; and, if you can picture all this, with a
washy, but clean stencilled pattern on the walls, you can form some idea of John
Barton's home.

38 A weaver's room

   Cleanliness and neatness are always the keynotes in such descriptions, whether in
the country or the town, a point implied by Mrs Gaskell but made by Dickens quite
explicitly. From those two virtues derive the tranquillity, comfort, and content of
domesticity. Occasionally a very clean housekeeper, like Mrs Joe Gargery in *Great
Expectations*, may possess 'an exquisite art of making her cleanliness more
uncomfortable and unacceptable than dirt itself',[116] rather as some people do their
religion; but for the most part both cleanliness and godliness are of the comfortable
variety among the working classes. Even in the eighteenth century, when interiors
(and people) were at every social level a great deal dirtier than they became in the
Victorian period, Defoe's Moll Flanders can forgive a multitude of sins, where
everything is 'so handsome and so clean'.[117] By the mid-nineteenth century, a dirty
and disorderly room signifies vice. Millais's painting of *Christ in the House of his
Parents* was deeply offensive to Dickens, apparently because its workaday
imperfections implied a far from Holy Family.[118] Part of his objection may also have
been that one's trade and one's home had in most cases parted company by that date,
a development that William Morris was later to deplore. The hand-loom weavers
were among the last to be driven into the factories. When one considers Godwin's
illustration (Fig. 38) and Disraeli's description in *Sybil* of such a room,[119] where the
loom is placed centrally 'so as to gain the best light which the gloomy situation could

afford', and the ailing wife and children lie on mattresses in the corners, it is not difficult to see why many, as well as Dickens, might have thought such a separation an improvement.

There were, as we have seen, quite practical reasons for valuing neatness and cleanliness in working-class homes: only neatness could make their narrow rooms in any sense comfortable (perhaps that is why the Bartons' houseplace seems crammed with furniture), and only cleanliness could preserve them – and hence their betters – from disease. It was not a lesson, according to Mayhew, that the poor in fact needed to learn, for he finds the same scrupulous cleanliness in the poorest of London tenements, where every object in sight from chairs to children seems to have been that moment newly scrubbed. But the representation of such interiors in the novel posed some problems. On the one hand, novelists like Disraeli and Kingsley, who wish to stress that the one nation has responsibilities towards the other, can sometimes seem unduly patronizing. The intrusiveness of attitudes like these is registered in Anne Brontë's *Agnes Grey* (1847), when the poor widow, Nancy Brown, feels badly caught out in a moment of negligence:[120]

> But the next day, afore I'd gotten fettled up – for indeed, miss, I'd no heart to sweeping an' fettling, an' washing pots; so I sat me down i' th' muck – who should come in but Maister Weston! I started siding stuff then, an' sweeping an' doing; and I expected he'd begin a calling me for my idle ways.

On the other hand, those like Mrs Gaskell and Dickens, who represent the poor as helping themselves, are liable to diffuse the intensity of the impression they wish to create. Alice Wilson's cellar dwelling with its brick floor 'so damp that it seemed as if the last washing could never dry up'[121] would not be far distant from the Davenports' if the nature of that 'dampness' were defined. But since, against the odds, Alice keeps her cellar as 'the perfection of cleanliness', the image is pleasing and does not impose itself in the same way on the reader's imagination. Frequent whitewashing or repapering, like John Barton's 'clean stencilled pattern', is often alluded to, no doubt because it made damp and derelict rooms look fresh and dry – but that is the way that they remain for the reader. By an irony, Disraeli and Kingsley, who have less intimate sympathy with the poor, tend to create more enduring impressions.

The frequency of fires in rooms like these is a related phenomenon; those that smoke or empty grates are much more frequent in the writing of social commentators. As William Atkinson observed in 1805, cottagers were more intelligent and industrious where fuel was cheap, for a comfortable fireside on winter evenings 'promotes social mirth, and instructive conversation'.[122] In *The Old Curiosity Shop* it is high summer, and Dickens himself does not mention a fire, but it is featured by one of his illustrators, within a chimneypiece much too solid and grand for a labourer's 'hut' (Fig. 39). One might with only slight exaggeration claim that firelight illuminates virtually every positive page in Victorian novels. Its importance lies not only in its welcome – and sometimes literally life-giving – warmth, but in the

39 Little Nell at the cottager's

light it provides. Mrs Barton only lights her redundant tallow candle because there are to be visitors, and Mrs Gaskell would prefer the room without it. To those for whom gas was out of the question, and candles or lamps were expensive luxuries, firelight was often the single source of light as well as heat, as George Eliot notes in *Adam Bede*: 'It was a pretty scene in the red fire-light: for there were no candles; why should there be, when the fire was so bright, and was reflected from all the pewter and the polished oak?'[123] She is particularly fond of describing interiors seen by its light, for the fire elicits the good housekeeper's virtues by its reflections in wood, pewter, and copper, the 'few bright saucepans and a kettle' noticed by little Nell. Rooms without fires are correspondingly bleak, as though the heart of the house had ceased to beat (a not infrequent simile). Although it seems in actuality to have been common enough, the empty hearth or inadequate smoking fuel, like Alice Wilson's 'damp coals, and half-green sticks',[124] is a poignant symbol in the novel, suggestive of every kind of deprivation.

It was no doubt because the fire was so important that the fireplace was so carefully tended and its mantelpiece lovingly 'dressed' both in fact and fiction. Even the blind, according to Mayhew, 'take great pride in their chimney-piece' because 'they like other people to see it'.[125] In *Sylvia's Lovers*, Mrs Gaskell emphasizes this well-kept hearth, 'of the same spotless whiteness as the steps; all that was black about the grate

40 A well-dressed mantelpiece

was polished to the utmost extent; all that was of brass, like the handle of the oven, was burnished bright'.[126] Penury, moral as well as physical, is signified in the Barton household when money is wanting to purchase the soap and brushes, black-lead and pipe-clay which had given the houseplace its cheerful look in more prosperous days.[127] Godwin illustrates a well-dressed mantelpiece (Fig. 40) which somewhat resembles the Toodles' in *Dombey and Son*: 'the castle on the mantel-piece with red and green windows in it, susceptible of illumination by a candle-end within; and the pair of small black velvet kittens, each with a lady's reticule in its mouth; regarded by Staggs's Gardeners as prodigies of imitative art.'[128]

It is in these prodigies of imitative art that Godwin discerns one of his social bridges, for he regards the love of art, exhibited even by the most miserable, as 'agreeable and cheering . . . evidence of striving upwards',[129] even though the former 'barbaric favourites' of the middle classes that have found their way to the firesides of the poor are not art 'of a very refined character'. Although the many pages of Mayhew are positively crammed with evidence that the poor had created a culture of their own, he seems none the less to share Godwin's view of art 'as a social bridge of no ordinary size and strength'. If the poor in model lodging-houses 'are kept in bondage, and made to *feel* that bondage',[130] a more enlightened view in relation to art wishes to persuade them 'to adorn their rooms *plentifully* with a better class of pictures'.[131] Loudon himself proposes a picture library, and the simple furniture he designs for cottages (Fig. 41), like Mrs Barton's Pembroke (Fig. 41a) and her round table with a branching leg (Fig. 41b), are direct descendants of Emma's two tables at Hartfield.[132] Conversely, he does not design a dresser like Mrs Barton's, a genuine piece of working-class furniture, but substitutes a sideboard for a neat cottage 'in which there is not much room' (Fig. 41c).[133] In course of time the poor seem to have accepted the image of their domestic life created by their betters. The Chartist, William Lovett, quotes with approval a description, written by a labourer's son in 1840, of the cottage of a (symbolic?) Widow Nest: 'I was so struck with the neatness of the cottage, the taste and order of the garden, the cheerfulness of the widow, and industry of the son, that on leaving the place I resolved to profit by what I had

41 Loudon's cottage furniture (a) Pembroke table (b) Dressing-table (c) Sideboard

witnessed.'[134] The whole description is an embodiment of middle-class values, not only in its moralistic conception of what such a home should be, but even in its prose. It is clear evidence of 'striving upwards'.

When little Nell enters the labourer's hut, we supposedly look around it with the eyes of the child. When Mrs Gaskell introduces us to the Bartons' lodging, we supposedly see it through the eyes of Mrs Barton. But neither passage is really written from a working-class viewpoint, for they impose middle-class values on working-class taste. No one could have been more attentive than Mrs Gaskell to that interior; one feels that she writes with a precise remembered image in her mind. No one could have been more sympathetic to the detail of the poor man's need, or more capable of vicarious imagination. Dickens knew at first hand from his own childhood what it was to live the life of the poor. But both reveal a trace of condescension and apology: his tea-tray is 'gaudy', its lady too red, her parasol too blue: hers is childish in its taste, its lovers scarlet against a background of bright green. This tone belongs to the omniscient middle-class author; indeed, Mrs Gaskell quite parts company with Mrs Barton when she mentions the deal Pembroke table: 'I cannot tell how far such a name can be applied to such humble material.' One is, however, convinced that all the objects she enumerates might really be found, in a time of full employment, in the actual houseplace of a Manchester worker. The dwarf clothes-press, corner cupboard, and eight-day clock that Dickens mentions are less convincing in a labourer's hut. Both are composing pictures, but her elements are genuine; his have the flavour of Mrs Cameron's idealized photographs of the poor at the mid-century, where, as Quentin Bell remarks with cruel truth, 'home is clearly the photographer's studio . . . furnished with props brought out for the occasion'.[135]

The prosperous had learnt to enter the houses of the poor, but they tended to see them with the eyes of well-intentioned visitors, like the 'twelve or fourteen monsters in broadcloth' who visit Wild Court, 'looking very much aghast' at what they find there. We observe the houseplace of the Bartons, or of the Higginses in *North and South*;[136] we inhabit the parlours of their middle-class complements, the Carsons[137] and particularly the Hales.[138] Comprehensive as Mrs Gaskell is, the eye selects what it is willing to see – bright geraniums, blue and white check curtains – both composing it into a picture and toning it down. Interiors are never quite so flamboyant in the novel as those described by Mayhew – an entire wall covered in holy pictures, the others papered in four different patterns;[139] in the novel they are 'arranged' by the author rather than the characters. The exceptions stand out, like Mucklebackit's cottage in *The Antiquary* (1816), which warrants the proverb 'The clartier [messier], the cosier'.[140] They are rarely found in fiction at a later date.

Poverty (as distinct from gamely 'making do' on a small income) is never so pleasing to the eye when it becomes part of middle-class experience. One could multiply examples, within the period covered by this book, from Richardson's exceptionally protracted and detailed description of the room in which Clarissa is imprisoned for debt,[141] to the many abrasive images of middle-class poverty in Gissing's *New Grub Street* (1891). The contrast can be succinctly demonstrated by the juxtaposition of two images, both of tea-tables, written a century apart, but surprisingly similar in their impact and even in their detail:

> Tea was nearly over and only the last of the second watered tea remained in the bottoms of the small glass jars and jampots which did service for tea-cups. Discarded crusts and lumps of sugared bread, turned brown by the tea which had been poured over them, lay scattered on the table. Little wells of tea lay here and there on the board and a knife with a broken ivory handle was stuck through the pith of a ravaged turnover.[142]

> She sat in a blaze of oppressive heat, in a cloud of moving dust; and her eyes could only wander from the walls marked by her father's head, to the table cut and knotched by her brothers, where stood the tea-board never thoroughly cleaned, the cups and saucers wiped in streaks, the milk a mixture of moats floating in thin blue, and the bread and butter growing every minute more greasy.[143]

The first passage, from Joyce's *Portrait of the Artist* (1914–15) is not at all surprising in its context; the second, from Jane Austen's *Mansfield Park*, is most unusual in her sparsely descriptive novels. Neither passage composes itself into a picture, like the multiple images of snowy cloths and simple fare in Dickens's working-class interiors; the detail is unsparing, not indulgent. Throughout the period of this book, the reduction of the prosperous to poverty invariably results in rooms that are painfully straitened: they are rarely bright homes, like those of the working class on even lower incomes. When those passages are compared, not only with the labourer's interior in *The Old Curiosity Shop*, but with Mrs Gaskell's account of Mrs Barton's houseplace, the extent to which the latter pair are pictures becomes apparent, despite Mrs Gaskell's fidelity to fact. Middle-class indigence disturbs the writer's expectations; working-class decency confirms them.

The interiors of the worthy poor in the Victorian novel are in consequence nearly always seen with the idealizing vision of an outsider. Only in the novels of Hardy and later of Lawrence does the reader see humble houses with the eyes of those who live in them. Hardy likes to remark, for example, on those signs of wear and tear whose beauty, as he says, is not visual but internal, since it inheres in long association – the rainbow-shaped stain left by a damp hat where it is hung up every evening upon a beam;[144] the greasy line marked by a succession of convivial shoulders against a wall[145] (a total contrast in its effect with the marks left by the head of Fanny's father). When in *Sons and Lovers* Lawrence describes Morel's solitary, self-indulgent breakfast, his mug of tea upon the hearth, his bread and bacon eaten from a newspaper on the fender with the aid of a clasp-knife, the image is neither aesthetic nor its contrary; the scene is an experience, less visual than sensuously satisfying.[146]

From the beginning, with Robert Owen's experiment at New Lanark, model housing had failed too often to accommodate the genius of those for whom it was intended. Cobbett fulminates against the grimness of New Lanark and its squares, built miles away from other habitations.[147] Such institutions, he asserts, should properly be used to incarcerate lawyers, and 'set the bobtailed brotherhood most effectually at work'. Model villages, both in fiction and in fact, do seem intended to 'improve' the poor into a middle-class image, if not to punish them on the model of the workhouse or the prison. Disraeli commends Mr Trafford, his ideal manufacturer in *Sybil*, for living in the middle of his model village.[148] He is an advance in this respect on Mr Millbank in the earlier *Coningsby*, whose house is removed half a mile from his factory, on the side of it opposite to his new estate.[149] Where Mr Millbank seeks to improve his employees by education – 'a library and a lecture-room; and a reading-hall, which any one might frequent at certain hours' – Mr Trafford, 'who comprehended his position too well to withdraw himself with vulgar exclusiveness from his real dependents', educates them with his own example: 'Proximity to the employer brings cleanliness and order, because it brings observation and encouragement.' Moreover, although he is 'the principal proprietor and proud of that character', like Mrs Thatcher he encourages his employees to buy their own houses.

One of the earliest model industrial settlements, Saltaire (Fig. 42), begun in 1851 in what was then the countryside of the Aire Valley, has the disadvantages to which Cobbett alludes, for its houses, despite their isolation, are distinctly urban, unrelieved by gardens front and back. Mr Trafford and Mr Millbank both provide gardens, but on the periphery of their villages; Sir Titus Salt (who lived elsewhere) provided a park on the banks of the Aire. Certainly he was in his way a model – his factory chimneys, like Mr Millbank's, were smokeless, as William Morris remarked approvingly[150] – and Saltaire is still a pleasant place to be, evidently felt to be so by those who live there, with its handsome public buildings, graceful church (Fig. 42a) and lions that failed to make Trafalgar Square. But it is also as deeply paternalistic as the model villages that Disraeli imagined; there are no pubs, for example, and one of the grander houses boasts a look-out (Fig. 42b) from which the (literal) overseer could convict those who went late to work or did their washing on Sundays with the evidence of his own eyes. It is, however, an interesting anomaly that Saltaire's present residents derive from their village an unusually intense sense of working-class identification.

There is, moreover, an unfortunate continuity between Saltaire and the depressing rows of 'improved' terraces that still house workers in English industrial towns. The railway towns, also built at the mid-century, are in their way a prosaic version of Saltaire, but the comments of one early railway enthusiast put one in mind of Coketown in *Hard Times*: 'A little red-brick town composed of 242 little red-brick houses – all running either this way or that at right-angles.'[151] When William Morris, nearer the end of the century, describes the buildings that 'cry out at you at the first glance, workmen's houses',[152] he seems to have the railway towns in mind; but his description of this 'wilderness of small, dull houses . . . roofed with thin, cold, purple-coloured slates', could be Conrad's London in *The Secret Agent*, another moral wilderness, despite the monotonous order of its streets: 'the enormity of cold, black, wet, muddy, inhospitable accumulation of bricks, slates, and stones, things in themselves unlovely and unfriendly to man'.[153] Doré's most notorious London scene,

(a) Focusing Saltaire

(b) Overseeing Saltaire

42 Saltaire

'Over London by Rail', is after all an image of *improved* housing, not of slums. Such buildings are imposed upon the poor; they are not an expression of their needs and hence their lives. This is why Dickens so often relishes the individual, and may sharply regret it when slum housing is swept away. The Toodle taste is demolished with Staggs's Gardens; their new accommodation in the railway company's own buildings does not merit description. It is presumably a replica of Coketown: 'Oh, woe the day! when "not a rood of English ground" – laid out in Staggs's Gardens – is secure!'[154]

With extensive slum-clearance in the later part of the century, the city-scape grew curiously ephemeral: 'the very houses seemed disposed to pack up and take trips.'[155] As Ruskin complained in 1849, the urban redevelopment of the time had the nomadic character without its advantages, losing liberty without gaining rest, and stability without the luxury of change.[156] It is perhaps no accident that Peggotty's boat in *David Copperfield* (1849–50), precisely because it is *not* designed to be stable, has one of the most delightfully detailed interiors anywhere in Dickens. 'If it had ever been meant to be lived in,' as David remarks, 'I might have thought it small, or inconvenient, or lonely; but never having been designed for any such use, it became a perfect abode.'[157] As time goes on, uniformity becomes more and more apparent, individuality correspondingly rare, until one arrives at the bargee's wife in *The Rainbow*, who does not understand the middle-class Ursula's excitement at the idea of living in a house that literally goes away, but is reconciled to it by her possession of a parlour and a plush suite at Loughborough.[158] One may sometimes feel, when reading Dickens and Lawrence, that everything Victorian philanthropists like Dorothea wished to provide for the workers in the end gave them everything but a home. As Ruskin said, 'There is a sanctity in a good man's house which cannot be renewed in every tenement that rises on its ruins.'[159]

Lord Salisbury, writing in 1883, might have been gratified by the bargee's wife, for he notes despondently that 'the approval of the new order of building is by no means universal or instinctive'.[160] As a housing reformer he knew from experience that older people particularly often preferred their mud hovels to new improved houses, even at the same rent. Earth and thatch were warmer than brick or slate; small buildings, if less wholesome, were easier to heat. In many cases the reformers had been prevented from pulling down old cottages and building new ones by the entreaties of the inhabitants. Only time and education could, he felt, remedy the situation. Lord Salisbury's discussion of working-class housing radiates concern and common sense; yet he assumes that there is little virtue in the type of house that the poor had evolved for themselves to suit their needs. How little the new ones suited working-class life is revealed by Lawrence in *Sons and Lovers*. He describes the miners' cottages as 'substantial and very decent', with little front gardens, porches, neat front windows, and dormers for the attics.[161] But that is the view from the front which the visitor sees, and those windows belong to rooms that are rarely inhabited. The parlour is only used on state occasions, and the bedrooms are part of waking life only in time of sickness, when the chill before the fire is lit is acutely felt. The kitchen or 'dwelling room' – one might almost say 'dwelling' – where Morel eats his solitary breakfast, is at the back; and the backs of the houses, facing inwards between the blocks, are another matter. The room in which the life of the house is passed therefore looks 'at a scrubby back garden, and then at the ash-pits'. As a result, 'the actual conditions of living in the Bottoms, that was so well built and that looked so nice, were quite unsavoury because people must live in the kitchen, and the kitchens opened on to that nasty alley of ash-pits'.

Little Nell and Mrs Barton, it should be noted, step straight through the front door into the central room, known in the north as the 'houseplace'. Even in a Manchester court, the Barton tenement is designed like the northern farms that Mrs Gaskell admires and the farm kitchens that delight George Eliot. It is the plan of the little houses in Saltaire, and the 'kitchen' as distinct from the 'parlour' houses in Port Sunlight at the end of the century – an indication that model villages were, in some respects at least, more enlightened than their derivatives. This plan allows the most lived-in room of the house to enjoy the best aspect and outlook. In this room the life of the house goes on, it has the fire, and the untidier aspects of existence are confined to the scullery. The parlour is a middle-class imposition, dating from the time of Jane Austen, when the possession of two reception rooms is the dividing line between the gentry and the rest. That is why poor Harriet, wistfully inclined to the farmer, Robert Martin, tries so hard to impress upon Emma the existence of '*two* parlours, two very good parlours indeed' at Abbey-Mill Farm.[162] Two parlours are certainly evidence of 'striving upwards', but this is an aim despised by George Eliot's working-class hero, Felix Holt:

> If I once went into that sort of struggle for success . . . I should become everything that I see now beforehand to be detestable. And what's more, I should do this, as men are doing it every day, for a ridiculously small prize – perhaps for none at all – perhaps for the sake of two parlours.[163]

It is only at Charterville, where in 1848 single-storey houses were designed and built by workers for workers, that a model plan is wholly rational (Fig. 43), suited to the actual lives to be lived within it. It dispenses with all that unused space, the parlour and the three cold, compulsory bedrooms, gathering all the rooms around the central sitting-room with the fire; this is entered from the front, but is screened by a porch. Certainly it retains a kitchen with sink, and a dining-room with stove, but its central room is clearly intended for daily use. The basis of the scheme was a lottery, advertised in the Chartist paper *Northern Star*; but the company collapsed within a decade, and almost all the winners lost their houses because their legal position was unclear,[164] although the houses themselves near Witney remain today (fetching as much as £130,000 in the present market). If the labourer's ideal home lived only briefly, even their less-than-ideal homes, like back-to-backs, which were often preferred to more model terraced housing by those who lived in them on account of their warmth, were pulled down by reformers throughout this century, until they were licensed to exist again in 1980.

43 Rational planning at Charterville

In the later years of Queen Victoria's reign, middle-class taste came increasingly to admire and even emulate many of those aspects of working-class buildings and interiors from which, in earlier decades, they had tried to wean the poor, constructing from them the middle-class idyll which will be described in a later chapter.[165] Their tendency to view such homes in terms of pictures led in itself to a desire to compose their own domestic contexts in similar ways. The taste for the picturesque certainly nurtured an admiration for vernacular architecture. Ruskin, for example, remarks that the untutored builder 'never thinks of what is right, or what is beautiful, but he builds what is most adapted to his purposes'.[166] Houses 'raised by the peasant where he likes, and how he likes' are 'therefore . . . frequently in good taste'.[167] It is these elements that create the beauty not only of the Westmoreland cottages that Ruskin is describing, which seem to be part of the hills from which they grow (Fig. 45); they are also the making of a village like Mrs Gaskell's beloved Knutsford – as it used to be.

An admiration for their architecture also led to an interest in their planning. The 'houseplace' of the simple northern workman was actually recommended for inclusion in middle-class homes,[168] just at the point where the workmen themselves had been actively persuaded into two parlours. Together with discovering the beauty of working-class architecture, as it was removed in order to improve it, the middle classes, profiting from Dutch painting,[169] came to admire their interiors, not the 'prodigies of imitative art', the spotted cats and illuminated castles that had percolated down from more prosperous parlours, but the more ordinary objects intended for everyday use. Where Loudon designs sideboards, but no dressers, for his cottages, Eastlake, as I have mentioned,[170] prefers the dresser to the sideboard in middle-class homes. The kettles and pans that draw the eye of little Nell are seen to have the beauty that inheres in use, although in the 1850s George Eliot writes of such interiors as a thing of the past.[171]

When Morris wrote of his imagined houses in *News from Nowhere* (1888) that they were 'alive and sympathetic with the life of the dwellers in them',[172] he pointed to an essential element in beauty that the best intentioned of the philanthropists had missed. He deplores the miserable face of the predominantly working-class city, which, by the close of the century, had come to house the workers of England with more space and conveniences than any other nation in Europe, precisely because it lacked that element: 'Bright as the spring morning is, a kind of sick feeling of hopeless disgust comes over you.'[173] Doubtless the houses that so nauseate Morris have their three bedrooms, their front parlour, and even a proper connection to the main sewer, but they are 'Poor with that poverty suggesting the starvation of every human need except mere bread'.[174]

Dorothea never builds her cottages, although, after the death of Mr Casaubon, her plans become yet more ambitious:

> I should like to take a great deal of land, and drain it, and make a little colony, where everybody should work, and all the work should be done well. I should know every one of the people and be their friend.[175]

'Then you *will* be happy, if you have a plan, Dodo,' her sister answers soothingly. But it never becomes more than a plan; even Mr Casaubon's fortune will not run to that, and Dorothea's ambitions meet the fate of more than one philanthropist brought face to face at last with discouraging facts. Eventually, she finds her happiness in marrying Will and leaves for London. Perhaps it was as well. One cannot be sure that she would have learnt the language of that other nation; and if she had not, would they have been her friend? In 1890 the first Act allowing local authorities to build houses for the poor was passed, and although at first few did, the number greatly increased after the passing of the Addison Act in 1919. The responsibility had passed from the Dorotheas. But it is worth noting that, at this period, the best designing, private and public alike – the model village at Port Sunlight at the turn of the century, for example, and the garden cities and suburbs of Edwardian times – really abandons the notion of urban building, in favour of a return to the rural and picturesque. The council houses in Figure 44 built by the Banbury RDC in 1920, in local stone around a central green that even had a pump, are an endeavour to recapture the unregulated beauty of a traditional English village like Knutsford. Dorothea would no doubt have found it ironic that the search, which began by turning its back on the picturesque, should eventually have discovered that, in its best efforts to create beautiful lives, it could not do better than make hygienic imitations of the picturesque cottages she had learnt to despise.

44 Picturesque council housing

4

Stories in stone
The houses of the past

The nostalgic affection shown by Victorian novelists for vernacular architecture and interiors can be only partly explained by their developing awareness, described in the previous chapter, of the conditions of the labouring poor. It is equally an expression of an increasing interest in the houses of the past, not only in those celebrated buildings that constitute the history of architecture, but in the small ones that Ruskin admired (Fig. 45), built to meet the needs of simple men. That sympathetic vision has become so much a part of our own imaginative response to ancient buildings that it is difficult now to conceive of a time when they either went unnoticed or were regarded with contempt. But the eighteenth century, by and large, despised old houses, which in its view wholly failed to satisfy the civilized needs of contemporary life, and should therefore be either altered or replaced. The way in which such buildings came to be valued for their own sake is not straightforward, for it seems to have been reached by three separate, though interconnected, routes; but it is from the conjunction of these three that the sense of a house as a life in itself is created.

In Hardy's description of Weatherbury Upper Farm in *Far from the Madding Crowd* (Fig. 46),[1] these elements can be quite clearly distinguished. He perceives the building at first with the eye of an architect and historian: 'Fluted pilasters, worked from the solid stone, decorated its front, and above the roof pairs of chimneys were here and there linked by an arch, some gables and other unmanageable features still retaining traces of their Gothic extraction.' Written into that sentence is the accumulated knowledge of two generations of historicism which had learnt to distinguish styles, where the eighteenth century and even the Regency had not, and had in consequence become convinced that country builders had continued through the centuries to build in an indigenous Gothic style. But the following sentence, which is atmospheric, has its roots in the eighteenth century's minor poetic tradition, descending from Milton's *Il Penseroso*, in which the imagination is drawn to contemplate 'divinest Melancholy', 'Ore laid with black staid Wisdoms hue'.[2] In a way that unmistakably recalls Hardy's own admiration for Crabbe's 'microscopic touch' – 'he gives surface without outline, describing his church by telling *the colour*

116

45 A Lakeland farm

46 Weatherbury Upper Farm

of the lichens'[3] – it is the neglect of the farm that makes it beautiful: 'Soft brown mosses, like faded velveteen, formed cushions upon the stone tiling, and tufts of the houseleek or sengreen sprouted from the eaves of the low surrounding buildings.' Yet the paragraph as a whole is more than an architect's description, or the poetic evocation of an ancient building in the tradition signified by the title of the novel, taken of course from Gray's *Elegy*. Houses, like men, have their histories of prosperity and vicissitude; and these impress themselves upon their features just as they do on those of the human face. Once 'the manorial hall upon a small estate around it, now altogether effaced as a distinct property', Weatherbury has been demoted to a farmhouse:

> A gravel walk leading from the door to the road in front was encrusted at the sides with more moss – here it was of the silver-green variety; the nut-brown of the gravel being visible to the width of only a foot or two in the centre. This circumstance, and the generally sleepy air of the whole prospect here, together with the animated and contrasting state of the reverse façade, suggested to the imagination that on the adaptation of the building for farming purposes the vital principle of the house had turned round inside its body to face the other way.

This third, distinct sense – of long-inhabited place, in which a building expresses both its past history and its present life – is a product neither of poetry nor architecture, but of the novel, developed particularly by Emily Brontë and Mrs Gaskell in their response to living places, like Wuthering Heights or Hope Farm in

Cousin Phillis (1865). The significance of such houses is not primarily historic, for they alter with, and thus express, the lives of those who inhabit them in the present. But their previous, more distinguished identity, like that of Weatherbury Upper Farm, frames those lives in a longer perspective of time and transience. The history of Hope Farm and Wuthering Heights, signified in the one by the grandeur of its gateposts, forming an unused approach to the front door,[4] in the other by 'a wilderness of crumbling griffins and shameless little boys' with the date of 1500 above the principal entrance,[5] does not dominate the sense of the house in either novel, for they each have much more to express of their present life. The same cannot be said of Weatherbury Upper Farm, or indeed of Hardy's other ancient – and not-so-ancient – houses. It is the peculiar intensity of his response that fuses the poetic and the historic visions with that living sense of long-inhabited place, so that his houses become something much more than mere settings: they are stories in stone.

'An object or mark raised or made by man on a scene is worth ten times any such formed by unconscious Nature,' Hardy noted in his diary in 1877. 'Hence clouds, mists, and mountains are unimportant beside the wear on a threshold, or the print of a hand.'[6] If his eye as a poet is drawn to these imperfections because 'art lies in making these defects the basis of a hitherto unperceived beauty',[7] they do even more to prompt the novelist's imagination, for the unwritten histories of countless lives are evoked by the mark on a wall, the wear on a newel post, the gleam of a drawer handle worn smooth by hands long buried. Worn thresholds, like the one at the 'hard-worked' end of Overcombe Mill, 'worn into a gutter by the ebb and flow of feet that had been going on there ever since Tudor times',[8] could tell a multitude of tales. A sycamore tree, whose roots form steps to a house with mullioned windows, suggests a poem in *Human Shows* (1925);[9] it also prompts a prose story, 'Interlopers at the Knap', in *Wessex Tales* (1888). Everywhere that evidence of passing feet haunts Hardy with a sense of tales untold:

> Here is the ancient floor,
> Footworn and hollowed and thin,
> Here was the former door
> Where the dead feet walked in.[10]

He refuses an invitation to the United States, not only because the newness of the new world, 'whose riper times have yet to be',[11] deters him, but because the 'prints of perished hands' detain him in the old:

> I trace the lives such scenes enshrine,
> Give past exemplars present room,
> And their experience count as mine.

As he once wrote of Tess and of 'all that have felt', beauty for Hardy inheres less in objects themselves than in what they symbolize. Tess herself, latterly so real a presence to him, is primarily a manifestation of place, not the 'unconscious nature' of the Vale of Blackmore, but of the almost conscious walls that have surrounded her from childhood: 'Part of her body and life it ever seemed to be; the slope of its dormers, the finish of its gables, the broken courses of brick which topped the chimney, all had something in common with her personal character.'[12]

This intense sensitivity to houses and their histories, visible in the traces left by former occupants, is not only a major source of Hardy's art, but also of his tragic sense of life. Tess herself is only once free of her personal history, and therefore briefly happy, when she and Angel, as fugitives among its dust-sheets, take refuge beneath the alien roof of Branshurst Court. But even that brief idyll cannot last:

> They will drag their house-gear ever so far
> In their search for a home no miseries mar;
> They will find that as they were they are,
>
> That every hearth has a ghost, alack,
> And can be but the scene of a bivouac
> Till they most their last – no care to pack![13]

'The worst of taking a furnished house', Hardy once wrote, 'is that the articles in the rooms are saturated with the thoughts and glances of others.'[14] He tried to escape his obsession by building himself an aggressively brand new-house, Max Gate. But ghosts are resilient. Not only were Romano-British urns and skeletons discovered when a well was sunk there, but imagination made of Hardy himself a ghost, haunting the occupants of his house in the year 2,000 despite their brave declaration:

> Some folk can not abide here,
>   But we – we do not care
> Who loved, laughed, wept, or died here,
>   Knew joy, or despair.[15]

But if the life of buildings, outlasting that of men, torments his imagination, it also inspires him; and if Hardy could not himself live in an old house, he wished to preserve them intact, even in their imperfections. In *Far from the Madding Crowd* it is the cavalier Sergeant Troy who regards Weatherbury Farm as rambling and gloomy, and plans to install sash-windows, remove the wainscot, and paper the walls.[16] Gabriel Oak, whose spirit is deeply rooted, likes the place as it is and resists the idea of renovation. The imperfections which tell so many stories are as expressive in a house as the lines on a human face.

It is surely because of his respect for the identity of old houses that so many of Hardy's fictional buildings can be readily identified. Weatherbury Upper Farm corresponds in every architectural detail of his description to Lower Waterston Farm (now Waterston Manor) near Puddletown (Fig. 46). This cannot be said of Wuthering Heights: although it has confidently been identified as Top Withens, it appears to be a rather grander house, sharing a number of its features with Ponden Hall (Fig. 58), supposedly the model for Thrushcross Grange, while possibly owing its cherubs and its griffins to yet a third, High Sunderland Hall.[17] Hope Farm has also been identified, with the house at Sandlebridge belonging to Mrs Gaskell's maternal grandfather, Samuel Holland, but the fictional house appears to be much smaller (it certainly does not boast fourteen bedrooms), and the resemblance does not seem to go much further than the gateposts.[18] On the other hand, it is still possible to drive round Hardy's Wessex and recognize many houses instantly, simply from his description. Oxwell Hall in *The Trumpet Major*[19] and Wellbridge Manor House in *Tess of the d'Urbervilles*[20] can, for example, be instantly recognized to the north of the A352 when travelling between Dorchester and Wareham. As Hardy himself claimed in the preface to *Tess*, all his descriptions in fiction of old English architecture were 'done from the real'.[21] That all these houses, and many others like them throughout England, are so carefully preserved today must owe much to the imaginative claim made for them in his novels. Certainly Oxwell Hall can no longer claim to be neglected, with 'all the romantic excellences and practical drawbacks which such mildewed places share in common with caves, mountains, wildernesses,

47 Enckworth Court

glens, and other homes of poesy that people of taste wish to live and die in'.[22] The fortunes of Weatherbury Farm have also taken an upward turn: it has been spared the sash-windows proposed by Sergeant Troy, and has been devotedly restored to all its original dignity. But, although its vital principle still turns the other way, its sengreen at least has vanished – for the present.

The eighteenth century would certainly have seconded Sergeant Troy's retort to Gabriel Oak: 'A philosopher once said in my hearing that the old builders, who worked when art was a living thing, had no respect for the work of the builders who went before them, but pulled down and altered as they thought fit; and why shouldn't we?'[23] Very few improvers in those days would have hesitated for a moment. Even the early Gothic enthusiasts either built themselves new houses, like Beckford, or, like Walpole, adapted those that already existed. Where buildings in the novel do retain their original form it tends to be for the wrong reasons. Delville Castle in *Cecilia*,[24] 'equally in want of repair and improvement', testifies to the arrogance of Mr Delville, and also to the depleted state of his purse. Cecilia complains that no taste has been shown in the disposition of its grounds, no opening contrived through its woods for distant views, while the interior is constructed 'with as little attention to convenience and comfort, as to airiness and elegance'. There can be no doubt what she would do with it, given her fortune. Wherever possible, Georgian and Regency gentlemen built new. If lumbered with an old house, without the means to raze it and start afresh, they would reconstruct it. If really impecunious, they would at least put a brave Palladian face on the old place.

In *The Hand of Ethelberta* (1876) Hardy describes the effect of one such eighteenth-century improvement, at Enckworth Court in fiction, Encombe in fact (Fig. 47).[25] The house is medieval in origin, but no attempt has been made to relate the old to the new addition, with the result 'that the hooded windows, simple string-courses, and random masonry of the Gothic workman, stood elbow to elbow with the equal-spaced ashlar, architraves, and fasciae of the Classic addition, each telling its distinct tale as to the stage of thought and domestic habit without any of those artifices of blending or restoration by which the seeker for history in stones will be utterly hoodwinked in time to come'. The eighteenth-century architect has aimed at illusion of a different kind: the staircase, made to look as light as biscuit-ware, is built of a freestone so heavy that it 'would have made a prison for an elephant if so arranged'; conversely, the massive blocks of red-veined marble lining the hall are owed exclusively to paint and plaster, while the apparently massive freestone of the exterior is a thin veneer, fastened to humble brick with copper cramps and dowels. As Hardy comments, 'It was a house in which Pugin would have torn his hair'; he might well have added Ruskin.

Pope, on the other hand, would have rejoiced at it, for he writes with enthusiasm to Martha Bount (c. 1724)[26] of the new wings with their Italian window-frames, attached by the first Earl of Bristol to the Castle at Sherborne, built originally by Sir Walter Raleigh in the closing years of Elizabeth's reign: 'If they were joind in the middle by a Portico covering the Old Building, [it] would be a noble Front,' he writes. 'The design of such an one I have been amusing myself with drawing.' By an irony, the castle may have formed part of Giles Winterbourne's view of Sherborne on a 'clear bright morning having the linear distinctness of architectural drawings, as if the original dream and vision of the conceiving master-mason were for a brief hour flashed down through the centuries to an unappreciate age'.[7] The hero of *The Woodlanders* cannot construe 'their eloquent look on this day of transparency', but it attracts his eye, where Pope, in an even less appreciative age, would not have seen it.

To Hardy, the only honest part of Enckworth Court is the medieval portion which has been degraded into offices; but the eighteenth century would never so have canonized the antique, at least where it related to indigenous buildings, not to ancient Greece or Rome. In his *Tour Through the Whole Island of Great Britain* Defoe does not waste many words on its architecture. His account of Cambridge, for example, is almost wholly devoted to the relationship between town and gown;[28] and while he remarks on the beauties of Ripon's market square and Minster, he is much more interested in the social aspects of medieval life.[29] Matthew Bramble, throughout his journeys in Smollett's *Humphry Clinker*, is actively dismissive of everything that predates the eighteenth century. Although he inspects the new architecture of Bath with critical care, he announces contemptuously: 'I never entered the Abbey church at Bath but once, and the moment I stept over the threshold, I found myself chilled to the very marrow of my bones.'[30] He makes the same objection to York Minster, which he regards as barbarous and saracenical, observing that the new Assembly Room (designed by Burlington), which seems to him to have been built on a design of Palladio, 'might be converted into an elegant place of worship'.[31] Old cathedrals in general would, he feels, offend anyone with a notion of propriety and proportion: 'the long slender spire puts one in mind of a criminal impaled, with a sharp stake rising up through his shoulder'.[32] It might be argued that Matthew Bramble is an eccentric, but the architect Robert Morris is equally contemptuous. He describes Westminster Abbey as 'a heavy, lumpish, unrefin'd Mass of Materials, jumbled together without Design, Regularity or Order',[33] while in Salisbury, although much wondered at, there is in his view 'nothing worthy of our Notice, but the Height of the Spire, and the prodigious expence Men have been at to perpetuate their Folly to future Times'.[34] Only 'the noble Structures of Antient *Rome*' and their derivatives are regarded by him as 'pure *Architecture*'.[35]

The conviction that 'Goths will always have a Gothic Taste'[36] was, moreover, slow to die. Although the medieval began to gain acceptance in the Regency, and the English past was in consequence no longer lumped comprehensively together as 'Gothic', later periods continued to be disparaged. Joseph Gandy, who in 1805 treats Palladian and Gothic as equal if different, nevertheless despises the wattle and daub of Tudor buildings:

What can be more frightful than the black and white daubings to successively projecting stories in some market-towns, as if they wished to shew all the deformities of the timbers, and exhibit the skeleton of the house? How strong is the contrast between the appearance of those and that of Bath and Oxford; the first all cheerfulness; the latter every thing that is grand, and almost sublime, in Architecture.[37]

Although in 1816 Scott adapts Pope in his affectionate description of Monkbarns, his Antiquary's house – 'the whole bore the appearance of a hamlet which had suddenly stood still in the act of leading down Amphion's, or Orpheus's, country dances'[38] – John Papworth in 1818 employs the same quotation for the opposite purpose, to deride the adventitious manner of Jacobean building.[39] This aversion to the old is even more marked in comments on the furniture of such buildings. In 1806 Repton wonders at 'the odd figures of our ancestors on canvas, and . . . the bad taste of old worm-eaten furniture',[40] reminding one of Jane Austen's dismissive attitude to portraits,[41] and the relative modernity with which her older houses are furnished. In *Mansfield Park* Elizabethan Sotherton contains the solid mahogany of George III, while in *Pride and Prejudice* only the portraits on the walls and the books in the library at Pemberley represent the preceding generations of Darcies.

An interest in the buildings of the English past, while leading ultimately to the informed precision of Hardy's first sentence describing Weatherbury Farm, first develops for reasons which have little to do with their architecture as such. When in

48 The Old Manor, Woodstock

1709 John Vanbrugh advanced his reasons 'for Preserving some Part of the Old Manor' at Woodstock (Fig. 48), he had no more than two to offer: that it had merit as a feature in the landscape – 'it wou'd make One of the Most Agreable Objects that the best of Landskip Painters can invent'[42] – and that it had value as a historical monument: '*I believe, though they may not find Art enough in the* Builder, *to make them Admire the beauty of the Fabrick* they will find Wonder enough in the Story, to make 'em pleas'd with the Sight of it.' He allows, one notices, no intrinsic merit to a building which, to judge from the drawing, Hardy would undoubtedly have celebrated. But in his concern that those who run eagerly to see fair Rosamund's bower should not be disappointed at finding that '*the Very footsteps of it Are no more to be found*', Vanbrugh reveals that he is himself to some extent a 'seeker for history in stones'. The Duchess of Marlborough, however, was not: 'This paper has something ridiculous in it to preserve the house for himself, ordered to be pulled down,' was her comment.[43] Those orders were carried out, but the paper itself was preserved because it related to the building of Blenheim (Fig. 2).

A belief that the indigenous buildings of the past have historical rather than architectural interest persists into the early nineteenth century. When Soane, for example, advocates that ruins (even those freshly built) should not be merely picturesque, but should recall real objects and events, he is reiterating Vanbrugh's two reasons for preserving the Old Manor.[44] Perhaps as a result of this emphasis on a building's history as distinct from its architecture, it is often clear that even the early advocates of Gothic have little sense of architectural period. 'Lord deliver me from this Gothic generation!' exclaims Scott's antiquary, Jonathan Oldbuck, 'A monument of a knight-templar on each side of a Grecian porch, and a Madonna on the top of it! – O *crimini!*'[45] As an eighteenth-century antiquarian he comments on anachronism, rather than architectural style, where Eastlake's similar dismissal in 1872 of the restoration, in Oldbuck's time, of Arundel Castle from ruins left by the Civil War is primarily stylistic: its Gothicism is, he claims, theatrical, and 'the most important elevation contains the anomaly of a Norman doorway surrounded by Perpendicular windows'.[46] But Oldbuck's own scholarship is not impeccable, although he measures decayed entrenchments and makes plans of ruined castles as a scholar should. His enthusiasm can run away with him, leading him to identify a Roman ruin in a dyke constructed only twenty years before. Pugin, similarly, may assail James Wyatt 'of execrable memory', for his alterations to the interior of Salisbury Cathedral,[47] but, to a modern eye, Wyatt's wish to create a great scenic effect is not far distant from Pugin's own histrionic style (as a young man he had designed stage sets for the theatre, including *Kenilworth* in 1831). Since the Gothic revival, each successive generation has persuaded itself that it has, for the first time, got the middle ages 'right', and each subsequent one has poured scorn on its predecessors. Such images of the past probably reveal more of the period that formed them than of the period they purport to represent.

Thus, if Oldbuck censures the solecisms of the first Gothic generation, and his creator, in the second, indicates the failings of his antiquary, Charles Eastlake, full of

Victorian confidence, finds much to criticize in Scott's numerous descriptions of medieval architecture;[48] but he does allow that the Waverley novels had an important part to play in quickening interest in buildings that had previously been regarded as 'all gloom and vulgar superstition', a description which tallies with the Gothic novel. It is certainly true that Scott never describes the buildings seen in his novels in anything like Hardy's meticulous and affectionate detail. His view of the church at Woodstock, which still exists, is as romantic and impressionistic as that of the Old Manor House, which, thanks to the Duchess of Marlborough, he had to imagine. And if one can take the narrative voice as his, he preferred in any case to imagine both, for a reason the Duchess herself would much have approved – that, being short of time, he made 'the magnificence of Blenheim' his priority.[49] Scott does, however, note the existence of such buildings as the church at Woodstock, as earlier writers, even on tours, had not. Not only that, but the type of tour which he is apt to provide for the reader is primarily of the architectural type, although conducted with transatlantic speed. In a single chapter of *Waverley* (1814), for example, the Castle of Stirling and its church (both redolent of chivalry), the venerable ruins of the palace at Linlithgow, and the grandeur and gloom of Edinburgh Castle all flash by, externally seen and historically described.[50]

Possibly Scott's greatest contribution lay in his interest in historical perspective, and in the living monuments history had left behind from all periods, not the middle ages only. Of the four novels that Kenneth Clark cites in *The Gothic Revival*,[51] apparently for their promotion of the Gothic taste, one, *Woodstock* (1826), is set in the seventeenth century; two, *The Abbot* (1820) and *The Monastery* (1820), at the close of the sixteenth; and only one, *Ivanhoe* (1819), in the middle ages as such, though at a period when architecture was Romanesque, not Gothic. Comparatively few of his novels are set in a strictly Gothic period, and even then are often located in countries other than England: *The Fair Maid of Perth* (1828) recreates fourteenth-century Scotland, *Anne of Geierstein* (1829) fifteenth-century Switzerland, and *Quentin Durward* (1823) fifteenth-century France. But if Scott did less than might be supposed to promote the taste for the English middle ages as such, he undoubtedly did more than is often remarked to develop a sense of period. He tends not only to cite actual buildings, but to do so in different chronological perspectives. *Woodstock*, for example, looks back from the nineteenth to the seventeenth century, which in turn looks back to the middle ages. In *The Betrothed* (1825), set in the Marches of Wales in the twelfth century, the reader is often enjoined to distinguish periods. The Garde Dolereuse is not to be confused with the Castle of Colwyn, for 'the length of time, and some geographical difficulties, throw doubts upon this ingenious conjecture'; Castell-Coch, on the other hand, is to be identified as Powis Castle, although now of course it looks very different.[52] There is a past within this past, however, for the heroine's aunt, the Lady Baldringham, observes the old ways, and not least in clinging to her antique Anglo-Saxon dwelling, a building quite as intimidating as the Gothic Udolpho is to Mrs Radcliffe's Emily, four fictional centuries later:

The house, for it could not be termed a castle, was only of two storeys high, low and massively built, with doors and windows forming the heavy round arch which is usually called Saxon; – the walls were mantled with various creeping plants, which had crept along them undisturbed – grass grew up to the very threshold, at which hung a buffalo's horn, suspended by a brass chain. A massive door of black oak closed a gate, which much resembled the ancient entrance to a ruined sepulchre, and not a soul appeared to acknowledge or greet their arrival.[53]

When Eveline does get in, by the simple expedient of ringing the doorbell – or rather, blowing the horn – she finds that the house is haunted by a particularly nasty ghost; it seems that, as in the nineteenth century, all Saxon and Norman families of note could boast at least of one and its related history. Scott was well aware that an interest in the past was not confined to his present: King René in *Anne of Geierstein* is shown to be as lovingly attentive to Roman antiquity as the eighteenth-century antiquary is to the Scottish.

For the most part, like the novelists that preceded him, Scott interests himself and the reader in great buildings, although his range, which includes manor houses and abbeys as well as castles, is more comprehensive than theirs had been. But he is also one of the first writers to note, and celebrate, that vernacular architecture which chiefly attracted Hardy's attention. In such instances, perhaps because he came to them freshly, his writing is more than usually specific. In *Rob Roy* (1817) Andrew Fairservice's dwelling is, for example, described as 'a snug comfortable Northumbrian cottage, built of stones roughly dressed with the hammer, and having the windows and doors decorated with huge heavy architraves, or lintels, as they are called, of hewn stone, and its roof covered with broad grey flags, instead of slates, thatch or tiles'.[54] Although, as revealed in the previous chapter, the interiors of such cottages were often much less comfortable than the passer-by had been led, by their external appearance, to expect, Scott often, as in this instance, contrasts the attractions of English vernacular architecture with the miserable hovels north of the border. He also admires the disposition of English villages, where the cottages, unlike those in Scotland (and some English estates), 'instead of being built in two direct lines on each side of a dusty high-road, stand in detached groups, interspersed not only with large oaks and elms, but with fruit-trees'.[55]

Scott is often attentive not only to architectural characteristics, but to their social and imaginative dimensions, as this example suggests. If he can be convicted of error and imprecision, it is largely because, when he began to write the Waverley novels, those who admired the products of the past were still at the stage of distinguishing functions, and had not yet arrived at periods of architecture and furnishing. His censure in *The Pirate* (1821) of those who 'make a medley of the caprices of the order, confounding the military, ecclesiastical and domestic styles of all ages at random', makes this clear.[56] The day of the amateur was soon to pass, however; in Eastlake's view, an age of ignorance was to be succeeded by an age of plagiarism.[57] After the foundation of the Camden Society in 1839, 'no one,' he says, 'was safe from critics, who knew to a nicety the orthodox *coiffure* of a thirteenth-century angel, and who damned a moulding that was half an hour too late'.[58] The early years of Queen Victoria's reign, during which the English architecture of the past was for the first time studied systematically and seriously, also produced a paradoxical disregard for the buildings they studied. When in 1845 the Camden Society declared for the 'middle-pointed' or decorated style of Gothic architecture, as distinct from Early English or the later Perpendicular, most advocates of Gothic followed suit. From the mid-century, 'th'improver's desolating hand' lay heavily on many medieval churches that lacked the requisite purity, a fashion in which Hardy as an architect was both to participate, and later, as a poet and novelist, to regret.[59] When Pugin wrote in 1836 that 'the mechanical part of Gothic architecture is pretty well

49 Improving the past

understood',[60] he also added, 'but it is the principles which influenced ancient compositions, and the soul which appears in all the former works, which is so lamentably deficient'. Despite the foundation of the Camden Society, the soul continued to evade capture, partly because so many early Victorians believed that imitation was at least as good as the real thing, and often better, a principle that could apply to furniture as well as buildings. Figure 49 shows two 'Mortuary' chairs, so named by the Victorians because they thought that the faces carved on the back rails portrayed the head of Charles I, executed in 1649. The chair to the reader's right, with its pumpkin face and death's head, is genuine Jacobean; the one to his left is Victorian, 'improved' by rather more regal physiognomies.

A reaction against Georgian architecture, and an admiration for the buildings of an earlier English past, predating the arrival of Palladio, had, however, undoubtedly come into being. To prefer a native to an alien architecture accorded with national pride in the expanding British Empire; to elevate the religious nature of the Gothic above the paganism of Greece and Rome obeyed the dictates of Christian morality. Where eighteenth-century novelists, as I have mentioned, tended either, like Smollett, to despise all pre-Georgian building, or, like Richardson, to associate it with dark doings, Victorian novelists tended in contrast to dismiss the architecture, not of the past, but of their immediate predecessors. Dickens, for example, remarks of a house in the time of George II that it was 'as stiff, as cold, as formal, and in as bad taste, as could possibly be desired by the most loyal admirer of the whole quartett of Georges',[61] where Agnes's ancient Canterbury house in *David Copperfield* is benign and unusually home-like, more 'spiritual' and clearly in good taste. Mrs Gaskell writes regretfully in her novel *Ruth* (1853) that, in an assize town in the eastern counties which had once been rich in Tudor buildings, 'the whole front of one side of the street was pulled down, and rebuilt in the flat, mean, unrelieved style of George the Third'.[62] There is no mistaking the quasi-religious note in her pleasure at finding that the interiors of those 'grand old houses' were 'too solidly grand to submit to alteration; so people were occasionally surprised, after passing through a commonplace-looking shop, to find themselves at the foot of a grand carved oaken staircase, lighted by a window of stained glass, storied all over with armorial bearings'. In this respect both architects and novelists undoubtedly owed much to Sir Walter Scott, whose novels had not only transmitted to them his enthusiastic interest in the past, but had also been an education in perspectives of time and the characteristics of different periods.

This interest in the past was not confined to architecture, but, as can be seen in the case of the 'Mortuary' chairs, extended to interiors as well. Henry Shaw's *Specimens of Ancient Furniture*, published in 1836 (the year of *Sketches by Boz* and Pugin's *Contrasts*), were drawn from actual examples in meticulous detail, in order that painters of historical subjects would not be guilty of anachronisms like 'the introduction of a wardrobe or a chair of the time of Queen Anne in the representation of an apartment of the reign of Henry the Sixth',[63] an accuracy already achieved, he claimed in his Prospectus, by designers of stage costume. It is

(b) Actual example

(a) Shaw's specimen

50

worth noting that his work is designed for artists, not collectors, although a number of his simpler examples are taken from Goodrich Court, the house of Sir Samuel Rush Meyrick, who writes the descriptions, and who appears to have observed 'period' himself in his domestic arrangement, for he comments on Plate 39 that the bedstead it depicts, with the date upon it of 1628, 'stands in what is termed, from the period of its furniture, the Charles the First's room, at Sir Samuel's residence'.[64] Since historical paintings tend to be concerned with significant events among the greatest with the grandest furniture, many of Shaw's specimens are grandiose, which perhaps does something to explain the monumental nature of much Victorian Gothic (Fig. 74). For example, in the absence of an actual specimen, he illustrates a late fifteenth-century 'buffet' or livery cupboard from an illuminated manuscript in the King's Library at Paris (Fig. 50a), although much simpler versions, like Figure 50b, were available in other medieval manuscripts and paintings.[65]

There is unfortunately no necessary contradiction between the factitious and the scholarly. Joseph Nash's depiction of the hall at Wakehurst in Sussex (Fig. 51), published in 1839, is not mistaken so much in its depiction of Jacobean architecture, armaments, and furniture as in the spirit of their representation. It reminds one that Nash's contemporaries liked to take from the past only those things that would accommodate themselves to the present, like the famous 'Knole settee' (Fig. 52), which is still in production, advocated by Eastlake because 'after 250 years of use, this sofa is still *comfortable*'.[66] Similarly, the hall at Wakehurst (Fig. 51) has clearly been assembled by a nineteenth-century gentleman with an eye to family life and a quite un-Jacobean comfort. The weapons on the wall, the design of the chairs and tables, the pattern on the matting, are only marginally anachronistic – the back legs of the dining chairs are slightly splayed where they should be upright, and the front ones are square where they should be turned – but the fault lies chiefly in their disposition. The hall has no connection with an age of spartan domesticity when weapons were for use, not show, and tables were unlikely to be covered with table-cloths. The table itself (and the family) should be larger. The figures, although clothed in appropriate costume, are unmistakably nineteenth-century in fancy-dress. They are as unconvincing as Disraeli's preposterous Lord Valentine with his dark blue eyes, who steadfastly refuses to 'don a Drury Lane cuirass' before his sovereign, and orders up the genuine article from his father's castle for her fancy-dress ball.[67]

If architects today are in no danger of surrounding a Norman doorway with perpendicular windows, as at Arundel, it is because the Victorians distinguished for them the characteristics of the particular styles; but the gains resulting in that period are not always obvious, at least where the imagination is concerned. With all their mistakes, Scott's novels persuade the reader that he has found his way into another period. His successors as writers of historical novels – Bulwer Lytton, Charles Reade, Charles Kingsley, Charlotte M. Yonge – were not enabled by their new knowledge to become more convincing, but the contrary. George Eliot's *Romola* (1862–3), perhaps the best historical novel of this period, is infinitely more precise than Scott's in its recreation of fifteenth-century Florence; but there is a deliberation in its description,

51 The hall at Wakehurst

an effort to arrive at details that are historically correct, which makes it feel what it
is – a work of studied reconstruction. The presence of antiquities in Bardo's room is,
for example, entirely appropriate to the context of a Renaissance humanist, but the
room itself has the air of a 'set piece', in which the painter's eye has co-operated with
the scholar's mind:[68]

> The voice came from the farther end of a long, spacious room, surrounded with
> shelves, on which books and antiquities were arranged in scrupulous order. Here
> and there, on separate stands in front of the shelves, were placed a beautiful
> feminine torso; a headless statue, with an uplifted muscular arm wielding a
> bladeless sword; rounded, dimpled, infantine limbs severed from the trunk,
> inviting the lips to kiss the cold marble; some well-preserved Roman busts; and
> two or three vases from Magna Grecia. A large table in the centre was covered
> with antique bronze lamps and small vessels in dark pottery. The colour of these
> objects was chiefly pale or sombre: the vellum bindings, with their deep-ridged
> backs, gave little relief to the marble, livid with long burial; the once splendid
> patch of carpet at the farther end of the room had long been worn to dimness; the
> dark bronzes wanted sunlight upon them to bring out their tinge of green, and the
> sun was not yet high enough to send gleams of brightness through the narrow
> windows that looked on the Via de' Bardi.

52 Original Knole settee

George Eliot encourages the reader's inner eye to linger on individual objects, persuading him, through the clarity of their detail, that, because each object is so fully itself, it is also more. Why, for example, is Bardo's room so like a sepulchre, with headless trunks and severed limbs, livid from long burial? (One remembers that the Victorians had a taste for memorial limbs in marble of dead infants.) Why are the colours uniformly pale and sombre, even the brilliance of the carpet worn to dimness? And why are textures so repellant, hard, chill, or metallic, even the well-handled vellum of the books made rebarbative by those deep-ridged backs? In the manner of the early Flemish painters,[69] the composition promotes thought rather than prompting response, persuading us of deliberate art, not spontaneous life.

On the other hand, George Eliot never makes the mistake of which Scott is constantly guilty – of making the past altogether too antique; of writing, as she once said of an ancient inn, 'in all moods and tenses except the indicative present'.[70] Whether in the twelfth, fourteenth, or eighteenth centuries, Scott's furniture is apt to be worm-eaten, his tapestries faded, and his buildings in a chronic state of disrepair. In *Rob Roy*, the library at Osbaldistone Hall, 'a gloomy room', although eagerly assembled in the late seventeenth century, has virtually disintegrated in the early years of the eighteenth: its oak shelves sag beneath the weight of folios and are worm-eaten, its tapestry is tattered, its grate rusty, and its tables, desks, and chairs, though huge and clumsy, still contrive to totter.[71] In *Old Mortality* (1816), the house at Milnwood, even in its best days and in a state of good repair, is cheerless and gloomy: 'the grass in the courtyard looked as if the foot of man had not been there for years; the doors were carefully locked, and that which admitted to the hall seemed to have been shut for a length of time, since the spiders had fairly drawn their webs over the doorway and the staples.'[72] If Ruskin complained that the Bradford manufacturers always wanted the newest and sweetest thing in pinnacles, Scott's characters might conversely have protested that they were never allowed anything not already old. Romola, on the other hand, could have put no such question to her creator, for George Eliot is, if anything, too careful to restore the city to the pristine purity of its Renaissance state. The marbles are fresh in their pink and white and purple, the Cathedral is free of stucco and its inlay only half-completed; the campanile looks forward to the future, not back to the past.[73] What is missing is that sense of living history which she can create so well elsewhere. It is, for example, captured much more fully in her description of St Ogg's in *The Mill on the Floss*, as it appeared in the nineteenth century: 'one of those old, old towns which impress one as a continuation and outgrowth of nature, as much as the nests of the bower-birds or the winding galleries of the white ants: a town which carries the traces of its long growth and history like a millenial tree.'[74] Although it has inherited a long past without thinking about it, and has no eye for the spirits that walk its streets, there is a felt connection between the original St Ogg, whose ferry-boat was guided by the Virgin, and the Catholic question which plagues the burghers in the quiet days of Mrs Glegg. *The Mill on the Floss* is not a historical novel, but the tone of such passages has much in common with Hardy's in *The Trumpet Major*, set in the reign of

53 Abbotsford

George III, where the indicative present co-exists contentedly with all the moods and tenses of the past. It is a poise that Scott, despite his multiple perspectives, never quite achieves.

Ruskin explains this failure by asserting that Scott was possessed less by the spirit of Hardy's first architectural sentence, than by the poetic spirit of his second, which to Ruskin is sentimental admiration, 'the kind of feeling which most travellers experience on first entering a cathedral by torchlight, and hearing a chant from concealed choristers; or in visiting a ruined abbey by moonlight, or any building with which interesting associations are connected, at any time when they can hardly see it'.[75] A certain amount of darkness and music in a minor key are calculated, he claims, to produce this effect on anyone: 'Even in its highest manifestation, in the great mind of Scott, while it indeed led him to lay his scenes in Melrose Abbey and Glasgow Cathedral, rather than in St Paul's or St Peter's, it did not enable him to see the difference between true Gothic at Glasgow, and false Gothic at Abbotsford.'[76] It is easy to see what Ruskin means when one looks at Abbotsford (Fig. 53), and Scott's description in *Rob Roy* of St Mungo's Cathedral in Glasgow[77] is largely dictated by sentimental uplift: 'The pile is of a gloomy and massive, rather than elegant, style of Gothic architecture; but its peculiar character is so strongly preserved, and so well suited with the accompaniments that surround it, that the impression of the first view was awful and solemn in the extreme.' It seems a little unfair, however, to suggest that Scott could not distinguish the architecture of St Mungo's from Abbotsford's; understandably, he did not want to live in a gloomy ecclesiastical pile, and chose his models from the military and domestic. Ruskin comes much closer to a diagnosis of Scott's weakness in another context, where he is discussing the emotional connotations of words like 'turret':[78]

> Take away from Scott's romances the word and idea *turret*, and see how much you would lose. Suppose, for instance, when young Osbaldistone is leaving Osbaldistone Hall, instead of saying 'The old clock struck two from a *turret* adjoining my bedchamber,' he had said, 'The old clock struck two from the landing at the top of the stair,' what would become of the passage?

Take away the turrets from Abbotsford and see how much you would lose. It is a word strongly coloured by the Gothic novel, and Scott, as a writer, can rarely resist the pleasures of a Gothic *frisson*, although, as a Regency gentleman, he saw no need to live in a house that generated continuous Gothic shudders.

It may seem unjust to connect with such imprecision Hardy's evocative second sentence, describing the overgrowth on Weatherbury Upper Farm. The point is really that its precision is of a totally different kind from that of his first, and that its antecedents lie in the eighteenth-century taste for the poetry of melancholy and solitude, and in the Gothic novel which this poetry helped to generate. Where Scott, like Hardy, is equally capable of both visions, the writers of the eighteenth-century novel ignored the architectural significance of old houses and treated them merely as keys to states of mind, equating antiquity, by and large, with evil, and rendering 'such remains mere objects for meditation and melancholy', as Cecilia remarks of Delville Castle.[79] 'Browner horrors' crowd so thickly around them that their characteristics as buildings are largely obscured. That phrase occurs in Pope's *Eloisa to Abelard*, and the engraving which formed the frontispiece to its second edition in 1720 (Fig. 54) suggests an architecture that would, to say the least, have been more at home in Pope's own London than among the forests of twelfth-century France. Richardson's *Pamela*, though not anachronistic to the same extent, is so in a similar way. The story is set in 1724, but Mr B's Lincolnshire house, which was built by his great-great-grandfather, must have been of a pre-Commonwealth date, in the reign of Charles I and Inigo Jones. But there is nothing, within or without, to suggest the Baroque flourish of its period. The house does in fact achieve an isolated example of external description, though these are very rare in Richardson, but its Gothic aspect is appropriate more to Pamela's apprehensions than its architecture: 'this handsome, large, old, and lonely mansion, that looks made for solitude and mischief, as I thought, by its appearance, with all its brown nodding horrors of lofty elms and pines around it'.[80]

Both in their atmospheric vagueness, and in their equation of antiquity with evil, the early Gothic novelists do not differ significantly from Richardson. Although Walpole attempts a pseudo-historicity in attributing his story to a black letter volume

54 Twelfth-century architecture to eighteenth-century eyes

of 1529, the Castle of Otranto possesses virtually no architectural features, although it is at least imaginable where Vathek's palace is not. With its secret passages and intricate cloisters, Otranto convinces as the image of an emotional state rather than as an actual place, while its frowning towers express everything that Ruskin claims is attached to such words. Mrs Radcliffe, as was indicated earlier,[81] is extremely vague on architectural period, and almost any one of her castles will do for them all:

> the twilight canopy of woods, the lonely grandeur of mountains, and the solemnity of Gothic halls, and of long, long galleries which echoed only the solitary step of a domestic, or the measured clink that ascended from the great clock – the ancient monitor of the hall below.[82]

Those who satirized this variety of 'sentimental admiration' were not necessarily unresponsive to ancient buildings. Jane Austen found much to admire in them, and was buried at last in Winchester Cathedral, which, as her sister then wrote, she had always loved. She could delight in a variety of old houses, in Donwell Abbey as in Northanger Abbey; on a grander scale in Sotherton, as, on a modest one, in Sanditon House. But all these have been adapted for modern living, and one can no more survive in an unspoilt Gothic castle than conduct one's life as though it were a Gothic novel, although, as I have mentioned,[83] she relished those too. Had Catherine Morland ever reached Blaise Castle, she would have found it even less to the Gothic taste than Northanger Abbey, for in 1795 Humphry Repton was preparing for her a surprise of a quite different kind. He concedes in his 'Red Book' that the place should have a gate 'in character with the castle to which it is the prelude', but largely in order that the stranger should be 'agreeably surprised to find that . . . he is not going to a mouldering castle whose ruined turrets threaten destruction, and revive the horrors of feudal strife, but to a mansion of elegance, cheerfulness, and hospitality'.[84] Furthermore, the building from which the mansion takes its name, to be seen in the view Repton had prepared from its dining-room windows (Fig. 24), is not, despite the foolish John Thorpe's assurances that it is 'the oldest in the kingdom',[85] anything more than an early Gothic folly (Fig. 55), built in 1766, with none of the long galleries and narrow, winding vaults that Catherine confidently imagines. The joke is surely quite deliberate: the Castle is as factitious as Catherine's emotions.

But where Jane Austen makes a real distinction between an ancient house with its past and present life, and those of the purely atmospheric variety, Peacock, in his satires on the taste, does not appear to differentiate. In *Headlong Hall* (1816) he christens his moss-grown castle 'Little Brain', while *Nightmare Abbey* (1818), although 'a venerable family mansion, in a highly picturesque state of semi-dilapidation',[86] elicits equally dilapidated attitudes, like Scythrop's melancholy and Mr Flosky's admiration for a past in which philosophical disagreements were resolved by roasting one's opponent. Victorian scholarship did, however, do much to modify the sentimental admiration that Jane Austen criticized, if not the adulation that Peacock disliked. Gothic novels did continue to be written, but it became a minor

55 Blaise Castle folly

genre, although one that remains an incidental presence in many writers, including Hardy himself. Significantly, however, it is the Gothic novelists in the Victorian period who seem to dislike old houses, whereas, in the novel of ordinary life, they are more often a poignant and consoling presence. One of Wilkie Collins's narrators, Marian, is quite explicit on this point when she comments on Blackwater House in *The Woman in White* (1860) that 'the main body of the building is of the time of that highly overrated woman, Queen Elizabeth'.[87] The galleries that Mrs Radcliffe admired are in her view 'hugely long', and are 'rendered additionally dark and dismal by hideous family portraits', every one of which she would like to burn. Again, in LeFanu's *Uncle Silas* (1864), Knowl is remembered as a happy house, but it does not seem one when the story begins there. On that November night, the wind is wailing in the ivied chimney, and the sombre room where the heroine, Maud Ruthyn, sits is made threatening by the angle which keeps half of it concealed. Nothing much goes on around the corner, but the reader is kept feeling that it may. The house belonging to Maud's cheerful cousin, Monica, to which the heroine escapes from the terrors of Bartram-Haugh, at first sight makes a positive impression as a 'pretty gabled house, beautified with that indescribable air of shelter and comfort which belongs to an old English residence, with old timber grouped around it, and something in its aspect of the quaint old times and bygone merry-makings, saying sadly, but genially, "Come in: I bid you welcome".'[88] That note of sadness is explained, however, when, belying its appearance (and its welcome), it goes on to talk of coffins, mortality, and the general law of decay.

If Dickens has been accused of a similar prejudice against old houses,[89] it must be because he sometimes writes like a Gothic novelist, and associates them in that vein with mystery, gloom, and evil. The Clennam house in *Little Dorrit*, whose 'gaunt rooms, deserted for years upon years, seemed to have settled down into a gloomy lethargy from which nothing could rouse them again',[90] is of this type. No floor is straight, the ceilings are begrimed by smoke and dust, the hearths are cold but soot still tumbles down the chimneys, 'the furniture, at once spare and lumbering, hid in the rooms rather than furnished them'. When Phiz illustrates the drawing-room (Fig. 56), he does allow a ray of light to penetrate, but only to point its finger at the chair left empty by Arthur Clennam's father, recently deceased, whose portrait hangs upon the wall behind. No doubt the contemporary veneration for former ages did make Dickens impatient, for he was an optimistic idealist, who tended to look to the future, not to the past. On the other hand, not only did he purchase for himself the Queen Anne house at Gad's Hill (Fig. 87), which he had coveted since childhood, but even in his earliest writing, as we have seen,[91] he insists that ancient houses and their furniture have voices which inspire him as a story-teller. Provided that those who live in them are innocent, his ancient buildings are often enchanting. Where the Clennam house lists because it is shortly (and symbolically) to fall, Agnes's Canterbury home in *David Copperfield* leans out purely from amiable curiosity, to see who is passing in the street below.[92] In Dickens's unfinished last novel, *The Mystery of Edwin Drood* (1870), the ancient houses of his cathedral city answer to the

56 The room with the portrait

attitudes of those within them. The gatehouse inhabited by the sinister Jasper is sinister too with its pendent ivy and creeper;[93] but the same elements, when they surround Crisparkle, are given a bright, attractive face.[94] His brickwork is harmoniously toned down by time, where Jasper's stones are insidiously decaying. When Datchery – in search, as he says, of 'something odd and out of the way; something venerable, architectural, and inconvenient', in a word, anything 'Cathedraly'[95] – becomes a tenant in Jasper's gatehouse, we are confident that, with such evidently good intentions, he will transform the character of his portion. For Dickens, the old cathedral city with its long history creates 'that blessed air of tranquillity . . . and that serenely romantic state of mind – productive for the most part of pity and forbearance – which is engendered by a sorrowful story that is all told, or a pathetic play that is played out'.[96] Cloisterham needs only a responsive mind to play upon. Jasper, clearly, is to produce a Gothic tale; Mr Crisparkle one suited to his name.

Although his views were later to change, Hardy's own early writing is clearly marked by the persuasions of his time: he shares with Dickens a tendency to connect the architecture of the past, by way of the Gothic genre, with 'vulgar gloom and superstition'; conversely, in common with that other strain in Victorian response, he

57 'Her Dilemma': Gothic scholarship and Gothic gloom

can regard it with an informed, even objective, eye. This duality is evident in his own illustration (Fig. 57) for a poem, 'Her Dilemma', written in 1866, in which a dying man asks the woman he loves to assure him that her feeling equals his. The scene is set

> in a sunless church,
> Whose mildewed walls, uneven paving stones,
> And wasted carvings passed antique research;
> And nothing broke the clock's dull monotones.[97]

In assuring him that her love is equal to his, the woman lies:

> But the sad need thereof, his nearing death,
> So mocked humanity that she shamed to prize
> A world conditioned thus, or care for breath
> Where Nature such dilemmas could devise.

Hardy's sketch is both a painful (even macabre) response to that dilemma, and the dispassionate dissection of a structure. The lovers are sketched like vertical effigies, their forms emphasized by the horizontal corpses and coffins beneath the floor; but the exact, objective detail of the arches, capitals, and pew ends expresses the careful student of medieval style.

In Hardy's first published novel, *Desperate Remedies* (1871), a related scene occurs. Edward Springrove is an architect, but also a Gothic hero. When the woman he loves marries another man, she turns from the altar to see him virtually pendent in the chantry chapel of the Aldclyffe family, with wild eyes, leaden orbits, sickly complexion, disordered hair, and 'spectre-thin', clinging to 'cadaverous marble' and surrounded by 'the reclining figures of cross-legged knights, damp and green with age'.[98] In the early pages of the novel, one of the characters remarks of the old manor house in which the tale is set, ' 'Tis jest the house for a nice ghastly hair-on-end story, that would make the parish religious,' adding hopefully, 'Perhaps it will have one some day to make it complete; but there's not a word of that kind now.'[99] Hardy certainly remedies the deficiency, with mysteries, midnight burials, secret hiding places, and even an execution to end up with – not Springrove's, naturally, but the Other Man's.

From the first, however, Hardy was an avowed medievalist, with an ardour equal even to Ruskin's. 'It was a street for a mediaevalist to revel in, toss up his hat and shout hurrah in, send for his luggage, come and live in, die and be buried in,' he writes of Lisieux in 1881.[100] By that time, certainly, his attitudes to the period had changed in one sense, for the early Hardy had been a restorer, not a preserver, and as he admits in the *Life* he came to regret what he had helped to destroy in the quest for the highest style of the middle-pointed. In 1867 he had assisted in the destruction and replacement of the church tower, north aisle, and transept of St Juliot in Cornwall, where he met his first wife, Emma. The story is told in *A Pair of Blue Eyes* (1873), where the iconoclastic vicar, Mr Swancourt, announces, 'We shall have a new one . . . a splendid tower – designed by a first-rate London man – in the newest style of Gothic art, and full of Christian feeling . . . not in the barbarous clumsy architecture of this neighbourhood.'[101] In the novel the destruction of the old one is regretted – 'It was an interesting piece of antiquity – a local record of local art'[102] – while in the *Life* Hardy wryly declares that he 'much regretted the obliteration in this manner of the church's history, and, too, that he should be instrumental in such obliteration, the building as he had first set eyes on it having been so associated with what was romantic in his life'.[103]

Although Ruskin himself did much to establish the orthodoxy of the middle-pointed, he had never been in favour of restoration. In *The Seven Lamps of Architecture* (1849), he states unequivocally:

> Do not let us talk then of restoration. The thing is a Lie from beginning to end. . . . Pull the building down, throw its stones into neglected corners, make ballast of them, or mortar, if you will; but do it honestly, and do not set up a Lie in their place.[104]

His writing sometimes seems to have a strong imaginative affinity with Hardy's – when, for example, he describes the difference between the beauty of a pastoral scene in Europe, and an endeavour to envisage it in the new world, which results only in 'blankness and chill': 'How cold is all history, how lifeless all imagery, compared to that which the living nation writes, and the uncorrupted marble bears!'[105] But the later Hardy's marble is not incorrupt; he values it particularly for its cracks and scratches, its amber tone:

> In the work of art it is the accident which *charms*, not the intention; *that* we only like and admire. Instance the amber tones that pervade the folds of drapery in ancient marbles, the deadened polish of the surfaces, and the cracks and the scratches.[106]

The love of the accidental interferes with the professional view: Somerset, the architect–hero of *A Laodicean* (1881), is distracted from measuring a church by the warmth of its stone, from observing a castle by the mosses on its walls, or a chapel by the markings on the pews.[107] Ruskin is never so distracted, and his image of the past is in consequence seen at high noon, uncomplicated by Hardy's sombre shadows. This is partly because they concentrated on different buildings, Ruskin on the cathedrals and palaces of the great, Hardy on the cottages, farms, and parish churches of the humble. The history of the first, though livelier in buildings, exists in written records; that of the second is *only* recorded in buildings, those moreover that 'had done nothing but wait, and had become poetical'.[108]

In his finest work, which certainly includes *Far from the Madding Crowd*, Hardy's response to old houses, within and without, is only in isolated sentences that of the dispassionate architect and scholar, whose eye restores a building to what it was, obliterating mentally what it has become. The burden of the past certainly informs the tragic sense of his novels, but his determinism is profoundly pondered and deeply felt: it makes no trite equation, as the Gothic novelists do, between mortality and crumbling stone. The eye that notes the moss and sengreen on the roof has much in common with the finest poetry in the tradition of *Il Penseroso*, but it is complemented by the novelist's sense of long-inhabited place, so that his description of those outbuildings is continuous with the sentences that follow, describing the altered life of Weatherbury Upper Farm. As the surviving witness of lives unchronicled elsewhere (one is recalled once more to Gray's *Elegy*), such buildings are introspective and elegiac; neither in personal nor in symbolic social life do they march with their times, as those historic houses of Disraeli, discussed in chapter 2, do with such energy. If they come to express something wider than themselves, it is the locality from which they grow, as though they were an outcrop of the rock itself. Where Mr Swancourt regards his church as barbaric, the narrative voice sees it, 'cutting up into the sky from the very tip of the hill', as 'a monolithic termination, of one substance with the ridge, rather than a structure raised thereon'.[109] To restore such a building, Hardy explains in his preface of 1895, 'seemed a not less incongruous act than to set about renovating the adjoining crags themselves'. The little Elizabethan houses on the Isle of Slingers, so affectionately described in *The Well-Beloved* (1892), before the reforming Pierston buys them and pulls them down because they are damp, appear in *The Trumpet Major* like a scree, tumbling down the flank of Portland Bill with 'the pleasant peculiarity of one man's doorstep being behind his neighbour's chimney, and slabs of stone as the common material for walls, roof, floor, pig-sty, stable-manger, door-scraper, and garden-stile'.[110] Old houses associate with the rock they stand on because they are built very often from that rock itself; they seem natural growths from the landscape that produced them (Fig. 45).

Hardy was by no means the first novelist to associate them with a regional sense of place. Although the earliest regional novels, like Maria Edgeworth's *Castle Rackrent* (1800), defined their locality by dialect rather than architecture, the Brontës, particularly Emily, had looked not only to idiom and landscape, but to local building. All three were great admirers of Scott, who had also gone some way in this direction; all, moreover, have some of the Gothic novelist's characteristics. But they are not enthusiasts for the merely historical, observing old buildings with Scott's antiquarian eye; nor, at their best, do they include them merely for the *frisson*. Even Anne, whose account of Wildfell Hall includes many Gothic exclamations – 'grim dark pile', 'desolate court', 'ruinous mass' – makes the Hall convincing as a living context. Although they are only partly identifiable, all their houses have the feel of the actual. They convince as places known from within, and known well; not visited merely, like those of Disraeli and Scott. They seem to be valued for what they are, and not merely on account of their antiquity or dignity.

Thornfield Hall, Jane Eyre's destination as a governess, is at once a literary and an actual house, dividing between the second and third floors. Everything above that line is distinctly Gothic: quite apart from the 'mystic cells' containing the mad and virulent Mrs Rochester, its third storey is furnished anachronistically. Its contents are said to be a hundred years old, and ought therefore to consist of Georgian mahogany, but the high-backed chairs, the tapestries and ornamental carving, the oak and walnut, are suggestive of Jacobean at the latest.[111] The inhabited rooms on the two lower floors are more convincing; it is not only that they are largely new-furnished, but also because they are a setting for life, not melodrama. The sense of actual place is even stronger in Charlotte Brontë's subsequent novel, *Shirley* (1849). At Fieldhead Hall, convincing people sit in the high-backed, old oak chairs, beside a hearth that is empty merely for the practical reason that a fire is unnecessary in summertime. The parlour is lined with oak, but the author is bracing about it: 'Very handsome, reader, these shining brown panels are; very mellow in colouring and tasteful in effect, but – if you know what a "Spring-clean" is – very execrable and inhuman.'[112] She even applauds the 'benevolent barbarian' who has painted the drawing-room panelling pinky white. Houses are not monuments, but places that people live in.

This practical, almost prosaic, sense of place is strongest of all in Emily Brontë's writing; so too is her perception of the relation between a building and the landscape that produced it. Her houses are less pretentious than her sisters', for Top Withens and Ponden Hall (supposedly the origin of Wuthering Heights and Thrushcross Grange respectively) are both modest houses which are, rather surprisingly, of much

58 Ponden Hall

the same date. In the novel, Thrushcross Grange with its civilized library, and its drawing-room, 'a splendid place' with crimson carpet and crimson-covered furniture, glittering chandelier and 'pure white ceiling bordered by gold', has Regency characteristics.[113] The actual house as it is today (Fig. 58), with its thick stone walls, stone-slated roof, its mullioned and transomed windows, is only a slightly grander version of a multitude of houses built in the Yorkshire dales in a style that is virtually unchanging from the sixteenth into the eighteenth century. But Ponden Hall had always boasted a fine library, its books including a first folio of Shakespeare, built up over generations of Heatons and used extensively by Emily Brontë. It had also been remodelled in 1801, the year that Lockwood gives for the story he tells. Emily Brontë has not only restored the house to the full glory of its Regency renovation, but has amplified its effect, for the main room at Ponden Hall must always have been similar to the houseplace she describes at Wuthering Heights. The glitter, crimson, and gilt, felt in the novel to be associated with Lockwood's mannered social world of the south, is appropriately discordant with the actual house, as much so as the first Catherine is within it.

Wuthering Heights, on the other hand, though somewhat grander and larger than Top Withens, is expressive of the unchanging life of the dales. Its scenes do not occur in the drawing-room or library, but in the great cheerful 'houseplace', typical of the north both in prosperous farms and labourers' cottages.[114] The centrality of this room is indicated by its name, and even more by its common abbreviation, to

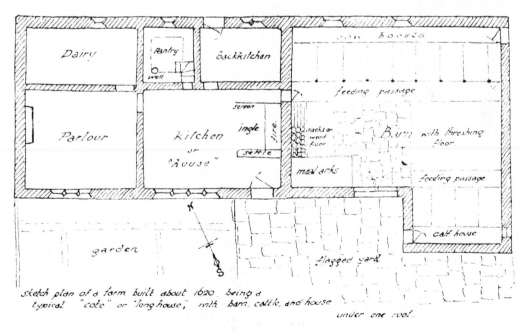

59 Plan of dales 'long house', c. 1620

'house'. As the plan of a typical dales long house of the seventeenth century indicates (Fig. 59), the front door opens directly into the houseplace, which also gives access to the upper floor, the other ground-floor rooms, and even the barns. The great fire is in consequence often screened by settles to either side; at Wuthering Heights they are curved and nearly enclose it, forming a room within a room. In *The Return of the Native* (1878), Hardy delightfully describes the role of the settle in the sitting-room at Bloom's End:[115]

> It is, to the hearths of old-fashioned cavernous fireplaces, what the east belt of trees is to the exposed country estate, or the north wall to the garden. Outside the settle candles gutter, locks of hair wave, and old men sneeze. Inside is Paradise. Not a symptom of draught disturbs the air; the sitters' backs are as warm as their faces, and songs and old tales are drawn from the occupants by the comfortable heat, like fruit from melon-plants in a frame.

The cooking was normally done over this fire, though the messier aspects of meals, their preparation and the washing-up, were performed in the back kitchen. Wuthering Heights (like Ponden Hall) is rather more grand as Lockwood describes it, for although, as he notes, the 'house' generally includes kitchen and parlour, he sees no sign of cooking as distinct from eating: 'One end, indeed, reflected splendidly both light and heat from ranks of immense pewter dishes, interspersed with silver jugs and tankards, towering row after row, on a vast oak dresser, to the very roof.'[116] Meals are eaten in the houseplace, and its adornment with related objects of everyday use confirms its traditional character. Even the sophisticated Lockwood finds the room attractive, although its furniture seems to him as primitive as the behaviour of its occupants.

As in the plan (Fig. 59), a parlour with a smaller fireplace may open off the houseplace, but the fire was only lit on state occasions, or in the event of births or deaths when it doubled as a bedroom. In *Sylvia's Lovers* Mrs Gaskell describes it as 'the sacred room of the house', dominated by the best bed which practically fills it;[117] she adds that, although her novel is historical, the room is still so regarded in retired farmhouses in the north of England. In Wuthering Heights, as at Thornfield Hall, the upper rooms are the Gothic part of the house, with their oak-cased beds, their neglect and undoubted damp. It may be significant that Heathcliff dies up there in the rain washing in through the open lattice, and not downstairs, with a proper sense of occasion, in the parlour.

The atmosphere of the houseplace at Wuthering Heights alters with the mood of its occupants. It is a warm and welcoming place at certain times and under Nelly's care; at others, during the reign of Zillah, it feels neglected and desolate. It is last seen in summer, its lattices open to the moonlit night, scented with the stocks and gilliflowers that the second Catherine and Hareton have planted beneath the windows. But even on that day of unusual warmth and calm, 'a fine, red fire illumined the chimney: the comfort which the eye derives from it renders the extra heat endurable'.[118] Nelly and Lockwood retreat to the open doorway, and the last part of the story is told there, not, like most of the rest, by the fireplace in the library at Thrushcross Grange. Its dominant figures, the first Catherine and Heathcliff, are no longer to be contained by houses; but Wuthering Heights, though about to be deserted, is allowed to make the final claim to the story.

The sense of a house as vividly inhabited, always itself, yet altering with the mood of those who live in it, is the particular creation of Emily Brontë. Wuthering Heights is felt to be an old house, but the point is never laboured. When Lockwood first enters it and notices the date of 1500 he wants to ask Heathcliff for a history of the place, but his host's attitude does not invite the enquiry and Emily Brontë makes no further allusion to it, for the age of the house is created by the life that is lived in it. Where, in the dale, Edgar reads in the seclusion of his library, and Lockwood later chats to Nelly across the same fireplace, the life of the houseplace at Wuthering Heights is communal: people come in from the moorland in search of warmth and food. We do not need to be told that generations have done so before; their presence is implied by the date over the door and the family names, Hareton Earnshaw. With its narrow windows deeply set in the walls, its corners defended with large jutting stones, it is at once a chronicle of human lives, and an outcrop, like Pennistone Crag, of the moorland around it.

The two discrete elements that had, until Emily Brontë's time, constituted the sense of the past – the generalized atmospherics of the Gothic novel, and the distanced but specific attention of the scholars – come to life in her account of Wuthering Heights because she brings to its representation the missing ingredient – the sense of long-inhabited place. This particular type of beauty is well defined by Vita Sackville-West in her novel, *The Edwardians* (1930), where candlelight reveals the old rooms at Chevron (Knole) to Anquetil:

> Their beauty, which he had thought to be exterior, became significant; they were quickened by the breath of some existence which they had once enjoyed, when no eye regarded them as a museum, but took them for granted as the natural setting for daily life.[119]

The houseplace at Wuthering Heights is superior in the sense that, unlike the rooms described at Chevron, it has always been intended for use, not show, and has been continuously inhabited. Mrs Humphry Ward in *Helbeck of Bannisdale* (1898) makes that distinction between the great house of her title and the working farm, Browhead, in the Lakeland fells above it: 'Here surely was something more human – more poetic even – than the tattered splendour of Bannisdale.'[120] Her heroine, Laura, is much less taken with its musty little parlour than with its kitchen, 'a room for winter, fashioned by the needs of winter', with fireplace, settle, and wall-cupboard carved with the date of 1679:

> By the help of that great peat fire, built up year by year from the spoils of the moss a thousand feet below, generations of human beings had fought with snow and storm, had maintained their little polity there on the heights, self-centred, self-supplied.

Earlier Victorian novelists, particularly George Eliot, Mrs Gaskell, and of course Hardy, had developed this response in their accounts of similar rooms. Mrs Poyser's kitchen in *Adam Bede*,[121] the houseplace at Hope Farm in *Cousin Phillis*,[122] the front sitting-room at Bloom's End in *The Return of the Native*[123] – all of them the central room in their respective houses – are memorable places. They do not belong in the houses of the great, or in the cottages of the very poor, but to those wealthy enough to inhabit houses built for successive generations, and poor enough to preserve what they inherit. Where the newly prosperous in Victorian novels prefer, like the Lintons at Thrushcross Grange, to have everything new-furnished, people like the Poysers, Holmans, and Yeobrights take pride in using the objects handled by their forebears. In *Over to Candleford* (1941) Flora Thompson describes one such householder, Dorcas Lane, at the close of the century, who has the taste 'to prefer good old oak and mahogany and brass, and the strength of mind to dare to be thought old-fashioned'.[124] The bedrooms still have their four-posters, the dresser shelves their pewter plates, and the grandfather clock in the kitchen still strikes the hours, as it had done on the day of Waterloo. Such houses have not been designed; they have simply grown.

It is significant that, apart from Hardy, all the novels cited for their description of the houseplace are by women. Hardy loved such rooms because he had lived in them, but the female novelists, apart from Flora Thompson, had not. Even the Brontës, although they often found their way into Tabby's kitchen, spent much of their time in the proper front parlour as a clergyman's daughters, even at Howarth, should. There are, however, very good reasons why women should enjoy the houseplace, even when they passed most of their life in sitting-rooms. The latter are 'polite' contexts, which deliberately ignore the staple activities of life – cooking, cleaning, and eating – where the houseplace discovers the beauty of these mundane occupations, and of the ordinary objects for everyday use connected with them. This is why George Eliot so much enjoyed Dutch painting, and if middle-class women did not themselves usually deal with the pans, pitchers, and onions that she admires[125] (Emily Brontë did make bread), they all supervised the running of the house, and performed duties that brought them into contact with them. They therefore knew much more intimately than men did 'the loving pains of life' and the textures of the commonplace.

There are other reasons why women should respond to old houses and their contents, not as architecture or antiques, but as living history. Most of them had to accept the contexts into which they were born, into which they married, or in which – as governesses, housekeepers, or companions – they earned their living. 'Sound' women – unlike Jane Austen's Mary Crawford, who decides to have Mansfield Park entirely new-furnished when contemplating marriage with Tom – accepted with good grace the contexts in which they found themselves, and took on their history as they took on their family. For sensitive natures, a wife's acceptance that she is no more than an episode in a life that pre-existed her and will continue after her, acquires a sacramental character. This is perceptively elicited by George Eliot in *Middlemarch* when Dorothea, betrothed to Mr Casaubon, visits her future home at Lowick Parsonage.[126] It is a somewhat gloomy house 'in the old English style', which needs children, flowers, open windows, 'and little vistas of bright things, to make it seem a joyous home'. But, although Mr Casaubon appeals to her for suggestions, Dorothea can see nothing to alter in it because 'everything seemed hallowed to her: this was to be the home of her wife-hood'. The more practical Celia chooses for her sister's 'boudoir' a room with a bow-window and pleasant outlook which had once belonged to Mr Casaubon's mother, 'where one might fancy the ghost of a tight-laced lady revisiting the scenes of her embroidery'. Dorothea's uncle, Mr Brooke, suggests 'new hangings, sofas, and that sort of thing', but his niece does not want to disturb the ghost of the lady, recognizing that the true ownership of the room is hers. But when, disillusioned by her wedding journey, she returns to her boudoir, she discovers that the room has also changed.[127] Its prospects and furniture seem shrunken; the tapestry stag has become a ghost in his blue-green world, and the volumes of polite literature look like imitations of books. The room now defines the circumscription of her lot, the stifling oppression of the gentlewoman's world: 'The duties of her married life, contemplated as so great beforehand, seemed to be shrinking with the furniture.' Dorothea did not wish to disturb the ghost of the tight-laced lady, but the room responds to her own tenantry despite her wishes.

It is the combination of these elements, beyond the middle of the nineteenth century, that endows the buildings of the English past with a life of their own in the English novel, so that they become characters rather than contexts. In Dickens's writing they are constantly personified: in the Clennam house rooms are 'plunged in lethargy', furniture 'hides'; in the house of Arthur Gride, the miser in *Nicholas Nickleby* (1838–9), chairs are 'of spare and bony make', 'lantern-jawed' presses 'totter' and 'cower', hangings 'creep together' and 'whisper', the clock on the stairs, 'with long lean hands and famished face', ticks 'in cautious whispers' and strikes the hour 'in thin and piping sounds like an old man's voice'.[128] The face and voice of Master Humphrey's clock are more genial, the pulse of its pendulum like a heartbeat, for its owner regards his furniture, not as 'inanimate objects', but as 'old and constant friends' with gentle, poignant stories of their own to tell.[129] George Eliot and Mrs Gaskell sense the life of old houses in a way that is more factual, less fictional. Like Weatherbury, the Hall Farm in *Adam Bede* has seen better days, for the great front door, which 'must once have been in the habit of shutting with a sonorous bang behind a liveried lackey',[130] is no longer opened: 'how it would groan and grate against the stone floor if it were!' Here, too, the building has turned itself around: 'the life at the Hall has changed its focus, and no longer radiates from the parlour', but from the farmyard and Mrs Poyser's kitchen at the back. Both George Eliot and Hardy generalize these discoveries about particular houses to alterations on a larger scale: he to the transformation of elegant town houses into shop fronts; she to that of a watering place into a port, 'where the genteel streets are silent and grass-grown, and the docks and warehouses busy and resonant'. Mrs Gaskell, who is always an unassuming writer, achieves this larger perspective almost imperceptibly, in terms of the ordinary habits of the family at Hope Farm, who no longer enter by the great gates and the front door.[131] The latter, 'handsome and all for show', is known as the 'rector'; the 'curate', which admits visitors directly to the houseplace, is reached by a pathway along the court wall, passing another indication of former dignity, 'a horse-mount, half covered with stone-crop and a little wild yellow fumitory'. In *Cousin Phillis* Mrs Gaskell is concerned with the impact of the railway upon traditional rural life; but this major alteration is seen within the context of other revolutions, equally poignant though long-past. She does not need to animate her houses artificially; by the accumulation of apparently slight details, she makes of them living history, and a searching, even tragic, insight into change.

In Hardy's finest writing the best of both these attitudes, factual and fictional, are fused together, so that his buildings have more personal identity than those of George Eliot and Mrs Gaskell, but less surreal personality than those of Dickens. Just as Weatherbury Upper Farm has a 'body' and 'vital principle', so Overcombe Mill in *The Trumpet Major*, 'hard-worked', 'round-shouldered', suggests the human form.[132] The stories told by such houses are historical: both have been manor houses, but while the first has declined into a working farm, the second has developed a split personality, one end 'a hard-worked house slipping into the river', the other, rented by Miller Loveday to Mrs Garland, 'an idle, genteel place . . . having no visible connexion with flour'. In these, as in all the novels of Hardy, such buildings are the features in which he may trace the detail of England's changing face. In his first story, *Desperate Remedies*, he describes a 'handsome specimen of the genuine roadside inn of bygone times', with its derelict outhouses and grass-grown stable yard: 'The railway had absorbed the whole stream of traffic which formerly flowed through the village and along by the ancient door of the inn.'[133] In *Jude the Obscure*, his last, that altered map is insistently traced: the great western highway is deserted, a place for the winds to play with straws and hay stems; railways have become the arteries that connect the country towns, and stations have altered their former orientation.[134]

The novelists' recognition that stories are told by the stones of ancient buildings thus creates a new, autonomous being for the house. Because their integrity as living things is acknowledged, the advocates of preservation triumph over iconoclasts like Sergeant Troy and the Duchess of Marlborough, and houses like the Old Manor at Woodstock are less often subjected to improvements, much less pulled down. In *Daniel Deronda* (1874–6) Sir Hugo Mallinger relishes the sight of a thirteenth-century doorway in the middle of a seventeenth-century front at Monk's Topping: 'To my mind,' he says, 'that is more interesting standing as it is in the middle of what is frankly four centuries later, than if the whole front had been dressed up in a pretence of the thirteenth century.'[135] Where the Old Manor at Woodstock was, to Vanbrugh's eye, a monument to the fame of fair Rosamund, quite modest cottages, by the Edwardian period, are treated, in the manner of Gray's *Elegy* and *Far from the Madding Crowd*, as memorials to unknown names and unwritten lives. Vernacular architecture, which had had no more than a claim to be picturesque a century earlier, had by then become the object of serious study, acquiring with that the right to preservation. 'The interest attaching to them is more nearly that of a living tradition than of an historical style,' a writer on architecture echoes the novelists in 1908. 'They have a breath of life about them for us today which is significant to an increasing number.'[136] What another such writer, Goodhart-Rendel, calls 'the tendency of lettered folk consciously to hark back to Gothic forms', gives way to an admiration for 'the tendency of unlettered folk unconsciously to build in a Gothic way'.[137] The arches connecting the chimneys of Weatherbury Upper Farm are an example of this unchanging style.

The growing admiration for such buildings was also extended to their furniture. In 1825 Cobbett had attended the sale of the contents of a farm in the weald of Surrey:

> Everything about this farm-house was formerly the scene of *plain manners* and *plentiful living*. Oak clothes-chests, oak bed-steads, oak chests of drawers, and oak tables to eat on, long, strong, and well supplied with joint stools. Some of the things were many hundreds of years old. But all appeared to be in a state of decay and nearly of *disuse*.[138]

They have been replaced by new mahogany, 'all as bare-faced upstart as any stock-jobber in the kingdom can boast of'. That oak is the 'primitive' furniture that Lockwood despises as better suited to a 'homely, northern farmer' than the gentleman that Heathcliff has become.[139] At the close of the nineteenth century, the period of which Flora Thompson writes in *Lark Rise to Candleford*, what she

60 Elizabethan and Jacobean nutcrackers

describes as 'the besieged generation' was still discarding 'the good, solid, hand-made furniture of their forefathers', not in favour of mahogany, but of 'the cheap and ugly products of the early machine age'.[140] But there are now many more interested travellers who, like Cobbett, recognize the value of the old work, casual callers who 'would buy a set of hand-wrought, brass drop-handles from an inherited chest of drawers for sixpence; or a corner cupboard, or a gate-legged table which had become slightly infirm, for half a crown'.

A reaction against the products of the machine age undoubtedly had much to do with this alteration. The taste for antiques, which inspires a drawing like that of the hall at Wakehurst (Fig. 51), is intensely self-conscious compared with the affection for the traditional and the useful which runs parallel with it. The appreciation of crafts long-practised and artefacts long-used was promoted by a distaste for the mechanical and a nostalgia for the work of hands. When Marx and Engels wrote in the *Communist Manifesto* of the proletariat, 'they smash to pieces machinery, they set

(b) Eastlake's sideboard

61 (a) Ponden Hall cupboard

factories ablaze, they seek to restore by force the vanished status of the workman of the middle ages',[141] they were romanticizing the age before machines and the dignity of early craftsmen. The origin, in the revival of the Gothic style, of the respect for ancient architecture and furnishing is evident in the Victorian conviction that the further back one goes, the better it gets. Godwin, for example, makes this point when he illustrates two nutcrackers (Fig. 60), one from the early years of Elizabeth's reign, the other from the time of Charles I. Both, he says, express an individuality not to be found in the mechanical products of the nineteenth century;[142] none the less, they are to be distinguished:

> In the older may be seen a remnant of the Mediaeval spirit. The bird in the foliage picking the nuts well carries out the idea of the headpiece and jaw. On the other, beyond the head, there is no attempt at that kind of decoration which conveys any idea.

Beyond the chaos of the Great Exhibition of 1851, it was this tradition that the Arts and Crafts Movement sought to revive. There is an obvious connection between the cupboard treasured by the Heatons of Ponden Hall for three centuries (Fig. 61a) and Eastlake's design for a dining-room sideboard (Fig. 61b), included in his *Hints on Household Taste*. The Heaton cupboard is the kind of object on which William Morris's eye alights in his *Dream of John Ball* (1888), which is set in the middle ages: 'A quaintly-carved sideboard held an array of bright pewter pots and dishes and wooden and earthen bowls.'[143] Eastlake's design is the sort of furniture which he sees in his vision of the future, *News from Nowhere* (1891): 'a few necessary pieces of furniture, and those simple, and even rude, but solid and with a good deal of carving about them, well-designed but rather crudely executed'.[144] Both preserve a proper distance from the Victorian Gothic furniture that Pugin derides (Figs. 74a, 74b); the admiration for vernacular buildings and interiors, by placing the emphasis on use, not show, had humanized Victorian retrospection.

In 1877 the Society for the Preservation of Ancient Buildings was formed by William Morris. In 1906 a paper, entitled 'Memories of church restoration', was read to the Society on Hardy's behalf. He notes in the *Life* that 'at the end of the lecture great satisfaction was expressed by speakers that Hardy had laid special emphasis on the value of the human associations of ancient buildings . . . since they were generally slighted in paying regard to artistic and architectural points only'.[145] That satisfaction would not perhaps have been felt had it not been for the affectionate and comprehensive portrayal of old houses in his novels, where even a thorough cleaning is regretted because it eradicates traces of visible history: 'the tawny smudges of bygone shoulders in the passage were removed without regard to a certain genial and historical value which they had acquired'.[146] In 1910 Hardy told the Corporation of Dorchester: 'Milton's well-known observation in his *Areopagitica* – "Almost as well kill a man as kill a good book" – applies not a little to a good old building; which is not only a book but a unique manuscript that has no fellow.'[147] When he claimed, a month before his death in 1928, that, if he were to have his life over again, he would prefer to be a small architect in a country town, he perhaps did not allow sufficiently for the extent to which, as a writer, he had trained the public eye to read and cherish those 'unique manuscripts'. Houses like Waterston Manor owe their preservation in no small part to their enduring purchase on the imagination as stories in stone, created by Hardy, not as architect, but as poet and novelist. He includes in his *Poems of the Past and the Present* the story of a man who refused to participate in the demolition of an Elizabethan house in Dorchester, was unemployed thereafter, and finally died. The stones of the house are dispersed and few remember it, but the poem itself establishes that memory and the significance of that action. The claim that Hardy makes for the man in his poem could be made in a different sense for his novels:[148]

His protest lives where deathless things abide!

5

Mrs Gereth's immorality
Middle-class taste and vulgarity

The previous three chapters have explored the various kinds of house that novelists looked at, rather than the type that they lived in themselves. Of those who have most to say about houses, only Disraeli possessed a great one of his own (Fig. 84), none had a poor one, and none, when choice became possible, elected to buy one earlier in date than the despised eighteenth century.[1] The interiors in which those novels were written were nearly all indomitably middle-class, but the much wider range of domestic contexts that writers imagine is indicative of more than an increasing social awareness of how other classes lived, or once had lived. Where Richardson and Jane Austen knew exactly where to find embodiments of taste, Victorian writers, losing confidence in great houses, looked about them, on every social level. They no longer knew in the same way what their houses should seem like, in what style they should be built, or how they should be furnished.

Their dilemma can be focused in a dozen years of Henry James's life and art. In 1885 he signed the lease for his first home, a fourth-floor flat in De Vere Mansions, a substantial Victorian building in Kensington. Given the high aesthetic taste so valued in his novels, the rooms were unexpectedly pedestrian, and he furnished them accordingly: 'large fat bourgeois sofas, solid tables and chairs: nothing original, "expectedness everywhere"'.[2] De Vere Mansions was not his final home, however; that was Lamb House in Rye (Fig. 62), more nearly a dream as the Victorians had come (with Hardy's assistance) to conceive it, acquired some twelve years later as 'a kind of little becoming, high door'd, brass knockered façade' to his life.[3] Its interior, with panelling, bow-windows, pedimented cupboards and window seats, lived up to the promise of that Georgian façade, and provided the inspiration for his own 'spoils', purchased with the advice of friends who knew about antiques. It became, according to H. G. Wells, 'one of the most perfect pieces of suitably furnished Georgian architecture imaginable'.[4]

James, therefore, was himself to experience what he called 'the fierce appetite for . . . the material odds and ends, of the more labouring ages', which he had analysed two years before in *The Spoils of Poynton* (1896);[5] just as, at De Vere Mansions, he had himself assembled the elements of that monumental Victorian

62 Lamb House

comfort which underlies the 'excrescences' and 'trumpery ornament' of the Brigstock taste in the antithesis of Poynton, Waterbath. James had acquired the idea for his story while still living in De Vere Mansions, when dining with friends one Christmas Eve, 'before the table that glowed safe and fair through the brown London night',[6] where his neighbour had spoken 'of such an odd matter as that a good lady in the north, always well looked on, was at daggers drawn with her only son, ever hitherto exemplary, over the ownership of the valuable furniture of a fine old house just accruing to the young man by his father's death'. His neighbour went on to say more, but James did not listen, seeing 'clumsy Life again at her stupid work'. He transformed the tale itself from life to art when renting a cottage, 'in its kind, perfection; mainly by reason of a small paved terrace which, curving forward from the cliff-edge like the prow of a ship, overhung a view as level, as purple, as full of rich change, as the expanse of the sea'.[7] The cottage was Point Hill, and the 'small red-roofed town, of great antiquity, perched on its sea-rock' which clustered beneath it was Rye, where he was to live to the end of his life.

The novella itself is certainly concerned with middle-class taste in England at the time, for its cast is drawn from the moneyed, but not aristocratic, inhabitants of the Home Counties. Nevertheless, there is something 'not quite English' in the whole conception, which reveals traces of the writer's indecision. Poynton itself, although

63 The spoils at Poynton

described as early Jacobean, is difficult to envisage; it never becomes more than what James calls it first, 'the matchless canvas for a picture'.[8] One cannot tell whether it has been in the Gereth family for generations, as is suggested by Mrs Gereth's compulsory retirement on her husband's death to a dower house, formerly occupied by a maiden aunt; or whether she and her husband not only furnished but purchased it together, as one might guess from the absence of portraits and inherited furniture. Even the spoils themselves are indefinite; the sparse detail suggests the Renaissance, and possibly the Baroque, of southern Europe, but the frontispiece chosen by James from the Wallace Collection for the New York edition (Fig. 63), 'a divine little chimney-piece, with all its wondrous garniture, a couple of chairs beside it, and a piece on either side, of the pale green figured damask on the wall',[9] is of eighteenth-century French furniture. Mrs Gereth, moreover, is not easily recognized as an English gentlewoman; she seems in fact to have been based upon the legendary Mrs Jack, an American who built a Venetian palace in Boston to house the spoils for which she scoured Europe. Waterbath, too, does not suffer so much from the ostentatious wealth one might have expected, as from the suggestion that it has been done on the cheap – implied by words like 'trumpery', 'scrapbook', 'gimcrack' – and that its failure lies largely in the unabashed, unfaltering wrongness of its selection.

To some extent the indefinites are those of an alien. One is never as certain of what one is meant to see in James's account of English houses and interiors as one is in the writing of English novelists, a distinction which operates in reverse across the Atlantic. An intricate web of allusion and assumption surrounds the subject of houses and their interiors, impenetrable to those not born in a certain country, and imperceptible to those who are. But, at least where Poynton is concerned, the vagueness seems also, to some extent, deliberate. The 'things', James wrote, 'would have to be presented, they would have to be painted – arduous and desperate thought; something would have to be done for them not too ignobly unlike the great array in which Balzac, say, would have marshalled them; *that* amount of workable interest at least would evidently be "in it"'.[10] But he does not treat them in anything like Balzac's detail; they remain deliberately impressionistic, no more than a suffusion of colour, light, and texture. As in the novels he wrote subsequently, in contrast with those that preceded *The Spoils of Poynton*, he does not attend so much to the thing itself as to its symbolism. Although the spoils do have a 'heroic importance', they are not themselves protagonists or antagonists. They are the ground over which middle-class taste and middle-class vulgarity fight it out.

Because he was untrammelled by the detail of specific objects, James moves more directly than other Victorian novelists to the question, which preoccupied so many of them, of what is and what is not good taste. This is not to imply that he in any way impugns the beauty of Poynton, much less to suggest that he is moved to defend the horrors of Waterbath. Where it is concerned merely with upholstery and furnishing, the Brigstock taste is at least as bad as Mrs Gereth's is good. The house itself, though 'bad in all conscience', has a setting that might have made it charming if only the Brigstocks had let it alone, but that is not how they had chosen to leave it: 'they had smothered it with trumpery ornament and scrapbook art, with strange excrescences and bunchy draperies, with gimcracks that might have been keepsakes for maidservants and nondescript conveniences that might have been prizes for the blind'.[11] Acres of varnish, comic water-colours, handy modern gadgets, a conservatory with a stuffed cockatoo on a tropical bough and a waterless fountain composed of shells stuck in with hardened paste, 'souvenirs of places even more ugly than itself and of things it would have been a pious duty to forget' – all these are among the intimate horrors of Waterbath, for the Brigstocks 'had an infallible instinct for gross deviation and were so cruelly doom-ridden that it rendered them almost tragic'.[12] Mrs Gereth escapes from its interior into the garden, where, despite her fears that the flowers will clash and the nightingales sing out of tune, she is revived (in the company of Fleda Vetch, who shares her discomfort) by the sight of 'the great tranquil sky, whence no cheap plates depended'.[13] Everything that Waterbath is, taste is not; Waterbath is its exact antithesis, its negative definition. It reminds one that books on the subject of taste tend to be books about vulgarity; it is so much easier to describe what one should not like than what one should.

The question of taste is not, however, confined to aesthetics, and when it comes to manners and even morals, Mona Brigstock is much more evenly matched with her future mother-in-law, Mrs Gereth; while her own mother, Mrs Brigstock, has an edge over them both. Mrs Gereth would no doubt have approved of Ruskin's unambiguous declaration:

> Taste is not only a part and an index of morality – it is the ONLY morality. The first, and last, and closest trial question to any living creature is, 'What do you like?' Tell me what you like, and I'll tell you what you are. Go out into the street, and ask the first man or woman you meet, what their 'taste' is, and if they answer candidly, you know them, body and soul.[14]

Ruskin, however, could not have approved of Mrs Gereth, provided he had observed the lady, rather than the arrangement of her house. It is a pointed irony that her son, Owen, should be as gifted with the moral taste she lacks, as he is defective in the aesthetic sense with which she is gifted. He may want to offer Fleda quite tasteless gifts – a massive clock, a table for breakfast in bed, a set of somebody's works in resplendent bindings – but he betrays a delicacy which goes to her heart in avoiding anything that would suggest that she has difficulty in making ends meet, a tact his mother never exercises.[15] Fleda herself, whose taste is at once moral and aesthetic, comes to depreciate the second after her exposure to the failures of her patroness in the first respect:

> The girl now had hours of sombre hope that she might never see anything 'good' again: that kind of experience was clearly so broken a reed, so fallible a source of peace. One would be more at peace in some vulgar place that should owe its *cachet* to a Universal Provider. There were nice strong simplifying horrors in West Kensington; it was as if they beckoned her and wooed her back to them.[16]

If the aesthetic and moral senses do not accord, does it then follow that they are divided?

This is not a question which would have occurred, at least in that form, to writers before the reign of Victoria, who would have assumed that the two were indivisible. As we have seen,[17] such words as 'elegance', 'refinement', and 'gentility' then spoke for themselves and required no definition, a consensus which, in itself, does much to explain the absence of sustained description in pre-Victorian novels. The relationship of taste to both morals and manners – for the second, according to Shaftesbury, is on the same footing as the first, but in a lower sense[18] – is also taken for granted. A lapse in taste and a moral lapse are virtually indistinguishable, and both are liable to result in a lapse in manners. Anna Howe's quick tongue is reproved by Clarissa on all three counts, as is Emma's by Mr Knightley on the occasion of the Box Hill picnic.

Richardson and Jane Austen would therefore have been unlikely to dispute Ruskin's claim, although they might have found his phrasing of it displeasing. Repton's formulation – 'the same principles which direct taste in the polite arts, direct the judgement in morality'[19] – would certainly have been more acceptable to both. They might also have regarded it as rather more realistic for, while neither creates a wholly admirable hero or heroine who lacks aesthetic taste and gentle manners, they are not so simple as to think that the reverse automatically holds true. In Lovelace and Henry Crawford equally, evident powers of aesthetic discrimination represent a potential self in the moral sphere that both conspicuously fail to realize. But Owen Gereth, with his delicacy of moral feeling and his total absence of aesthetic taste, would have seemed to both writers a curious anomaly. Mrs Gereth would also have surprised them, because her good taste does not extend to good manners, let alone to morals. But Fleda Vetch and Mona Brigstock, the one a personification of good taste on every front, the other as wholly representative of vulgarity, would have been easily recognized.

'The taste of beauty and the relish of what is decent, just, and amiable perfects the character of the gentleman and the philosopher,' Shaftesbury wrote in his *Characteristics* (1711),[20] 'and the study of such a taste or relish will, as we suppose, be ever the great employment and concern of him who covets as well to be wise and good as agreeable and polite.' Taste, in the eighteenth century and Regency, is not regarded as a 'gift of nature', with which a man either is or is not born; it has to be acquired, a 'grace of art', the product of assiduous application. Even Pamela, rising from honest peasant stock, is not seen as one of nature's gentlewomen. She is a credit to her education, conferred on her by her former mistress, Mr B's late mother, who has unintentionally fashioned for herself a suitable daughter-in-law. The study of taste is Clarissa's great employment, and Anna Howe admries her arduous regime of self-improvement. On the other hand, although 'to advantage dressed', nature remains the touchstone of excellence. In relation to building and planting as well as literature, Pope invokes the 'just Standard' of '*Nature Methodiz'd*' as 'the *Source*, and *End*, and *Test* of *Art*'.[21] Although transplanted from the field to the garden, Pamela must still remain a flower;[22] Clarissa is moreover acclaimed because '*nature* was her *art*, her *art* was *nature*'.[23] When Sir Charles Grandison undertakes improvements on his country estate, he does so in a manner Pope would have approved: affirming that art is the handmaid of nature, he does not force the second, but aids her, without letting the first be seen.[24]

Although one may feel that a nature so improved upon is scarcely natural at all in a post-Romantic sense, Pope's injunctions, often quoted and interpreted as he intended, remain the principles of designers into the Regency.[25] Plaw's frontispiece to his *Rural Architecture* in 1802 (Fig. 64), is explained by him as follows: 'The

64 Taste improving Rural Simplicity

subject is Taste, accompanying Rural Simplicity, and pointing to one of the most beautiful Scenes this County can boast of, viz. The Lake of Winandermere; on the largest Island in which, is built a circular Villa after a design of the Author's.'[26] The landscape, sketched by Mr Barrett, is unmistakably romantic; but the villa, supplied by Mr Deare, 'Sculptor at Rome', is its antithesis. Beyond the Romantics, nature refused to be methodized to the same extent, and most high Victorians would have regarded it as sacrilege to erect such a building in such a setting (they might even have been gratified to hear that its form is now to be mass-produced as a liqueur bottle).

In this, as in other respects, Jane Austen remains a true Palladian, untouched by Rousseau. She would undoubtedly have agreed with Knight, who affirms in his *Principles of Taste* (1805) that 'All refinement of taste . . . arises, in the first instance, from this faculty of improved perception.'[27] Her heroines, particularly Fanny and Anne Elliot, are properly responsive to natural beauty, but their taste is without romantic spontaneity. Their creator, like Repton, evidently believed that true taste is 'an appeal to the understanding, which is able to compare, to separate, and to combine, the various sources of pleasure derived from external objects'.[28] When Fanny rhapsodizes over the shrubbery, she relates her enthusiasms to reflections on time, change, and memory;[29] when Anne enjoys a walk in autumn, 'that season of peculiar and inexhaustible influence on the mind of taste and tenderness',[30] she meets the occasion with 'musings and quotations'.

That note of moderation, that tendency to do what the comparative eye suggests and what comparable gentlefolk have previously done, typifies the approach of Jane Austen's morally stable characters to acquiring, improving, or furnishing a middle-class home. Most houses are not chosen by their occupants but devolve upon them, because they belong to an estate or at least to a family. In consequence they are all that such houses should be – the outward sign of the income and status of those who live in them. Parsonages presented more of a problem, for the church had only come to be regarded as a proper calling for the sons of gentlemen towards the end of the eighteenth century. At its beginning, most of the clergy had lived in cottages, often augmenting their pittance with weekday farming, like Fielding's Parson Trulliber, who is discovered 'stript into his waistcoat, with an apron on, and a pail in his hand, just come from serving his hogs'.[31] By its end, because clerical incomes from glebe farms had been greatly increased by enclosures and agricultural improvement,[32] most were gentlemen who left the service of hogs to others. The problem of matching a clergyman's residence to his calling was often resolved by building vicarages in a Gothic style, as in Papworth's *Rural Residences* (Fig. 65), a practice to which Ruskin later objects.[33] The upright Edmund Bertram, whose parsonage at Thornton Lacey is not new-built, is quite prepared to give it 'the air of a gentleman's residence' by moving the farmyard (he is not, after all, a farmer like Parson Trulliber); but Henry Crawford undoubtedly exceeds the appropriate bounds in wishing 'to raise it into a *place*', so that 'from being the mere gentleman's residence, it becomes, by judicious improvement, the residence of a man of education, taste, modern manners, good

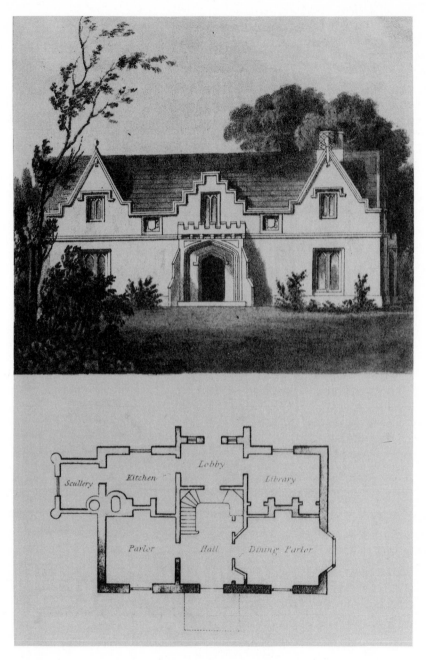

65 A Gothic vicarage

connections'.[34] It is not only that the improvements he contemplates – turning the house to face the other way, and constructing around it a park and even a lake – are much too expensive for a parson's purse: for a clergyman to masquerade as a squire, deluding the traveller's eye as Henry proposes, offends against good taste in the moral sense, however elegant the 'place' he has in mind may be.

A house appropriate to a gentleman needs no description. Cleveland, 'a spacious, modern-built house', belonging to the Palmers in *Sense and Sensibility*, is defined by that which makes it like, not unlike, other houses of its kind: 'It had no park, but the pleasure-grounds were tolerably extensive; and like every other place of the same degree of importance, it had its open shrubbery and closer wood walk.'[35] Jane Austen does not describe its architecture, but we can safely assume that it is classical, no doubt resembling Plaw's design for a small country house (Fig. 14), for its offices too have been planted out. For her, as for her eighteenth-century predecessors, ostentation, declaring that one is a cut above one's equals, is in itself a definition of vulgarity. In 1731 Pope had put paid to the exhibition of wealth in his Fourth Moral Essay addressed to Burlington:

> At Timon's villa let us pass a day,
> Where all cry out, 'What sums are thrown away!'
> So proud, so grand, of that stupendous air,
> Soft and Agreeable come never there.
> Greatness, with Timon, dwells in such a draught
> As brings all Brobdignag before your thought.[36]

The rule of taste and its restraints, which this Essay did so much to establish, endures well into the Regency. In 1805 Knight, in his *Principles of Taste*, appears to echo Pope when he remarks that, although 'the ponderous extravagances of Vanbrugh . . . are never contemptible in the whole' (Fig. 2), nevertheless 'in later works of the same kind . . . equal expense has been incurred to produce objects similar to what we may reasonably suppose a cabinet-maker of Brogdignag would have made for Gulliver's nurse'.[37]

Before the accession of Queen Victoria, novelists are less likely than Pope to identify ostentation with unduly conspicuous wealth; they define it rather as the endeavour to present yourself, your house, or your possessions as other than they actually are or should properly be. Although they render an otherwise graceful dining-room ludicrous, Smollett is chiefly amused by a set of Vandyke family portraits to which periwigs have been added to bring them up to date, particularly since they match ill with the unreformed straight boots below, the painter having tried and failed to dispute the price with the Squire before descending to the footwear.[38] Mrs Radcliffe's Emily is distressed to find the beams and wainscot of the Gothic hall at Epourville painted white and decorated with frivolous ornaments, but because the renovation is insensitive, rather than because it is unduly rich: 'everything that appeared denoted the false taste and corrupted sentiments of the present owner'.[39] Jane Austen notes pretension frequently, but almost always in relation to manners. The new Mrs Elton's frequent references to Maple Grove, her brother's 'seat', are vulgar, rather than the house itself which does not appear.[40] Mr Collins also offends in emphasizing the attractions of his house, not because its interior is intrinsically tasteless, but because he evidently wishes to make Elizabeth feel what she has lost in refusing his hand, by requiring admiration for each piece of his furniture, from the sideboard to the fender, or pointing out his views with a minuteness which leaves 'beauty entirely behind'.[41]

It is in Jane Austen's last, unfinished novel, *Sanditon*, that the reader begins to feel that this long consensus of taste is under strain. It is no longer possible to interpret with confidence the appearance of houses in a strange locality. Mr Parker, catching sight of 'the neat-looking end of a Cottage, which was seen romantically situated among woods on a high Eminence at some little Distance',[42] insists that it must be the residence of the surgeon, for, as he remarks to Mr Heywood, 'excepting your own, we have passed none in this place, which can be the Abode of a Gentleman'. He is hard to convince, despite Mr Heywod's assurance that it is 'as indifferent a double Tenement as any in the Parish, and that my Shepherd lives at one end, & three old women at the other'. Designs for cottages, which can be adapted either to house two working-class families or one middle-class couple (Fig. 6), are apt to confuse social distinctions. Mr Parker is himself an enthusiast who is busy confusing them, for he is a landed gentleman turned property developer, who plans to transform his ancestral acres and the quiet seaside village of Sanditon into a facsimile of nearby Eastbourne, which had had equally modest beginnings. He is not alone in moving with his time. Sir Edward Denham, the local baronet, is a devotee of the Romantics: influenced no doubt by Byron, he has learnt to model himself on Lovelace, not Sir Charles, feeling 'that he was formed to be a dangerous Man – quite in the line of the Lovelaces';[43] he is moreover 'running up' for himself 'a tasteful little Cottage Ornée, on a strip of Waste Ground'.[44] His aunt by mariage, Lady Denham, 'born to Wealth but not to Education',[45] who is Mr Parker's partner in the proposed development, is not herself above ostentation of the grosser variety, for her 'Entrance Gates were so much in a corner of the Grounds or Paddock, so near one of its Boundaries, that an outside fence was at first almost pressing on the road – till an angle *here*, & a curve *there* threw them to a better distance'.[46] The regulated social life, composed of two or three houses of importance in Jane Austen's villages, is thrown into confusion when Sanditon blossoms into a resort.

Under the impact of a new social mobility, taste and morality are tending to part company: as a result, the word itself begins to define merely what everyone claims and no one has. When Peacock's Mr Gall declares in *Headlong Hall*, 'there is, in fact, no such thing as good taste left in the world',[47] the company proves his point by protesting severally:

'O, Mr Gall!' said Miss Philomela Poppyseed, 'I thought my novel –'
'My paintings,' said Sir Patrick O'Prism –
'My ode,' said Mr Mac Laurel –

'My ballad,' said Mr Nightshade –
'My plan for Lord Littlebrain's park,' said Marmaduke Milestone, Esquire –
'My essay,' said Mr Treacle –
'My sonata,' said Mr Chromatic –
'My claret,' said Squire Headlong –
'My lectures,' said Mr Cranium –
'Vanity of vanities,' said the Reverend Doctor Gaster, turning down an empty egg-shell; 'all is vanity and vexation of spirit.'

Where Jane Austen uses the phrase 'a matter of taste' to indicate a consensus, our modern usage already seems to be developing, in which it merely implies 'each to his own'. The vexation of spirit that, as a result, afflicts the Victorian gentleman when faced with the choice of style for his house is dramatized by Robert Kerr in 1864:

> A bewildered gentleman may venture to suggest that he wants only a simple comfortable house, 'in no style at all – except the comfortable style if there be one'.
>
> The architect agrees, but they are all comfortable. 'Sir, you are paymaster, and must therefore be pattern-master; you choose the style of your house just as you choose the build of your hat; – you can have *Classical* [Fig. 66a], columnar or non-columnar, arcuated or trabeated, rural or civil, or indeed palatial; you can have *Elizabethan* [Fig. 66b] in equal variety; *Renaissance* ditto; or, not to notice minor modes [Fig. 66c] *Mediaeval* [Fig. 66d] in any one of its multifarious forms, eleventh century or twelfth, thirteenth or fourteenth, whichever you please, – feudalistic or monastic, scholastic or ecclesiastic, archaeologistic or ecclesiologistic, and indeed a good many more.'
>
> 'But really, I would much rather not. I want a plain, substantial, comfortable *Gentleman's House*; and, I beg leave to repeat, I don't want any *style* at all. . . . I am very sorry, but if you would kindly take me as I am, and build my house in *my own style* –'[48]

This problem would not have perplexed the poor gentleman fifty years earlier, as Kerr observes, but he does not, as others did, attribute this to the collapse of agreed canons of taste; he ascribes it rather to an increase in knowledge. In the Regency, despite two centuries of antiquarianism, the entire kingdom would not, he claims, have had the knowledge of one head in twenty by 1864: 'We live in the era of *Omnium-Gatherum*; all the world's a museum, and men and women are its students.'[49]

It is revealing, however, that Kerr's house is always the same one, appearing on each occasion in a different costume: architectural ornament is applied to a building; it is not a necessary expression of that building itself. Twenty-five years later it reminds J. J. Stevenson 'of a fish dinner at which, cod, skate, and haddock all tasted the same, having been all cooked with the same lard'.[50] He might more appropriately

(a) Classical

(b) Elizabethan

(c) A minor mode

(d) Medieval

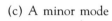

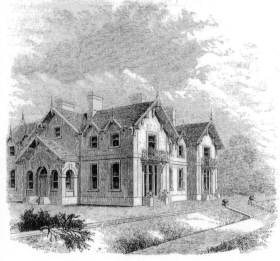

66 Choosing a style

have described it as the same fish disguised each time with a different sauce. 'Private judgement runs riot,' Pugin had complained in 1843;[51] 'every architect has a theory of his own, a beau ideal he has himself created; a disguise with which to invest the building he erects,' usually the result of his latest travels to the Alhambra, Rome, or the Nile. 'We want no new style of architecture,' Ruskin protests, 'but we want *some* style.'[52] Bewildered clients, like Kerr's gentleman, should not be forced to send, as the Bradford manufacturers did, for 'an architectural man-milliner' like him who can tell them 'the leading fashion; and what is, in our shops, for the moment, the newest and sweetest thing in pinnacles'.[53]

But the embarrassment of choice in architectural style was nothing compared with that encountered when furnishing one's interior. As I have mentioned,[54] furnishings in the Victorian period came to dominate the architectural definition of a room partly because, with the arrival of the machine age, so much more could be obtained for so much less; keeping abreast with fashion became a preoccupation, and rooms in consequence were crammed with objects. As Quentin Bell remarks, 'even if we look into comparatively humble dwellings where each object of virtue represents a material sacrifice, the portraits mounted on velvet and framed in gold, the flocked wall paper, the ornately carved chairs, the settee, the rubber plant, the antlered hat-rack, the commode, the what-not, represent a whole-hearted love of beauty which has never been surpassed'.[55] The spoons in Figure 67 were simple Georgian ones, until the Victorians stamped them with fruit and inscribed them with foliage. According to Rosamund Watson, in the year of *Poynton*'s publication, the mistress of the house 'has even been known in an excess of enthusiasm to paint posies of marguerites and red poppies across a Chippendale table',[56] a habit which distresses Gabriel Betteridge, the house steward in *The Moonstone* (1868), because the griffins and cupids with which his mistress has decorated her boudoir remain unpleasantly in his head for hours after he has done with the pleasure of looking at them.[57] It would not, however, be true to say, as I may have implied, that eighteenth-century furnishing was always restrained; on the contrary, some of it, influenced by the taste for Chinese, Indian, and Gothic, was positively Rococo. But even so, there was much less of it, and its design often assimilated it to the architecture. It is the discrepant nature of the multitudinous items in Victorian rooms, each of them contending for attention, which constitutes what George Eliot describes, by contrast with the eighteenth century, as 'the restlessness of vulgar furniture'.[58] The idea is so rarely entertained that there could be too much, even of very good things.

The high Victorian interior is, however, something of a paradox: on the one hand chillingly formal, on the other feverishly exuberant. Where householders felt they could leave nothing out, they possibly sensed that they had to keep it down, to impose an order – there being no taste to offer one – upon an anarchy of elements. In the first view, everything is shrouded and protected by dustsheets, draperies, and antimacassars. Mrs Brigstock, 'determined to rise', unwisely brings with her to Poynton 'a "lady's magazine" purchased at the station, a horrible thing with patterns of antimacassars, which, as it was quite new, the first number, and seemed so clever,

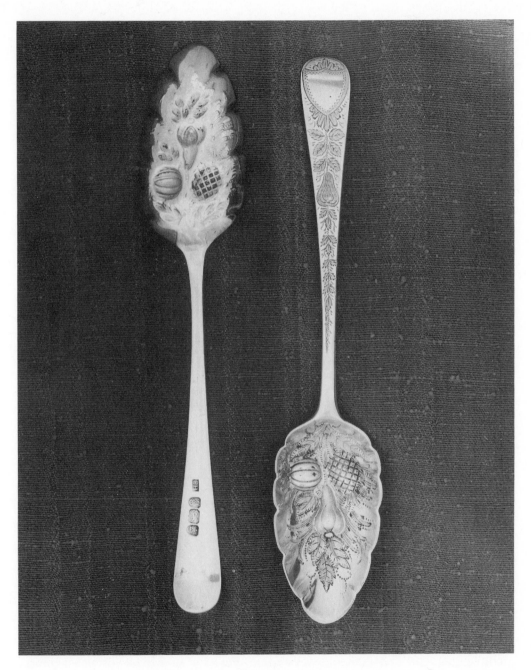

67 Victorian ornamentation of Georgian spoons

she kindly offered to leave for the house'.[59] Mrs Gereth will of course have none of it: 'For heaven's sake don't let your mother forget her precious publication, the female magazine with the what-do-you-call-'em? – the grease-catchers. There!'[60] She tosses it after them and Mona, with the reflexes of a good sport, contrives to catch it. In the second view, the Victorian interior, when unswathed, is a riot of animal, vegetable, and even mineral life, much of it pretending to be what it is not. In Figure 68 the reader is invited to identify the objects illustrated; answers are given in the list of illustrations. A visitor (to Waterbath, of course, rather than Poynton) might knock for admission on the head of a goat, and wipe his feet on a Newfoundland dog,[61] before advancing onto a leopard-skin simulated in oil cloth.[62] He might place his card on a tray held out by a bear, and hang his topper on Bell's seat of antlers, beside a lady's hat, fashioned from a whole pheasant.[63] While awaiting his summons to the drawing-room, he might warm his hands upon a suit of armour (Fig. 68c),[64] and admire the wainscot of marble with which the walls are papered[65] by the light of a torch extended to him by a stuffed monkey.[66] And that is only the beginning.

Eastlake does, however, draw a firm distinction between the rooms 'above stairs' (drawing-room and bedrooms), where everything is extravagant and flimsy, and those 'below stairs' (dining-room and possibly library) where it is gloomy and substantial.[67] Above stairs, flowers, bouquets and garlands of them, were common in carpets, while Brobdignagian convolvuli, trained on trellises,[68] might adorn the walls of quite modest households. One might have thought that, between the walls and the carpet, there would have been sufficient vegetation, but many invited the garden into the house, perhaps to compare the artificial with the actual. Animal motifs were also common: human faces (although enclosed in picture frames) might feature in the carpet,[69] and Rosamund Watson illustrates a chair (Fig. 69) in which the sitter's back rests on somebody's nose, his hands on the backs of lions, while bodiless birds transport him to the ceiling.[70] At one period there was even a fashion for animal furniture, where an elephant might function as a cosy corner, or the skull of a hippopotamus as an armchair.[71] Mineral life could be collected on the 'what-not', or on that quintessential piece of Victorian furniture, the protean chiffonier (Fig. 70). The word itself meant 'a collector of scraps', and, aided by the what-not, that was just what it did, the 'scraps' themselves no doubt resembling the 'very recherchy lot – a collection of trifles for the drawing-room table' (including a heart-shaped box which becomes in sequence an ornamental double flower and a book of riddles), auctioned off by Mr Trumbull at an earlier date to the inhabitants of Middlemarch.[72] To this temple of the domestic affections, the fireplace functioned as the shrine and focus. The mantelpiece, properly tasselled and draped, is the altar, sporting family photographs like Mrs Gaskell's (Fig. 95), or, like the humble one that James describes in *The Princess Casamassima*, adorned with 'a design, partly architectural, partly botanical, executed in the hair of Miss Pynsent's parents', flanked 'by a pair of vases, under glass, containing muslin flowers'.[73] In summer, when there was no fire, the grate below would be elaborately decorated: in the house

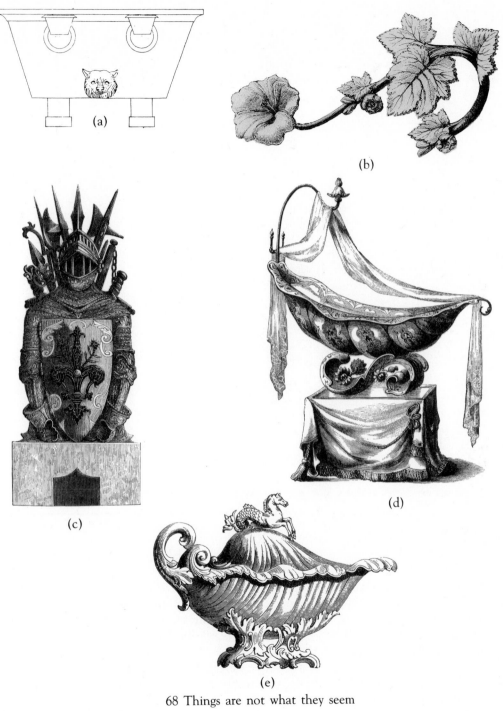

68 Things are not what they seem

69 Animate chair

of the newly-wed it might, for example, be given a bridal aspect with white velvet, a wreath of orange-blossoms in oil, and maidenhair fern.[74]

Where the furnishings of the drawing-room, dominated by green and gold, with walnut furniture and chairs with round seats, betoken feminine fuss, the dining-room is made of sterner stuff: it will have chairs with square seats, a turkey carpet, red flock wallpaper, huge curtain rails (though with no increase in strength), enormous flowers as finials, and curtains so long that they have to be looped up and can seldom be drawn.[75] The pictures on the walls will not be the anodyne subjects of the drawing-room, but will often exhibit flesh, sometimes of the human variety: 'such large framefuls of expensive flesh-painting in the dining-room, that Mrs Larcher was

70 The protean chiffonier

nervous until reassured by finding the subjects to be Scriptural'.[76] The wine cooler on the sideboard, like Sir Brian Newcome's 'immense receptacle' shaped like a Roman sarcophagus (Fig. 68a),[77] might represent a different fate of flesh, but the life of the room, in the vegetable and animal sense, was to be found in the silver and crockery. Each candle might rise from a rose as artificial as the flowers in the vases,[78] or a caravan of camels might 'take charge of the fruits and flowers and candles, and kneel down to be loaded with salt'.[79] Alternatively, it could be brought to you by a mule in its panniers, or a sea-nymph might proffer it to you 'on a shell just fresh from the ocean, or you found it in a bird's nest; by every guest a different pattern'[80] (Eastlake is driven to wonder why the Martyrs' Memorial has never been adapted to form a pepperpot).[81]

Nothing as interesting will occur in the library, which is, after all, bound to be fitted with books. Even the Claverings' decorators add no more than 'wonderful easy-chairs' (so that Sir Francis may get his sleep after dinner among 'solemn bronzes in the severe classic style')[82] to the ponderous oak and traditional turkey carpet which endured throughout the century: 'Time was when the possession of a Turkey carpet was . . . the outward and visible sign of financial and respectable grace,'[83] writes Rosamund Watson, confirming the general view of contemporary critics that the library was, on the whole, the least objectionable room in the house. Nothing, however, could do away with the bulbous curves of the woodwork, short of the chisel which Ursula Brangwen, an Edwardian in reaction, asks her father to take to the bulging oak chimney-piece in their late Victorian house in Beldover.[84] The source of her distaste, 'that sort of important paunch' and 'the stout inflated prosperity' it symbolizes, leads one to reflect on the suggestiveness of the human form in much Victorian furniture; it is the less surprising that tablecloths covered the table's legs to ankle-length, veiling them decently.

Such items would not of course be found in every house, or at the one time: one of them, indeed, Sir Brian Newcombe's sarcophagus (Fig. 68a), belongs, both in fact and in fictional period, to the Regency. But they serve to indicate the disarray into which the rule of taste had fallen. There were no rules to tell one what should be included or excluded. 'Let us not criticize what all condemn,' Disraeli wrote in 1847:[85]

> But how remedy the evil? What is wanted . . . is, a man. Shall we find a refuge in a Committee of Taste? Escape from the mediocrity of one to the mediocrity of many? We only multiply our feebleness, and aggravate our deficiencies. . . . Suppose an architect were hanged? Terror has its inspiration as well as competition.

The 'man' (if not the martyr) did present himself, in the person of Ruskin, whose *Seven Lamps of Architecture* appeared two years later. He was too doctrinaire to appeal to every writer on taste: Edith Wharton, for example, regarded him as a dubious exponent of the causes and effects of beauty.[86] But his seven lamps or principles do have much in common with those of mid or late Victorian writers like Eastlake and Morris, and although they relate primarily to architecture, they have equal relevance to interiors, as Ruskin himself quite often indicates. In almost every particular, the Victorian house offends against them. The Lamp of Sacrifice dispenses with 'fineries or formalities' – cornices of ceilings, graining of doors, fringing of curtains. 'I speak from experience,' Ruskin asserts. 'I know what it is to live in a cottage with a deal floor and roof, and a hearth of mica slate; and I know it to be in many respects healthier and happier than living between a Turkey carpet and gilded ceiling, beside a steel grate and polished fender.'[87] The Lamp of Truth disposes of everything that is not what it seems, 'the gilded or bronzed wood, the painted iron, the wretched upholstery of curtains and cushions'.[88] The Lamp of Power banishes the meanness of contemporary domestic architecture, and the trashiness of its 'very rechercy' contents: 'How small, how cramped, how poor, how miserable in its petty neatness is our best!'[89] Although in Ruskin's view all ornament should have its origin in natural forms, and he is lavish with it, provided it is in places where people do not work but rest, he observes that, seen by the Lamp of Beauty, 'unnatural arrangements are just as ugly as unnatural forms'.[90] That disposes of the flowers and faces underfoot, and the trellis work festooned with convolvuli on the walls. Since, seen by the Lamp of Life, good work is hard work, and moreover, work that is enjoyed, all short, cheap, and easy ways of doing things result in bad work.[91] The Lamp of Memory is opposed to novelty, and scorns the transiently fashionable: 'I cannot but think it an evil sign of a people when their houses are built to last for one generation only.'[92] Finally, in accordance with the Lamp of Obedience, heterogeneity is abandoned in favour of a single agreed style.[93] The contents of Waterbath, indeed Waterbath itself, are totally demolished, and we are left – not, indeed, with Poynton – but with a version of that cottage with its hearth of mica slate, excluding the probable meanness of its architecture.

If the founders of the Arts and Crafts Movement had a great deal in common with Ruskin, it is not, however, equally clear that the views of the novelists always coincided with those of the aesthetes. The mules and sea-nymphs which transport the salt appear, for example, on the table of Sidonia, Disraeli's paragon of taste in *Tancred*. Those very features of Victorian interiors that the aesthetes despised were, as I have already mentioned,[94] precisely those that the imagination found irresistible in fiction, even – or especially – at their worst. There was so much to focus the eye and stimulate the mind that it was difficult to wish anything away. A writer like Dickens may censure this type of tableware in fiction, yet indulge himself in similar ways in fact. The caravan of camels, for example, belongs to the Veneerings in *Our Mutual Friend*, where it illustrates the taste of a mushroom man who wants to make an impression, and has been helped to create one by the Heralds' College, which has discovered for him a crusading ancestor. But, although Dickens pokes fun at the camels, he evidently enjoys them; and although they are not found on the modest tables of his ideal homes in fiction, their relatives – the candlesticks of simulated roses and the artificial flowers – were found upon his actual dinner table by Mrs Carlyle: 'quantities of *artificial* flowers . . . the very candles rose each out of an artificial rose! Good God!'[95] 'Such getting up of the steam' was, she thought, 'unbecoming to a literary man who *ought* to have his basis elsewhere than on what the old Annandale woman called "Ornament and grander" '. But it was the literary man to whom the animacy and variety of interiors was such a source of imaginative discovery and delight that even the most absurd of Victorian fashions can find a home within his novels somewhere. The fashion for rubber plants and aspidistras pales by comparison with the specimens cultivated by Mrs Pipchin, the seaside landlady in *Dombey and Son*, who boasts 'half-a-dozen specimens of the cactus, writhing round bits of lath, like hairy serpents; another specimen shooting out broad claws, like a green lobster; several creeping vegetables, possessed of sticky and adhesive leaves; and one uncomfortable flower-pot hanging to the ceiling, which appeared to have boiled over, and tickling people underneath with its long green ends, reminded them of spiders'.[96] The vogue for animal furniture could have suggested Mr Venus's extraordinary shop in *Our Mutual Friend*, where tea is brewed and muffins toasted beneath the glassy gaze of alligators, dogs, and ducks, encephalitic babies and 'humans warious'.[97]

It even seems at times as though Dickens is mounting a campaign against the purists, who could be purer even than their Regency predecessors. Jane Austen, for example, has no objection to natural objects in unnatural places, and actually complains that the leaves on her new set of Wedgwood ware, 'especially in such a Year of fine foliage as this', ought to be larger: 'One is apt to suppose that the Woods around Birmingham must be blighted.'[98] Eastlake, on the other hand, shares Ruskin's view, for he affirms that 'a carpet, of which the pattern is shaded in the imitation of natural objects, becomes an absurdity when we remember that if it were really what is pretends to be, no one could walk on it with comfort'.[99] He appears to echo the unattractive Mr Gradgrind in *Hard Times*, who insists that 'Taste is only another name for Fact,'[100] and that walls should not, in consequence, be papered with horses, or floors carpeted with flowers. The reader's sympathy is, however, directed to Sissy Jupe, who is used to horses in her domestic environment (the circus), and would have no objection at all to treading on carpet-flowers: 'It wouldn't hurt them, sir. They wouldn't crush and wither if you please, sir. They would be pictures of what was very pretty and pleasant.'

Ten years after Pugin attempted to establish a standard of taste in his broadside, *Contrasts*, which, like Ruskin's writing, tends to identify it with morality, Dickens adopts the same title for a chapter in *Dombey and Son*,[101] which firmly inserts a wedge between them, distinguishing the man of taste from the moral man. His man of taste is Mr Carker, Dombey's manager; his moral man is Mr Carker, his humble junior, and the homes of the two are deliberately contrasted. The house of Mr Carker the manager, though small in itself, is Taste writ large:

> The first is situated in green and wooded country near Norwood. It is not a mansion; it is of no pretensions as to size; but it is beautifully arranged and tastefully kept. . . . The simple exterior of the house, the well-ordered offices, though all upon the diminutive scale proper to a mere cottage, bespeak an amount of elegant comfort within, that might serve for a palace. This indication is not without warrant; for, within it is a house of refinement and luxury. Rich colours, excellently blended, meet the eye at every turn; in the furniture – its proportions admirably devised to suit the shapes and sizes of the small rooms; on the walls; upon the floors; tingling and subduing the light that comes in through the odd glass doors and windows here and there. There are a few choice prints and pictures, too; in quaint nooks and recesses there is no want of books.

Jane Austen would not have cared for this cottage *ornée*, with its irregular rooms and unpredictable windows; she, who would never couple refinement with luxury, would not have been surprised to find that the prints and pictures are of 'one voluptuous cast – mere shows of form and colour'. Nor is Dickens, but for the very different reason that the good taste of the whole is much too marked. The element of arrangement, suggesting a carefully assembled façade, persuades the reader of its dishonesty.

The home of Carker the junior, radiating truth in its poverty, is more briefly described:

> The second home is on the other side of London, near to where the busy great north road of bygone days is silent and almost deserted, except by wayfarers who toil along on foot. It is a poor, small house, barely and sparely furnished, but very clean; and there is even an attempt to decorate it, shown in the homely flowers trained round the porch and in the narrow garden.[102]

It is part of the new suburban desolation, 'only blighted country, and not town', an example of that cramped domestic building, miserable in its petty neatness, that Ruskin deplores. But where the elegant house of Carker the manager is subtly tainted with its owner's personality, the house of the junior is 'honest', an expression of the affections, and therefore not merely a building, but a 'home'. In Jane Austen's novels, as in the case of Mrs Smith in *Persuasion*, we are often made sharply aware that narrow and tasteless lodgings produce defects in temper; in Dickens's novels, it is often the other way about.

Most Victorian novelists, in this respect at least, would agree with Dickens. If they do not go quite as far as he did, either in life or in art, there is a consensus that the genuinely good-hearted are unlikely to be rich, and are most unlikely to create unlovely homes. Effectively they reverse Ruskin's proposition, 'Tell me what you like, and I'll tell you what you are.' The good cannot produce ugly interiors, and, if they do, something is wrong with their goodness rather than their taste. What they value may have no intrinsic beauty: 'Very commonplace, even ugly, that furniture of our early home might look if it were put up to auction; an improved taste in upholstery scorns it; and is not the striving after something better and better in our surroundings, the grand characteristic that distinguishes man from the brute?'[103] Such family accumulations elevate the affections above any aesthetic ideal of new-born taste, for 'heaven knows where that striving might lead us, if our affections had not a trick of twining round those old inferior things – if the loves and sanctities of our life had no deep immovable roots in memory'. This is not memory in Ruskin's sense, where the products of the past are valued because they are better, not simply because they are old; such objects are valued by the novelists because they are old, although they are not better. Certainly they also have their principles – not seven lamps, but five commandments, each with its contrary injunction – but these are based upon moral, rather than aesthetic convictions. It is the quality of the occupant's moral character that is at test in his interior, not the degree of his aesthetic taste.

The first prohibition undoubtedly relates to ostentation, especially where it is of the moneyed kind. The collapse of Victorian taste had, after all, much less to do with the battle of styles or their proliferation, than with technological and social change.

The new fortunes of the Industrial Revolution, and the increasing social mobility that resulted from it, destroyed those traditions that decided for you what your house should be. In 1804, when Bartell describes the *nouveau riche* or 'city men' who aspire to a house in the country and the status of gentlemen, he actually objects to their conformity in wanting a reduced version of the mansions of their betters, 'a snug or a neat little box . . . the most formal thing that imagination can conceive'.[104] New wealth and good – or at least conservative – taste are not at that date antithetical; there is no implication in Jane Austen's novels that her new fortunes – Bingley's, Weston's, Gardener's – go to create unacceptable homes. But by 1831, when Peacock published *Crotchet Castle*, the *nouveau riche*, with the encouragement of designers like Bartell, had learnt to indulge the romance and novelty that he recommends. Mr Crotchet, whose father, like Dick Whittington, had walked from Scotland to London with his 'surplus capital not very neatly tied up in a not very clean handkerchief',[105] makes his own fortune on the stock market and translates some of it into a castellated villa to which he gives the name of 'Castle' because it is built on the site of a Roman *castellum*. His rustic neighbours instantly transform him into 'Squire Crochet of the castle', although 'he could not become, like a true-born English squire, part and parcel of the barley-giving earth'. For the remainder of the century, the 'ornament and grander' that accompanies new wealth, particularly the sort that speaks its cost and little else, is constantly assailed, and not without reason. The Victorian house in the 'castellated style' that Pugin satirizes (Fig. 71a) is not dissimilar from the one designed by Lamb (Fig. 71b) and reproduced in Loudon's *Encyclopaedia*.

The tendency of new fortunes to equate possessions with conspicuous wealth rather than evident taste is noticed by Mrs Gaskell in the very detail of their speech. The conversation of the industrialists' wives in Milton reminds Margaret Hale of a childhood game in which as many nouns as possible are introduced into a single sentence: 'They took nouns that were signs of things which gave evidence of wealth – housekeepers, under-gardeners, extent of glass, valuable lace, diamonds and all such things; and each formed her speech so as to bring them all in, in the prettiest accidental manner possible.'[106] In Mrs Thornton's drawing-room, where that conversation occurs, the interior itself illustrates Margaret's observation, for every corner (duly unveiled for the social occasion) is so filled with ornament that it becomes a weariness to the eye.[107] Others, like Dickens's Mr Podsnap, who 'could tolerate taste in a mushroom man who stood in need of that sort of thing, but was far above it himself', allow wealth to speak, quite simply, for itself: 'Everything said boastfully, "Here you have as much of me in my ugliness as if I were only lead; but I am so many ounces of precious metal worth so much an ounce; – wouldn't you like to melt me down?" '[108] Later in the century, the older generation of the Forsytes has the same attitude to property. Jolyon does not even like the suite of dark green velvet and carved mahogany in his study, but consoles himself with the reflection that it will appreciate in price: 'It was pleasant to think that in the after life he could get more for things than he had given.'[109] He does not realize how long he will have

71 (a) Pugin's satire on modern castellated mansions

(b) Lamb's design for same

to wait, but then, time is no consideration in eternity. Swithin loves luxury and ormolu, but again his chief pleasure in his more colourful context is based upon 'the knowledge that no one could possibly enter his rooms without perceiving him to be a man of wealth'.[110] 'Great wealth is often the sign of vulgar ignorance,' Canon Barnett wrote in *The Ideal City* in 1893.[111] 'Its owners know so little that they find excitement in ostentation, in making a greater show than their neighbours, and in leaving bigger fortunes.' This passion, he adds, has grown up in the nineteenth century because it has brought so much more within the reach of the many, and persuaded men that they are worth what they have.

It is no wonder that the Victorian novelists make an equation between relative poverty and taste. They counter ostentation with restraint, a virtue that limited means, to some extent, impose. Mrs Gaskell often censures 'the taste that loves ornament, however bad, more than the plainness and simplicity which are of themselves the framework of elegance'.[112] It is in the rooms of the relatively poor that she finds the second, like those of the kindly Bensons, where, although 'the furniture looked poor and the carpets almost threadbare. . . there was such a dainty spirit of cleanliness abroad, such exquisite neatness of repair, and altogether so bright and cheerful a look about the rooms – everything so above-board – no shifts to conceal poverty under flimsy ornament – that many a splendid drawing-room would give less pleasure to those who could see evidences of character in inanimate things'.[113] George Eliot makes the point even more explicitly, in relation to the Meyrick household in *Daniel Deronda*, of which she remarks that 'it is pleasant to know that many such grim-walled slices of space in our foggy London have been, and still are the homes of a culture the more spotlessly free from vulgarity because poverty has rendered everything like display an impersonal question'.[114] Even Dickens is apt to make the same equation where his more admirable characters are concerned, and the ambitious Bella Wilfer in *Our Mutual Friend* has to practise the domestic virtues in a cottage on a small income, before Rokesmith allows her to give them scope in an affluent house. A virtuous middle-class interior whose poverty is not seen as a virtue, like the wretched, poverty-stricken room belonging to Mr Crawley, the curate of Hogglestock, is something of an exception.[115] Trollope, like Jane Austen, is realist enough to acknowledge that genteel penury is in some ways worse than destitution.[116]

The second commandment – do not have rooms for show – relates to the two-parlour complex. The possession of two is already established in Jane Austen's time as the minimum qualification for middle-class status.[117] An example is Mr Collins's parsonage at Hunsford, which seems to resemble Papworth's design (Fig. 65). One can understand from his plan why Elizabeth should wonder at Charlotte's choosing what Papworth calls the 'library' as the common sitting-room. She soon perceives the answer – that Mr Collins has appropriated Papworth's dining-parlour as his study, in order to secure a view of the road, and the possible approach of his patroness, Lady Catherine; if his wife were to enjoy that view, Mr Collins would join her all too frequently.[118] In houses like this and those with only two reception rooms, the dining-parlour would often serve for common use, for two parlours made possible different modes of life, as Jane Austen observes in her uncompleted novel, *The Watsons* (c. 1803). Tom Musgrove, who loves to take people by surprise when they are not expecting him, on one occasion finds the boot on the other foot, 'when instead of being shown into the usual little sitting room, the door of the best parlour, a foot larger each way than the other was thrown open, & he beheld a circle of smart people whom he c^d not immediately recognize arranged with all the honours of visiting round the fire'.[119] In contrast with the Victorian period, however, both rooms seem to have been in frequent use: Jane Austen, having rejoiced at her brother's possession of two parlours at Henrietta Street, immediately shows both of them to be occupied; 'We are now all four of us young Ladies sitting round the Circular Table in the inner room writing our Letters, while the two Brothers are having a comfortable coze in the room adjoining.'[120] In the eighteenth century one could retire to one's closet; in the Regency one could not. The possession of two public rooms was therefore vital to accommodate different activities in small houses, and to provide an escape from the company of Mr Collins, or the chatter of poor Miss Bates, who has only one.

But because best parlours were identified with gentility, those with social aspirations longed to have them. In 1825 Cobbett describes, with his usual trenchancy, the new farmhouses built along those lines: 'mere painted shells, with a Mistress within, who is stuck up in a place she calls a *parlour*, with, if she have children, the "young ladies and gentlemen" about her: some showy chairs and a sofa (a *sofa* by all means): half a dozen prints in gilt frames hanging up: some swinging book-shelves with novels and tracts upon them.'[121] The house is now much too neat for a labourer with dirt on his boots to enter, and everything proclaims to an observer 'that there is here a constant anxiety to make a *show* not warranted by the reality'. This transmutation is succinctly expressed in a rhyme of the time:

Man to the plough,	Man tally ho',
Wife to the cow,	Miss piano,
Girl to the yarn,	Wife silk and satin,
Boy to the barn,	Boy Greek and Latin,
And your rent will be netted.	And you'll all be gazetted.[122]

It is the story that George Eliot tells in *The Mill on the Floss*, with the additional irony that poor Tom hates the classics and much prefers the barn.

By Queen Victoria's accession, although more people than ever before possessed front parlours, they tended to be reserved strictly for show, by both the middle classes and the workers. Possibly the need for two rooms was less keenly felt because the upper rooms were no longer out-of-bounds during the day and bedrooms were more freely used. The new Mrs Gibson, in Mrs Gaskell's *Wives and Daughters*, refurnishes the bedrooms of her daughter Cynthia and her stepdaughter Molly, so that they are adapted for waking as well as sleeping life; she evidently considers it to be 'modish', but Molly prefers the old-fashioned room of her childhood.[123] In any event, one writer after another deplores the fact that the front parlour has degenerated into a shrine. In Harriet Martineau's *Deerbrook* (1839), for example, the rooms that look out upon the road are those for use – the dining-room where Mrs Rowland sits during the day, and the little blue parlour where her daughter Sophia supposedly reads history and practices her music.[124] The drawing-room 'was so dull, that it was kept for company; that is, it was used about three times a-year, when the pictures were unveiled, the green baize removed, and the ground-windows, which opened upon the lawn, thrown wide, to afford the rare guests of the family a welcome from birds and flowers'. Mrs Joe Gargery in *Great Expectations* also has a 'little state parlour', although she is a blacksmith's wife; it is only unveiled at Christmas time and passes the rest of the year 'in a cool haze of silver paper, which even extended to the four little white crockery poodles on the mantelshelf, each with a black nose and a basket of flowers in his mouth, and each the counterpart of the other'.[125] Maggie Tulliver's Aunt Pullet in *The Mill on the Floss* is the kind of farmer's wife that Cobbett railed against, for her front door mats are not intended for use, and her scraper is spotless, with a deputy to do the dirty work.[126] Her best room is kept locked, its furniture like corpses in white shrouds, and everything not shrouded with its legs upwards. To the end of the century, this is the universal standard of respectability, practiced by the Bingleys in George Moore's *Esther Waters* (1894), and imposed by them upon the neighbourhood. They use their drawing-room, with its 'substantial tables, cabinets and chairs, and antimacassars, long and wide, china ornaments and glass vases', only on Sundays, when the family gathers there to sing hymns around the piano.[127]

Whole towns constructed on front-parlour principles are dismal places. Wilkie Collins describes 'the clean desolation, the neat ugliness, the trim torpor of the streets of Welmingham', a town 'in the first stage of its existence, and in the transition state of its prosperity', where the civilized desolation of the street is repeated in each neat front parlour with its flaring paper on the walls, its bible in the exact centre of the largest table, and its furnishings which naturally include a sofa and a chiffonier.[128] Designers are at one with novelists in their dislike of the front parlour. In his book on *House Architecture*, George Stevenson laments in 1880: 'With its cold walls and ceiling, its tawdry finery, and gimcrack furniture, the ordinary drawing-room is often one of the most uncomfortable rooms in the house.'[129] It is not, he says, intended to be lived in, for everything is too fine and flimsy for wear. It spends most of its time swathed in brown holland, 'the books on the round table in the centre of the room (without which, no ladies' drawing-room is considered to be complete), radiated at equal distances around its circumference'. Its only purpose lies 'in producing that consciousness of being as good as our neighbours, in which consists so much of the happiness of life'.

'Good' can mean 'morally speaking', or 'economically', and relates to taste only in the sense that the word no longer has any other definition. Mrs Gaskell is particularly aware that the new industrial class that has developed in the north requires a new *social morality* if it is to express itself in acceptable interiors. The

Thorntons' dining-room in *North and South* is objectionable partly because its overladen table contrasts uncomfortably with the Higginses', with whom we spent the previous chapter.[130] The flaring yellow damask and brilliant carpet of the drawing-room present 'a strange contrast to the bald ugliness of the look-out into the great mill-yard', over which the looming mill-house casts a shadow and darkens the summer evening prematurely. Margaret has seen that drawing-room before, when it perfectly illustrates Stevenson's observations, down to the circular table with its books, radiating like the spokes of a wheel: 'Wherever she looked there was evidence of care and labour, but not care and labour to procure ease, to help on habits of tranquil home employment; solely to ornament, and then to preserve ornament from dirt or destruction.'[131]

The truly good, as distinct from the consciously moral, do not have sitting-rooms or parlours in the least like this. Theirs are places where the visitor feels welcome instead of wondering if he has wiped his boots. Their rooms don't have 'Hands off!' written all over them; they express ease and occupation. Mrs Gaskell, like Dickens, is fond of contrasts, although not quite to the same end. The moralistic Bradshaws in *Ruth* have a formal drawing-room quite as uncomfortable and ostentatious as the Thorntons',[132] which contrasts with the patient poverty of the Bensons',[133] as the Thorntons' does with the Hales'. The wealthy Carsons' house in *Mary Barton* is more pleasing,[134] but the young ladies can find nothing to do in their comfortable, well-lit drawing-room, although the impoverished quarters of the city that surrounds them offer plenty of occupation for those with a social conscience. Although they do not seem to have an unused parlour, their drawing-room again is less attractive than the humble houseplace of the Bartons in their better days,[135] largely because it is less fully used. When Wilson calls on the Carsons in search of help, he is, after some hesitation, invited into the library – Mr Carson, after all, was once himself a mill-hand – but he remains suspended in the doorway, since he is not asked to sit down, let alone eat with them.[136] Both master and man are welcomed in the Hales' sitting-room, and although their maid, Dixon, is relieved when the second, Nicholas Higgins, takes off his boots and arrives in his socks, he is instantly invited to join them at tea.[137] That room makes an impression on Robert Thornton which specifically contrasts with the one in which he has just left his mother, not her formal drawing-room with its excess of ornament, but the dining-room where she commonly sits. In contrast with the Hales' sitting-room, the latter is 'twenty times as fine; not one quarter as comfortable'. It is handsome, ponderous, and dazzling with its mirrors and gilding, where the Hales' room[138] exhibits 'a warm, sober, breadth of colouring, well-relieved by the dear old Helstone chintz-curtains and chair covers', together with accents upon natural things: pale green birch, ivy, and copper-beech in a white vase; oranges and ruddy apples heaped on leaves and placed on a white table-cloth. Mrs Thornton, who has always been a worker, and continues to be so beyond her elevation to the bourgeoisie, allows evidence of 'feminine habitation' to extend no further than her corner. The 'lived-in look' cultivated by the aristocracy (Fig. 18) is avoided by her, since apparent idleness is a better indication of her

72 Madeline's parlour

arrival at middle-class respectability. The Hales, on the other hand, make their occupations evident: an open davenport stands in the window, 'pretty baskets of work stood about in various places; and books, not cared for on account of their binding solely, lay on one table, as if recently put down'.

The lived-in look can of course be fabricated. Loudon, who feels that the appearance of idleness makes rooms look dismal, suggests how the slothful may counterfeit employment: 'This effect would be produced by the daily papers, and some periodical works, and open letters received in the morning on the principal tables; and, on other tables, some of the blotting books might be open: the inkstands not thoroughly in order, with some unfinished writing and open books or portfolios, would give at least the appearance of industry.'[139] Such 'foolish tricks' are, he says, often used by idle people, and Dickens's Mrs Badger in *Bleak House* appears to be an example of the type, for she sits 'surrounded in the drawing-room by various objects, indicative of her painting a little, playing the piano a little, playing the guitar a little, playing the harp a little, singing a little, working a little, reading a little, writing poetry a little, and botanising a little'.[140] Like her colouring (for she also rouges a little), Mrs Badger evidently puts it on; but the virtuous, both among the workers and the middle classes, do not have to resort to subterfuge in order to disguise what Loudon calls 'the bad taste of indolence'.[141]

One does not have to look far in the Victorian novel to discover that evidence of useful occupation is essential to a middle-class interior. In *Nicholas Nickleby*, Madeline Bray's parlour is one such room (Fig. 72); and Dickens, like Nicholas, is positively overwhelmed by the evidence it offers of her character:

> But how the graces and elegances which she had dispersed about the poorly furnished room, went to the heart of Nicholas! Flowers, plants, birds, the harp, the old piano whose notes had sounded so much sweeter in bygone times; how many struggles had it cost her to keep these two last links of that broken chain which bound her yet to home! With every slender ornament, the occupation of her leisure hours, replete with that graceful charm which lingers in every little tasteful work of woman's hands, how much patient endurance and how many gentle affections were entwined! He felt as though the smile of Heaven were on the little chamber.[142]

Heaven could not always have smiled on the work of women's hands in that period; but then, one is confident that good people, like the Meyricks in *Daniel Deronda*, would be bound to produce something pleasant when they set out to embroider their own cushions.[143] Victorian novelists agree upon this point: good people make pleasant rooms because they use them. Few, however, focus the significance of that quite so sharply as Mrs Gaskell, for it is in rooms like the Hales' that she begins to demolish the seemingly insuperable barriers between class and class, discovering a closer affinity in the taste of those who exhibit the same humanity, than in those who merely share the same status.

The third commandment – be not dirty or untidy – is rarely applied overtly to a middle-class home. In an age that employed more domestic servants than any before or since, every middle-class house, however modest, engaged at least one pair of hands to do the dirty work. The injunction has more relevance, as we have seen, when it comes to the landlords of working-class tenements.[144] In the eyes of Tom Thurnall, the doctor in Kingsley's novel, *Two Years Ago*, those who permit dirt among the poor offend against the fifth of the Lord's commandments, 'Thou shalt not kill.'[145] But, if cleanliness rarely needs to be enjoined in relation to a middle-class interior itself, it is nevertheless an unstated priority. The disorder in the house of Mrs Jellyby, who is preoccupied to the exclusion of everything else with the conversion to Christianity of the natives of Borrioboola-Gha, is censured by Dickens in *Bleak House* because charity should begin at home, not only in her immediate household, but in the disorder of London that surrounds it.[146] No one can hope to put the world in order who does not first put his or her own house in order.

The complementary injunction – be neat and clean, but neither to excess – is more often featured. On the one hand, no admirable interior fails in this respect: the 'exquisite neatness' of the Bensons, the 'spotlessness' of the Meyricks are moral virtues. Scott sees them as synonymous with taste, for, in censuring the absence at the Dinmonts' house 'of all those little neatnesses which give the eye so much pleasure in looking at an English farm-house', he goes on to observe that there were 'evident signs that this arose only from want of taste'.[147] Charlotte Brontë makes the same equation when she commends Frances Henri's little room in *The Professor*: 'poor the place might be; pure truly it was; but its neatness was better than elegance'.[148] On the other hand (as in the case of the working class), those housekeepers who make neatness and cleanliness transcendent virtues may repel not only visitors but their own household. Mrs Thornton's domestic puritanism, which announces like the Pharisee 'I am not as other men', implies a Christianity that lacks compassion. Mrs Holman at Hope Farm in *Cousin Phillis* possesses the contrary art – of making the order and cleanliness of her houseplace comfortable. Although 'everything that ought to be black and polished in that room was black and polished . . . and such things as were to be white and clean, were just spotless in their purity', the shovelboard, the well-read books, the work-baskets all indicate that it is thoroughly, and enjoyably, lived in.[149] When her visitor begins to draw his model for a new turnip-cutting machine with a charred stick on the surface of the dresser, 'scoured to the last pitch of whiteness and cleanliness', Mrs Holman tries to conceal beneath her interest in his plan some furtive experiments with a duster, to see how easily it will come off.[150] 'Ignoble neatness', as Eastlake calls it,[151] is the kind that inhibits life within a house, like Mrs Thornton's 'icy, snowy discomfort'.

It is sometimes said that 'comfort', to which the fourth commandment relates, is the keynote of Victorian interiors. Certainly the frequency with which the word is used,[152] together with the emphasis on upholstery (exemplified in the fashion for the cosy corner), supports the point. John Gloag even suggests that a philosophy of comfort came to replace educated taste, although the substitution went unnoticed.[153] Neatness and comfort are often paired as adjectives when Dickens is describing the interiors of which he approves. Mr Pickwick's rooms in Goswell Street, 'although on a limited scale, were . . . of a very neat and comfortable description'.[154] When at the end of the novel he moves to his own more spacious house in Dulwich, he declares that 'It has been fitted up with every attention to substantial comfort', while to his visitors it appears 'so beautiful, so compact, so neat, and in such exquisite taste'.[155]

On the other hand, even in Dickens's novels, excessive comfort can suggest corrupt indulgence. That warning note is struck in the word 'luxury' applied to the house of Carker the manager; it is also heard in the description of Steerforth's room in *David Copperfield*, which is rather too much 'a picture of comfort, full of easy chairs, cushions and foot-stools'.[156] Similarly, in George Eliot's *Felix Holt*, when Harold refurnishes Transome Court and makes his mother into 'grandmamma on satin cushions',[157] he does unwitting damage to his domestic life. If Mrs Thornton's interior, though containing plenty of upholstery, is not comfortable in the proper sense, since it seems a sacrilege to sit upon it, too much inviting ease, at the other extreme, may weaken the moral backbone. Physical comfort has to be justified by its spiritual dimension. Edward Clayhanger, at the end of the period, is surprised by its degree in the Orgreave drawing-room, compared with the stiff middle-class respectability of his own home; but the effect of 'extraordinary lavish profusion' is redeemed because it is also 'faded and worn, like its mistress'.[158] It bears the marks, as she does, of twenty-five years' loving care for a large family.

Finally (the fifth commandment), many writers seem to prefer evidence of long association to the expression of any more abstract concept of taste. If they do not assail the term itself with Dickens's vehemence, they do mistrust it for related reasons. In Charlotte Brontë's *Shirley*, for example, Mr Yorke's interior should be pleasing: 'There was no splendour, but there was taste everywhere – unusual taste – the taste, you would have said, of a travelled man, a scholar, and a gentleman.'[159] But his creator tells us quite specifically that Mr Yorke is without the organs of veneration and comparison, and has too little of those of benevolence and ideality – in a word, he lacks imagination.[160] It is as though, to the Victorian sensibility, some conscious notion of how things should look interferes with the unconscious way in which a room may grow; that the first is always in danger of deceit, of thinking yourself superior to others, where the second is invariably honest, expressive of the values of the heart. Mr Yorke is not Soames Forsyte, whose taste is only another way of making money by choosing the right things in advance of the market; but his gift is confined to the eye. He may arrange a house, but cannot make a home.

It is the consciously tasteful who insist on furnishing quite new, or indeed, at a later period, quite old. Already in Jane Austen's novels, where the second never happened, and the first cannot have occurred so frequently, those whose impulse lies in that direction are those whose moral sense is weak. It is a characteristic of her more admirable characters that they cling to old associations, where those relate to things as well as persons. In the former schoolroom at Mansfield Park, Fanny gathers around her objects that have no other claim to beauty: a faded footstool covered by her cousin Julia, 'too ill done for the drawing-room'; a collection of family portraits, 'thought unworthy of being anywhere else'; and her sailor brother's sketch of his ship, 'with HMS *Antwerp* at the bottom, in letters as tall as the main-mast'.[161] Such objects are valued purely because of their associations: 'Every thing was a friend, or bore her thoughts to a friend.' George Eliot, who has already been quoted in this connection,[162] is convinced that these objects with their old associations are the ground in which the moral being may take root: 'There is no sense of ease like the ease we felt in those scenes where we were born, where objects became dear to us before we had known the labour of choice, and where the outer world seemed only an extension of our own personality: we accepted and loved it as we accepted our own sense of existence and our own limbs.'[163] Maggie's devotion to such things is her anchor, and even Tom is humanized by the return to his old home, 'where the pattern of the rug and the grate and the fire-irons were "first ideas" that it was no more possible to criticise than the solidity and extension of matter'.[164] When the mill is sold, both Tom's parents lose part of their identity. For Mr Tulliver, it is the place 'where all his memories centred, and where life seemed like a familiar smooth-handled tool that the fingers clutch with loving ease';[165] now his fingers have nothing to close upon. His wife is equally bewildered, for 'the objects among which her mind had moved complacently were all gone – all the little hopes, and schemes, and speculations, all the pleasant little cares about her treasures which had made the world quite comprehensible to her for a quarter of a century, since she had made her first purchase of the sugar-tongs, had been suddenly snatched away from her, and she remained bewildered in this empty life'.[166] Objects hallowed by past associations give the soul its bearing; those who lose them – even more, those like Gwendolen Harleth, who never had them[167] – are spiritually adrift.

It is interesting to ask how Poynton and Waterbath relate to these criteria. Of neither house could one use the word 'restraint'; however, in terms of ostentation, Waterbath offends much less than Poynton, although it must in justice be added that Mrs Gereth does not love her 'things' merely on account of the price they would fetch, though that to the Brigstocks is the sole value of Poynton's contents. Waterbath also scores in terms of use, for Poynton is a show-piece and is covered in linen shrouds much of the time. James does not descend to cleanliness and neatness, while comfort is seen as a matter of attitude. Mrs Gereth is acutely *un*comfortable at Waterbath, but because of its ugliness, not its spotlessness or (one assumes) an absence of easy chairs. Conversely, the Brigstocks are ill-at-ease at Poynton because of their awareness that they are supposed to 'rise' when the house is forced upon them 'as a subject for effusiveness'.[168] But it is in terms of association that Waterbath and the Brigstock taste really come into their own. Mrs Gereth may rail against 'the "household art" and household piety of Mona's hideous home', but the only justification for most of its contents, like those in Fanny's East Room, is that of 'an interesting remembrance connected with' them. Poynton, on the other hand, is a collector's piece rather than a home. Its rooms are not inhabited in the course of the story; the reader, like Fleda, is conducted around it, more as though it were a museum. Its contents have been collected and arranged purely on grounds of taste, not need or use. Fleda may discover that Poynton is 'the record of a life', but she might equally have seen it as the record of a career.

In resorting to the past, Mrs Gereth in any case bypasses the issue of contemporary taste, for although she feels that much might be done with Waterbath, she never indicates what that might mean in contemporary terms. In 1897 the collecting of antiques was a relatively recent passion. The interest in earlier furniture, originating in the reign of William IV, had not necessarily meant that one tried to acquire it; more probably, one would order whole rooms reproduced in a particular historical style, Elizabethan, say, or Jacobean. Many Victorian novelists, as we saw in the previous chapter, were responsive to interiors of those periods, but such furniture is usually seen *in situ*, in the houses, great or humble, that first acquired it. Thus the narrator in the novella *A Phantom Lover* by Vernon Lee (1886) admires a Jacobean interior because it impresses him with all that is 'natural, spontaneous', and has nothing about it of 'the picturesqueness which swell studios have taught to rich and aesthetic houses'.[169] It has not, in other words, been contrived, but has simply grown. Like Mr Yorke's, Mrs Gereth's arrangement of her house is unduly self-conscious.

The real attempt made in the later Victorian period to achieve a modern style which would honour the consensus of principles already outlined was, of course, the Arts and Crafts Movement. Its finest spokesman, William Morris, formulates them all. The instinct for possession leads, he claims, either to sheer vexation, or to a chain of pompous circumstances: 'I have never been in any rich man's house which would not have looked the better for having a bonfire made outside of it of nine-tenths of all that it held.'[170] He advocates simplicity with a vehemence more than equal to the novelists': 'Simplicity of life, begetting simplicity of taste, that is, a love for sweet and lofty things, is of all matters most necessary for the birth of the new and better art we crave for; simplicity everywhere, in the palace as well as in the cottage.'[171] He also advocates neatness, but on their terms: 'though all rooms should look tidy, and even very tidy, they ought not to look too tidy'.[172] When he describes the kind of drawing-room he approves, its contents are determined chiefly by use: 'First a bookcase with a great many books in it: next a table that will keep steady when you write or work at it: then several chairs that you can move, and a bench that you can sit or lie upon: next a cupboard with drawers.'[173] Apart from pictures or painted walls, a small carpet and fresh flowers, no more is needed: 'a drawing room ought to look as if some kind of work could be done in it less toilsome than being bored'.[174] The comfort of his rooms is of the spiritual rather than the physical variety: they are suited to life, and there is nothing in them which would 'make a simple man shrink'. But although his ideal of living space appears to conform with the convictions of Mrs Gaskell and many other novelists, when the fireplace that Nesfield designed for Farnham Royal and the type of room that it implies (Fig. 73) are compared with Mrs Gaskell's own fireplace and room in Manchester (Fig. 95), they do not seem to have very much in common. Her interior is certainly not over-

73 Fireplace at Farnham Royal

stuffed or ostentatious, but, with its restlessly discrepant elements and its altar-like fireplace, it is unmistakably middle-class Victorian. His, on the other hand, although more richly ornamented, is harmonized by an aesthetic vision, and its fireplace is convivial, not memorial.

The Arts and Crafts Movement does not, however, present itself as a 'style', with that fatal self-consciousness that comes to be associated with the word 'taste'. Although it is clearly retrospective, as Eastlake's settles and inglenook both indicate, it looks back to the past for a pattern of domestic life, rather than a unifying style as such. Earlier Gothic furniture was retrospective in the second sense, seeking the pictorial rather than the practical; as Pugin's satire on the taste indicates (Fig. 74a), it was not calculated at all for ordinary life: 'A man who remains any length of time in a modern Gothic room, and escapes without being wounded by some of its minutiae, may consider himself extremely fortunate.'[175] His satire is no exaggeration, for, as he admits, he has 'perpetrated many of the enormities' himself, inflicting them on the queen at Windsor Castle; moreover, it is certainly no worse than the 'mediaeval court' at the Great Exhibition (Fig. 74b). In contrast, objects like Eastlake's dining-room sideboard (Fig. 61b), although visually pleasing, look back to the past primarily for objects of practical use.

Art Nouveau, which developed in the last quarter of the century, does not correspond at all to the mid-Victorian principles of the novelists, although it owed a good deal to the Arts and Crafts Movement – some designers, indeed, were common to both. Known to the furniture trade as the 'Quaint Style', it set out to create a specifically non-historical movement, and made an excessive use of decoration, to which form, comfort, and practicality were all subordinated. It did of course have its literary originators and adherents, and was apt, in the satirical view, to become conflated with the Arts and Crafts Movement:

> With red and blue and sagest green
>   Were walls and dado dyed,
> Friezes of Morris' there were seen
>   And oaken wainscot wide.
> Now he who loves aesthetic cheer
>   And does not mind the damp
> May come and read Rosetti here
>   By a Japanese-y lamp.[176]

The main difference is that, along with the past, Art Nouveau throws off those notions of responsibility which, for Morris and the mid-Victorian novelists, had done much to determine what an acceptable domestic interior should include. Wilde's creation, Lord Henry Wotton, delights in the 'Japanese effect' which makes him think 'of those pallid jade-faced painters of Tokio who, through the medium of an art that is necessarily immobile, seek to convey the sense of swiftness and motion'.[177] It is the same attitude, of art for art's sake, which leads him to argue 'that if one man were to live out his life fully and completely . . . I believe that the world would gain

(b) The 'mediaeval court' at the Great Exhibition

74 (a) Pugin's satire on modern Gothic furniture

such a fresh impulse of joy that we would forget all the maladies of mediaevalism'[178] – maladies which, for him, are associated with conversations about feeding the poor and the necessity of model lodging-houses. Like Arnold, he advocates (instead, not as well) a return to the Hellenic ideals of 'sweetness and light'. One wonders whether his name is intended to recall that of the seventeenth-century writer, Sir Henry Wotton, an advocate of the classical, who thought that the principles of architecture should be three: commodity, firmness, and *delight*.

In this respect at least there is a real distance between Art Nouveau and the Arts and Crafts Movement; but Morris himself may have invited that conflation, for, despite the vigour of his opinions, he is not nearly as prescriptive as Ruskin had been. His injunction – '*Have nothing in your houses that you do not know to be useful, or believe to be beautiful*' – can include a great deal when one reflects upon it.[179] It is, for example, perfectly illustrated by 'Boffin's Bower' in *Our Mutual Friend*.[180] Mr Boffin's part of the room is a practical region of 'sand and sawdust'; it extends between, and includes, the two settles, each with a table before it, to either side of the fire, and contains only those things that he knows to be useful: books, tumblers, 'certain squat case-bottles of inviting appearance', a bowl of sugar, a steaming kettle, and 'compensatory shelves on which the best part of a large pie and likewise of a cold joint were plainly discernible among other solids'. Mrs Boffin's area, facing the fire, is carpeted with flowers and the 'glowing vegetation' she believes to be beautiful. Her 'flowery land' is ornamented with 'stuffed birds and waxen fruits under glass shades', with a sofa, footstool, and little table, all garish in taste and colour, though expensive. To Mr Wegg's eye, they have 'a very odd look beside the settles and the flaring gaslight pendent from the ceiling'; but the room not only obeys Morris's precept – it is a perfect example of marital accommodation, and of 'doing as one likes', the vice for which Arnold castigates the English.[181]

It is impossible, however, to castigate Mr and Mrs Boffin, though their goodness of heart, in this case, is clearly *not* productive of good taste. 'Doing as one likes' Arnold sees as the battle-cry of those, mostly across the Atlantic, who oppose what they describe as the 'religion of culture'. But, as the century drew to its close, others joined with Dickens in opposing the criteria of taste implied in 'sweetness and light',[182] finding in its antithesis, vulgarity, more convincing evidence of honesty and truth.

When in 1861 Thackeray remarks upon 'the ugly room, the ugly family, the kind worthy people',[183] he is indicating a contrast, not a connection. When in 1864 Kerr alludes to the 'incredible worship of the Ugly' which is developing, it is clear that he is identifying an aberration.[184] It is a different case when Meredith's new woman, Clara, affirms in 1879: 'I can imagine learning to love ugliness. It's honest. However young you are, you cannot be deceived by it.'[185] Both her developing preference, and her justification for it, would have dumbfounded Jane Austen, but taste never recovers the moral strength it could still claim into the Regency. The animate, vigorous, vulgar world of the first period of mass production, its ability to reach to the pockets of people who had not in the past been rich enough to choose, and the democratic nature of that appeal led eventually to a different orthodoxy. Thus Forster says of Rickie, the hero of *The Longest Journey* (1907): 'He did not love the vulgar herd, but he knew that his own vulgarity would be greater if he forbade it ingress.'[186] Taste had acquired the stigma of class, rather than wealth, and was equally despised by those who did not have it, and by those who knew what it was, but suffered from social conscience.

Rickie, as a child, has learnt how cruel taste can be, for his father leaves his mother, who 'had not the gift of making her home beautiful; and one day, when she bought a carpet for the dining-room that clashed, he laughed gently, said he "really couldn't," and departed.'[187] As an adult, he is led to wonder, when staying with the Ansells, among the endless, incompetent family portraits, the texts, and the harp in luminous paint, 'whether one of the bonds that kept the Ansell family united might not be their complete absence of taste – a surer bond by far than the identity of it'.[188]

Victorian novelists, as we have seen, suspected taste when it was pursued for its own sake; they were, however, willing to apply the word to simple households which earned the title 'home'. For Edwardian novelists, the two have become effectively incompatible: the bonds of truth which make a home cannot be formed where taste predominates. Its dishonesty may come in various forms: ' "Of course, Soames is a connoisseur", said Aunt Juley hastily: "he has wonderful taste – he can always tell beforehand what's going to be successful." '[189] It can be a covering for unhealthy sentiments, as it is with Ford's Mrs Duchemin, who has too much of it,[190] or James's Madame de Vionnet, whose *mise-en-scène* is a seduction in itself.[191] Just as Fleda Vetch comes to rely upon 'the strong, simplifying horrors in West Kensington', so Margaret Schlegel in Forster's *Howards End* learns to dislike the taste of intellectual Chelsea – 'those decorative schemes that wince, and relent, and refrain, and achieve beauty by sacrificing comfort and pluck'[192] – because Chelsea despises those who are of the world, not of the mind. She turns with relief to her equivalent of West Kensington – the Wilcox dining-room: 'After so much self-colour and self-denial, Margaret viewed with relief the sumptuous dado, the frieze, the gilded wallpaper, amid whose foliage parrots sang.'[193] Although she knows quite well that her own furniture could not withstand it, 'those heavy chairs, that immense sideboard loaded with presentation plate, stood up against its pressure like men'. While taste has become virtually synonymous with immorality, ostentatious wealth is at least good-hearted, overt, and – in that sense – honest. Mr Podsnap has grown acceptable.

Mr Podsnap does, however, lack heart in the generous sense, and those who put their confidence in vulgarity identify it with the life of the affections. Not far from Waterbath, either in time (for eleven years divide them), or in place (for both are in the south of England within reach of London), is the Honeychurches' Windy Corner, described in Forter's *A Room with a View*. It too is built in countryside of incongruous splendour, takes its name from another of the four elements, and is furnished (to judge from the varnish) from the same emporia. Mrs Gereth, having escaped from the awful Brigstock interior, begins to reflect what she might have made of the house, having 'taken the fine hint of nature'.[194] Cecil Vyse, a visitor to Windy Corner, whose aesthetic sensibilities are equally anguished, throws open the curtains (drawn to protect the new carpets), to gaze out past a rustic bench to an incomparable view, and consider how the drawing-room might be improved: 'With that outlook it should have been a successful room, but the trail of Tottenham Court Road was upon it.'[195] Waterbath, if undistinguished, is not an ugly house; Windy Corner is:

> The situation was so glorious, the house so commonplace, not to say impertinent. The late Mr Honeychurch had affected the cube, because it gave him the most accommodation for his money, and the only addition made by his widow had been a small turret, shaped like a rhinoceros' horn, where she could sit in wet weather and watch the carts going up and down the road.[196]

So far one might be viewing Windy Corner with the disparaging eye of James himself, if not with the satiric vehemence of Mrs Gereth. But Cecil Vyse is a man of small account in Forster's eyes, while the Honeychurches have the gift of life:

> So impertinent – and yet the house 'did,' for it was the home of people who loved their surroundings honestly. Other houses in the neighbourhood had been built by expensive architects, over others their inmates had fidgeted sedulously, yet all these suggested the accidental, the temporary; while Windy Corner seemed as inevitable as an ugliness of Nature's own creation. One might laugh at the house, but one never shuddered.[197]

Neither Forster nor the Honeychurches themselves deny the vulgarity of Windy Corner; but being conventional, concerning oneself with puddings, hydrangeas, and boilers, allowing the odd bone to lie on a Maple's chair in the drawing-room – in a word, allowing that Nature may herself be ugly – create the life that eludes Cecil Vyse and for which his aesthetic soul craves. As Lucy Honeychurch concludes, he understands beautiful things, but, because he does not understand people, is unable to transform aesthetic taste into life.[198]

The advocates of ugliness sometimes seem to miss the fact that vulgarity can be dishonest too; that it can be adopted, like taste, as a façade. In her story, 'Janet's Repentance', George Eliot describes façades of both kinds. She expects to find in a clergyman's study an expression of clerical taste, 'where the general air of comfort is rescued from a secular character by strong ecclesiastical suggestions in the shape of the furniture, the pattern of the carpet, and the prints on the wall; where, if a nap is taken, it is in an easy chair with a Gothic back, and the very feet rest on a warm and velvety simulation of church windows'.[199] To deny an imputation of luxury by disguising it in clerical taste is one kind of dishonesty; Mr Tryan's actual and very ugly little study is deception of the opposite variety: 'The man who could live in such a room, unconstrained by poverty . . . must have chosen that least attractive form of self-mortification which wears no haircloth and has no meagre days, but accepts the vulgar, the commonplace, and the ugly, whenever the highest duty seems to lie among them.'[200] George Eliot gives Mr Tryan the benefit of the doubt; James is less sparing of his Princess Casamassima, who can create, wherever she goes, 'the most charming room in Europe', and chooses to go slumming in Madeira Crescent instead. It is her way of proving that she has identified her lot with the poor, but she does not convince that true man of the people, Paul Muniment, who comments blandly as he inspects her room:

> 'You've got a lovely home.'
> 'Lovely? My dear sir, it's hideous. That's what I like it for,' she hastened to explain.
> 'Well, I like it, but perhaps I don't know the reason. I thought you had given up everything – pitched your goods out of window for a grand scramble.'
> 'It's what I *have* done. You should have seen me before.'[201]

Paul, who admits he would give his nose for similar deprivation, concludes unkindly that she has 'a great deal left, for a person who has given everything away'. In the case of the Princess, one concludes, her taste is more truthful than her assumption of vulgarity.

Lucy Honeychurch is driven in the end to believe that 'good taste and bad taste were only catchwords, garments of diverse cut'.[202] Fleda Vetch, because she is gifted with taste where Lucy is not, comes, as the novel does, to a different, and quintessentially Victorian, conclusion. For there is a third house in *The Spoils of Poynton*, the modest Ricks, once the home of a maiden aunt, the dower house into which Mrs Gereth is driven by Owen's marriage to Mona. Mrs Gereth, from the first, despises Ricks; but Fleda, from the first, finds much to admire in it:

> 'Why it's charming!' she exclaimed a few hours later, turning back again into the small prim parlour from a friendly advance to the single plate of the window. Mrs Gereth hated such windows, the one flat glass sliding up and down, especially when they enjoyed a view of four iron pots on pedestals, painted white and containing ugly geraniums, ranged on the edge of a gravel path and doing their best to give it the air of a terrace.[203]

But Fleda is ready to forgive the plate glass and the geraniums because Ricks as a whole expresses the personality of the maiden aunt:

> The place was crowded with objects of which the aggregation somehow made a thinness and the futility a grace; things that told her they had been gathered as slowly and as lovingly as the golden flowers of the other house. She too, for a home, could have lived with them; they made her fond of the old maiden-aunt; they made her even wonder if it didn't work more for happiness not to have tasted, as she herself had done, of knowledge.[204]

At the end of the story, Mrs Gereth returns all the spoils to Poynton, which promptly and symbolically burns down. In their place she digs out from the barn the maiden aunt's despised possessions, and rearranges them around the house. The 'wretched things', as Mrs Gereth calls them, instantly acquire a beauty of their own; unconsciously, she has used her taste to express the personality that loved them in the first place. Mrs Gereth regards the result as 'just like Waterbath', but no comparable quality of character is expressed in the Brigstock house. Fleda admits that it is not the great chorus of Poynton, but she reproaches Mrs Gereth for her blindness:

> 'You're not, I'm sure, either so proud or so broken as to be reached by nothing but that. This is a voice so gentle, so human, so feminine – a faint far-away voice with the little quaver of a heart-break. You've listened to it unawares.'[205]

The beauty of Ricks resides in the impression it gives 'of something dreamed and missed, something reduced, relinquished, resigned: the poetry, as it were, of something sensibly *gone*'.[206] Mrs Gereth is rewarded for her own sacrifice, for she too has dreamt of something – Poynton – and has resigned it in giving up the 'things'. The interior of Ricks is now entirely truthful, as it never was when arrayed in Poynton's grandeur.

In its final condition, Ricks is a house that would have appealed to Charlotte Brontë and Mrs Gaskell, to Dickens and George Eliot, far more than the perfect interior of Poynton. They would have understood, as Mrs Gereth cannot, Fleda's warm response to the poor lady's setting:

> 'Beautiful things?' Mrs Gereth turned again to the little worn bleached stuffs and the sweet spindle-legs. 'That's the wretched things that were here – that stupid starved old woman's.'
> 'The maiden-aunt's, the nicest, the dearest old woman that ever lived?'[207]

It may be true that the Victorians' houses were memorials to personality rather than shrines of taste. But perhaps they were, after all, not so wrong in believing that the living space of a congenial personality, one which shared with Morris the conviction that 'the true secret of happiness *lies in taking a genuine interest in all the details of daily life*',[208] could not, in a final analysis, prove uncongenial to the eye. Our current version of 'doing as one likes', expressed in the assertion 'It's all a matter of taste', denies any content, moral or otherwise, to that word itself. The Victorians restored to taste the moral content it had once had, if in a different form. Where in the eighteenth century good taste implied good morals, for the Victorians the expression of good morals *was* good taste.

6

Barton Cottage and the 'perfect pastoral'
The middle-class idyll

Although the Victorian novelists seem to agree on the characteristics of a pleasant middle-class interior, it is not always clear that this is where they or their characters really want to live. Like the Meyricks' in *Daniel Deronda*,[1] such interiors are won from urban desolation, 'grim-walled slices of space' in inner cities, an environment against which the imagination rebels. The division in feeling between where one actually lives and where one would like to is apparent in Mrs Gaskell's letters. In the summer of 1849 she writes to Catherine Winkworth, wanting to know what her lodgings on the Isle of Wight are like: 'Grand proper rooms, I dare say, as dull as dust, with no amusing warming-pans, nor crockery, nor spurs, nor dresser, as Selina and we had at the Lakes; our dear charming farm-kitchen at Skelwith was worth a dozen respectable properly-furnished rooms.'[2] But it is to those respectable rooms that Mrs Gaskell herself has to return, in order to settle 'down into soberness'. In the spring of that year she had herself been staying in lodgings in Stratford-upon-Avon, which, unlike those she envisages in the Isle of Wight, met with her definition of delight: 'a cottage where one's head was literally in danger of being bumped by the low doors, and where the windows were casements: where the rooms were all entered by a step up, or a step down: where the scents through the open hall door were all of sweet briar and lilac and lilies of the valley'.[3] Commenting on her London lodgings, she adds with regretful affection: 'Cd. there be a greater contrast to dear, charming, dingy dirty Panton Square?' Victorian paintings of such idyllic cottages were numerous, and still find their way on to many greetings cards today (Fig. 75). It would not be in the spirit of the game to suggest that such cottages are probably damp and dark, that thatch is a fire-hazard, and that all those flowers do not usually burst into bloom simultaneously.

One of the most memorable descriptions in the Victorian novel of this idyll, capturing both its potency and its factitiousness, is that of the painting on the wall of Mrs Plornish's shop parlour in *Little Dorrit*.[4] The shop itself is in Bleeding Heart Yard, a hunting lodge in the reign of Elizabeth, in that of Victoria a tenement for the nomadic poor. Mrs Plornish has given heart to the dismal present with an image from the rural past, 'a little fiction' in which she 'unspeakably rejoiced'. The wall of

75 The perfect pastoral

the parlour has been painted to resemble a cottage, including in it the real door and window, despite their 'highly disproportioned dimensions'. The cottage has all those characteristics that such fictions still display in advertisements: sunflowers and hollyhocks 'flourishing with great luxuriance', thatch of course, a faithful dog 'flying at the legs of the friendly visitor', a cloud of pigeons, a densely smoking chimney indicating 'good cheer within, and also, perhaps, that it had not been lately swept'. The door, when it is shut, exhibits a brass plate with the inscription: 'Happy Cottage, T. and M. Plornish'. It is of no account to Mrs Plornish that, when her husband leans against it to smoke his evening pipe, his hat blots out the pigeon-house, his back swallows up the dwelling, and his hands in his pockets uproot the garden and lay waste the countryside: 'No poetry and no Art ever charmed the imagination more than the union of the two in this counterfeit cottage charmed Mrs Plornish.' To come into the shop when it is shut and hear her father singing inside the cottage is 'a perfect Pastoral to Mrs Plornish, the Golden Age revived'. It is, however, significantly difficult to translate this cottage from mental into visual image, for the first part of the description seems to suggest that it is painted on the inside of the parlour wall; the second, like the illustration (Fig. 76), that it is painted

76 Happy Cottage

on the outside. It is even less possible for Mrs Plornish to translate her fiction into reality; and perhaps, as Dickens intimates, such idylls only remain so in dreams.

If one goes back just over half a century, to Jane Austen's *Sense and Sensibility*, the contrast in attitude to the Dashwoods' cottage in Devon is dramatic. Barton Cottage is satisfactory only in so far as it avoids the character of a 'perfect pastoral', and matches up to the convenience of a respectable middle-class home:

> As a house, Barton Cottage, though small, was comfortable and compact; but as a cottage it was defective, for the building was regular, the roof was tiled, the window shutters were not painted green, nor were the walls covered with honeysuckles. A narrow passage led directly through the house into the garden behind. On each side of the entrance was a sitting room, about sixteen feet

square; and beyond them were the offices and stairs. Four bedrooms and two garrets formed the rest of the house. It had not been built many years and was in good repair.[5]

Mrs Dashwood has been expelled from her husband's estate by her stepson on his father's death. She and her daughters have to make do with Barton Cottage as the minimum that will house their family with some appearance of gentility. In these circumstances Mrs Dashwood's daughters are more accommodating than Mrs Davilow's in *Daniel Deronda* who has to protest: 'It is not so very bad. There are two little parlours and four bedrooms. You shall sit alone whenever you like.'[6] The Dashwood sisters in the Regency do not expect this degree of privacy, but responses in Jane Austen's characters do divide between those whom it suits to romanticize Barton as a cottage, and those who see its real defects as a house. John Dashwood, who wants to do as little as possible to help his mother and sisters, declares that Barton Cottage is 'the most complete thing of its kind . . . that ever was'.[7] Mr Palmer, whose pocket is not in question, remarks that the parlour is very low-pitched and its ceiling crooked.[8] Willoughby, who has no intention of living in one, asserts that a cottage is 'the only form of building in which happiness is attainable';[9] Eleanor, who does, retorts that the stairs are dark and narrow while the kitchen smokes. The cottage does much to sort out character: it indicates, for example, the fickleness of Willoughby, and the substance of Mr Palmer, concealed inside his ungracious exterior.

The most obvious reason why Jane Austen satirized the middle-class vogue for cottages where Dickens sympathized with it lies in the different places where they spent most of their lives, and where their respective characters spend most of theirs – she in the country, he in the city, in accordance with the actual shift in population between her generation and his. For the Victorians, sobre reality exists in the dingy dirty city, where the aspiration of middle-class taste is in practice upwards, to interiors yet more respectable and more properly furnished. But a nostalgia, in which even the apostles of vulgarity share, envisages a very different setting for life: its imaginative yearning is outwards, to houses that are rural, rooted, and unpretentious. The middle-class ideal parts company with its working idea of an actual home; in consequence, the perfect pastoral is not undermined by its exposure to reality, as it was for Jane Austen.

But that is not sufficient by itself to explain why, in Dickens's time, the dream of a cottage should have proved so tenacious, although it rarely offered a form for actual life; while in contrast, before the reign of Queen Victoria (although, as we shall see, some romantic souls did delight in ideas of seclusion and simplicity), no one of gentle birth yearned to see more of a working farm than its exterior. It is equally relevant to note that, at that earlier time, middle-class life had more of its own stabilities and traditions: successive generations might inhabit the same house, hold the same living, enter the same profession, or go into the services; social mobility into the class was more limited. In the subsequent industrial and post-Romantic age, when fortunes earned in trade became more general, memories of a rural life, responsive to seasonal change, acquired the potency of a lost inheritance. The independent yeoman (a class that was rapidly diminishing), with his life on the land and his happy capacity to be at once farmer and gentleman, exercised an attraction that Jane Austen could not have imagined. Wuthering Heights is one such combination of manor house and working farm; Stone Court in *Middlemarch* is another, 'looking as if it had been arrested in its growth toward a stone mansion by an unexpected budding of farm-buildings on its left flank, which had hindered it from becoming anything more than the substantial dwelling of a gentleman farmer'.[10] To a class more mobile and more rapidly losing its traditions than the one above, and even the one below it, the rank of yeoman offered a satisfying, if theoretic, historical form. It had the additional advantage that it seemed to include in it all those features of other types of house that the middle classes admired but did not live in. The possession of land, especially through inheritance, linked the yeoman's cottage to the houses of the great; while its simplicity of life, its naturalness, connected it with the houses of the poor. Those authentically old, and even those that simulated age, seemed to establish the owner in a locality and a tradition.

But the most attractive aspect of the cottage was its solution to the problem of taste. Those who could not afford the expensive simplicity of Farnham Royal (Fig. 73), and developed in their city dwellings ill-assorted rooms like Mrs Gaskell's (Fig. 95), were exonerated from the labour of choice, for everyone (except the farmer) approved the traditional furniture of farm-kitchens, the 'amusing' warming-pans, crockery, and dresser. The idea of the cottage escaped the restrictions of urban respectability, and its simple interior, as in Ruskin's Welsh cottage with the hearth of mica slate, could be made to correspond much more readily to the novelists' criteria of taste. But even when realized in stone or oak, authentically old and not a new-built cottage *ornée*, the idyll remains a 'wonderful deception'. If built originally with the solidity to last, dwellings which the middle class continues to describe as 'cottages' were invariably intended for those with means in excess of a cotter's. Very few genuine cottages survive; those that are described as such are mostly farms. Yet the idea became the dream solution of many people, a majority of them much more sophisticated than Dickens's 'poor woman', Mrs Plornish. From the working class, through the various levels of the middle class, up to the aristocracy itself, the cottage idyll possessed, and still possesses, the imagination of many city-dwellers. It is not a workable solution to the lives that most people actually lead; it is a daydream of the lives they would like to lead.

In order to trace the genesis of the idyll, one must go right back to the close of the seventeenth century. Although Restoration drama was, on the whole, hard upon country life (those who come from the country are almost invariably bumpkins), there is nevertheless already a sense that that is where virtue and health reside, as well as boredom.[11] But, as the new century advances, an increasing number of gentlemen begin to build Palladian houses in the country in order to look after their estates; the debate between the merits of urban and rural existence intensifies in consequence. Matthew Bramble, for example, makes it perfectly clear where his allegiance lies by stating unequivocally the difference between his 'country comforts' and his 'town grievances':[12] no 'clear, elastic, salutary air' but 'steams of endless putrefaction'; no 'virgin lymph' but 'the mawkish contents of an open aqueduct, exposed to all manner of defilement' of which 'human excrement is the least offensive part'; no fresh bread, made from his own wheat and baked in his own oven, but 'a deleterious paste, mixed up with chalk, alum and bone-ashes'. City life, in other words, has come to be equated with pollution; country existence with the pure and wholesome.

Gentlefolk began in consequence to occupy themselves and banish boredom by dabbling in the more acceptable countryside activities. Pastoral pursuits, of the kind that Clarissa cultivates in her milkmaid's dress,[13] were thought to lend charm to a lady. As Papworth remarks on his design for a dairy house not unlike the one at Blaise, 'When the fashionable amusements of the town are relinquished for those of the country, there are few so interesting to the female mind as the dairy.'[14] He is not sure whether such enthusiasms are the result of poetry, or have 'a real existence' born of nature, but thinks on the whole that the two have been combined by taste, 'for there are few residences, whose possessors have been acknowledged to lead in the walks of polished fancy or pictorial beauty, where the dairy has not formed an agreable feature in the order of its rural offices'. Even Pamela, who might be supposed to have had enough of the real thing before her translation, appreciates a visit to a dairy house, regarding it as suitable to the lady she has become, although the most natural thing about it is Mr B's natural daughter.[15] We never visit the dairy house in *Clarissa*, which perhaps betrays its precarious existence as a mental image rather than a real alternative; but the reader is taken to the poultry yard at Harlowe Place, where Clarissa tends her grandfather's favourite fowls. John Plaw's description of a poultry house or aviary, 'intended to be erected on a lawn, in front of a neat cottage villa',[16] indicates just how distant these activities were from those in an actual hen-house in a farmyard. The building itself is designed to be a pretty focus from a drawing-room window; and the occupation proposed for its mistress, 'occasionally to feed [the birds] . . . by which they become very familiar and tame', seems hard on the fowls, although it shows the lady to advantage. It is the kind of thing that Jane Austen's Mary Crawford, who detests real farmyards, might well have done, for she appreciates the effect of naturalness, if not the fact.[17]

Such places are designed, however, to be an extension of the garden, rather than serving as an actual house. Initially, as seen in chapter 3,[18] the cottage, like the Gothic ruin, had been treated chiefly as a feature in the landscape. The Vicar of Wakefield learns to enjoy the life of a yeoman because he has to, not because he has chosen it; and, although he puts a brave face on the matter, his cheerful tone emphasizes in itself that his lot is a bad one:

My house consisted of but one story, and was covered with thatch, which gave it an air of great snugness; the walls on the inside were nicely white-washed, and my daughters undertook to adorn them with pictures of their own designing. Though the same room served us for parlour and kitchen, that only made it the warmer. Besides, as it was kept with the utmost neatness, the dishes, plates, and coppers, being well scoured, and all disposed in bright rows on the shelves, the eye was agreably relieved, and did not want rich furniture.[19]

Poised midway between poverty and plenty (with sufficient space for the respectability of three bedrooms), the vicar and his family do, however, enjoy, in their 'little republic' of twenty acres, all the peace of mind that is supposed to attend upon their way of life. The novelty of all that gleaming copper has not had time to wear off through impatience with the scouring, before they tumble down another rank in their descent through society. Occasionally Fielding's travellers encounter gentlemen who have deliberately adopted rural solitude; but these do not attempt to lead a yeoman's life, and the quality of their existence depends upon the state of mind that led them to seek seclusion in the first place. Because, in *Tom Jones*, the Man on the Hill is a misanthropist, his 'house or cottage, for it might be called either without much impropriety', is scarcely a centre of hospitality for benighted travellers.[20] The Mr Wilson whom Joseph Andrews encounters has a rather different history; his house, as a result, is so warmly welcoming, his version of rural existence so idyllic, that a dog has to be shot in order to provide the appropriate *memento mori* in Arcadia.[21]

As the Gothic slowly insinuated itself into the house, however, so the householder gradually inserted himself into the cottage, as the rule, rather than the exception. The picturesque taste undoubtedly had much to do with the vogue. Richard Knight was not alone in preferring the 'real scenes' and domestic images of the Dutch painters to the towering scenery of Salvator Rosa; and the cottage growth that seems a part of nature to the methodized nature of Capability Brown in the parks of the great.[2] Those like James Malton, who advocate the building of middle-class cottages, make the taste for the picturesque the ground of their argument. In his *Essay on British Cottage Architecture* (1798), he quotes from 'the production of a friend, replete with Cottage imagery':[23]

> At the door of my straw-cover'd cot
>   The rose and the jessamine blend;
> Each tree that o'ershadows the spot
>   Is dear to my heart as a friend!
> Its course, from the first noble donor,
>   From father to son can we trace;
> For ages the seat of fair honour,
>   Content, independence, and peace.
> The trav'ller, at fast falling night,
>   The smoke of its chimney surveys,

77 A 'refined' cottage

> And journeys with bosom more light,
>   Secure of refreshment and ease;
> For fortune permits to extend,
>   Though she gives no superfluous store,
> A jug, and a crust, to a friend,
>   A morsel to gladden the poor.

It is of course 'a most wonderful deception', for the cottage is not seen from within through the eyes of its occupant, but with those of a passer-by, educated in the picturesque and the pastoral poetry of the eighteenth century. The voice is imagining a situation, not describing the actual; it is too educated to have a place in the genealogy it describes, and would, at that date, be most unlikely to buy up an actual cottage for adaptation to a gentleman's life. Like the clients for whom Malton is writing, his friend would much more probably commission a cottage *ornée* of the type designed by Pocock (Fig. 77) for 'persons of refined manners and habits'.[24] It includes a conservatory and a verandah in which to walk at wet seasons. Far from looking like the one that Knight describes in *The Landscape*, its chimney choked with ivy, its roof covered with reeds and mosses (in Malton's view, 'the most happy description of some of the exterior furniture of a Cottage, that I remember ever to have met with in any of our poetical authors'),[25] the neat thatched roof is in meticulous order, and a rustic trellis is provided to restrain the 'mantling vine'. With two parlours and four bedrooms, it is, like Barton Cottage, clearly intended for a gentleman's lifestyle. One remembers that the double/single cottage (Fig. 6) allows two parlours and a separate kitchen to a middle-class couple, where a family of labourers is supposed to combine the activities of all three within one living-room.

At this period, the interior of the cottage *ornée* has little contact with the peasant life; it is 'natural' only in a very cultivated sense. One of the most delightful examples ('*tout à fait riant*', as one writer describes the type),[26] designed by Papworth for two ladies in the Lake District, includes a minute description of its proposed interior.[27] Its version of nature is one unknown to the Romantic poets, and its riot of plant life, real and simulated, is of a tropical luxuriance that would shame the fells around it. The interior walls are to be adorned with trellis-work, both real and simulated; in the drawing-room it is to be divided by painted pilasters with oriental flowers twining about them. Tints are to be dominantly autumnal, but the draperies are to be patterned with sage-green leaves and blue and white flowers. Upright flower-stands are to be placed in every corner; others hang from each step of the staircase where they may twine up the banisters and hang in festoons from the ceiling. Because the whole effect is to be totally 'natural', even the books in the book-room must forgo any touch of gilding on their spines, as this would introduce a note of artifice.

Yet artifice, outside as well as inside, is characteristic of the cottage *ornée*. In the first place, as in Papworth's description of that Lakeland interior, writers tend to discuss their designs as though they were painting a picture, not building or

78 Aiming upwards

furnishing a house. Even the more sober among them, like Edmund Bartell,[28] who eschews façades of trellis-work because they produce too dressed an appearance, and Gothic windows because they conflict with simplicity, place their emphasis on colours and textures that will harmonize with the countryside. Secondly, the type was artificial because no one assumed that gentlemen would welcome those aspects of rural simplicity that the painters featured: worn thatch, small windows, and cramped accommodation. They may disguise their generous dimensions, as in Figure 77, but their neatness and the studied quality of their design reveal them for what they really are: residences for those who do not labour, not those who do.

The appeal of the cottage *ornée* was partly based on the wide spectrum of social rank it could accommodate. At the one extreme, it might house an aristocrat playing the shepherd; at the other, as aspiring gentleman on less than a gentleman's income. Where most cottages assumed the appearance of the class below them, a few might counterfeit the architecture of the class above them, as in Figure 78 where the style of the building makes it perfectly clear that the owner is not the gardener who is rolling the lawn. While, at this lower end of the scale, no designer parts company with two parlours and three bedrooms, at the upper extreme a very grand house indeed could masquerade as 'humble'. The largest of them at this period, designed by Nash for George IV, was the Royal Lodge in Windsor Park (Fig. 79), known as the King's Cottage, which cost £200,000 to build, furnish, and equip. Princess Lieven managed to detect in it 'a habit of unspoiled magnificence, which left behind the

79 Aiming downwards

sentiment of *une charmante béatitude*'.[29] In Victoria's reign, the label 'cottage' was attached to Ascott (1874–6) with its thirty bedrooms,[30] and Disraeli describes in 1850 a 'morning fête' at Rosebank, Lady Londonderry's country cottage by the Thames, 'where to render the romantic simplicity complete Lady Londonderry, in a colossal conservatory, condescended to make tea from a suite of golden pots and kettles'.[31] In a ballad by Coleridge and Southey, the Devil detects the fault in cottages of this type:

> He saw a cottage with a double coach-house,
>   A cottage of gentility;
> And the Devil did grin, for his darling sin
>   Is pride that apes humility.[32]

Had the Devil encountered Papworth's cottage (Fig. 78), he might have remarked the contrary sin, of those whose architectural pride attempts to veil a humble income.

Jane Austen's eighteenth-century predecessors were divided in their novels between those who preferred country life and those who advocated the city. It is not surprising either that Matthew Bramble should praise the pastoral existence of a former landowner who enjoys 'the perfection of content' in 'a small convenient farmhouse, having a little garden which he cultivates with his own hands';[33] or that Sterne, for most of his life a country-dweller, should admire a little French farmhouse with twenty acres and a *potagerie*.[34] Conversely, it is predictable that Dr Johnson, an ardent city-man, should regard such idylls of happiness as a delusion. When Rasselas finds himself among true shepherds, Imlac remarks with prophetic scepticism that this 'is the life which has been often celebrated for its innocence and quiet'; on closer acquaintance, the Princess pronounces the shepherds to be envious savages.[35] When they find the hermit whom Rasselas hopes may have the secret of happiness, an educated man who has chosen the pastoral life deliberately, they discover that he cannot wait to leave it for the city; far from improving the character, he declares, 'The life of a solitary man will certainly be miserable, but not certainly devout.'[36] It was a danger of which some designers were aware: Dearn, for example, offers a genteel version of the back-to-back, so that future hermits may live with a companion, while deluding themselves that they enjoy a rural solitude since the other house will be invisible. In this way, he hopes to protect from disappointment those 'who picture to themselves a state of happiness in the country, to which their past habits, and indeed the very nature of things, are equally averse'.[37]

Once the vogue for the cottage *ornée* is introduced, novelists contemporary with Jane Austen seem to align themselves in a different way, for their attitude to it is no longer determined primarily by their preference for country as opposed to city; they are either romantic or realistic, those with sensibility or those with sense. Mrs Radcliffe, as one would expect, falls into the first group, for her novels are full of little pastoral idylls, although these, for the most part, are externally seen. Emily's visit to La Voisin's cottage is, for example, composed like a contemporary painting:[38]

against the background of the cottage itself 'on the edge of a little green' with 'cattle and a few sheep reposing under the trees', the old man sits on his bench beside the door, near a table laden with wine, fruit, and bread; his son-in-law is playing a pipe; his grandsons (fine and rosy to a boy) are eating their supper, lovingly tended by their mother. Fanny Burney, on the other hand, is so outraged by the spectacle of a cottage *ornée* that she launches into a rare descriptive paragraph in order to assail its pretentiousness,[39] which in this case culminates in the attic storey with a very small Venetian window, whose minute panes of glass and glazed tiles represent 'dogs and cats, mice and birds, rats and ferrets, as emblems of the conjugal state'. Despite his pleasure in humble houses, whether of the middle or working class, Scott is another realist when it comes to the fashion. Colonel Mannering, for example, censures Julia's romanticism along those lines: 'If she thinks of love and a farm, it is a *ferme ornée*, such as is only to be found in poetic description, or in the park of a gentleman of twelve thousand a year.'[40]

No one, however, assails the cottage taste with quite the vehemence and consistency of Jane Austen, from her earliest writing to her last. Even her *Juvenilia* include 'A Tale' where the hero is asked to accommodate his brother, four ladies, and their numerous servants in a genuine cottage comprising two rooms and a closet.[41] He solves the problem with two 'noble Tents', the construction of which is 'both simple and elegant – A couple of old blankets, each supported by four sticks' which give 'striking proof' of his 'taste for Architecture'. In her final novel, *Sanditon*, both the cottage and the villa *ornée* are pilloried: the first is 'run up' with as much expedition as Wilhelmus's tents; the second – because Mr Parker despises his ancestors for building in holes – is perched so perilously upon its hilltop that his wife complains that they are 'literally rocked' in bed on windy nights.[42]

But it is in *Sense and Sensibility* that she makes her most sustained assault on the cottage idyll. The very title of the novel suggests the demarcation between those who face the actualities, and those who disguise them in a picturesque form. Apart from Barton itself, which is the better for appearing to be the house it is and not a cottage, there are instances both of 'the pride that apes humility', and the humble income that assumes unwarranted pride. Robert Ferrars, who is fond of drawing up 'plans for magnificent cottages',[43] and who moreover advises everyone to build one although he settles finally in town himself,[44] is an example of the first. He informs Eleanor (who is of course accustomed to two parlours, each 16 feet square), that there can be no problem of space in cottages, as he has assured his friend, Lady Elliott, who feared she would not have room in hers to hold a dance: 'I immediately saw that there could be no difficulty in it.'[45] The solution is quite simple: the dining parlour will easily accommodate eighteen couples; the library can be used instead for refreshments and tea; while the supper can be set out in the saloon. 'If people do but know how to set about it,' he concludes, 'every comfort may be as well enjoyed in a cottage as in the most spacious dwelling.' Although, as we have seen, his description does not exaggerate the actual dimensions of some 'cottages', Eleanor only agrees with him because she does not feel he deserves the compliment of rational opposition. As an example of the alternative deception, Mrs Jennings is confident that her cousin Lucy, if she marries Edward on a bachelor's income, will still contrive to be quite 'snug' in a cottage like Barton 'or a little bigger – with two maids and two men'.[46]

Jane Austen's objection to middle-class cottages has nothing to do with their location; she spent most of her life in the countryside, and it is clear that that is where her preference lay too. Her congenial character Anne Elliot suffers a 'very determined' sense of 'disinclination' on her approach to Bath with her 'first dim view of the extensive buildings, smoking in rain'.[47] Even in fine weather Jane Austen shared this reaction: 'The sun was got behind everything,' she writes in a letter, 'and the appearance of the place from the top of Kingsdown was all vapour, shadow, smoke, and confusion.'[48] Only flawed characters, like Mary Crawford and Lady Susan, regard a country village as an 'insupportable spot'.[49] The basis of her objection to the cottage *ornée* lies elsewhere – in her abhorrence of dishonesty. In her view, houses – like people – should appear to be what they actually are; those who deceive draw trouble on themselves and on society. Marianne's sensibility is largely spared because she deludes only herself: she reads into Willoughby's admiration for Barton Cottage a willingness to marry for love and not for money. But characters who profess to yearn for life in a cottage are usually duplicitous, involving others, like Robert Ferrars, Lucy, and Willoughby himself. Isabella Thorpe in *Northanger Abbey* is another example of the type; she is also after money, and while she declares that 'A cottage in some retired village would be ecstasy',[50] she defines what she really means in her next sentence: 'There are some charming little villas about Richmond.' Only in *Mansfield Park* does William seem to be forgiven for envisaging future happiness in a cottage with Fanny;[51] but then, he is still too young to know any better. In the architectural dimension, the cottage *ornée* confuses social distinctions, as at Uppercross and Sanditon;[52] and where these are confused, it is difficult for people to know what is true, moral, or even proper. It is interesting that Jane Austen should never have assailed in the same way the pretentious houses of the moneyed classes, although some were certainly built in the years in which she wrote her novels (Fig. 17); Rosings itself, in *Pride and Prejudice*, is only made objectionable because Mr Collins insists on detailing the cost of the glazing and enumerating the articles of plate.[53] Such houses were at least what they appeared to be – the property of families with fortunes; the cottage *ornée*, whether built with a fortune or without one, was attempting to disguise those facts.

Possibly because social distinctions had in any case been confused by his time, the case in Dickens is almost the reverse of this: the cottage is more 'truthful' and more wholesome than many unequivocally middle-class homes. By that period, of course, the 'genuine' cottage had become more popular than the cottage *ornée* (a preference that Jane Austen would have found even less explicable), and while an old building in the city may be sinister, cottages in the country never are: they are refuges for innocence, like that of Oliver Twist or little Nell. Honeysuckle and jessamine cluster round their lattices, and eyes wearied by city-scapes look out on quiet perspectives of garden, meadow, and woodland. But genuineness is not confined to age; those 'wonderful deceptions', the new-built cottages of the middle classes, have for Dickens the same virtue of honesty, although that word itself is now used in a sense quite different from Jane Austen's: it implies truth to oneself, not one's society. There is one in *Little Dorrit*, belonging to the honest Mr Meagles, whose cottage at Twickenham is 'just what the residence of the Meagles family ought to be'.[54] Jane Austen would certainly have thought it absurd in Mr Meagles to pull down part of a respectable brick house, in order to adapt the remaining portion to form a cottage; but in Dickens's view he is merely suiting his accommodation to the assorted characters of his household, with 'a hale and elderly portion to represent Mr. and Mrs. Meagles, and a young picturesque, very pretty portion to represent Pet', their daughter. Even the later addition of a conservatory corresponds to a fourth character, their volatile servant, Tattycoram, her temperament being indicated by 'the uncertain hue of its deep-stained glass', and her dependence by its position, sheltering against the cottage wall. One is not surprised to find that indoors 'it was just large enough and no more; was as pretty within as it was without, and was perfectly well arranged and comfortable'. When you do not have the real thing, to counterfeit the perfect pastoral in the suburbs is, for Dickens, just as good. The generous Garlands in *The Old Curiosity Shop* have a similar cottage at Finchley, named 'Abel' after their son;[55] the soft-hearted Wemmick in *Great Expectations* exhibits his real good nature solely in his cottage *ornée*, the miniature castle at Walworth.[56] Only taste that is too good, like that of Mr Carker the manager, can destroy the truth-to-the-self of such counterfeit cottages.[57]

But even for Dickens the genuinely ancient building, probably a yeoman's rather than a cottager's, has a distinct edge over the cottage *ornée*; and the latter had had itself, from the beginning, connotations of age built in, as it were, with the thatch, the dormer windows, and the calculated irregularities. The importance of antiquity to the idyll must surely have arisen because it seemed to confer upon the middle classes that stability of status which only a family lineage can supply. It is significant that the poem 'replete with cottage imagery' by Malton's friend should feature the idea of lineage so prominently, though his *British Cottage Architecture* is intended for clients building new.[58] Genuine yeoman houses were suggestive to the Victorians of all the virtues formerly attributed to the middle class, for if they were uncertain of what their houses should be, this was partly because they no longer knew what values their class should itself exhibit. The locksmith's house in *Barnaby Rudge* (a historical novel, set in the late eighteenth century) is a prime example of the type, indifferent to the grandeurs above it, compassionate to the needy below it.[59] It is full of character, self-effacing, but (unlike Kerr's gentleman) completely confident in its 'own style': 'a modest building, not very straight, not large, not tall; not bold-faced, with great staring windows, but a shy blinking house, with a conical roof going up into a peak over its garret window of four small panes of glass, like a cocked-hat on the head of an elderly gentleman with one eye'. It has no need to refer itself to other houses, particularly to anything above it: 'It was not built of brick or lofty stone, but of wood and plaster; it was not planned with a dull and wearisome regard to regularity, for no one window matched the other, or seemed to have the slightest reference to anything besides itself.' The confidence that comes from standing squarely on one's own foundations, of answering to no one but oneself, is felt to be a proper middle-class ambition, unpretentious, honest, individual.

In the Victorian novel, the cottage itself is often conflated with the farm or yeoman's house, a fact which in itself has relevance. Mrs Gaskell's Lakeland farm at Skelwith is of the same type as her lodging at Stratford, which is undoubtedly not the 'cottage' that she calls it. A similar imprecision occurs today where quite substantial dwellings are described as 'cottages' when they are in the country, while much smaller ones may be called 'houses' simply because they have a town address. As I have said, probably very few of the houses described as 'cottages', both then and now, were ever anything less than yeoman houses; but it is nevertheless at the upper end of the scale that notions of lineage become most marked. For the Victorian and Edwardian middle classes, tradition and descent continued to be an essential aspect of the idyll. The Earnshaw family originally built Wuthering Heights in 1500; the Heatons of Ponden Hall had lived on that spot from the sixteenth century. Hope Farm had belonged to the Holmans for generations; its original had been in Mrs Gaskell's family since 1718. Even in connection with Howards End, a more recent and more modest building, Forster makes the point quite explicitly in relation to Mrs Wilcox who has inherited it, for she does not belong to the young people, and their motor, in the present, but to the house and the trees that overshadow it from the past.[60] She is not high born, but she cares about her ancestors, and thus deserves the name of 'aristocrat': 'One knew that she worshipped the past, and that the instinctive wisdom the past can alone bestow had descended upon her – that wisdom to which we give the clumsy name of aristocracy.'

To men who had newly achieved independent means and the rank that went with them, a cottage or farmhouse, relating to the land, conferred an air of stability upon an abrupt ascent. Trollope devotes a novel to that aspect of the taste, although he is less interested in houses than many of the novelists contemporary with him, and is moreover contemptuous of the cottage idyll: 'A flat Eden I can fancy it, hemmed in by broad dykes, in which cream and eggs are very plentiful, where an Adam and an Eve might drink the choicest tea out of the finest china, with toast buttered to perfection, from year's end to year's end; into which no money troubles would ever find their way, nor yet any naughty novels.'[61] If his novel *Orley Farm* is concerned with a lawsuit and 'money troubles', rather than with the house which is at their centre, that is precisely because the issue of social mobility occupies the foreground of his attention. The possession of Orley Farm confirms the uncertain status of Lucius Mason and his mother, whose own forebears 'were thoroughly respectable people in the hardware line'.[62] As he explains in his *Autobiography*, it was based on Julian's Hill, 'a farmhouse on the land', where Trollope's family (whose status was also somewhat uncertain) had lived for a number of years in his own childhood.[63] Its

80 Orley Farm

importance to him is indicated by the frontispiece to the first edition (Fig. 80), where the place, 'just as it was when we lived there, is to be seen . . . having had the good fortune to be delineated by no less a pencil than that of John Millais'. According to the novel, originally the house 'was not fitted for more than the requirements of an ordinary farmer', but was gradually extended and ornamented, as Millais's illustration suggests, 'till it was commodious, irregular, picturesque and straggling'.[64] The lowest portion is the original farmhouse, and the highest includes the addition of dining-room, drawing-room, and bedroom, on each of its three floors successively. Nature unifies its various stages since 'the face of the house from one end to the other was covered with vines and passion-flowers, for the aspect was due south; and as the whole of the later addition was faced by a verandah, which also, as regarded the ground floor, ran along the middle building, the place in summer was pretty enough'.[65] Like its mistress, the house has risen from humble origins but has not quite parted with its original identity. The building itself traces the history of the family's ascent in society; it is a record of the changing fortunes of Lady Mason and her late husband. *Orley Farm* is less often read today than the Barchester or Palliser novels, but according to Trollope's own reckoning, its sales at the time when he wrote his *Autobiography* were only exceeded by those of *Can You Forgive Her?*[66]

Like the locksmith's in *Barnaby Rudge*, the exteriors of such houses cock a snook, as it were, at the houses of the great. Their interiors, those at least that they were traditionally supposed to have, look with a kindly eye on the artefacts of those who labour below them. As I have mentioned,[67] there is a definite connection in George Eliot's novels between her admiration for paintings of Dutch interiors, and her description of traditional farmhouse kitchens, where beauty, animate and inanimate, is seen to reside in evidence of wear. Ruskin was certainly one of those whom she accuses of imposing aesthetic rules which refuse to such subjects the title 'art', for he despised the Dutch painters as 'men of facts', and their paintings as the mere depiction of objects.[68] George Eliot, on the other hand, valued them precisely because of this fidelity to the actual:

> All honour and reverence to the divine beauty of form! Let us cultivate it to the utmost in men, women, and children – in our gardens and in our houses. But let us love that other beauty too, which lies in no secret of proportion, but in the secret of deep human sympathy.[69]

One of the subjects that she mentions in the second category – 'those heavy clowns taking holiday in a dingy pot-house, those rounded backs and stupid weather-beaten faces that have bent over the spade and done the rough work of the world' – recalls paintings like Bruegel's *Wedding Banquet* (Fig. 81), with its faithful representation of quite ordinary objects, pottery crocks, wooden boards, and brooms. Jane Austen's sensible Edward does not like the kind of art fostered by the picturesque, of watch-towers and groups of banditti;[70] George Eliot does not *dislike* the madonnas and angels of which Ruskin approves, but her preference, though unstated, clearly goes

81 'The faithful representation of commonplace things'

to those Dutch depictions of the everyday. She has at least in common with Jane Austen a habit of connecting the actual with the true.

Perhaps for this reason, she does not suggest, as many others did, that the middle classes should cultivate the style of the cottage and farm in their homes and gardens. Where Godwin is cheered at the mid-century by the evidence that middle-class taste is percolating downwards, Lethaby, writing in that century's final year on carpenter's furniture, wishes that that influence would take the opposite direction.[71] Like George Eliot, he perceives a continuity between the traditional work of country craftsmen and a certain type of art, alluding specifically (as others included in the Arts and Crafts Movement did) to Dürer's depiction of St Jerome in his study (Fig. 82): 'Compare the dignity of serene and satisfying order with the most beautifully furnished room you know: how vulgar our *good taste* appears and how foreign to the end of culture – Peace.' The peace of St Jerome's study – like that of Mrs Poyser's kitchen, the houseplace at Hope Farm, or Ruskin's cottage – is created, as it were, from the same materials. Nothing pretends to be what it is not; wood and stone are not painted, papered, or carpeted. Everything is for use, nothing for show, but each everyday object becomes an ornament: the slippers beneath the bench, the scissors in the rack, the hour-glass, the hat, the candlesticks. Where, into Jane Austen's time, architecture had dominated furnishing, while beyond it furnishings had dominated architecture, this room strikes a perfect balance between the two for neither dominates the other. It was a balance that the Arts and Crafts Movement strove for – and indeed sometimes achieved in their own interiors.

In his earliest novel, *The White Peacock* (1911), Lawrence contrasts a traditional farm kitchen not unlike this with one of the 'improved' variety. The second, though clean, sparkling, and warm with bright red chintzes, is spoilt 'by green and yellow antimaccassars, and by a profusion of paper and woollen flowers', both evidence of its attempt to rise in the world.[72] In contrast, the traditional kitchen, 'that looked so quiet and crude', is 'a home evolved through generations to fit the large bodies of the men who dwelled in it, and the placid fancy of the women'.[73] It also resembles the houseplace at Hope Farm in *Cousin Phillis*, but where Mrs Gaskell recognizes that the traditional life such rooms express is passing, Lawrence is less of a realist (unless the title of the chapter, 'A prospect among the marshes of Lethe', indicates a doubt), for he allows his heroine to find in that kitchen her real home and her escape from the present:

> It is rare now to feel a kinship between a room and the one who inhabits it, a close bond of blood relation. Emily had at last found her place, and had escaped from the torture of strange, complex modern life.[74]

The difference is partly that Phillis has never tried modern life, and Emily has; but it is also one of period. In 1865 the forward current was still strong; in 1911 it had begun to eddy.

Cottages designed for the late Victorians and Edwardians, by architects like Voysey and Ernest Gimson, were both literally and figuratively more weighty than

82 St Jerome's study

83 Rooksnest: Howards End

the playful cottages of the Regency. Like Lutyens's grander houses, they aimed at assimilation to the countryside by the use of traditional local materials; but their owners were not, like his, drawn from that part of the middle class that was aiming upwards. According to Girouard,[75] they 'came to the country to walk through it rather than hunt and shoot through it, and wanted to get to know country characters rather than country society'. But despite their traditional architecture, uncomfortable furniture, and even an occasional houseplace included in the plan, they were often consciously progressive. Like Kingsley's hero, Lancelot, who lives at an earlier date in a cottage *ornée*,[76] they felt that society needed to be changed, and their politics were radical rather than conservative.

One could say much the same for the Schlegels, in their complex relationship with Howards End; but although their attitude to country life is much of the kind that Girouard describes, they are drawn to the house chiefly by its modest antiquity. It was, above all, the quality of age that became the main attraction of the farm or cottage to the middle classes, a priority which still exists today. Howards End is based on Rooksnest (Fig, 83), Stevenage, where Forster spent the happiest parts of his own childhood: 'The house is my childhood and safety. Three attics preserve me,' he once wrote.[77] Both in fact and in fiction it had been a farmhouse: Mr Wilcox complains that such converted farms 'don't really do, spend what you will on them'.[78] Attempts to build an alpine rockery and a garage have both failed; 'And, inside the house, the beams – and the staircase through a door – picturesque enough, but not a place to live in.' The Schlegels, who had anticipated that Howards End, true to the Wilcox taste, 'would be all gables and wiggles, and their garden all gamboge-coloured paths',[79] are delighted by just those aspects of the house that Mr Wilcox dislikes. They are particularly responsive to those that link it with country life, in the agricultural, not the hunting and shooting, sense, of course: the native oaks and elms; the orchard trees, the adjacent meadow, and the smell of hay; the teeth embedded in the bark of the tree which testify to local superstition. The Schlegel furniture, expressive of Chelsea taste, is arranged by the clairvoyant Miss Avery around the house as though that was where it had always been meant to be.[80] Margaret, the spiritual descendant of Mrs Wilcox, comes into her own, and the novel ends with Helen's celebration of the hay-crop. Like Lawrence's Emily, both the Schlegels have found their place – and their Lethean refuge from modern life.

The rural idyll can never quite disengage from an element of role-play. Even when invested in a real building, it remains as much an escapist dream, a piece of stage-setting for the life one would like to lead, as the Dairy at Blaise or Mrs Plornish's 'Happy Cottage', painted on the wall of her front parlour. Emily may have flour on her brown arms, and Helen whisps of hay in her wind-blown hair, but neither belongs fully in the country life with which they have chosen to identify. When Jane Eyre, a penniless fugitive from Thornfield Hall, looks in through the window of the Riverses' kitchen, she sees the haven that such interiors were to become to the middle-class imagination: a sanded floor, clean scoured, a walnut dresser, pewter plates reflecting the fire, and an elderly woman, 'somewhat rough-looking, but scrupulously clean, like all about her'.[81] To these, however, she gives no more than cursory attention, for 'in them there was nothing extraordinary'. It is the two young women seated by the hearth, 'ladies in every point', who attract her attention. The old servant, Hannah, is in her proper place; but the two ladies, Diana and Mary Rivers, do not belong in that kitchen. For the period with which this book is concerned, they never did. Rooksnest had a hall which Forster described as 'the pride of the house'.[82] It had once been the central room or great farm kitchen, with an open fireplace and a great chimney; but that had already been filled in with 'a wretched little grate' before Forster's mother took the house. In the novel, Miss Avery furnishes this room with the contents of the Schlegel library, and adapts it to the patterns of middle-class life. There is, in other words, no going back.

It is revealing, in this connection, to consider the kinds of house that the novelists who have had most to say in these chapters elected to live in when they had the money to choose. Those who were not inspired by the cottage idyll – Richardson, Disraeli, and Henry James – seem to have acquired just what they wanted. Richardson typified middle-class success in his period, with the house he had built in White Lyon Square and a villa at Fulham. Disraeli aimed higher. 'What does Ben know of Dukes?' his father is said to have asked when *The Young Duke* was published;

84 Hughenden Manor: Disraeli

but his son was determined to know them and had set his sights on the great country house that would match with his future acquaintance. Hughenden Manor (Fig. 84), originally a late eighteenth-century house with 750 acres, acquired by him in 1848, was everything he wanted, especially when Lamb (responsible for Fig. 71b) improved it with Gothic ornament fourteen years later. Disraeli remained for the rest of his life devoted to the place, and spent as much time there as he could, enjoying the role of landed gentleman: 'When I come down to Hughenden I pass the first week in sauntering about my park and examining all my trees, and then I saunter in the library and survey the books,' he wrote.[83] Henry James never had the money to aim so high, but one feels that his house in Rye (Fig. 62) was, on a small scale, all that he had admired in greater houses such as Medley, Mertle, and Gardencourt.

The cottage enthusiasts are another matter. Hardy, who did so much to instruct the public eye in the beauty of vernacular architecture, who had been born and had spent the early part of his life in a cottage at Higher Bockhampton which is a perfect realization of the idyll (Fig. 85), could only bear to live in a new-built house, as I have mentioned.[84] Max Gate is no more than a typical middle-class dwelling of its period which would be more at home in Muswell Hill than in Dorset. George Eliot's choice was also bourgeois, contemporary, and disappointing, despite its country setting and 'Old English' style; spacious and respectable is the best one can say of

85 Hardy's birthplace

86 'The Heights': George Eliot

87 Gad's Hill Place: Dickens

88 'The Lawn': Mrs Gaskell

'The Heights' at Witley which enchanted her (Fig. 86).[85] Mrs Gaskell and Dickens both bought eighteenth-century houses, properly modernized of course, but still a surprising choice given their mutual contempt for the 'banal architecture of that period',[86] although Dickens made his as irregular as possible: 'My little place is a grave red-brick house, which I have added to and stuck bits upon in all manner of ways, so that it is as pleasantly irregular, and as violently opposed to all architectural ideas, as the most hopeful man could possibly desire.'[87] Perhaps, as others have discovered, a style to look at and a space to live in struck them both as distinct requirements. Dickens's Gad's Hill (Fig. 87), as Angus Wilson remarks, 'was never, and is not today, more than a pleasant if somewhat inconveniently situated gentleman's house';[88] none the less, as Dickens explains in a letter of 1857, it was the fulfilment of a childhood dream:[89]

> Down at Gad's Hill, near Rochester, in Kent – Shakespeare's Gad's Hill where Falstaff engaged in the robbery – is a quaint little country house of Queen Ann's time. I happened to be walking past, a year or a half or so ago with my sub-editor of *Household Words*, when I said to him: 'You see that house? It has always a curious interest for me, because when I was a small boy down in these parts I

89 Chawton 'Cottage': Jane Austen

thought it the most beautiful house . . . ever seen. And my poor father used to bring me to look at it, and used to say that if ever I grew up to be a clever man perhaps I might own that house.'

The effect of this chance conversation was to give Dickens the opportunity of buying it. A sadder story attaches to the purchase of Mrs Gaskell's dreamed-of house, 'The Lawn', near Alton (Fig. 88). It was to be a surprise to her husband on his retirement, when its purchase on credit (of which he would not have approved) would have been completed. But in the event she died there, before that date was reached, while celebrating its acquisition at family tea around the drawing-room fire.[90] With its garden, shrubbery, French windows, and plentiful rooms, it is, like Gad's Hill, a house that many, now as well as then, would regard as pleasant but unexceptional. No one of these houses has more in common with the idyll than a rural position; all are unmistakably middle-class, all could exist in the suburbs of a city, and all are within easy reach of London, in relation to the transport of their time.

It is a final irony that Jane Austen, who alone assailed the cottage taste from first to last, should be the only one of these writers to have settled finally in what the middle classes today describe as a cottage (Fig. 89). It was not her own choice, but belonged to her brother's secondary estate at Chawton; it offered many of those characteristics that are felt to be attractive in her novels. Chawton is her ideal village of two or three families, including the great house; moreover, the road from London to Winchester passed outside it, so there was plenty to look at. From the first, it seems to have met with her approval:

> Our Chawton home, how much we find
> Already in it, to our mind;
> And how convinced, that when complete
> It will all other Houses beat
> That ever have been made or mended,
> With rooms concise, or rooms distended.[91]

She does not, one notes, refer to it as a cottage. Jane Austen would have shared Cobbett's indignation at Cheltenham:

> There is '*Liverpool-Cottage, Canning-Cottage, Peel-Cottage*'; and, the good of it is, that the ridiculous beasts have put this word *cottage* upon scores of houses, and some very mean and shabby houses, standing along, and making part of an unbroken street![92]

William Morris once suggested that the houses we live in should suggest the lives we lead or want to lead.[93] The cottage is unfailingly attractive because it expresses the life that many would like to lead. On the other hand, the houses in which the middle class actually lived more nearly expressed the lives that they actually led. Of necessity, most of them were city-dwellers, leading the sort of social life that involved two parlours and limited contact with the kitchen. The Victorian and Edwardian terraced houses that sprang up in their thousands around English cities were well adapted to that way of life.[94] If they did not excite enthusiasm, either among novelists or designers, it was because the life they implied was, in itself, unsatisfying. Houses may be determined by the life we lead, but to some extent they also determine our lives. As in the case of Mrs Plornish, the perfect pastoral was an escape, in imagination at least, from that tyranny.

7

Immaterial walls
The psychology of living space

The discussion of living space has so far been confined to its conscious aspects; but houses also have a subconscious being, both in themselves and in the minds of their owners, of which novelists are much more keenly aware than architects or designers. In the twenty years that divide Dickens's first novel from Jane Austen's last one, the consciousness of living space not only changes its nature, a revolution described in the first chapter,[1] but its unconscious being alters too. Before the publication of *Persuasion* in 1818, houses are conceived as walls defining space, and their contents are infrequently described; beyond the publication of *Sketches by Boz* in 1837, objects positively jostle for attention, while the walls that contain them become almost invisible. In the earlier period, the psychology of living space is more intensely felt than in the later, as though that concentration upon things repressed the sense of a house as a psychic entity. But if its subconscious being, as a result, is less apparent in the later period, it is not lost; rather, it is diffused in discrete objects or their accumulation. It is the purpose of this chapter to elicit some of its implications in both periods.

The novels of Richardson make an obvious starting-point: not only is he the first writer of fiction to be really interested in living space; he also shows a greater responsiveness to its psychological dimension than any subsequent novelist. It is relevant here to return to the question, which has only been answered so far in general terms,[2] of why he specifically never pauses to describe it, particularly since his novels leave the contrary impression. If one asks the casual reader whether the detail of houses and their contents plays an important part in them, he will probably answer 'Yes'. Millais's response to *Sir Charles Grandison* as 'pure pre-Raphaelitism',[3] ot Leslie Stephen's as 'a sort of Dutch painting of extraordinary minuteness',[4] confirms that that is the impression his novels create. But, as we have seen, sustained description, particularly where it relates to interiors, is extremely rare in Richardson's writing, although a vivid sense of location – whether in rooms, on staircases, in passages, or as forming the containment of a house – is a central and recurrent sensation for his readers. The texture that Millais and Stephen describe is not created by objects, but by the minutiae of emotions and attitudes. The critic may rightly insist that he has none of 'the nineteenth century's love of detailed description of rooms' or of 'firmly realized setting',[5] but no writer could be more aware of the importance and significance of houses.

Why does he then persistently refuse to furnish them, especially since he himself considered that he was introducing a new and more realistic type of writing?[6] He could certainly have done so had he wished to, for occasional passages in his novels show that he can use most effectively the expressive relationship between human beings and the things with which they surround themselves. Aunt Nell's reception of a letter from Sir Charles anticipates the exclamatory rejoicings of Miss Bates in *Emma* on hearing from Jane Fairfax: 'Look you here niece; Look you here! – But I sha'n't shew you *all* he writes. – On go the spectacles – for she will not for the world part with the Letter out of her hands.'[7] Eventually she folds it up and tucks it in her letter-case, which, in the absence of other correspondence, contains 'bits and ends of ribbands, patterns, and-so-forth, of all manner of colours, faded and fresh; with intermingledoms of gold-beaters skin, plaisters for a cut finger, for a chopt lip, a kibe, perhaps for corns; which she dispenses occasionally very bountifully, and values herself, as we see at such times by a double chin made triple, for being not unuseful in her generation'. Compared with this, one of Richardson's rare descriptions of an interior, the 'elegantly furnished' drawing-room at Grandison Hall,[8] is a decorator's inventory: 'It is hung with a light green velvet, delicately ornamented; the chairs of the same; the frames of them gilt; as is the frame of a noble cabinet in it.' One might deduce from such a passage that he was simply uninterested in houses and furniture, rather like Trollope, who provides a chapter titled 'The Duke in his study' merely with a mantelpiece, and one named 'A family breakfast-table' with no more than a kidney:[9] 'Descriptions of scenes and places . . . [have] not been usual with me', he observes with truth in his *Autobiography*.[10] Richardson's own life, however, suggests the opposite. When in 1752 he built himself a house in White Lyon Court, distinct for the first time from his business premises, he became so absorbed in its progress that he scrutinized the workmen daily through a 'spy-window' in his original house.[11] Although he rarely travelled, he was reciprocally interested in the houses of his correspondents, requesting from Lady Bradshaigh a painting of her house in Lancashire, and from her sister, Lady Echlin, a sketch of her Irish retreat, Villarusa.[12]

The answer to these apparent contradictions may well lie in his own statement, 'I never wrote from what I saw by the bodily eye',[13] and his avowed purpose: to dispense with the pomp and parade of romance, the improbable and the marvellous, in order to 'promote the cause of religion and virtue' by his innovatory realism.[14] Verisimilitude, as it relates to what the eye perceives, was not his object in itself; because his truth was inward, he registered environments only as they played on the receptive sensibility. For example, both he and the impeccable Sir Charles take an almost excessive interest in 'improvements', but the material results of such an interest are of less significance than the spiritual implications of the word itself. Dr Bartlett, Sir Charles's agent in such matters, is 'in Heaven, while on Earth' when his patron's estates in both kingdoms are improving; Sir Charles communicates this news to Harriet as 'the friend of my Soul'. Material circumstance does not cease to be important, but it expresses itself as a moral, not a physical, presence. It is revealing that Richardson's rare descriptions of place should coincide either with exceptionally intense states of mind, or with unusually relaxed ones, for the larger (and the best) parts of his novels are written in states of suspension, before situations have resolved themselves into the alternatives of bliss and catastrophe. 'How apt one is to engage every thing in one's distress, when it is deep!' remarks the married Pamela, 'and one wonders too, that things animate and inanimate look with the same face, when we are greatly moved by any extraordinary and interesting event.'[15] In such states of uncertainty the mind revolves, not the objects as such, but their ambiguous psychological significance.

The fashion for formal description in Victorian fiction, perhaps because it owed so much to painting, does not add as much to the fictional description of living space as one might expect. When a room is conceived as a picture it is apt, as I have remarked,[16] to become a still life, a place to look at, not a space to live in. In the novels of Richardson and Jane Austen, on the other hand, the reader is made keenly aware of the presence of four walls by the disposition of people within a room. Interiors in their novels thus exist as human situations, not (as so often subsequently) merely as arrangements of furniture like the scene on a stage before the characters enter. Stage scenery may in fact have made some contribution to this distinction between psychological and physical realism. The Victorian stage, like the Victorian novel and the Victorian interior, was detailed and cluttered. Charlotte Brontë, in the person of Jane Eyre, makes the connection: 'A new chapter in a novel is something like a new scene in a play; and when I draw up the curtain this time, reader, you must fancy you see a room in the George Inn at Millcote, with such large figured papering on the walls as inn rooms have; such a carpet, such furniture, such ornaments on the mantel-piece, such prints; including a portrait of George the Third, and another of the Prince of Wales, and a representation of the death of Wolfe.'[17] In this comparison, the Restoration and eighteenth-century stage, like the rooms contemporary with it, was sparsely furnished, the definition offered by the walls dominating the furniture within them, as they continued to do into the Regency. The china closet in *The Country Wife*, that room within a room where the supposed eunuch, Horner, cuckolds his friends, becomes a space symbolic of sexual potency. 'I cannot make china for you all,' Horner retorts to Lady Fidget's announcement: 'We women of quality never think we have china enough.'[18] In a similar vein, referring to the advances of Mr B, Pamela exclaims: 'Hey, you know, *closet* for that, Mrs Jervis.'[19] Richardson's novels frequently allude to the stage – conversations may even be set down as dramatic dialogue – but perhaps he owes most of all to the playwright's stagecraft, for such dramatizations occur particularly where the manoeuvring between various rooms or parts of rooms is emphasized, as in Lovelace's invasion of Clarissa's lodging in Hampstead. As in the drama, one is almost always witnessing scenes within four walls, yet their texture, in itself, has little importance. But their presence – in a psychological sense – undoubtedly does. Do they enclose or exclude? Are they protective or constraining? Do they define a haven or a prison?

Richardson was not the first, and certainly not the last, to ask that question. In Defoe's *Journal of the Plague Year* (1722) the narrator continually refers to houses as prisons: 'here were so many prisons in the town as there were houses shut up',[20] But he sometimes also refers to them as havens: 'I rejoiced to see that such little sanctuaries were provided for so many families in a time of such desolation.'[21] Obviously enough, when a house is closed up by the authorities because its occupants are suffering from plague, it is a prison; when the family itself closes the house in order to keep the plague at bay, it is a sanctuary. But on a more metaphoric level that question continues to be rehearsed throughout the time-span covered by this book, if in different forms, corresponding to the architecture and domestic mores of a given period, and their relation to the world outside. In Jane Austen's novels, as in the social houses of the Regency, society does not, like the plague, have to be kept at bay as it does in Richardson's novels. Her rooms, like his, are sparsely furnished; but her emphasis is not, like his, so much on walls as on the movement between external and internal life. In the Victorian novel, as in the Victorian house, society is again regarded as an infection from which the home is a protection; but attention shifts from walls or space to furniture, precluding some types of significance but inviting others. In every period, the house has psychological significance.

Before examining the elements that constitute our living space – gardens, windows, furniture, and so on – it is useful to consider some of the ways in which the house, when conceived in terms of the psyche, may express relationships, professions, individual people, and social structures through its identity with the body itself, conceived in those various senses. Novelists, indeed, were not alone in regarding a house as a psychological rather than a physical entity: to some extent architects did so themselves, though their symbolism, like Jane Austen's, has a social cast. In Richardson's own time, the architect, Robert Morris, speaks of houses as 'little Commonwealths of Families'.[22] William Lethaby, writing at the close of the nineteenth century, sought to connect the symbolism of the house not merely with human society, but with the universe itself: 'the development of building practice and ideas of world structure acted and reacted on one another'.[23]

The novel is normally rather less ambitious, and, because it and the house are both domestic, it is more often directly expressive of that social institution, marriage, than of society as such, much less the cosmos. In Jane Austen's stories, for example, the phrase 'a comfortable home' is peculiarly insistent. We are told in the first sentence of *Emma* that she already has a comfortable home; it is a declaration of Jane Austen's theme, for why then marry? – a question that Emma later puts to Harriet. But her situation is atypical among Jane Austen's women. For most of them that phrase defines their ambition for the future, and is virtually synonymous with marriage. 'I ask only a comfortable home,' Charlotte Lucas pleads with Elizabeth in an effort to justify her engagement to the preposterous Mr Collins.[24] In the event, their communal possession of the parsonage at Hunsford does confer a mutual style and interest on that improbable pairing. For the ill-assorted majority, a comfortable home is a great improver of relationships: in *Sense and Sensibility* Mrs Palmer is a shade less silly when at Cleveland, and her husband much less sardonic than when abroad; Lady Bertram's indolent stupidity does not embarrass Sir Thomas when she disposes herself permanently on the sofa at Mansfield. The Victorian emphasis on 'things' as distinct from walls also comes into its own where marriage is concerned. With a total absence of Jane Austen's caution, Harriet Martineau in 1839 describes the significant relation of furniture and matrimony: 'On this table, and by this snug fireside, will the cheerful winter breakfast go forward, when each is about to enter on the gladsome business of the day; and that sofa will be drawn out, and those window-curtains will be closed, when the intellectual pleasures of the evening – the rewards of the laborious day – begin.'[25] Despite its fulsomeness, the passage captures well the sense in which the house presents both the self to society and society to the self, as a reflection of social priorities on the one hand, as an escape from them on the other: 'Here they will first feel what it is to have a home of their own – where they will first enjoy the privacy of it, the security, the freedom, the consequence in the eyes of others, the sacredness in their own.'

The way in which a house can make a marriage is finely caught in an Edwardian painting by John Lavery (Fig. 90). The vertical lines of pictures, curtains, fireplace, clock, mirror, and fireside seat correspond to those of the woman; the horizontal lines reflect the angle at which her husband sits. 'Things' give this rather formal relationship their backbone; but there is a horizontal emphasis in the woman too, in the line of her hat, and in the arm that extends towards her husband, though the hand declines to reach him. Thackeray describes one such marriage in *Lovel the Widower* (1861): 'We would have been semi-attached as it were. We would have locked up that room in either heart where the skeleton was, and said nothing about it, and pulled down the party wall and taken our mild tea in the garden.'[26] In his comment on Lavery's painting, Quentin Bell stresses 'the fine tonal "rightness" of it all';[27] tone in another sense sustains the relationship. As Trollope remarks in *Doctor Thorne*, some marriages are especially suited to winter, when the gleaming upholstery of the new furniture in the new house compensates for the absence of a closer bond.[28]

But if 'things' can sustain a relationship, they can also trap it, like a prison. Walter Sickert's painting, *Ennuie* (Fig. 91), relentlessly traces the oppressive 'oneness' of marriage, for, although they face in different directions, the couple appear as literally one flesh. The well-known face of ordinary things becomes insistent and bizarre; the patterns on wall and table-cloth reiterate. This sensation is sharply registered in Conrad's story, 'The Return', which is about a house and the failure of a marriage.[29] Before the marriage is threatened, the detail of the furnishing – glimmering stair-rods, red carpet, thick curtains – compose the haven of the home, affirmed against the bleak city outside. Once the husband knows that his wife is unfaithful to him,

90 'Things' sustain a marriage

similar elements have an altered aspect: the glow of the fire only throws into relief the bars of the grate, 'black and curved, like the charred ribs of a consumed sacrifice'; the light from a lamp under a wide shade of crimson silk has in 'the warm quality of its tint something delicate, refined and infernal'; the beat of the clock answers regularly to the husband's footsteps, 'as if time and himself, engaged in a measured contest, had been pacing together through the infernal delicacy of twilight towards a mysterious goal'.

In this story, as in many of its period, the surrounding city with its 'grim, impenetrable silence of miles of walls', perpetually threatens (like the plague) to swallow down the individual lives of city-dwellers. For the Victorians, society had been transformed quite out of recognition by the speed of the Industrial Revolution, in ways that seemed to have escaped human control. To the ills that followed upon it they had no agreed answer, except the personal values defined by family life. 'In a house we all feel of the proper proportions,' Wilde remarks. 'Everything is subordinated to us, fashioned for our use and our pleasure.'[30] But if the marital home is seen as a haven from the urban world, the house itself cannot outlast the marriage; once the second is threatened, the first begins to disintegrate, like a ship. It is no accident that the capacity in seamen to create a cabin ashore makes for stable relationships; it is one that particularly delights both Jane Austen and Dickens, although she is largely confident in society, and he, like most Victorians, is not. Admiral and Mrs Croft in *Persuasion* are shown to be capable of transforming any house, even the icy grandeurs of Kellynch Hall, into a home. The seagoing men in Dickens's novels, like Peggotty in *David Copperfield* and Mr Tartar in *The Mystery of Edwin Drood*, keep their homes on land 'like the inside of the most exquisite ship that ever sailed'.[31] Mr Tartar, particularly, seems to have discovered that the city itself is an ocean, upon which our permanent homes are always adrift, for the security and stability of foundations is not to be found among heaving waters; they belong with the disciplines and restraints that a man can impose on his own life, an art in which seamen are particularly skilled.

Nautical housekeeping also has a particular attraction because the man, his professional life, and his home are all so clearly expressive of each other – a truth more evident to Victorian novelists with their varied interiors, than to their predecessors, who assumed a consensus of taste. But this interrelation between people and houses, houses and people, is felt in many other aspects of life. Henry James is particularly apt to see people as buildings, especially in *The Golden Bowl*, which, as its title suggests, is centrally concerned with the symbolism of objects. Prince Amerigo's 'dark blue eyes . . . resembled nothing so much as the high windows of a Roman palace, of an historic front by one of the great old designers, thrown open on a feast-day to the golden air'.[32] His expression is said to light up the 'brave architecture' of his face. The Americans, Adam Verver and his daughter Maggie, enjoyed a relationship that 'resembled a good deal some pleasant public square, in the heart of an old city';[33] when the prince marries Maggie he intrudes into that square like 'a great Palladian church, say – something with a grand

91 'Things' become a trap

architectural front'.[34] Adam Verver's personal architecture has much more modest models: his face 'resembled a small decent room, clean-swept and unencumbered with furniture';[35] his eyes, although blue like the prince's, are 'ample and uncurtained windows' which stamp 'the place with their importance, as the house-agents say'.[36] The architecture of the two men is expressive, in its turn, of the contrasting societies that they represent, for Verver's unencumbered rooms and ample windows personify American simplicity, honesty, and cash, where the prince's Palladian presence, with its element of illusion and its distance from ordinary life, has the grandeur and archaism of European civilization.

In James's writing, people tend to be scaled up to buildings and furniture. It is, for example, a compliment to describe Mrs Lendon as 'a large occasional piece of furniture', for she is 'one of the solid conveniences that a comfortable house would have'.[37] In Dickens's writing, people are instead scaled down to things: the 'innocent piece of dinner furniture that went upon easy castors', known as a Twemlow in *Our Mutual Friend*, is slow to reveal itself as a man.[38] As was mentioned in chapter 4,[39] Dickens's houses are often more animate than their occupants, and sometimes even more vociferous, but this may have its serious aspect too. When Richard Carson likens his existence to 'living in an unfinished house, liable to have the roof put on or taken off',[40] it is an ominous reminder that Bleak House, too, stood open to the weather when its master, Tom Jarndyce, blew his brains out, and that many other houses have grown derelict because of the protracted Jarndyce case in Chancery.

It is not surprising that houses and interiors should come to express so much about their occupants in novels, when they are so often designed in life to do just that, particularly in the Victorian period. As Veblen reiterates in his *Theory of the Leisure Class* (1899), the possessions with which people surround themselves are intended primarily to make statements about their status and affluence. This truth was certainly not lost on the novelists, although they pursue it in more subtle ways. Madame Merle, in James's *Portrait of a Lady*, responds to Isabel's declaration that she doesn't care about her suitor's house by observing:

> That's very crude of you. . . . Every human being has his shell and you must take that shell into account. . . . I've a great respect for *things*! One's self – for other people – is one's expression of oneself; and one's house, one's furniture . . . – these things are all expressive.[41]

In the event, Isabel fatally misreads Gilbert Osmond's carefully designed milieu, attributing to that unscrupulous and avaricious man the subtlety of tone and the 'atmosphere of summer twilight' that she perceives in his 'things'.[42] But perhaps Madame Merle was not mistaken, for a more experienced reader of 'things' might have noticed that that picture was much too carefully composed.

Gilbert Osmond's interior is clearly intended to make a statement, albeit a false one, about the kind of man he is; but in the houses of those with less aesthetic sensibility, or in private rooms which are not designed for public view, interiors may make unconscious disclosures, which their occupants do not intend for the visitor's eye. Rickie, the hero of Forster's *The Longest Journey*, is 'extremely sensitive to the inside of a house, holding it an organism that expressed the thoughts, conscious and subconscious, of its inmates'.[43] He scarcely needs to interpret the Pembrokes' conscious house, with its works of art, its microscope and books, for it declares itself: 'I am not quite like other houses, yet I am perfectly comfortable.'[44] On the other hand, Rickie's own 'perishable home' in Cambridge is an expression of his subconscious: 'With his head on the fender and all his limbs relaxed, he felt almost as safe as he felt once when his mother killed a ghost in the passage by carrying him through it in her arms.'[45] Rather than her arms, the walls of his room, given his foetal position, are suggestive of his mother's womb.

Forster is of course writing after Freud had begun to publish; hence the acknowledged importance of the subconscious. But Freud was always ready to concede that he was merely formulating insights achieved long before in fictions: 'How hard it is for a psychoanalyst to discover anything new that has not been known before by some creative writer', he laments,[46] quoting later, in the same work, from *Tristram Shandy* where Sterne anticipates him in attributing significance to apparently random and unimportant actions: 'There are a thousand unnoticed openings . . . which let a penetrating eye at once into a man's soul.'[47] It is an interesting choice, for Sterne himself constantly relates the objects within four walls to mental states.

In his interpretation of dreams, Freud also owed much to a psychoanalytic predecessor, K. A. Scherner. In his book, *Das Leben des Traumes* (1861), Scherner argues that dream images are related to physical stimuli, and that the organs of the body are in dream consistently represented by the attributes of a house and its furnishings. While Freud acknowledges that 'the one typical – that is regular – representation of the human figure as a whole is a *house*', he accuses Scherner of wanting 'to give this symbol a transcendent importance it does not possess'.[48] However that may be, the form of the human body is a principle in much Palladian architecture, where the left side mirrors the right, but the front does not reflect the rear; where central features, like the door or nose, are single, but features to either side of them, like windows or eyes, are paired. According to Ackerman, Palladio himself 'compared the dwelling to the human body, the noble and beautiful parts of which the Lord ordained to be exposed, and the ignoble but essential parts to be hidden from sight'.[49] When Roger Pratt comments in 1650 on his design for Coleshill, 'Let the fairest room above be placed in the very midst of the house, as the bulk of a man is between his members',[50] he is recognizing this principle, although in his plan, as in others of Palladio, there is an exact correspondence between front and rear.

Freud suggests, moreover, that houses in dreams are male and female: that those with smooth walls correspond to men, those with ledges and balconies to women.[51] It may not be wholly fanciful to suggest that the four-square houses with their smooth façades, inspired by Palladio in the eighteenth century, correspond (with their horizontal emphasis, attached to the male in the paintings of Sickert and

Lavery) to a male-dominated domestic world. For the Victorians, a woman is the presiding genius who makes a home, and their predominant style is Gothic, with its irregular façade and vertical emphasis. Margaret Wilcox, in Forster's *Howards End*, is convinced that houses, in themselves, are either male or female;[52] it is not a matter of the sexual distribution of a household. If Queen Victoria were to give a dinner party for pre-Raphaelite painters and poets, the atmosphere would not, she affirms, be in the least artistic: 'Heavens, no! The very chairs on which they sat would have seen to that.' So with their own house, despite the presence of their brother – 'it must be feminine, and all we can do is to see that it isn't effeminate' – while the Wilcox house in Ducie Street, notwithstanding Mrs Wilcox, is 'irrevocably masculine, and all its inmates can do is to see that it isn't brutal'. Victorian writers on architecture are apt to complain that (male) Palladian style dominates the occupants; they recommend the (female) Gothic, because it supposedly accommodates itself to the needs of those within it.

The novelist's conviction that a house is a living organism, that it has a human face, and a human history of vicissitude and change, has already been discussed.[53] But it is worth recalling again Hardy's statement about Tess's childhood home: 'Part of her body and life it ever seemed to be.'[54] Returning to it at the time of her mother's illness, she notices that 'a stupefaction had come into [its] features'.[55] For Richardson, the house or room are virtually interchangeable with the body, and the same questions can apply to both: is one at ease in the flesh or in the house? is one imprisoned by them? In the motto he wrote for Lady Echlin's grotto at Villarusa – 'Tho' in this little Cell the Body seems confin'd/ Nor Earth, nor Seas, nor Skies, can bound th'outsoaring Mind' – the four walls, like the body itself, become a cell, from which the mind or spirit seek to free themselves.[56]

In examining the elements that constitute a house, it makes obvious sense to begin with the garden, for it bears much the same relation to the house that dress does to the body. Veblen would argue that dress, like the other possessions of the leisure class, testifies solely to status and affluence; but just as dress itself may convey many other meanings, the relation of the house to what surrounds it may be more complex. In *The Gentleman's House*, Robert Kerr distinguishes two types of garden: the classical which originated in Italy, and the picturesque or Gothic which is typically English.[57] The first he associates with grandeur and the Palladian houses of the eighteenth century, implying that they exhibit man's mastery of nature. The second he connects with charm, the Victorian taste for the Gothic, and a submission to the natural as master. As with houses, a sexual alignment readily suggests itself.

Kerr's distinction does not really hold for the great landscape gardeners of the eighteenth century, who were after all much less formal than the Italians; not does it quite apply to the successors of Capability Brown in the nineteenth, who were often less picturesque than he implies. But his categories can be usefully adapted to suggest the two relations a garden may have to a house. The grandeur and scale of the eighteenth century and Regency park mediates between the house and the world on

92 The extrovert house

to which it opens. It controls nature, in the sense that the house is made the focus of the landscape, and may even set its stamp upon it, as in Constable's painting of Malvern Hall in 1809 where the image of the house is reflected in the lake below it (Fig. 92). The second type of garden is an extension of the house; it does not look out to a larger world, but is introspective. It is often surrounded by high walls or hedges, and is as private as the house itself. For Ruskin, with his quintessentially Victorian ideal of womanhood, kept 'within her gates, as the centre of order, the balm of distress, and the mirror of beauty', this type of garden is the appropriate setting where she may 'play with the fringes of its guarded flowers, and lift their heads when they are drooping, with her happy smile upon her face . . . because there is a little wall around her place of peace'.[58] Atkinson Grimshaw's painting suggests the symbolism of gardens like this (Fig. 93). Its hedges are high, its garden door firmly closed; it relates to the house as the woman does to the lily beside her, and the circular path with the flowering bed inside it has a suggestively uterine shape. Gardens, blossoms, and flowers are, according to Freud, symbols of the female genitals:[59] while certain of his patients reserve 'an architectural symbolism for body and genitals', in other cases 'the circle of ideas centring round plant-life . . . may just as readily be chosen to conceal sexual images'.[60] This suggests why Victorian architecture liked to invite the garden into the house, by means of plate-glass windows, conservatories, and the cultivation of indoor plants. It did not extend 'home' through the mediation of the garden into the outside world as the eighteenth century had done.

Although he is writing in the mid-eighteenth century, and his gardens give no sign of being either picturesque or natural, Richardson's are evidently of the enclosed type like the more formal gardens in the early part of the century. They never encourage that grand sweep of the eye, afforded in *Tom Jones* by Mr Allworthy's, whose prospect is closed only by an arm of the sea, and a ridge of wild mountains, their peaks among the clouds.[61] Although most of Richardson's houses are grand country seats, which would encourage the reader to expect vistas like these, in keeping with his century's developing taste, his gardens are distinctly deficient in prospect. Like his houses, they create a sense of firm enclosure within high walls. Pamela (like one of Freud's patients)[62] has great difficulty in scaling those in Lincolnshire, and when she finally acquires a key and lets herself out, she populates the pasture beyond them with a 'horrid' bull with 'firey saucer eyes' and locks herself in again.[63] Although she discovers that the bull is merely a cow, she makes no further attempt at escape. The house and the garden may be her prison, but, like Harriet when captured by Harcourt in *Sir Charles Grandison*, her frantic attempts at escape are largely for effect, 'For whither could I go?' Richardson's gardens in fact propose the same question as his houses: are they havens, or are they prisons? The same question could be asked of the garden at Harlowe Place, for when Clarissa escapes through its door to Lovelace and immorality, she discovers that her new, extended prospect is 'pathless and lonesome', and looks back towards those garden walls which were once her prison like a banished Eve towards Eden.[64]

93 The introvert house

There is, however, nothing particularly natural about Richardson's gardens. Despite her rustic origin, Pamela purports to believe that sunflowers are scented, that beans will grow overnight, and that common weeds are garden flowers. Rather than plants, his gardens sprout a multitude of little buildings – alcoves, grottoes, and summer-houses – which serve the same purpose as his closets indoors. This is of course more in keeping with the period's taste: Robert Morris particularly recommends the 'unspeakable Raptures' that such retreats induce in those who are given to thought and contemplation.[65] Richardson's little buildings function even more frequently as sets for seduction. It is in the summer-house in Bedfordshire that Mr B first besieges Pamela 'with frightful eagerness',[66] a performance his nephew repeats after her marriage. Such places promote the type of rapture that Morris has in mind only when, as Mr B's firmly wedded wife, she creeps up the stairs 'of this once frightful place' in order to kneel down and offer thanks.[67] 'My prison is become my palace!' she declares, 'and no wonder everything wears another face!'[68] For the first time she notices that the garden, although more confined than that in Lincolnshire, does boast a pretty canal, a fountain, and a cascade. She even begins to make excursions outside it.

The atmosphere of Richardson's gardens is heavy with sexual implication; in Jane Austen's one takes in fresh air with as much vigour as she herself did: 'I enjoy [this exquisite weather] all over me, from top to toe, from right to left, Longitudinally, Perpendicularly, Diagonally', she writes in a letter to Cassandra.[69] Characters in her novels take frequent walks, both in their grounds and outside them. Seizing a bright spell is a preoccupation on uncertain days. The grounds of her houses, whether on the scale of Pemberley Park, which is ten miles round, or in the shrubberies of Hartfield and Mansfield Parsonage, adapt nature, by the introduction of gravelled paths, to the convenience and enjoyment of the walker. Although much more natural than Richardson's, in that they include a good deal of vegetable life, Jane Austen's gardens always mediate between the house and the world around it. Where his novels begin their life within an individual mind enclosed in a closet, a four-walled recess within a four-walled house in a walled garden, hers are conceived in a community, its associations, and its location. Her houses always have names, where his commonly do not; moreover, where his normally have no exterior context, hers are often approached from the outside, through the grounds that surround them. Pemberley, although in itself not ostentatious, is certainly the centre of the scene: 'a large, handsome, stone building, standing well on rising ground, and backed by a ridge of high woody hills'.[70] That corresponsive sense of building and context, that a house should look out upon its setting while its setting should emphasize the house at its centre, is essential to all her buildings beyond the Restoration. The individual is part of a family, the family of a wider community; family and community in their turn form the frame for individual development.

The doors of a house, especially those that connect with the world outside, have a particular significance for the earlier novelists. Getting in and out of them in Jane Austen's houses normally presents no problem; apart from the gate between the garden at Sotherton and the park beyond it,[71] they do not seem to be encumbered with locks and keys. They are simply 'Inlets of Men', as Wotton put it,[72] permitting an easy commerce with the outside world: 'the young people, meeting with an outward door, temptingly open on a flight of steps which led immediately to turf and shrubs, and all the sweets of the pleasure-ground, as by one impulse, one wish for air and liberty, all walked out'.[73] Richardson, like Freud, saw considerably more in doors than that. Especially in *Clarissa*, they are constantly being locked and unlocked, while keys and keyholes have a marked significance. 'Windows, and doors in and out of rooms, take over the meaning of orifices in the body,' Freud wrote, extending the symbolism of the room, 'and the question of the room being *open* or *locked* fits in with this symbolism, and the *key* that opens it is a decidedly male symbol.'[74] There is something of that in the incident at Sotherton, where the movement from the garden into the park, necessitating a key, invites the dangers that Clarissa encounters when she escapes from the protective garden walls of Harlowe Place. Richardson, however, is much more insistent and explicit.

Where Clarissa retains her keys, she feels secure; where she surrenders them, she is imperilled. When Lovelace offers to approach her in the Ivy House in the gardens of Harlowe Place, she is made falsely confident by the knowledge that, if he can unlock the door from outside, she must unbolt it from within. Even when she finds herself outside that fatal door, she is deluded by the sight of the key into thinking that she can readmit herself again at will. In an attempted escape from her lodgings at Mrs Sinclair's, she seems to have taken a lesson from Lovelace, for he hears her '*unbolt, unlock, unbar* the door; then, as it proved afterwards, put the key into the lock on the outside, lock the door and put it in her pocket'.[75] But in the interim, Clarissa's lost virginity is nowhere more poignantly registered than in her confused cry: 'O Lovelace! if you could be sorry for yourself, I would be sorry too – but when all my doors are fast, and nothing but the keyhole open, and the key of late put into that, to be where you are, in a manner without opening any of them – O wretched, wretched Clarissa Harlowe!'[76] In one sense, Clarissa is referring to her imprisonment, to her inability to reach Lovelace when the doors are locked and even the keyhole blocked. In another, almost counter-sense, she is alluding to his penetration of her privacy, and, by a latent sexual implication, to her rape and her lost maidenhead. The two are, however, connected, for his enforced possession of her precludes, once and for all, her approach to him.

The Victorian novel contains plenty of doors, but they have much less significance than those in Richardson's novels, or even Jane Austen's. External doors tend to stand open in the countryside (where perpetual summer apparently reigns), especially if the owner is open-hearted; conversely, they are often closed in towns, where householders are more often tight-fisted and careful of their property. Within the house, partly because Victorian rooms usually had the one door which could be firmly shut,[77] they are mostly used as a definition of privacy. In Henry James's story, *The Other House* (1896), Mrs Beever's early Victorian mansion promotes her rigid morality by enclosing private conversations.[78] Conversely, the new house with its habitable hall 'full of "corners" and communications', not to mention a superfluity of doors, tends to break down the barriers of morality with those of privacy.[79]

Windows, however, are another matter, for their significance increases from the Regency onwards. Richardson takes significantly less interest in them than in doors, locks, and keyholes – as does Freud – no doubt because they are commonly regarded as the eyes of a house, and do not have the same obvious sexual symbolism. Not only creative writers like James, but writers on architecture like Henry Wotton, equate the window with the eye: 'We must take heed to make a House (though but for civil Use) all Eyes, like *Argus*';[80] their primary purpose, in his view, is the admission of light, but too many of them will make a house cold in winter, too hot in summer. In Richardson's novels windows serve a number of purposes, but rarely those they primarily exist for – to admit light and entice the eye outwards. His characters tend to treat windows as though they are closets whose walls are opaque; they retire into them chiefly to read private letters, or conceal emotion. When they do look out, it is not to enjoy the prospect, but in search of those outside, as Harriet spies out the approach of Sir Charles, or Pamela, besieged by Lady Davers, throws up the sash to appeal to Mrs Jewkes. At this point Pamela escapes through the window, as Clarissa tries to do in Mrs Sinclair's London house. Clarissa's two attempts upon those windows are the more dramatic because they are not, in the eighteenth century, supposed to serve as doors, and have iron railings before them as she discovers. Her isolation from the outside world, though surrounded by the teeming pavements of London, is dramatically emphasized by an uncharacteristic loss of decorum when she appeals in vain to passers-by: 'For the love of God, good honest man! For the love of God, mistress . . . a poor, poor creature, said she, ruined –.'[81]

But unless they are very startled, as in this instance, Richardson's houses normally keep their eyes closed. Windows had grown larger in the course of the eighteenth century, but this had not reflected an increasing interest in the view so much as the increasing window-tax, which was based on number, not on size. Jane Austen's, in contrast, almost always keep theirs open, possibly because, whatever the location of their fictional houses, he wrote his novels in town, she hers in the country. Her characters, like his, may retreat into windows and for similar reasons, but this is not encouraged as a habit. Emma is relieved when the unsociable Mr John Knightley 'seemed early to devote himself to the business of being agreeable', instead of 'drawing his brother off to a window';[82] and though Fanny does well to hide her feelings at Mansfield by turning 'farther into the window', she does better in composing them with the aid of 'the scene without, where all that was solemn and soothing, and lovely, appeared in the brilliancy of an unclouded night'.[83] One is always aware in Jane Austen's novels that her houses look *out* of their windows, and that prospect is a priority among her characters. George Emerson remarks, in Forster's *Room with a View*, that all 'men fall into two classes – those who forget views and those who remember them, even in small rooms'.[84] Jane Austen's men and women definitely belong in the second category. On entering Pemberley, Elizabeth turns quickly away from her 'slight survey' of the dining-parlour to enjoy the view from its windows, which is much more carefully detailed by Jane Austen than the furniture; moreover, as they pass into other rooms, 'from every window there were beauties to be seen'.[85] Conversely, one is instantly made aware on entering Elizabethan Sotherton that 'the situation of the house excluded the possibility of much prospect from any of the rooms'.[86] Responsiveness within a house to climatic and seasonal change is keenly felt. Outlook may emphasize melancholy and solitude: 'A cold stormy rain set in, and nothing of July appeared but in the trees and shrubs, which the wind was despoiling, and the length of the day, which only made such cruel sights the longer visible.'[87] But spirits can recover with the climate: on the following afternoon the weather clears and Emma instantly goes out 'with all the eagerness which such a transition gives'.[88] Views from inside are all important in the novels; they can redeem a house as confined internally as Barton Cottage, or their absence detract from one as spacious as Sotherton.

The social nature of Jane Austen's houses is also emphasized by the fact that her characters more often resort to windows to watch the world go by (or, better still, come to call), than to admire the beauties of nature. When Catherine's post-chaise returns her unexpectedly from Northanger Abbey to Fullerton, 'the whole family were immediately at the window; and to have it stop at the sweep-gate was a pleasure to brighten every eye and occupy every fancy'.[89] We are told in *Emma* that Highbury Parsonage is too hard upon the road for elegance, but so too was the Austens' house at Chawton, and she evidently enjoyed it. With the end of the Winchester term she remarks in a letter to her nephew: 'We saw a countless number of Postchaises full of Boys pass by yesterday morn^g – full of future Heroes, Legislators, Fools, and Villains.'[90] Village or town houses enjoy freedoms here that her great country houses do not share; there is little watching of this kind from Mansfield Park.

Windows, which became so much larger with the arrival of plate glass and more numerous with the departure of the window-tax at the mid-century, have much more significance than doors for the Victorians, although not quite of the kind that they had for Jane Austen. As I have already mentioned,[91] her attitude to the enlargement of windows, especially where they became doors, was ambivalent. She enjoyed looking out, or going out of them, but disliked the sense that others might look in or even come in by them, since that would signify a social life that had become rather too relaxed and informal for comfort. Surprisingly – in view of their much greater emphasis on privacy – the Victorians seem to shed these inhibitions, possibly as a result of urban living where the spectacle of one's neighbours was unavoidable. Characters are not only seen at fictional windows, but may gaze without embarrassment from the outside in. The natural and human shows outside are often enjoyed by them as they are by Jane Austen's characters, but they acquire a further significance for the story-teller's art. Glass itself, a barrier both impenetrable and invisible, becomes an emblem for the tantalizing relationship between the quasi-autonomous story and the watching eye.

The scene in *Wuthering Heights* where Catherine and Heathcliff look in through the windows of Thrushcross Grange is one of the earliest manifestations of this insight. The world they see within is 'heaven', to which they feel they have a greater right than the quarrelsome Edgar and Isabella. But when Catherine is taken inside, Heathcliff instantly recognizes that she has entered the wrong story: 'if Catherine had wished to return, I intended shattering their great glass panes to a million of fragments, unless they let her out'.[92] But Catherine is, for the time, perfectly happy; it is only later that she realizes that Thrushcross Grange is her prison, and that her paradise lies in the moorland world outside. There is a great deal of broken glass in *Wuthering Heights*, as though the author herself wished to break down the barriers between her interlinking stories, and perhaps her own relation to the world she creates. In the case of little Hans, Freud interprets the smashing of windows as a substitute for prohibited relationships.[93]

To stand outside a house and look in through its windows is to write a story of lives one does not know. Silas Wegg in *Our Mutual Friend* does exactly that, and is most put out when Mr Boffin buys the house and threatens his fiction. When he finally gets inside 'Our House', as he has come to call it, and finds it 'in all particulars as different from his mental plans of it . . . as it well could be', he still refuses to part with its imagined history and form: 'So tender were his lamentations, that the kindly Mr Boffin was quite sorry for him, and almost felt mistrustful that in buying the house he had done him an irreparable injury.'[94] Phiz's illustration of Mr Pickwick and Sam Weller, seen through a Gothic window (Fig. 94), suggestively expresses this relation of reader and writer to their fiction. It is moreover noticeable that frame and curtains are suggestive of a stage.

If one looks with care at that illustration, however, it becomes quite hard to tell which side of that window we are on. Stories can occur when one looks out as well as in. There is much simultaneous looking into and out of windows in *Dombey and Son*, where Florence gazes wistfully out at the life she would like to live, of the 'rosy children' in the house across the street, and they in turn look out of their windows – not at her, but at the varied life in the street below – for both may be stories.[95] Hardy's story, 'A Changed Man', is related by an invalid watcher at an oriel window with 'a raking view of the High Street'.[96] Events in Conrad's novel, *Chance* (1913), are continually observed or deduced from what is seen through windows. It was left to the Edwardians, possibly in response to the Queen Anne style, to reinstate the distinction between outside and inside, by abandoning plate glass and dividing windows into small leaded panes.

It is the fireside, however, even more than the window, which promotes story-telling in the Victorian novel. Florence Dombey spends much of her maiden life looking out of windows, but even more of it looking into fires, trying to detect the shape of her future in its shifting flames. For others in that novel, like the ruined Alice who no longer has a future to look forward to, the fire prompts confessions of the past.[97] This great Victorian institution is virtually the invention of that period, for when one returns to the novels of Richardson and Jane Austen, the absence of fires is almost chilling. Richardson scarcely ever mentions them; they do nothing to promote the letters written by his heroines, despite the fact that eighteenth-century

94 Mr Pickwick's window

closets, even very small ones, were provided with fireplaces (Fig. 96a). Jane Austen does allude to them occasionally, but for reasons quite different from those of Dickens. When Sir Thomas causes a fire to be lit in the old schoolroom, Fanny's retreat at Mansfield Park, he is extending to her his paternal care, and it preys upon her conscience – as it is meant to, for he wants her to marry Henry Crawford. Even then, Fanny muses over 'that too great indulgence and luxury of a fire upstairs',[98] rather than sitting, as Florence Dombey does, over the fire itself. Jane Austen herself wrote her novels in public rooms, partly because there were no fires upstairs at Chawton. When she is visiting her brother's more affluent house, Godmersham Park, she savours before breakfast the indulgence and luxury of an upstairs fire just as Fanny does: 'very snug, in my own room, lovely morn^g, excellent fire, fancy me'.[99] But sitting over fires, either individually or as a family group, seems to be another matter. If one turns back to Repton's two representations of the parlour (Figs 7a, 7b), it is clear that neither arrangement of the room centres around the hearth. The formal circle of empty chairs in the old parlour is not gathered around the fire, but to one side of it. In the Regency version, the old man has his nose in a book and his slippers in the hearth, but the rest of the family is distributed in little groups around the room, according to their different occupations. It is the privilege of age to sit by the fire: Jane Austen rejoices when she graduates to a chaperon, 'for I am put on the Sofa near the Fire & can drink as much wine as I like'.[100] For the young, it is another matter. Both in Richardson's novels, which value the benefits of solitude, and in Jane Austen's, which acknowledge social claims, a certain distance from the fireside is a necessary discipline.

In contrast, the hearth is at the very centre of Victorian story-telling, not least because the narrative voice often speaks explicitly from that position to its hearers or readers. Where Angus Wilson calls it 'that great Dickensian institution, the cheerful domestic fireside',[101] Leavis quotes from Santayana rather less kindly – 'In every English-speaking home, in the four quarters of the globe, parents and children would do well to read Dickens aloud of a winter's evening' – in order to convict the novels of an essential lack of 'sustained seriousness'.[102] 'Family entertainment', as the video merchants of today describe the classics, is certainly an aspect of the fireside, but it does not necessarily preclude the serious. *Wuthering Heights*, which Leavis admires, is related largely by Nelly Dean from the fireside at Thrushcross Grange; Henry James, a structural part of Leavis's Great Tradition, acknowledges its relation to story-telling: 'She knew more than she could have told you, by the upstairs fire, in a whole dark December afternoon.'[103] That relation of fire and tale, narrator and story, is finely caught by Ford Madox Ford, as the setting necessary for his 'saddest story', which accidentally acquired the title *The Good Soldier*: 'So I shall just imagine myself for a fortnight or so at one side of the fireplace of a country cottage, with a sympathetic soul opposite me.'[104] From time to time they will go out to admire a moon as bright as in Provence, and then return 'to the fireside, with just the touch of a sigh because we are not in that Provence where even the saddest stories are gay.' But then, they are not sitting by that cottage hearth either. When the reader discovers, in the final chapter, that he is beside the fire in the great hall at Branshaw with the mad girl interjecting 'Shuttelcocks', he perceives yet another story, neither gay nor sad, but positively macabre.

But the fireside is also more than a setting for story-telling in the novels of Dickens: the fire itself has a sacramental symbolism, connected with both marital fidelity and the steady flame of love, and even with 'the sacred fire from heaven'.[105] Lethaby identifies it with the umbilicus: 'In the rites of Greece and Rome it was the hearth that was specially identified with the omphalos and so in Latin we have "focus", and in French "foyer", at once hearth and centre.'[106] Neither Freud nor Scherner connect the fire as such with the heart, but there is no mistaking this significance in Victorian novels. The hearth is the life-giving centre of the domestic affections; those who are deficient in human feeling almost always have low fires or empty grates.

The significance of public rooms differs between these periods and writers in much the same way as the hearth. Given that all his novels are concerned with 'high life', Richardson's houses are remarkably unsociable, although they make much of the disposition of rooms common in large houses in his time. When in 1756 Sir Isaac Ware advocates a typical suite of saloon, ante-chamber, drawing-room, bedchamber, and dressing room,[107] the order he describes has an ascending, not descending, order of importance for the visitor. Only very welcome guests indeed can penetrate beyond public or semi-public rooms to the innermost sanctum of them all, the closet.[108] The state of Pamela's fortunes can thus be gauged by the rooms to which her harassed father is admitted when he visits her.[109] But Richardson's public rooms are rarely used like this to welcome in the world; on the contrary, they feature mostly as the arena in which his characters defend their right to privacy. Clarissa, forced from her closet into public rooms at Harlowe Place, spends her time repelling the unlovely Soames, 'sitting asquat' in his chair and pressing her hoop, or setting 'his splay feet in an approaching posture'.[110] When in lodgings, the dining-room becomes the battleground where she defends her virginity and Lovelace urges his right to penetrate her closet privacies. Even in acute distress, she seeks the protection of its public nature: 'She rushed by her own apartment into the dining-room: no terror can make her forget her punctilio.'[111] Sir Charles is also a master of that virtue, and does battle through a whole series of rooms – drawing-room, two parlours, and his study – before expelling, by non-violent means, the intrusive Mrs O'Hara and her husband: 'This house, in which, however, you are an intruder, Sir, is your protection.'[112]

Where Richardson's novels were, as we have seen,[113] both written in his closet and dramatized there in the minds of his heroines, Jane Austen wrote hers in public rooms of what went on around her. Her drawing-rooms are desolate only when they are empty; they are normally crowded not only with family but with visitors, when they become places of infinite dramatic potential, in the delicate and disciplined negotiation between private need on the one hand, and public duty on the other. Fanny may, for example, retreat with her headache to a distant sofa at Mansfield Park, but is quickly recalled from concealment to her place and her work at the table.[114] Sources of light, like the fire or the candles on the piano, serve to divide such rooms between their convivial centres and their cooler, ill-lit recesses. Where a relationship is suspected and approved, others may be 'too honourable to listen' to what passes between couples in the corners, like Mrs Jennings in *Sense and Sensibility*;[115] but where one is not suspected or is undesired, privacy can never be secure. For those beyond marriageable age, the drawing-room thus supplies all the bystander's privilege of spectacle; but for those whose destiny is undecided, it can be an arduous testing-ground. Whatever her wishes, a woman cannot initiate; if she moves her seat, she must have a reason for doing so: Eleanor, in the incident referred to, goes to the window 'to take more expeditiously the dimensions of a print'. If she does achieve privacy, she may not retain it if it gives rise to remark; and she may have difficulty in securing it at all, if duty keeps her at the piano or behind the teapot.

From her first to her last published novel, Jane Austen is at her best in describing scenes that are set in public rooms. In *Persuasion* they are particularly frequent, and their nuances are explored with painful amplitude. The ambiguity of Anne's situation exacerbates the discomforts of such occasions; she has not yet achieved the sofa by the fire, but, as an unmarried woman whose looks have faded, she is treated in most households as a convenience; constant demands and domestic noise prey on her nerves. Others may regard her as an onlooker, and she may try to cultivate that disposition, but her sensitivity to Captain Wentworth's presence is intensified, as well as shielded, by public indifference. His unspoken awareness of her and hers of him, her literal inability to draw closer (when they are divided on the sofa by the ample and tearful Mrs Musgrove), his unguarded impulses of renewed affection – when, for example, he removes a troublesome nephew – all trace the gradual second growth of their relationship without an explicit word on either side. The culminating scene of many, in the Musgroves' dining-room in their Bath hotel, is painful in its suspense. Anne catches the slightest sound from Wentworth's corner; after overhearing (as she intended) her conversation in the window, his abrupt exit desolates her; his return, on the pretext of finding his gloves, revives her; his covert delivery of a personal letter consumes her with impatience, but she cannot rush to her closet with it as one of Richardson's heroines would have done; she must trust to Mrs Musgrove's preoccupation in order to read it, and to Charles's fraternal negligence in order to reply to it. The draft for chapter 23,[116] where all is made explicit in a tête-à-tête devised by Admiral Croft in his empty drawing-room, is clearly inferior, for the disciplines and constraints of public rooms are a most effective means of intensifying emotion and increasing the moral stature of Jane Austen's heroines. That sensitivity to the needs of others, the ability to subordinate personal concerns to public demands, to remain outwardly composed while inwardly turbulent, to be frank without obtrusiveness, truthful without impertinence, patient enough to await opportunity, and sufficiently brave to seize it when it offers – all these compose the moral strength of an Anne Elliot, and eventually secure for her Wentworth's hand.

95 Mrs Gaskell's drawing-room in Manchester

Public rooms in Victorian novels rarely achieve this degree of social complexity, or even attempt it. The constraints of social life on any scale are associated with the mansions of the rich,[117] and are felt to be opposed to the values of the heart and the sense of 'home'. On the other hand, middle-class rooms, as we have seen,[118] become much more diverse and expressive of the values, individual and familial, of the occupants, as in Mrs Gaskell's contrast between reception-rooms for show, like Mrs Thornton's, and those that speak a quality of life, like the sitting-room in the Hales' Manchester lodgings. Mrs Gaskell's own drawing-room, at Plymouth Grove in Manchester (Fig. 95), is evidently of the second type. The fireplace features prominently, and is surrounded with personal mementoes; books, piano, flowers, writing materials speak for quiet, cultivated occupations; heavy curtains protect the family room from the obtrusive urban world outside. But the dominant mode of the time speaks for values much closer to Mrs Thornton's – if one can generalize. James's Merton Densher certainly thinks he can, as he takes stock of Mrs Lowder's early or mid-Victorian room (he is not sure which) with Edwardian, and moreover American, eyes:

> He had never dreamed of anything so fringed and scalloped, so buttoned and corded, drawn everywhere so tight and curled everywhere so thick. He had never dreamed of so much gilt and glass, so much satin and plush, so much rosewood and marble and malachite. But it was above all the solid forms, the wasted finish, the misguided cost, the general attestation of morality and money, a good conscience and a big balance.[119]

Where Richardson's public rooms are psychic entities, and Jane Austen's are spaces furnished with human figures, in Victorian rooms the furniture and upholstery take over.

Freud defines the significance of rooms in dreams quite unambiguously: they 'are usually women; if the ways in and out of them are represented, this interpretation is scarcely open to doubt'.[120] His observation has evident relevance to rooms that are primarily private, like Rickie's womb-like 'perishable home' in Cambridge, and rather less to public rooms like Mrs Lowder's, which are designed to make a statement to the outside world. For this reason, it is the sparsely furnished closets of Richardson, rather than the heavily furnished sitting-rooms of the Victorian novel, that explore the psychological significance of rooms most insistently. It is not always easy (even for Richardson) to decide what is and what is not a closet. In 1756 Isaac Ware seems to regard it as a walk-in cupboard – 'There are a multitude of things that must be always at hand, and never in sight; and these are what furnish closets'[121] – a definition which Jane Austen is beginning to accept in the Regency, when these personal retreats came to be regarded as vulgar.[122] Johnson gives a similar definition in his dictionary, but also describes it as 'a small room of privacy or retirement', as it had been in medieval and Elizabethan houses. Richardson's own use of the term is elastic, at one extreme describing a housekeeper's store-cupboard[123] or a walk-in wardrobe;[124] at the other, Mr B's library in Bedfordshire, with its outer door opening

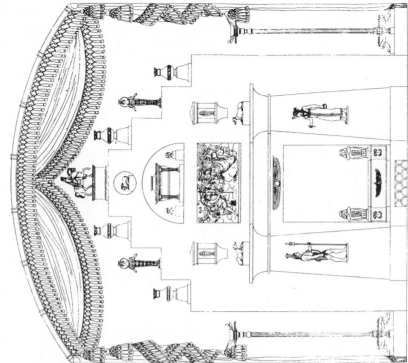

(b) Regency closet as curtained alcove

96 (a) Eighteenth-century closet at Strawberry Hill

into the garden.[125] Generally speaking, however, he uses the word of a room with a single door and a specific owner: Sir Charles has a closet like Walpole's or Hope's (Figs 96a, 96b) for his curiosities[126] (though Hope's in the Regency is more like a curtained alcove with a fireplace); Harriet as Lady Grandison has one, too, for her personal effects. The psychological significance of the room for Richardson is, however, clear enough: rooms are defined as closets when they are felt to enclose; they thus become the definition of a woman's right to privacy – that is, to her virginity – before marriage, and her liberty after it only to receive her husband as she wishes. Conversely, when the right to privacy is violated, the closet becomes a prison, not a sanctuary.

The closet is insistently featured in all Richardson's novels, but its significance differs in each. Because Pamela is initially a servant, her experience of closets is more various than that of Clarissa or Harriet, for the female sanctuary where the lady can resist ambush is a trap for her maid, whose master employs it as a base for those activities which, in Ware's terms, should be always at hand but never in sight. As Pamela's fortunes improve, the closet changes its status along with her own. As a maid in Bedfordshire she does not possess one, but writes her letters in her attic bedroom. As a potential mistress in Lincolnshire she acquires one, but without achieving the lady's right to privacy: Mrs Jewkes regards it as her duty to 'rummage' her there.[127] As a wife her claim to privacy is fully allowed: on her wedding night Mr B sends up a message 'desiring to know whether [he] may attend upon me in my *closet*; and hinting to me, that however, he did not expect to find me *there*'.[128] On her marriage, rooms which were prisons come to signify her freedom. When she is given her late lady's closet in the house in Bedfordshire for her own use, she employs herself there 'in thankfulness, prayer and meditation'.[129] Throughout this part of the novel, Pamela is constantly running into closets of every description, as into their equivalent in the garden, in order to throw herself on her knees and offer thanks.

Confinement and freedom are consecutive attitudes to the closet in *Pamela*; in *Clarissa* they are simultaneous truths. Unlike the maid, the lady is always confident of her right to the closet's privacy, which Clarissa affirms whenever it is threatened. On the other hand, that threat is never removed; no marriage ceremony lifts the siege, or removes her need to stand on the defensive. At Mrs Sinclair's, she immediately possesses herself of two closets, a dark and a light one, and checks their security.[130] But once Lovelace has penetrated both her closets, Clarissa's spiritual progress is charted by her acceptance of ever decreasing physical range, together with the gradual relinquishment of all personal claims. Her initial instinct was towards a wider freedom: her imprisonment at Harlowe Place precipitated her escape through the garden door into the perilous world beyond. Thereafter she discovers, as Lovelace does from a contrary direction, that physical and mental liberation have little connection. Her lodgings become increasingly confined, yet her final simple room above the glove-shop is the only one to afford her freedom of action and mind. Movement is no longer seen as a solution; she first accepts her restriction to the house, then to her 'closet-duties' above stairs; subsequently she confines herself to bed, and finally to the coffin, which she describes as her 'palace' and 'last home'. In a sense quite different from Pamela's, her 'palace', too, is the transformation of her 'prison-house'. Clarissa also learns to surrender her keys, and the contents of her closet are, by her will, deliberately offered to the public eye. Paralleled with her abnegation of her right both to privacy and to personal space is Lovelace's increasingly frantic movement: 'So I have them all prisoners, while I range about as I please,' he remarks.[131] But where Clarissa discovers liberation in her confinement, freeing the mind from the restrictive walls of her closet like the soul from the body, Lovelace finds only confinement in his freedom.

To the perceptions of *Clarissa*, *Sir Charles Grandison* offers both a postscript and a conclusion. The postscript emphasizes that the virtuous need have nothing to fear from the exposure of closet privacies. Sir Charles positively urges the sceptical to station themselves in closets, in order that they may overhear 'private' conversations. His invitations are most frequent in Italy, possibly on the principle of doing in Rome as Rome does. For this he earns his hostess's warm approval: 'O Chevalier! you are equally prudent and generous! Why won't you be one of us? Why won't you be a Catholic?'[132] One recalls Charlotte Brontë's contempt for such papistical practices in *Villette*, but Sir Charles is rightly confident that eavesdroppers will hear no ill of him.

The conclusion is more comprehensive than this postscript, for it generalizes the predicament of Richardson's three heroines to the position of women more generally considered. Lovelace, for example, makes a sustained analogy between Clarissa and a captured bird, forced to sing in her cage;[133] but Charlotte Grandison (Lady G), who enters her cage of her own accord, is equally sensitive to the parallel: 'My Lord, to be sure, has dominion over his bird. He can choose her cage. She has nothing to do, but sit and sing in it.'[134] Charlotte is riled because Lord G has chosen the 'cage', their London house, without consulting her: 'Does not he, by this step, make me his chattels, a piece of furniture only, to be removed as any other piece of furniture, or picture, or cabinet, at his pleasure?'[135] Even in her happiness, Harriet expresses very similar fears about marriage: 'Her name sunk, and lost! The property, person and will, of another, excellent as the man is.'[136] It is part of Sir Charles's excellence, however, that he is acutely sensitive to this vulnerability in the opposite sex. Where Lord G outrages Charlotte by 'invading' her 'retirement' in her closet (though the poor man only wants to express his 'odious rapture'), Sir Charles is careful never to offend in this way, as Harriet ardently records.[137] A mutual regard for each other's privacy is for Richardson the keystone to a successful marriage. Harriet may be appalled, on the eve of her wedding, by the sacrifice of identity that marriage entails, but she soon accommodates herself to her new condition as 'the declared mistress of this spacious house', and not least because the closet that Sir Charles has prepared for her allows a perpetuation of her independence.[138] An acceptance of her bounds is essential to female strength, but these bounds should first be made acceptable. Enclosure is sanctuary where it can exclude; where it cannot, it is imprisonment.

In Richardson's novels, a woman's retention of closet privacies is a mark of female strength; in Jane Austen's, it tends, on the contrary, to denote a moral weakness.

Men and women still possess their sanctums: Sir Thomas has his 'own dear room', Mr Bennet his library; Fanny establishes herself in the old schoolroom, Mrs Bennet in her dressing-room. But in the cases of Sir Thomas and Mr Bennet, their tendency to retreat from family life seems to account in part for the disasters that befall their daughters. Mr Bennet is himself outraged when, on Lydia's elopement, his wife confines herself to her dressing-room:

> 'This is a parade,' cried he, 'which does one good: it gives such an elegance to misfortune! Another day I will do the same; I will sit in my library, in my night cap and powdering gown, and give as much trouble as I can.'[139]

Catastrophe has drawn him from his sanctum; public appearances must be sustained, and a state of undress has its unethical aspect.

Fanny's beloved East Room might seem to be an exception. Jane Austen rarely follows her characters into privacy, but here she does; her rooms are rarely described in any detail, but this one is. To some extent the East Room, by atoning for them, indicates the deficiencies of Mansfield, where too much importance is attached to public form, too little to inward life. It is significant that, when Edmund and Mary want knowledge of their own hearts, they should come to the East Room in search of it. But Fanny's tendency to retire upstairs, as much at Portsmouth as at Mansfield, is also an indication of her weakness. She is an outsider in both houses, physically as incapable of tolerating the disorder of the one as she is mentally unable to sustain the formality of the other. She is not criticized as severely as Lady Susan, the heroine of Jane Austen's brief epistolary novel, who solicits private colloquies in dressing-rooms, and even invites them in her own with the opposite sex. Nevertheless, if the East Room indicates the failings of Mansfield, it also signifies those of Fanny herself. Where for Richardson the ordeals of morality are largely private, for Jane Austen virtue is only meaningful where it can survive a public test.

In Richardson's novels the reader, quite as much as the characters, has the run of the house, from attic to basement, from salon to closet, although he is never in any doubt as to which of these is public and which private. In Jane Austen's houses one is invited only into those rooms that a guest might enter. These may occasionally, in case of illness, include a dressing-room, but never a bedroom as such, or indeed a kitchen. Such rooms are as neatly effaced from her novels, though not from her letters, as the earliest lavatories, disguised as wardrobes, were from the rest of the house. In the Victorian novel the movement between rooms that are public and those that are private has much less significance. This is partly because they are not defined in that way, but instead according to their multitudinous functions. Because novelists are domestically more comprehensive and do not confine themselves to respectable households, certain social inhibitions are relaxed, and the reader is treated less as a guest than as one of the family, with a similar run of the house. Unless they contain death-beds, there are, however, certain inhibitions in the case of middle-class bedrooms which do not apply with Richardson. Trollope, for example, regards it as improper to take the reader into Mrs Grantley's bedroom, and

97 *The Awakening Conscience*

escorts him instead into the Doctor's dressing-room, to listen to their conversation through a half-open door.[140] In other respects, the Victorian novel is domestically quite as wide-ranging as Richardson's, more so indeed as one descends the social scale.

It should now be quite apparent that the symbolism of rooms for Richardson is invariably sexual, where for Jane Austen it is always social, reflecting the manners and mores of her time. It might also seem that the Victorian novel, by its concentration on physical objects rather than walls as a definition of space, tends to exclude both types of implication. Undoubtedly, the language of objects is of a different kind; but it can be equally expressive and relate in a different way to Richardson's own question, is the room a haven or a prison? In this context, it is in relation to furniture that the Victorian novel comes into its own.

On 25 May 1854 *The Times* published a letter from Ruskin in which he defended Holman Hunt's painting *The Awakening Conscience* (Fig. 97), by interpreting the language of that cluttered love-nest. Its symbolism, one might think, is scarcely cryptic: the cat, whose eyes replicate the lover's; its prey, the dying bird; the half-naked female leaning on the clock; the painting of the woman taken in adultery – all these, although recorded with the distinctness and precision of earlier paintings like that of Quinten Massys (Fig. 11), scarcely call for the same degree of interpretation. But Ruskin's comments on the furniture, which expand upon Hunt's own explanation of his painting, pursue less immediately obvious implications, suggested by the song the girl has been singing – 'Oft in the stilly night', with its fond memories of an earlier home:

> There is not a single object in all that room – common, modern, vulgar (in the vulgar sense, as it may be), but it becomes tragical, if rightly read. That furniture so carefully painted, even to the last vein of the rosewood – is there nothing to be learnt from that terrible lustre of it, from its fatal newness; nothing there that has the old thoughts of home upon it, or that is ever to become a part of home? Those embossed books, vain and useless – they also new – marked with no happy wearing of beloved leaves.[141]

This is the dilemma of Gwendolen Harleth, the source of her moral frailty in *Daniel Deronda*.[142] She has no childhood home, 'endeared to her by family memories', as the Meyricks do in the same novel; she has spent too much of her earlier life 'roving from one foreign watering-place or Parisian apartment to another, always feeling new antipathies to new suites of hired furniture'.[143]

The Awakening Conscience has, moreover, a further connection with the Victorian novel, for Pamela's generalized recognition that in distress the familiar assumes a different face is made specific by Hunt and by the writers of his time: in the words of Henry James, 'objects took on values not hitherto so fully shown';[144] in those of Ruskin, 'the most trivial objects force themselves upon the attention of a mind which has been fevered by violent and distressful excitement'. The love-nest has been a haven from a disapproving world; but while the lover still reclines easily (and horizontally) within it, the surrounding objects reveal a falsity that preys upon his mistress, who starts up (vertically) as though to escape the room. The altered face assumed in distress by the familiar is subtly traced by Mrs Gaskell in the rather different situation of Cousin Phillis. The quiet of the houseplace, the measured clock, 'perpetually clicking out the passage of the moments', speak for permanent content when we first enter it.[145] But when Holdsworth has deserted Phillis, these very same elements form an oppressive claustrophobia: 'The clock on the stairs – the minister's hard breathing – was it to go on for ever?'[146] In a related way, 'the complexion even of external things' seems 'to suffer transmutation' on Tess's wedding night, as she confesses her past to Angel Clare:[147]

> All material objects around announced their irresponsibility with iteration. And yet nothing had changed since the moments when he had been kissing her; or rather, nothing in the substance of things. But the essence of things had changed.

Perhaps because Victorian rooms were so often memorials to personality, this alteration in the essence of things, so that objects become obtrusive, discrete, and inimical, is often keenly sensed in emotional states, and especially when the personality that gave them a composite meaning has left or died. Dickens writes, of the departed Barnaby and his mother, that it was strange how vividly their decaying furniture 'presented those to whom it had belonged, and with whom it was once familiar'.[148] In *Bleak House* George Rouncewell comments on the empty rooms of Lady Dedlock: 'Rooms get an awful look about them when they are fitted up, like these, for one person you are used to see in them, and that person is away under any shadow.'[149]

Henry James once remarked that 'objects and places, coherently grouped, disposed for human use and addressed to it, must have a sense of their own, a mystic meaning proper to themselves, to give out'.[150] When death or disaster strikes a household, and its furnishings are dispersed, auctioned off, or sold to junk shops, each abandoned piece becomes as helpless as a severed human limb. 'It is disgusting', Guy Mannering remarks at an auction, 'to see the scenes of domestic society and seclusion thrown open to the gaze of the curious and vulgar.'[151] It is a spectacle which never fails to stir the Victorian imagination, even in those who take very little interest in interiors. Charles Reade, for example, makes central to his novel, *Hard Cash*, one particular house, Albion Villa; but he only once bothers to describe its contents, and that is when they become tragic and emblematic, beneath the hammer of the auctioneer.[152] Perhaps the most moving of Hardy's many poignant elegies, Mother Cuxom's over Susan Henchard, centres itself upon this insight: 'And all her shining keys will be took from her, and her cupboards opened; and the little things a' didn't wish seen, anybody will see.'[153] At the other extreme, the loneliness of furniture can be made a truth about the wilderness that a desolate city and civilization have become, as in Conrad's view of a second-hand furniture shop in the streets of London, 'where, deep in the gloom of a sort of narrow avenue winding through a bizarre forest of wardrobes, with an undergrowth tangle of table legs, a tall pier-glass glimmered like a pool of water in a wood'.[154] It is as though the city, in dissolving, has reverted to primeval forest.

The distress felt at the fate of furniture in so many Victorian novels is an indication of the degree to which their notion of 'home' depended on the combination of movable elements by a presiding personality, usually individual but sometimes familial. When that is gone, the walls do not – as it were – stand alone; while those objects that filled them, when seen as discrete items, lose the qualities they possessed in combination: 'articles which, properly and decently arranged, look creditable and handsome, have then a paltry and wretched appearance'.[155] One might even suspect that the very solidity of Victorian interiors was partly the result of an effort to disguise their transient nature; while the Edwardian recognition of the transience of all that solidity finally set the whole notion of 'home' adrift.

When Will and Anna Brangwen in *The Rainbow* purchase their second home at Beldover, a suburban villa built by the wife of a colliery manager, that solidity is its characteristic: ' "Good and substantial," was the keynote.'[156] The widow's hearty oak, her Wilton carpet, large round table, and Chesterfield 'covered with glossy chintz in roses and birds' combine their 'common good taste' with the Brangwens' more exclusive one (good prints, grey walls), to give an impression of superior 'culture'. In her generation, Anna delights in the solidity and size of the sunny rooms, but to her daughter, Ursula, their ordinariness is only made tolerable by a more refined touch. In Lawrence's subsequent novel, *Women in Love*, the house is dismantled, and in its vacant state grows insubstantial:

> The sense of walls, dry, thin, flimsy-seeming walls, and a flimsy flooring, pale with its artificial black edges, was neutralising to the mind. Everything was null to the senses, there was enclosure without substance, for the walls were dry and papery. Where were they standing, on earth, or suspended in some cardboard box?[157]

Ursula and Gudrun are shocked: 'It is too appalling. What must we be like if we are the contents of *this*?' In rejecting the house, they deny the values of their parents' generation, refusing marriage, an address, and an establishment: 'The little grey home in the west', Ursula quotes ironically, and Gudrun replies, 'Doesn't it sound grey too?'

But a commitment to the transient and evanescent, which Birkin advocates,[158] Ursula echoes, and Lawrence made himself, is not as easy as it seems. In the strongly autobiographical novel, *Kangaroo*, written of the war years, Harriet (the equivalent of Lawrence's wife, Frieda) improvises a home in a whole succession of flimsy rented interiors, contriving 'that air of pleasant distinction which a woman who knows how to do it finds so easy, especially if she has a few shawls and cushion-covers and bits of interesting brass or china'.[159] Harriet, we learn, never travels without these necessities. Similarly, although Gudrun has declared that she could not 'bear to be married and put into a house',[160] she cannot bring herself to part entirely with the invitation to stability expressed in the Victorian ideal of 'home', although she conceives it ironically, in terms of conventional and inferior art.

She suddenly conjured up a rosy room, with herself in a beautiful gown, and a handsome man in evening dress who held her in his arms in the firelight, and kissed her. This picture she entitled 'Home'. It would have done for the Royal Academy. (Fig. 90)

The hero of *Aaron's Rod* (1922) – which to some extent forms a trilogy, spanning the war years, with *The Rainbow* and *Women in Love* – is, in the aftermath of war, exhausted rather than appalled by such notions. He leaves his family, and remains 'glad not to have a cosy hearth and his own arm-chair'; yet he continues to think of 'his wife and children at home'. 'Home' and the meaning of relationships are, as we have seen, closely related; we know they have changed, but do not yet know what they will become.

The elements that constitute a home were of course reassembled after the First World War, and again after the Second. The house has continued to have a central significance in the art of the novelist; but its meaning is different, which is why the period with which this book is concerned ends at 1914. The Victorian notion of home, although so familiar, is no longer really available to us, and it is that fact that prompts one to end, not with its disappearance, but with its heyday, in asking how and why that notion had possessed the domestic imagination of the nation for so long. Much has already been said about the value of old associations, which root the affections from our earliest years, through the visible significance of things, in the values of family and fireside.[161] The collapse of that particular type of stability is traced by Lawrence, for whereas Tom Brangwen lives as an adult in the home of his childhood, his stepdaughter, Anna, inhabits three separate houses when marriage takes her from the Marsh Farm, each corresponding to an alteration in her husband's social status; while her children do not grow up, as she had done, in the one house and among the same objects. As a consequence, the confidence, indivisible from the Victorian fireside, that, if the world without is storm and sea, the house within is a secure and peaceful haven is no longer accessible as it once was.

It is no coincidence that the Victorians produced so many paintings connected with fishermen and lifeboatmen which directly dramatize both the haven itself and the threat that faces it from the world without. *A Hopeless Dawn* (Fig. 98), painted by Frank Bramley in the last quarter of the century, is an example: the candle gutters in the early light, the Windsor chair remains empty, the meal laid on the spotless cloth still waits for the father who will not return. One could parallel scenes like this with many pages in the Victorian novel, where the world within and the threat without are contrasted. As might be expected, there are many such passages in Dickens's *Christmas Books*, that season being the high festival of hearth and home. The Ghost of Christmas Present actually takes Scrooge out to a lighthouse, to prove that true homes may even be found in the heart of the tumult: 'Even here, two men who watched the light, had made a fire, that through the loophole in the thick stone wall shed out a ray of brightness on the awful sea.'[162] It has been remarked that

98 *A Hopeless Dawn*

Dickens never approved of any organization or institution, with the sole exception of what is now the Great Ormond Street Hospital for children. But he is by no means the only Victorian writer to feel that the answer to the seemingly insuperable ills that Victorian society had generated could only be found in the values of home, since only there would the sole available ethic – Christianity – remain a wholly reliable moral touchstone. Technological revolution, both then and now, is not least disturbing because social values previously held prove quite inadequate to the new situation. Where does one begin, if not in the manageable world defined by the home? This was certainly where the most socially conscious writers – Dickens, Disraeli, Kingsley, and Mrs Gaskell – looked for their answers.

Especially in Dickens's novels, the outside world of the city is apt to become phantasmagoric, as though it escapes the grasp of sanity: 'It seemed as if the street were absorbed by the sky, and the night were all in the air.'[163] The world of the happy home is totally different; it is, by definition, within our grasp. Many Victorian novelists take pleasure in housekeeping, expressed as the control of a miniature world, which is indeed the main pleasure of keeping house. The seaman's interior, as I have mentioned, does this to perfection, 'everything being stowed away as if there were an earthquake regularly every half-hour'.[164] But, like Captain Cuttle, Dickens's seamen tend to be bachelors. The articulation of Bleak House is a more significant example, for John Jarndyce has no natural family; in defiance of the social system (in this case, Chancery), he has assembled one from the goodness of his heart. Within that renovated house, which like Tom Jarndyce has blown its brains out, he prepares an individual space suited to each of the three victims of the system (Esther's, as one would expect, has a conspicuous fireplace),[165] attempting to reconcile them beneath a single roof; what the law has sundered, this one man joins together. As a whole, the house is like its master: it keeps the miseries of the larger world at bay by accommodating them within a single room, the Growlery, but is elsewhere wholly unpredictable, as delightful and full of surprises as Mr Jarndyce is himself, provided that the wind is not in the east. Esther, with her pleasant cares and her everlasting keys, certainly flourishes in Bleak House, but its miniature descendant, presented to her by Mr Jarndyce on her marriage, is even more fulfilling. The pleasure of having one's world entirely within one's control is indivisible from this type of home; a doll's world is a safe place to be, and the reduction in its detail gives it delicacy. Such places are frequently savoured in Dickens's novels: Abel Cottage, belonging to the benevolent Mr Garland in *The Old Curiosity Shop*, is one instance, tiny within and without, boasting 'such a kitchen as was never before seen or heard of out of a toy-shop window, with everything in it as bright and glowing, and as precisely ordered too'.[166] The gratifications of a larder lined with jars of preserves, of a linen cupboard stacked with immaculate sheets, of shining pots and pans awaiting the fire, are felt in the work of many other novelists. The miniature scale is, for example, equally emphasized in Charlotte Brontë's account of the house that M. Paul prepares in *Villette* for Lucy Snow.[167] There is a little couch and a little chiffonier in the salon, a little kitchen with a little stove, a diminutive set of earthenware in a small cupboard and 'two pretty cabinets of sleeping-rooms'. The storm without removes M. Paul abruptly from the story, but Lucy is left secure within her nest. It is difficult not to entertain the suspicion that Charlotte Brontë, who tends to dismember her heroes by various methods, subconsciously left no room for M. Paul. Harriet Martineau rather gives the game away when she remarks, 'Women do inevitably love house-keeping, unless *educational*, or other *impediments* interfere with their natural tastes.'[168]

But it is rather too easy to make fun of the Victorian ideal of 'home'. Even Ruskin in 'Queens' Gardens' seems to build his walls in the confidence that they will give those within them the necessary strength to look outside to 'the whole world in wilderness' beyond them. Esther's keys may jingle irritatingly through *Bleak House*; but her obsession with them, unlike Clarissa's, is more than personal; they represent her effort to keep the household which Jarndyce has assembled together in amity beneath one roof. In this she is only partially successful, for the world outside proves almost too much for his experiment, assailing it with smallpox which spreads from the 'perishing blind houses, with their eyes stoned out' which have been left by Chancery to rot in Tom-all-Alone's. The Victorian house may, like Richardson's, be frequently defined against the sexual threat; but the adulterer is subsumed into the larger image of a society from which the house must be defended if there is to be any hope of reforming that society itself. The situation is closer to our own than to Jane Austen's, whose doors are often opened so that society may reform the house.

Neither period had, however, to endure the bleak definition of much modern architecture – that the house is a machine for living in. Both, though in different ways, would have known what a lie that was. The equation, in the first place, quite fails to perceive the essential connection between the house and play; with delight, that is, rather than with efficiency. The image with which I began, the Dairy House at Blaise, emphasizes the fact that houses are fictions of how life ought to be; and Nash did not stop with the Dairy but extended his fiction from the individual to society in the creation of Blaise Hamlet (Fig. 99). Every one of this group of nine cottages *ornées* is individual designed – with their multiple garden seats – to delight the inhabitant; and (although the front doors face away from one another, apparently in order to minimize gossip) all are gathered around a central green. Because he sees it as 'responsible for some of the worst sentimentalities of England', Nikolaus Pevsner is rather hard upon Blaise Hamlet: 'Its progeny is legion and includes Christmas cards and tea-pots.'[169] But he also comments on its 'kind of fairy village green', and asks the question: 'Why then are we not irritated but enchanted by it?' One answer is surely the smallness of its scale and the thought that has gone into its making; another that it has, almost to excess, that element of play that is often conspicuously lacking in modern building. As Wemmick observed in fiction of his miniature castle at Walworth, 'If you have an idea, carry it out and keep it up';[170] one remembers that, in fact, William Burges provided his larger castle with a real portcullis that actually worked.[171] It seems a pity that, in the absence of this element in modern building, people have to make do with its image on Christmas cards and teapots.

99 Blaise Hamlet

But there is an even stronger reason why the house cannot be regarded as a machine for living in: houses themselves do not allow it. No building, however new, can be totally divided from its history, even where designers have forgotten it. The arrival of electricity, central heating, and television has changed our houses more than we assume. With the disappearance of the hearth as the major source of light, heat, and interest, the Victorian notion of 'home' is unavailable, and the relation of the house to the world outside it is now of a different kind. Moreover, as Edith Wharton once remarked, 'The survival of obsolete customs which makes the study of Sociology so interesting, has its parallel in the history of architecture.'[172] Everyman is perhaps happier *not* to know that the balls on the gateposts of his suburban villa represent the skulls of Celtic sacrifice;[173] that his three underused bedrooms, expensive to heat and light, are needed to prevent him from committing incest;[174] that the height of his ceilings and the extent of his windows, in conforming to the building regulations, accept a mistaken theory of infection (Fig. 34c), in allowing the fatal miasma room for itself or modes of escape.[175] The dimensions of my own Jacobean house (Fig. 100) are adjusted to cattle, not to people; its three bays, each measuring roughly 18 by 15 feet, compose the space determined before the Norman Conquest as adequate to house two pairs of oxen.[176] Houses, whether old or new, as

100 Manor House, Wilsill

we have seen, have a distinct being of their own. They are no more like machines than people themselves are.

As Margaret Schlegel says, houses are in consequence 'saucy things' with an independent will. They are as slippery as language, which also alters in ways its users cannot control in response to technological and social change. Again like language, they commit us to ideas we may not want to entertain, and refuse to accommodate those we might prefer. The novel is invincibly domestic, partly because it functions like the house as a little world we think we can control. When it applies its language to the house, it makes continual discoveries, bringing to consciousness aspects of our environment that normally go unrecognized. To some extent, the novelist, like the architect and the designer, is an unconscious interpreter; one cannot, for example, quite believe that Richardson would have recognized his own discoveries. But those discoveries are no less real for that. In Dickens's *Battle of Life*, Dr Jeddler remarks, in order to console his daughters, who are over-sensitive to both: 'A real home is only four walls; and a fictitious one, mere rags and ink.'[177] It is plain, however, that he makes that comment only because his family knows so well that it is not true.

Notes

Where practical, references to primary sources existing in multiple editions are given by section. Full reference to a secondary source or particular edition is given the first time a work is mentioned; thereafter, the reader is referred to the original entry by chapter and note number, thus: *Clarissa* (1, 1).

1 The Dairy House at Blaise

1 Samuel Richardson, *Clarissa*, Everyman, 4 vols, London, 1932, reprinted from the 4th edition of 1751, vol. IV, p. 497.
2 Philip Larkin, 'Home is so sad', in *The Whitsun Weddings*, London, 1964.
3 From the publication *Common Sense*, quoted by John Dixon Hunt and Peter Willis (eds), *The Genius of the Place*, London, 1975, p. 19.
4 Samuel Richardson, *Pamela*, Everyman, 2 vols, London, 1914, vol. II, pp. 1, 36.
5 Quoted in T. C. Duncan Eaves and Ben D. Kimpel, *Samuel Richardson: a Biography*, London, 1971, pp. 496–7.
6 See James Chambers, *The English House*, London, 1985, p. 127.
7 Jocelyn Harris (ed.), *The History of Sir Charles Grandison*, Oxford English Novels, 3 parts, London, 1972, part II, p. 291.
8 See *Samuel Richardson: a Biography* (1, 5), pp. 72–5; Richardson not certainly the sole editor.
9 Sir Henry Wotton, *The Elements of Architecture*, 1624, part I, following 'Of Chimnies'.
10 Robert Morris, *Lectures on Architecture*, part I, 2nd edn, 1759, part II, 1st edn, 1736, Farnborough, 1971, pp. 23–4.
11 ibid., p. 144.
12 See James S. Ackerman, *Palladio*, Harmondsworth, 1966, pp. 40–53.
13 John Cornforth, *English Interiors 1790–1848*, London, 1978, p. 16.
14 Adam Smith, *The Theory of Moral Sentiments*, 1759, quoted in Peter Thornton, *Authentic Décor: the Domestic Interior 1620–1920*, London, 1984, p. 102.
15 Oliver Goldsmith, *The Vicar of Wakefield*, chs 1, 19.
16 *Clarissa* (1, 1), vol. III, pp. 444–5. See also Fanny Burney (almost never descriptive), who details an impoverished interior in *Camilla* (1796), bk II, ch. 13.
17 John Milton, *Il Penseroso*, ll. 155–60.

18 Quoted in Christopher Hussey, *English Gardens and Landscapes 1700–1750*, London, 1967, p. 43.

19 William Congreve, *The Way of the World*, IV, iv.

20 Batty Langley, *New Principles of Gardening*, quoted in *The Genius of the Place* (1, 3), p. 180.

21 Title page to Paul Decker, *Gothic Architecture Decorated*, 1759, Farnborough, 1968.

22 Jean-Jacques Rousseau, *Discours sur l'origine de l'inégalité*, 1755.

23 Horace Walpole, *A Description of the Villa of Mr. Horace Walpole at Strawberry Hill*, 1784, Farnborough, 1964, Preface, p. iv.

24 Horace Walpole, *The Castle of Otranto*, ch. 1.

25 Sir John Soane, *Lectures on Architecture*, 1809–36; publication of Sir John Soane's Museum no. 14, 1929, p. 172.

26 See pp. 73–82.

27 John Papworth, *Rural Residences*, 1818, Farnborough, 1971, p. 25.

28 John Plaw, *Sketches for Country Houses, Villas and Rural Dwellings*, 1800, Farnborough, 1972, p. 13.

29 Letter to Cassandra Austen, 14 October 1814.

30 Letter to Cassandra Austen, 1 December 1798.

31 Letter to G. H. Lewes, 11 January 1848.

32 Mrs Radcliffe, *The Mysteries of Udolpho*, ch. 1.

33 Letter to Cassandra Austen, 30 January 1809.

34 Letter to Anna Austen, 9 September 1814.

35 Q. D. Leavis makes this observation in 'Jane Austen: novelist of a changing society', but argues that the changes at Uppercross are welcome to Jane Austen; *Collected Essays*, vol. I, *The Englishness of the English Novel*, Cambridge, 1983, pp. 26–60.

36 Jane Austen, *Persuasion*, ch. 5.

37 *Lectures on Architecture* (1, 25), p. 126.

38 ibid., p. 190.

39 *Persuasion*, ch. 5.

40 Jane Austen, *Pride and Prejudice*, chs 8, 10.

41 *Persuasion*, ch. 5.

42 *Authentic Décor* (1, 14), p. 157.

43 Jane Austen, *Northanger Abbey* (1818), ch. 20.

44 Jane Austen, *Emma* (1816), ch. 41.

45 ibid.

46 See pp. 42–3.

47 Letter to J. Edward Austen, 16 December 1816.

48 Charles Dickens, *Sketches by Boz*, 'The Boarding House', ch. 1.

49 Charles Dickens, *The Old Curiosity Shop*, ch. 1.

50 See John Gloag, *A Short Dictionary of Furniture*, London, revised edn 1969, pp. 809, 811.

51 *Authentic Décor* (1, 14), pp. 228–9.

52 ibid., p. 221.

53 William Makepeace Thackeray, *Pendennis*, ch. 37.

54 See pp. 49–51, 84–6.

55 See Robert Furneaux Jordan, *Victorian Architecture*, Harmondsworth, 1966, p. 110.

56 Charles Dickens, *Martin Chuzzlewit* (1843–4), ch. 2.

57 Charles Dickens, *Great Expectations* (1860–1), ch. 27.
58 J. C. Loudon, *An Encyclopaedia of Cottage, Farm, and Villa Architecture and Furniture*, London, new edn 1839, p. 2.
59 ibid., p. 763.
60 See pp. 73–82.
61 See pp. 70–8, 81.
62 Mrs Norris's 'White House', which seems to have two bedrooms (apart from servants' garrets), Jane Austen, *Mansfield Park*, ch. 3.
63 See pp. 122–4
64 See pp. 135–6.
65 Charles Dickens, *Sketches by Boz*, Characters V, 'The Parlour Orator'.
66 Olive Cook, *The English Country House*, London, 1974, p. 214.
67 Charles Dickens, *Dombey and Son* (1847–8), ch. 36 (ironically titled 'House-Warming').
68 ibid., ch. 6. See also pp. 106, 178–9.
69 Included in Viscount Ingestre (ed.), *Meliora*, First Series 1853, London, 1971 reprint, p. 261.
70 *Great Expectations*, ch. 25.
71 See pp. 36, 56.
72 See pp. 36–8, 56–9, 86–7.
73 Charlotte M. Yonge, *The Young Stepmother*, ch. 10.
74 William Morris, *Lectures on Art and Industry* (1881–94), *Collected Works*, vol. XXII, New York, 1966, pp. 362–5.
75 *The Young Stepmother*, ch. 10.
76 Charles Eastlake, *Hints on Household Taste*, 3rd revised edn, London, 1872, p. 49.
77 George Eliot, *Scenes of Clerical Life* (1857), 'Mr Gilfil's love-story', ch. 19.
78 See pp. 217–19. Although *The Wedding Banquet* was painted by Bruegel in *c.* 1568, it is, in this respect, closely related to the Dutch painting of the seventeenth century in which the Victorians most delighted.
79 See Erwin Panofsky, *Early Netherlandish Painting*, The Charles Eliot Norton Lectures 1947–8, New York, Hegerstown, San Francisco, and London, 1971, vol. I, p. 354.
80 ibid., p. 144. See also Larry Silver, *The Paintings of Quinten Massys*, Oxford, 1984, pp. 136–7.
81 Henry James, *The Golden Bowl* (1904), ch. 25.
82 E. M. Forster, *Howards End*, ch. 33.
83 See chapter 6, especially pp. 200, 219–22, 227–8.
84 Walter Crane, 'The Revival of Design', in *Arts and Crafts Essays*, Arts and Crafts Exhibition Society, London, 1899, p. 2.
85 D. H. Lawrence, *Women in Love*, ch. 26.
86 ibid., Preface.
87 Ford Madox Ford, *A Man Could Stand Up* (1926), part III, ch. 1.
88 Included in the 1977 Abinger edition of E. M. Forster, *A Room with a View* (1908), p. 211.
89 *Howards End*, ch. 17.
90 Fay Weldon, *Letters to Alice*, London, 1984, Letter 4.

2 Aspects of Chesney Wold

1 See p. 21.
2 True of Richardson, Fanny Burney, Jane Austen, Mrs Radcliffe; largely true of Fielding, Smollett; not true of Defoe, Sterne.
3 See pp. 68–70, 86–93.
4 Charles Dickens, *Bleak House*, ch. 18.
5 See Angus Wilson, *The World of Charles Dickens*, Harmondsworth, 1972, pp. 37–8.
6 *Bleak House*, ch. 2.
7 ibid.
8 ibid., ch. 43.
9 ibid., ch. 37.
10 ibid., ch. 40.
11 ibid., ch. 28.
12 ibid., ch. 41.
13 ibid., ch. 18 (within a page of the idyllic description of Chesney Wold with its delusive rest).
14 ibid., ch. 6.
15 ibid., ch. 12.
16 ibid., ch. 66.
17 ibid., chs 7, 64.
18 See pp. 36–8.
19 See Mark Girouard, *Life in the English Country House*, New Haven, Conn., and London, 1978, p. 2.
20 The aristocrat's responsibility in towns chiefly concerned planning; few took much interest in their town, as distinct from their country, houses. See John Summerson, *Georgian London*, revised edn, Harmondsworth, 1978, pp. 122–3.
21 *Samuel Richardson: a Biography* (1, 5), pp. 405–6.
22 ibid., p. 491.
23 *The History of Sir Charles Grandison* (1, 7), part III, p. 285.
24 ibid., p. 286.
25 ibid.
26 *The Elements of Architecture* (1, 9), part II.
27 Henry Fielding, *Tom Jones* (1749), bk I, ch. 4.
28 *The History of Sir Charles Grandison* (1, 7), part III, p. 96.
29 Fanny Burney, *Camilla*, bk VI, ch. 4.
30 Tobias Smollett, *Humphrey Clinker* (1771), Letter to Sir Watkin Phillips, London, 10 June.
31 Jane Austen, *Pride and Prejudice*, ch. 43.
32 Jane Austen, *Sense and Sensibility*, ch. 42.
33 *Georgian London* (2, 20), p. 144.
34 From *The Architecture of Roger Pratt*, quoted in *Life in the English Country House* (2, 19), p. 138.
35 ibid.
36 Jane Austen, *Mansfield Park*, ch. 39.
37 ibid., ch. 9.

38 *Remarks on Forest Scenery*, in *The Genius of the Place* (1, 3), p. 338.
39 *Mansfield Park*, ch. 6.
40 Humphry Repton, *An Enquiry into the Changes of Taste in Landscape Gardening*, 1806, Farnborough, 1969, p. 56.
41 *Mansfield Park*, ch. 8.
42 *Sense and Sensibility*, ch. 30.
43 William Cobbett, *Rural Rides* (1822–6, published together 1830), 30 November 1822.
44 *Georgian London* (2, 20), p. 122.
45 *English Interiors 1790–1848* (1, 13), p. 13.
46 *Clarissa* (1, 1), vol. I, p. 170.
47 *Mansfield Park*, ch. 5.
48 *The History of Sir Charles Grandison* (1, 7), part III, p. 278.
49 *Pride and Prejudice*, ch. 43.
50 *Mansfield Park*, ch. 9.
51 *Pride and Prejudice*, ch. 43.
52 ibid., ch. 8.
53 Jane Austen, *Emma*, ch. 42.
54 See Jane Aiken Hodge, *The Double Life of Jane Austen*, London, 1972, p. 95.
55 Letter from Jane Austen to Cassandra, 3 November 1813.
56 Letter to Cassandra, 8 November 1800.
57 Letter from Jane Austen to Francis Austen, 3 July 1813.
58 Jane Austen, *Persuasion*, ch. 6.
59 ibid., ch. 13.
60 *An Enquiry into the Changes of Taste in Landscape Gardening* (2, 40), p. 65.
61 See p. 15.
62 *Rural Rides*, 11 November 1825.
63 *Encyclopaedia* (1, 58), p. 8.
64 ibid.
65 Augustus Welby Northmore Pugin, *An Apology for the Revival of Christian Architecture* (1843), pp. 38–9.
66 See *The English Country House* (1, 66), p. 215.
67 See Mark Girouard, *The Victorian Country House*, Oxford, 1971, pp. 6–7.
68 Matthew Arnold, *Culture and Anarchy* (1869), ch. 3.
69 *Bleak House*, ch. 2.
70 For example, Geoffrey Best, 'Social change and taste in mid-Victorian England', Victorian Society Report, 1963, p. 2.
71 Benjamin Disraeli, *The Young Duke*, bk I, ch. 9.
72 Benjamin Disraeli, *Sybil*, subtitle.
73 See *Life in the English Country House* (2, 19), pp. 52–3.
74 *Tom Jones*, bk I, ch. 4.
75 Mrs Radcliffe, *The Mysteries of Udolpho*, chs 3, 32.
76 *Lectures on Architecture* (1, 10), pp. 66–9.
77 *Lectures on Architecture* (1, 25), p. 145.
78 R. W. Chapman (ed.), *The Oxford Illustrated Jane Austen*, vol. VI, *Minor Works*, London, 1969, pp. 428–30.
79 Jane Austen, *Northanger Abbey*, ch. 7.
80 ibid., ch. 5.

81   *Sybil*, bk II, ch. 1.
82   ibid., bk II, ch. 12.
83   Benjamin Disraeli, *Coningsby*, bk III, ch. 4.
84   ibid., bk IX, ch. 1.
85   ibid., bk III, ch. 2.
86   See p. 13.
87   *Coningsby*, bk III, ch. 2.
88   *Sybil*, bk IV, ch. 5.
89   *Coningsby*, bk III, ch. 4.
90   A formulation repeated three times in *Sybil*.
91   *Coningsby*, bk III, ch. 3.
92   *Sybil*, bk II, ch. 5.
93   Karl Marx and Friedrich Engels, *Manifesto of the Communist Party*, I, 'Bourgeois and Proletarians'.
94   *Sybil*, bk II, ch. 5.
95   *Coningsby*, bk III, ch. 4.
96   See *Life in the English Country House* (2, 19), Fig. 169 and p. 290.
97   Charles Kingsley, *Yeast*, ch. 13.
98   ibid., ch. 6.
99   Charles Kingsley, *Two Years Ago*, ch. 8.
100 *Yeast*, Epilogue.
101 ibid.
102 Jane Austen, *The History of England* (1791), *Minor Works* (2, 78), p. 142.
103 *English Gardens and Landscapes 1700–1750* (1, 18), comment on Plate 185.
104 *Lectures on Architecture* (1, 25), p. 82.
105 *Emma*, ch. 42.
106 George Eliot, *Daniel Deronda*, ch. 16.
107 ibid., ch. 36.
108 ibid.
109 ibid., ch. 16.
110 ibid., ch. 12.
111 ibid.
112 Anthony Trollope, *An Autobiography* (written 1875–6, published posthumously 1883), ch. 13.
113 Anthony Trollope, *The Prime Minister* (1875–6), ch. 19, titled 'Vulgarity'.
114 Anthony Trollope, *Can You Forgive Her?* (1864–5), ch. 80.
115 ibid., ch. 27.
116 ibid., ch. 22.
117 *An Apology for the Revival of Christian Architecture* (2, 65), p. 2.
118 George Eliot, 'Mr Gilfil's Love-Story', ch. 3.
119 ibid., ch. 4.
120 ibid.
121 ibid., ch. 2.
122 ibid.
123 ibid., ch. 4.
124 *The Victorian Country House* (2, 67), p. 10.
125 *Bleak House*, ch. 7.
126 Anthony Trollope, *The Small House at Allington* (1862), ch. 1.
127 *Encyclopaedia* (1, 58), pp. 791–2.
128 *The Small House at Allington*, ch. 1.
129 Robert Kerr, *The Gentleman's House or How to Plan English Residences from the Cottage to the Palace* (1864), London, 2nd edn 1865, p. 68.
130 *The Victorian Country House* (2, 67), pp. 11, 19–22.

131 *Gentleman's House* (2, 129), pp. 63–4.
132 ibid., p. 67.
133 ibid., p. 116.
134 ibid., p. 130.
135 *Coningsby*, bk III, ch. 2.
136 *Gentleman's House* (2, 129), p. 254.
137 ibid., p. 229.
138 ibid., p. 195.
139 See pp. 86–7.
140 *Gentleman's House* (2, 129), p. 392.
141 ibid., p. 203.
142 *Life in the English Country House* (2, 19), p. 285.
143 See pp. 86–7.
144 See *Authentic Décor: the Domestic Interior 1620–1920* (1, 14), p. 218.
145 *Gentleman's House* (2, 129), p. 121.
146 *Coningsby*, bk III, ch. 2.
147 *Gentleman's House* (2, 129), p. 107.
148 William Morris, *Lectures on Socialism* (1883–94), *Collected Works*, vol. XXIII, New York, 1966, pp. 199–200.
149 William Makepeace Thackeray, *Pendennis*, ch. 22.
150 *Rural Rides*, 17 November 1822.
151 *Gentleman's House* (2, 129), pp. 67–8.
152 Mrs Gaskell, *Wives and Daughters*, ch. 2.
153 Letter to Marianne Gaskell, 13 and 14 September 1857.
154 Charles Dickens, *Barnaby Rudge*, ch. 13.
155 Charles Dickens, *A Tale of Two Cities*, bk II, ch. 23.
156 Other examples: Satis House in Charles Dickens, *Great Expectations*; Thornfield Hall in Charlotte Brontë, *Jane Eyre* (1847); Stancy Castle in Thomas Hardy, *A Laodicean* (1881); Poynton in Henry James, *The Spoils of Poynton* (1897).
157 Anthony Trollope, *Barchester Towers* (1857), ch. 15.
158 George Eliot, *Felix Holt*, ch. 34.
159 *Daniel Deronda*, ch. 31.
160 Charles Dickens, *Little Dorrit* (1856–7), bk II, ch. 12.
161 Anthony Trollope, *Doctor Thorne* (1858), ch. I.
162 Anthony Trollope, *The Duke's Children* (1880), ch. 37.
163 *Barchester Towers*, ch. 22.
164 *The Small House at Allington*, ch. 1.
165 See p. 80.
166 *Daniel Deronda*, ch. 10.
167 ibid., ch. 9.
168 ibid., ch. 31.
169 Henry James, *The Princess Casamassima* (1886), ch. 22.
170 Henry James, *The Portrait of a Lady* (1881), ch. 9.
171 Henry James, *The Wings of the Dove* (1902), bk V, ch. 1.
172 In 'James and the house beautiful', *Collected Essays*, vol. 2, *The American Novel and Reflections on the European Novel*, Cambridge, 1985, Q. D. Leavis argues that 'those were gone who deserved not to stay', a debatable point.
173 In *The Princess Casamassima* and Henry James, *The Golden Bowl* respectively.

174 Henry James, *The Awkward Age* (1899), ch. 17.
175 In *The Portrait of a Lady* and *The Spoils of Poynton* respectively. On Poynton, see below pp. 159–60.
176 *The Princess Casamassima*, ch. 22.
177 ibid.
178 Henry James, *The Tragic Muse* (1890), ch. 13.
179 *The Portrait of a Lady*, ch. 9.
180 *The Wings of the Dove*, bk V, ch. 1.
181 Conversation with Margaret Jourdain, quoted in Pamela Hansford-Johnson, *I. Compton-Burnett*, British Council Bibliographical Series, 1951, p. 36.
182 Ivy Compton-Burnett, *A Heritage and its History*, ch. 11.
183 ibid., ch. 12.
184 Ben Jonson, 'To Penshurst', ll. 45–8, in *The Forrest* (1616).
185 In the Tietjens tetralogy, Ford Madox Ford, *Parade's End*, particularly *Last Post* (1928).
186 In Ford Madox Ford, *The Good Soldier* (1915).
187 ibid., part IV, ch. 3.
188 D. H. Lawrence, *Women in Love*, ch. 8.

3   Dorothea's cottages

1 George Eliot, *Middlemarch*, ch. 3.
2 See p. 38.
3 William Makepeace Thackeray, *Pendennis*, ch. 62.
4 Henry Fielding, *Tom Jones*, bk V, ch. 5.
5 Fanny Burney, *Diary of Madame d'Arblay* (1842–6), vol. II, p. 183.
6 Jane Austen, *Emma*, ch. 10.
7 ibid., ch. 23.
8 Charles Dickens, *Hard Times*, bk II, ch. 6.
9 Anthony Trollope, *The Prime Minister*, ch. 73.
10 *Middlemarch*, ch. 3.
11 ibid.
12 *Encyclopaedia* (1, 58), p. 354.
13 Printed in John Gloag, *Mr Loudon's England*, Newcastle, 1970, p. 203.
14 Quoted in R. J. Brown, *The English Country Cottage*, London, 1984, p. 39.
15 Oliver Goldsmith, 'The Deserted Village' (1770), ll. 275–6, 281–2.
16 See M. Batey, 'Nuneham Courtenay', *Oxoniensia* XXXIII, 1968, pp. 108–24. Other contenders include Lissoy in Ireland. Auburn is probably a composite representation of the problems of rural depopulation.
17 Quoted in *The English Country Cottage* (3, 14), p. 45.
18 Uvedale Price, *Essays on the Picturesque* (1810), vol. II, Farnborough, 1971, p. 346.
19 See *The English Country Cottage* (3, 14), p. 43.
20 *Encyclopaedia* (1, 58), p. 811.
21 See pp. 39–40.
22 *Encyclopaedia* (1, 58), p. 766.
23 ibid., p. 811.
24 *Middlemarch*, ch. 3.
25 William Cobbett, *Rural Rides*, 30 November 1822.

26 ibid., 31 October 1822.

27 ibid., 31 August 1823.

28 Subject of chapter 6 below.

29 James Malton, *An Essay on British Cottage Architecture* (1798), Farnborough, 1972, Introduction, p. 6.

30 Mrs Radcliffe, *The Mysteries of Udolpho*, ch. 32.

31 Richard Payne Knight, *An Analytical Inquiry into the Principles of Taste*, 4th edn (1808), Farnborough, 1972, p. 146.

32 *Middlemarch*, ch. 9.

33 ibid., ch. 22.

34 In *The Genius of the Place* (1, 3), p. 363.

35 *Sketches for Country Houses, Villas and Rural Dwellings* (1, 28), note to Plate V, p. 10.

36 Richard Payne Knight, *The Landscape*, bk II, ll. 288–93.

37 Jane Austen, *Sense and Sensibility*, ch. 18.

38 *An Enquiry into the Changes of Taste in Landscape Gardening* (2, 40), p. 133.

39 *Rural Residences* (1, 27), p. 10.

40 Joseph Gandy, *Designs for Cottages, Cottage Farms, and Other Rural Buildings* (1805), Farnborough, 1971, Introduction, p. i.

41 ibid., p. vi.

42 ibid., p. i.

43 William Shenstone, 'Unconnected Thoughts on Gardening' (1764), in *The Genius of the Place* (1, 3), p. 292.

44 *Sense and Sensibility*, ch. 18.

45 Jane Austen, *Northanger Abbey*, ch. 26.

46 *Encyclopaedia* (1, 58), p. 812.

47 Mrs Gaskell, *North and South*, ch. 3.

48 ibid., ch. 46.

49 Charles Dickens, *Christmas Books, The Chimes* (1845), the third quarter.

50 *Middlemarch*, ch. 12.

51 ibid., ch. 39.

52 Benjamin Disraeli, *Sybil*, bk II, ch. 12.

53 Quoted in *The English Country Cottage* (3, 14), pp. 49–50.

54 Thomas Gray, *Elegy Written in a Country Churchyard* (1751), 1. 23.

55 Edmund Bartell, *Hints for Picturesque Improvements in Ornamented Cottages* (1804), Farnborough, 1971, p. 116.

56 John Wood, *A Series of Plans for Cottages or Habitations of the Labourer either in Husbandry, or the Mechanic Arts, adapted as well to Towns as to the Country* (1781), Farnborough, 1972, Introduction, p. 3.

57 William Godwin, *Caleb Williams*, vol. I, ch. 6.

58 *Series of Plans for Cottages* (3, 56), Introduction, p. 3.

59 Charles Kingsley, *Yeast*, ch. 6.

60 ibid., ch. 3.

61 ibid., ch. 13.

62 *Essays on the Picturesque* (3, 18), vol. II, p. 221.

63 *North and South*, ch. 15.

64 B. Kirkham Gray, *Philanthropy and the State*, London, 1908, p. 68.

65 George Godwin, *London Shadows*, London, 1854, pp. 1–2.

66 Charles Dickens, *Little Dorrit*, bk I, ch. 3.
67 *London Shadows* (3, 65), p. 2.
68 Friedrich Engels, *The Condition of the Working-Class in England*, 'The Great Towns'.
69 Mrs Gaskell, *Mary Barton*, ch. 3.
70 ibid., ch. 6.
71 *The Condition of the Working-Class in England*, 'The Great Towns'.
72 W. Nassau, Senior, *Letters on the Factory Act* (1837), quoted in Friedrich Engels, ibid.
73 *Sybil*, bk III, ch. 4.
74 *London Shadows* (3, 65), p. 7.
75 George Godwin, *Town Swamps and Social Bridges*, 1859, Leicester, 1972, p. 12.
76 *Mary Barton*, ch. 6.
77 *The Condition of the Working-Class in England*, 'The Great Towns'.
78 Henry Roberts, *The Dwellings of the Labouring Classes*, 3rd edn, London, 1853, p. 3.
79 *Town Swamps and Social Bridges* (3, 75), p. 6.
80 See Humphry House, *The Dickens World*, Oxford, 1960, p. 167.
81 Quoted by Alexander Stewart, *The Medical Aspects of Sanitary Reform*, 2nd edn 1867, in Alexander Stewart and Edward Jenkins, *Medical and Legal Aspects of Sanitary Reform*, Leicester, 1969, p. 47.
82 Charles Dickens, *Bleak House*, ch. 11.
83 *London Shadows* (3, 65), p. 53.
84 In *Medical and Legal Aspects of Sanitary Reform* (3, 81), pp. 85–6.
85 Charles Kingsley, *Alton Locke*, ch. 35.
86 Charles Dickens, *Our Mutual Friend*, ch. 3.
87 *Mary Barton*, ch. 2.
88 *London Shadows* (3, 65), p. 6.
89 Henry Mayhew, *London Labour and the London Poor*, 1861–2 edn, New York, 1968, vol. I, p. 48.
90 John Ruskin, *Sesame and Lilies* (1864), Lecture I.
91 See Royston Lambert, *Sir John Simon 1816–1904 and English Social Administration*, London, 1963, pp. 49–55.
92 *Alton Locke*, ch. 35.
93 Quoted by J. N. Tarn, *Working Class Housing in Nineteenth Century Britain*, Architectural Association Paper no. 7, 1969, p. 3.
94 Charles Dickens, *The Old Curiosity Shop*, ch. 38.
95 *The Legal Aspects of Sanitary Reform* (in *Medical and Legal Aspects of Sanitary Reform*) (3, 81), p. 96.
96 *Town Swamps and Social Bridges* (3, 75), p. 16.
97 *The Dwellings of the Labouring Classes* (3, 78), p. 67.
98 Letter to Charles Eliot Norton, 5 April 1860.
99 *The Dwellings of the Labouring Classes* (3, 78), p. 68.
100 Letter to Angela Burdett-Coutts, 16 March 1852.
101 See *Working Class Housing* (3, 93), pp. 14–16; J. N. Tarn, *Five Per Cent Philanthropy*, Cambridge, 1973, pp. 30–1.
102 *Mr Loudon's England* (3, 13), p. 115.
103 *The Dwellings of the Labouring Classes* (3, 78), p. 57.
104 *Town Swamps and Social Bridges* (3, 75), p. 21.
105 *Working Class Housing* (3, 93), p. 18.

106 'Conversion of a heathen court', 'Wild Court tamed', in Charles Dickens (ed.), *Household Words*, no. 247, 16 December 1854, pp. 409–13; no. 283, 25 August 1855, pp. 85–7.

107 'Wild Court tamed' (3, 106).

108 ibid.

109 See *Five Per Cent Philanthropy* (3, 101), pp. 72–3; E. Moberley Bell, *Octavia Hill: a Biography* (1942), London, 1965, pp. 77–85.

110 Patrick Geddes, *Civics as Applied Sociology*, part I, 1904, included in Helen E. Meller (ed.), *The Ideal City*, Leicester, 1979, p. 105.

111 Charles Dickens, *Dombey and Son*, ch. 34.

112 *The Condition of the Working-Class in England*, 'The Great Towns'.

113 *Mary Barton*, ch. 2.

114 *The Old Curiosity Shop*, ch. 15.

115 *Mary Barton*, ch. 2.

116 Charles Dickens, *Great Expectations*, ch. 4.

117 Daniel Defoe, *Moll Flanders* (1722), Everyman, London, 1930, p. 143.

118 See *The Dickens World* (3, 80), pp. 126–8.

119 *Sybil*, bk II, ch. 13.

120 Anne Brontë, *Agnes Grey*, ch. 11.

121 *Mary Barton*, ch. 2.

122 William Atkinson, *Views of Picturesque Cottages with Plans* (1805), Farnborough, 1971, Introduction, p. viii.

123 George Eliot, *Adam Bede* (1859), ch. 34.

124 *Mary Barton*, ch. 2.

125 *London Labour and the London Poor* (3, 89), vol. I, p. 400.

126 Mrs Gaskell, *Sylvia's Lovers* (1863), ch. 7.

127 *Mary Barton*, ch. 10.

128 *Dombey and Son*, ch. 6.

129 *Town Swamps and Social Bridges* (3, 75), p. 18.

130 *London Labour and the London Poor* (3, 89), vol. I, p. 317.

131 ibid., p. 319.

132 *Emma*, ch. 41.

133 *Encyclopaedia* (1, 58), p. 301.

134 William Lovett, *Chartism: a New Organization of the People* (1840), Leicester, 1969, p. 100.

135 Quentin Bell, *Victorian Artists*, London, 1975, p. 43.

136 *North and South*, ch. 13.

137 *Mary Barton*, ch. 6.

138 *North and South*, ch. 10.

139 *London Labour and the London Poor* (3, 89), vol. I, p. 47.

140 Sir Walter Scott, *The Antiquary*, ch. 26.

141 See pp. 6–7.

142 James Joyce, *A Portrait of the Artist as a Young Man*, ch. 4.

143 Jane Austen, *Mansfield Park*, ch. 46.

144 Thomas Hardy, *Under the Greenwood Tree* (1872), part II, ch. 6.

145 Thomas Hardy, *The Trumpet Major* (1880), ch. 16.

146 D. H. Lawrence, *Sons and Lovers* (1913), ch. 2.

147   *Rural Rides*, 10 August 1823.
148   *Sybil*, bk III, ch. 8.
149   Benjamin Disraeli, *Coningsby*, bk IV, ch. 3.
150   William Morris, *Hopes and Fears for Art* (1877–81), *Collected Works*, vol. XXII, New York, 1966, p. 71.
151   Quoted in *Five Per Cent Philanthropy* (3, 101), p. 149.
152   *Lectures on Art and Industry* (1, 74), pp. 375–6.
153   Joseph Conrad, *The Secret Agent* (1907), ch.3.
154   *Dombey and Son*, ch. 15.
155   ibid.
156   John Ruskin, *The Seven Lamps of Architecture* (1849), 'The Lamp of Memory', section 3.
157   Charles Dickens, *David Copperfield* (1849–50), ch. 3.
158   D. H. Lawrence, *The Rainbow* (1915), ch. 11.
159   *The Seven Lamps of Architecture*, 'The Lamp of Memory', section 3.
160   Lord Salisbury, 'Labourers' and Artisans' Dwellings', 1883, reprinted in Andrew Mearns, *The Bitter Cry of Outcast London*, Leicester, 1969, p. 114.
161   *Sons and Lovers*, ch. 1.
162   *Emma*, ch. 4.
163   George Eliot, *Felix Holt*, ch. 27.
164   See Crispin Paine and John Rhodes, *The Worker's Home, Small Houses in Oxfordshire through Three Centuries*, Oxfordshire Museums Service, Publication no. 10, Oxford, 1979, p. 27.
165   See pp. 200–28.
166   John Ruskin, 'The cottage', ch. 4. of *The Poetry of Architecture*, 1892, reprinted from *Architectural Magazine* 1837–8.
167   ibid., ch. 5.
168   See p. 221.
169   See pp. 27, 217–19.
170   See p. 26 and Fig. 61b.
171   George Eliot, *Scenes of Clerical Life*, 'Mr Gilfil's love-story', ch. 19.
172   William Morris, *News from Nowhere*, ch. 2.
173   *Lectures on Art and Industry* (1, 74), pp. 375–6.
174   *The Secret Agent*, ch. 13.
175   *Middlemarch*, ch. 55.

4   Stories in stone

1   Thomas Hardy, *Far from the Madding Crowd* (1874), ch. 9.
2   John Milton, *Il Penseroso*, ll. 12, 16.
3   Florence Emily Hardy, *The Life of Thomas Hardy 1840–1928*, 1962, 1975 reprint with corrections, London, 1975, p. 284. The *Life* is substantially the work of Hardy, not his second wife.
4   Mrs Gaskell, *Cousin Phillis*, part I.
5   Emily Brontë, *Wuthering Heights*, ch. 1.
6   *Life of Thomas Hardy* (4, 3), p. 116.
7   ibid., p. 114.

8   Thomas Hardy, *The Trumpet Major*, ch. 3.
9   Thomas Hardy, 'One who Married above Him', in *Human Shows* (1925).
10 Thomas Hardy, 'The Self-Unseeing', in *Poems of the Past and the Present* (1902).
11 Thomas Hardy, 'On an Invitation to the United States', in *Poems of the Past and the Present*.
12 Thomas Hardy, *Tess of the d'Urbervilles* (1891), ch. 50.
13 Thomas Hardy, 'Starlings on the Roof', in *Satires of Circumstance, Lyrics and Reveries* (1914).
14 *Life of Thomas Hardy* (4, 3), p. 254.
15 Thomas Hardy, 'The Strange House (Max Gate AD 2000)', in *Late Lyrics and Earlier* (1922).
16 *Far from the Madding Crowd*, ch. 35.
17 Winifred Gérin, *Emily Bronte*, London, 1971, pp. 82–4, 224–5.
18 Winifred Gérin, *Elizabeth Gaskell*, London, 1976, pp. 11–12.
19 *The Trumpet Major*, ch. 6.
20 *Tess of the d'Urbervilles*, ch. 34.
21 ibid., addition of 1895 to the Preface to the fifth and subsequent editions.
22 *The Trumpet Major*, ch. 6.
23 *Far from the Madding Crowd*, ch. 35.
24 Fanny Burney, *Cecilia*, bk VI, ch. 1.
25 Thomas Hardy, *The Hand of Ethelberta*, ch. 38.
26 In *The Genius of the Place* (1, 3), pp. 208–9.
27 Thomas Hardy, *The Woodlanders*, ch. 5.
28 Daniel Defoe, *Tour Through the Whole Island of Great Britain*, Letter 1.
29 ibid., Letter 8.
30 Tobias Smollett, *Humphrey Clinker*, Letter to Dr Lewes, Scarborough, July 4.
31 ibid.
32 ibid.
33 *Lectures on Architecture* (1, 10), p. 49.
34 ibid., p. 50.
35 ibid., p. 51.
36 Sir John Clerk of Penicuik, 'The country seat' (1731), in *The Genius of the Place* (1, 3), p. 203.
37 *Designs for Cottages* (3, 40), Introduction, p. v.
38 Sir Walter Scott, *The Antiquary*, ch. 3.
39 *Rural Residences* (1, 27), pp. 41–2.
40 *An Enquiry into the Changes of Taste in Landscape Gardening* (2, 40), p. 4.
41 See p. 40.
42 In *The Genius of the Place* (1, 3), p. 121.
43 ibid., editor's note, p. 119.
44 *Lectures on Architecture* (1, 25), p. 154.
45 *The Antiquary*, ch. 16.
46 Charles Eastlake, *A History of the Gothic Revival* (1872), Leicester, 1970, p. 60.
47 A. W. N. Pugin, *Contrasts*, 1841 edition, p. 38.
48 *A History of the Gothic Revival* (4, 46), pp. 112–13.
49 Sir Walter Scott, *Woodstock* (1826), ch. 1.
50 Sir Walter Scott, *Waverley*, ch. 39.

51 Kenneth Clark, *The Gothic Revival*, 1928, Harmondsworth, 1964, p. 58.
52 Sir Walter Scott, *The Betrothed*, ch. 1.
53 ibid., ch. 13.
54 Sir Walter Scott, *Rob Roy*, ch. 18.
55 Sir Walter Scott, *The Heart of Midlothian*, ch. 30.
56 Sir Walter Scott, *The Pirate*, ch. 31.
57 *A History of the Gothic Revival* (4, 46), p. 89.
58 ibid., p. 137.
59 See pp. 143–4.
60 *Contrasts* (4, 47), p. 43.
61 Charles Dickens, 'The Haunted House' (1859), a short story in two chapters, ch. 1.
62 Mrs Gaskell, *Ruth*, ch. 1.
63 Henry Shaw, *Specimens of Ancient Furniture*, London, 1836, p. 2.
64 ibid., p. 40.
65 Hieronymus Bosch, *The Seven Deadly Sins*, 1475–80; Caxton presenting his Recuyell of the Histories of Troy to Margaret, Duchess of Burgundy, engraving attributed to the Master of Mary of Burgundy, c. 1474.
66 *Hints on Household Taste* (1, 76), p. 161.
67 Benjamin Disraeli, *Sybil*, bk IV, ch. 5.
68 George Eliot, *Romola*, ch. 5.
69 See p. 27.
70 George Eliot, *Felix Holt*, ch. 28.
71 *Rob Roy*, ch. 10.
72 Sir Walter Scott, *Old Mortality*, ch. 38.
73 *Romola*, ch. 3.
74 George Eliot, *The Mill on the Floss*, bk I, ch. 12.
75 John Ruskin, *The Seven Lamps of Architecture*, Preface to the 2nd edn, 1855.
76 ibid.
77 *Rob Roy*, ch. 19.
78 John Ruskin, *Lectures on Architecture and Painting*, 1854 (delivered 1853), Lecture I.
79 *Cecilia*, bk VI, ch. 1.
80 *Pamela* (1, 4), p. 92.
81 See p. 13.
82 Mrs Radcliffe, *The Mysteries of Udolpho*, ch. 35.
83 See p. 46.
84 *The Genius of the Place* (1, 3), p. 361.
85 Jane Austen, *Northanger Abbey*, ch. 11.
86 Thomas Love Peacock, *Nightmare Abbey*, ch. 1.
87 Wilkie Collins, *The Woman in White*, Second Epoch, ch. 1.
88 Joseph Sheridan LeFanu, *Uncle Silas*, ch. 42.
89 *The World of Charles Dickens* (2, 5), pp. 192–4.
90 Charles Dickens, *Little Dorrit*, bk I, ch. 5.
91 See p. 22.
92 Charles Dickens, *David Copperfield*, ch. 15.
93 Charles Dickens, *The Mystery of Edwin Drood*, ch. 2.
94 ibid., ch. 6.
95 ibid., ch. 18.

96 ibid., ch. 6.
97 Included in Thomas Hardy, *Wessex Poems and Other Verses* (1898).
98 Thomas Hardy, *Desperate Remedies*, ch. 13, section iii.
99 ibid., ch. 5, section i.
100 Thomas Hardy, *A Laodicean*, bk VI, ch. 1.
101 Thomas Hardy, *A Pair of Blue Eyes*, ch. 31.
102 ibid.
103 *The Life of Thomas Hardy* (4, 3), p. 79.
104 John Ruskin, *The Seven Lamps of Architecture*, 'The Lamp of Memory', section 19.
105 ibid., section 2.
106 *The Life of Thomas Hardy* (4, 3), p. 191.
107 *A Laodicean*, chs 1, 3, 14.
108 Thomas Hardy, *Jude the Obscure*, part II, ch. 2.
109 *A Pair of Blue Eyes*, ch. 4.
110 *The Trumpet Major*, ch. 34.
111 Charlotte Brontë, *Jane Eyre*, ch. 11.
112 Charlotte Brontë, *Shirley*, ch. 11.
113 *Wuthering Heights*, ch. 6.
114 See pp. 112, 219–21.
115 Thomas Hardy, *The Return of the Native*, bk II, ch. 6.
116 *Wuthering Heights*, ch. 1.
117 Mrs Gaskell, *Sylvia's Lovers*, ch. 12.
118 *Wuthering Heights*, ch. 32.
119 Vita Sackville-West, *The Edwardians*, ch. 2.
120 Mrs Humphry Ward, *Helbeck of Bannisdale*, ch. 4.
121 George Eliot, *Adam Bede*, ch. 6.
122 *Cousin Phillis*, part I.
123 *The Return of the Native*, bk II, ch. 6.
124 Laura Thompson, *Lark Rise to Candleford* (1939), ch. 27.
125 *Adam Bede*, ch. 17.
126 George Eliot, *Middlemarch*, ch. 9.
127 ibid., ch. 28.
128 Charles Dickens, *Nicholas Nickleby*, ch. 51.
129 Charles Dickens, *Master Humphrey's Clock* (1840–1), ch. 1.
130 *Adam Bede*, ch. 6.
131 *Cousin Phillis*, part I.
132 *The Trumpet Major*, ch. 2.
133 *Desperate Remedies*, ch. 8 section iii.
134 *Jude the Obscure*, part III, ch. 2.
135 George Eliot, *Daniel Deronda*, ch. 35.
136 W. Curtis Green, *Old Cottages and Farm Houses in Surrey*, London, 1908, p. 1.
137 H. S. Goodhart-Rendel, 'English Gothic architecture of the nineteenth century', *Journal of the RIBA*, vol. XXXI, no. 11, 1924, p. 322.
138 William Cobbett, *Rural Rides*, 20 October 1825.
139 *Wuthering Heights*, ch. 1.
140 *Lark Rise to Candleford*, ch. 6.
141 Karl Marx and Friedrich Engels, *Manifesto of the Communist Party*, part I.

142   *Town Swamps and Social Bridges* (3, 75), p. 46.
143   William Morris, *A Dream of John Ball*, ch. 2.
144   William Morris, *News from Nowhere*, ch. 9.
145   *The Life of Thomas Hardy* (4, 3), p. 331.
146   *The Trumpet Major*, ch. 16.
147   *The Life of Thomas Hardy* (4, 3), p. 352.
148   'A Man', in *Poems of the Past and the Present*.

5   Mrs Gereth's immorality

 1   See pp. 222–7.
 2   Leon Edel, *The Life of Henry James*, Harmondsworth, 1977, vol. I, p. 756.
 3   Letter to A. C. Benson, quoted in *The Life of Henry James* (5, 2), vol. II, p. 243. The door is 9 feet high.
 4   H. G. Wells, *Experiment in Autobiography*, 1934, ch. 8, section ii.
 5   Henry James, *The Spoils of Poynton*, Preface to vol. X of the New York edition.
 6   ibid.
 7   ibid.
 8   *The Spoils of Poynton*, ch. 2.
 9   Letter from James to the Keeper of the Wallace Collection, quoted in Leon Edel's Introduction to *The Spoils of Poynton*, London, 1967, p. 22.
10   *The Spoils of Poynton*, Preface to vol. X of the New York edition.
11   *The Spoils of Poynton*, ch. 1.
12   ibid.
13   ibid.
14   John Ruskin, *The Crown of Wild Olive*, 1866, Lecture II.
15   *The Spoils of Poynton*, ch. 6.
16   ibid., ch. 12.
17   See pp. 5–6.
18   Lord Shaftesbury, *Characteristics of Men, Manners, Opinions and Times* (1711), Treatise VI, Miscellany III, ch. 2.
19   Humphrey Repton, *Fragments on the Theory of Landscape Gardening* (1816), quoted in *The Genius of the Place* (1, 3), p. 372.
20   *Characteristics*, Treatise VI, Miscellany III, ch. 1.
21   Alexander Pope, *An Essay on Criticism* (1711), ll. 69, 89, 73.
22   *Pamela* (1, 4), vol. II, p. 91.
23   *Clarissa* (1, 1), vol. IV, p. 500.
24   *The History of Sir Charles Grandison* (1, 7), part III, p. 95.
25   See *Hints for Picturesque Improvements in Ornamental Cottages* (3, 55), p. 82.
26   John Plaw, *Rural Architecture or Designs from the Simple Cottage to the Decorated Villa* (1802), Farnborough, 1971, p. 3.
27   *An Analytical Inquiry into the Principles of Taste* (3, 31), p. 100.
28   *An Enquiry into the Changes of Taste in Landscape Gardening* (2, 40), pp. 47–8.
29   Jane Austen, *Mansfield Park*, ch. 22.
30   Jane Austen, *Persuasion*, ch. 10.
31   Henry Fielding, *Joseph Andrews* (1742), bk II, ch. 14.
32   See *The English House* (1, 6), pp. 163–5.

33 *The Crown of Wild Olive*, Lecture II.
34 *Mansfield Park*, ch. 25.
35 Jane Austen, *Sense and Sensibility*, ch. 42.
36 Alexander Pope, Fourth Moral Essay, ll. 99–104.
37 *An Analytical Enquiry into the Principles of Taste* (3, 31), p. 180.
38 Tobias Smollett, *The Adventures of Peregrine Pickle* (1751), ch. 105.
39 Mrs Radcliffe, *The Mysteries of Udolpho*, ch. 2.
40 Jane Austen, *Emma*, for example ch. 33.
41 Jane Austen, *Pride and Prejudice*, ch. 28.
42 Jane Austen, *Sanditon*, ch. 1.
43 ibid., ch. 8.
44 ibid., ch. 3.
45 ibid.
46 ibid., ch. 12.
47 Thomas Love Peacock, *Headlong Hall*, ch. 10.
48 *The Gentleman's House* (2, 129), pp. 340–1.
49 ibid., p. 342.
50 J. J. Stevenson, *House Architecture*, London, 1880, vol. I, p. 9.
51 *An Apology for the Revival of Christian Architecture* (2, 65), p. 1.
52 John Ruskin, *The Seven Lamps of Architecture*, 'The Lamp of Obedience', section 4.
53 *The Crown of Wild Olive*, Lecture II.
54 See pp. 16–18.
55 *Victorian Artists* (3, 135), p. 4.
56 Rosamund Watson, *The Art of the House*, London, 1897, p. 151.
57 Wilkie Collins, *The Moonstone*, The Story, First Period, ch. 8.
58 George Eliot, *Daniel Deronda*, ch. 12.
59 *The Spoils of Poynton*, ch. 3.
60 ibid., ch. 4.
61 G— L—, *The Science of Taste* (1879), quoted in Jerome Hamilton Buckley, *The Victorian Temper: a Study in Literary Culture*, Cambridge, Mass., 1951, p. 134.
62 *Hints on Household Taste* (1, 76), p. 51.
63 John Gloag, *Victorian Taste*, London, 1962, pp. 151–3.
64 C. J. Richardson, *Picturesque Designs for Mansions, Villas, Lodges, &c., &c.*, London, 1870, pp. 94–6.
65 *Hints on Household Taste* (1, 76), p. 52.
66 *Victorian Taste* (5, 63), p. 154.
67 *Hints on Household Taste* (1, 76), pp. 73–4.
68 ibid., p. 14.
69 Edith Wharton and Ogden Codman Jr., *The Decoration of Houses*, New York, 1897, p. 101.
70 *The Art of the House* (5, 56), p. 53.
71 *Victorian Taste* (5, 63), p. 155.
72 George Eliot, *Middlemarch*, ch. 60.
73 Henry James, *The Princess Casamassima*, ch. 4.
74 John Gloag, *Victorian Comfort* (1963), Newton Abbot, 1973, p. 105.
75 *Hints on Household Taste* (1, 76), p. 97.
76 *Middlemarch*, ch. 60.

77 William Makepeace Thackeray, *The Newcomes* (1853–5), ch. 14.
78 Letter from Jane Carlyle to Jeannie Welsh, 17 May 1849.
79 Charles Dickens, *Our Mutual Friend*, ch. 2.
80 Benjamin Disraeli, *Tancred* (1847), bk II, ch. 14.
81 *Hints on Household Taste* (1, 76), p. 289.
82 William Makepeace Thackeray, *Pendennis*, ch. 37.
83 *The Art of the House* (5, 56), p. 97.
84 D. H. Lawrence, *The Rainbow*, ch. 14.
85 *Tancred*, bk II, ch. 10.
86 *The Decoration of Houses* (5, 69), pp. 33–4.
87 *The Seven Lamps of Architecture*, ch. 1, section vii.
88 ibid., ch. 2, section xvi.
89 ibid., ch. 3, section xxiv.
90 ibid., ch. 4, section xii.
91 ibid., ch. 5, section xxiv.
92 ibid., ch. 6, section iii.
93 ibid., ch. 7, passim.
94 See p. 23.
95 Letter to Jeannie Welsh, 17 May 1849.
96 Charles Dickens, *Dombey and Son*, ch. 8.
97 *Our Mutual Friend*, bk I, ch. 7.
98 Letter to Cassandra, 6 June 1811.
99 *Hints on Household Taste* (1, 76), p. 48.
100 Charles Dickens, *Hard Times*, bk I, ch. 2.
101 *Dombey and Son*, ch. 33.
102 ibid.
103 George Eliot, *The Mill on the Floss*, bk II, ch. 1.
104 *Hints for Picturesque Improvements* (3, 55), p. 60.
105 Thomas Love Peacock, *Crotchet Castle*, ch. 1.
106 Mrs Gaskell, *North and South*, ch. 21.
107 ibid., ch. 20.
108 *Our Mutual Friend*, bk I, ch. 11.
109 John Galsworthy, *The Man of Property* (1906), ch. 2.
110 ibid., ch. 3.
111 *The Ideal City* (3, 110), p. 58.
112 *North and South*, ch. 7.
113 Mrs Gaskell, *Ruth*, ch. 19.
114 *Daniel Deronda*, ch. 18.
115 Anthony Trollope, *The Last Chronicle of Barset* (1867), ch. 4.
116 The case of those middle-class characters who are reduced to indigence is a different matter, see pp. 107–8.
117 See p. 112.
118 *Pride and Prejudice*, ch. 30.
119 *The Oxford Illustrated Jane Austen* (2, 78), p. 355.
120 Letter to Cassandra, 16 September 1813.
121 William Cobbett, *Rural Rides*, 20 October 1825.

122 Quoted in E. J. T. Collins, *Victorian Rural England*, Victorian Society Third Conference Report, 1965, p. 9.
123 Mrs Gaskell, *Wives and Daughters*, ch. 16.
124 Harriet Martineau, *Deerbrook*, ch. 1.
125 Charles Dickens, *Great Expectations*, ch. 4.
126 *The Mill on the Floss*, bk I, ch. 9.
127 George Moore, *Esther Waters*, ch. 20.
128 Wilkie Collins, *The Woman in White*, Third Epoch, ch. 8.
129 *House Architecture* (5, 50), vol. II, p. 59.
130 *North and South*, ch. 20.
131 ibid., ch. 15.
132 *Ruth*, ch. 17.
133 ibid., ch. 19.
134 Mrs Gaskell, *Mary Barton*, ch. 18.
135 ibid., ch. 2.
136 ibid., ch. 6.
137 *North and South*, ch. 37.
138 ibid., ch. 10.
139 *Encyclopaedia* (1, 58), p. 799.
140 Charles Dickens, *Bleak House*, ch. 13.
141 *Encyclopaedia* (1, 58), p. 799.
142 Charles Dickens, *Nicholas Nickleby*, ch. 46.
143 *Daniel Deronda*, ch. 39.
144 See pp. 52, 82–3, 94, 98–9
145 Charles Kingsley, *Two Years Ago*, ch. 14.
146 *Bleak House*, ch. 4.
147 Sir Walter Scott, *Guy Mannering* (1815), ch. 25.
148 Charlotte Brontë, *The Professor* (1857, but written 1846), ch. 19.
149 Mrs Gaskell, *Cousin Phillis*, part I.
150 ibid., part II.
151 *Hints on Household Taste* (1, 76), p. 106.
152 See p. 23.
153 *Victorian Taste* (5, 63), p. 7.
154 Charles Dickens, *Pickwick Papers*, ch. 12.
155 ibid., ch. 57.
156 Charles Dickens, *David Copperfield*, ch. 20.
157 George Eliot, *Felix Holt*, ch. 1.
158 Arnold Bennett, *Clayhanger* (1910), bk II, ch. 7, section ii.
159 Charlotte Brontë, *Shirley*, ch. 3.
160 ibid., ch. 4.
161 *Mansfield Park*, ch. 16.
162 See p. 179.
163 *The Mill on the Floss*, bk II, ch. 1.
164 ibid.
165 ibid., bk III, ch. 9.
166 ibid., bk IV, ch. 2.

167 See p. 259.
168 *The Spoils of Poynton*, ch. 3.
169 Vernon Lee, *A Phantom Lover*, ch. 2.
170 *Hopes and Fears for Art* (3, 150), p. 48.
171 ibid., p. 24.
172 ibid., p. 113.
173 ibid., p. 76.
174 ibid., p. 113.
175 A. W. N. Pugin, *The True Principles of Pointed or Christian Architecture*, London, 1841, p. 40.
176 Quoted by John Betjeman, *A Pictorial History of English Architecture*, London, 1970, p. 89.
177 Oscar Wilde, *The Picture of Dorian Grey* (1890), ch. 1.
178 ibid., ch. 2.
179 *Hopes and Fears for Art* (3, 150), p. 76.
180 *Our Mutual Friend*, bk I, ch. 5.
181 Matthew Arnold, *Culture and Anarchy*; title of ch. 2.
182 ibid.; title of ch. 1.
183 William Makepeace Thackeray, *The Adventures of Philip*, vol. I, ch. 16.
184 *The Gentleman's House* (2, 129), p. 368.
185 George Meredith, *The Egoist*, ch. 16.
186 E. M. Forster, *The Longest Journey* (1907), ch. 2.
187 ibid.
188 ibid., ch. 3.
189 John Galsworthy, *In Chancery* (1920), ch. 12.
190 In Ford Madox Ford, *Some Do Not* (1924).
191 In Henry James, *The Ambassadors* (1903).
192 E. M. Forster, *Howards End*, ch. 18.
193 ibid.
194 *The Spoils of Poynton*, ch. 1.
195 E. M. Forster, *A Room with a View*, ch. 8.
196 ibid., ch. 18.
197 ibid.
198 ibid., ch. 17.
199 George Eliot, 'Janet's Repentance', ch. 11, in *Scenes of Clerical Life*.
200 ibid.
201 *The Princess Casamassima*, ch. 36.
202 *A Room with a View*, ch. 13.
203 *The Spoils of Poynton*, ch. 5.
204 ibid.
205 ibid., ch. 21.
206 ibid.
207 ibid.
208 William Morris, *Signs of Change* (1885–6), Collected Works, vol. XXIII, New York, 1966, p. 94.

6 Barton Cottage and the 'perfect pastoral'

1 George Eliot, *Daniel Deronda*, ch. 18.
2 Letter to Catherine Winkworth, 21 August 1849.
3 Letter to Eliza Fox, 29 May 1849.
4 Charles Dickens, *Little Dorrit*, part II, ch. 13.
5 Jane Austen, *Sense and Sensibility*, ch. 6.
6 *Daniel Deronda*, ch. 21.
7 *Sense and Sensibility*, ch. 33.
8 ibid., ch. 19.
9 ibid., ch. 14.
10 George Eliot, *Middlemarch*, ch. 12.
11 For example, John Vanbrugh, *The Relapse* (1696).
12 Tobias Smollett, *Humphrey Clinker*, Letter to Dr Lewis, London, 8 June.
13 See p. 1.
14 *Rural Residences* (1, 27), p. 89.
15 *Pamela* (1, 4), vol. I, pp. 431–41.
16 John Plaw, *Ferme Ornée or Rural Improvements* (1795), Farnborough, 1972, note to Plate 8.
17 Jane Austen, *Mansfield Park*, ch. 6. (Mary Crawford disparages the proximity of the farm-yard); ch. 7 (she poses at the window against a natural background).
18 See pp. 73–8.
19 Oliver Goldsmith, *The Vicar of Wakefield*, ch. 4.
20 Henry Fielding, *Tom Jones*, bk VIII, ch. 10.
21 Henry Fielding, *Joseph Andrews*, bk III, chs 2–4.
22 Richard Payne Knight, *The Landscape*, bk I, ll. 225–44; bk II, ll. 1–76, 288–93.
23 *An Essay on British Cottage Architecture* (3, 29), p. 5.
24 W. F. Pocock, *Architectural Designs for Rustic Cottages, Picturesque Dwellings, Villas &c.* (1807), Farnborough, 1972, p. 8.
25 *An Essay on British Cottage Architecture* (3, 29), pp. 5–6.
26 T. D. W. Dearn, *Sketches in Architecture* (1807), Farnborough, 1971, p. 9.
27 *Rural Residences* (1, 27), pp. 48–52.
28 *Hints for Picturesque Improvements in Ornamented Cottages* (3, 55), pp. 6–12.
29 Quoted in Terence Davis, *The Architecture of John Nash*, London, 1960, p. 25.
30 See *The Victorian Country House* (2, 67), p. 53.
31 Quoted in Robert Blake, *Disraeli* (1966), London, 1978, p. 298.
32 Samuel Taylor Coleridge and Robert Southey, 'The Devil's Thoughts' (1799), ll. 21–4.
33 *Humphrey Clinker*, Letter to Dr Lewis, Cameron, 6 September.
34 Laurence Sterne, 'The Supper', in *A Sentimental Journey* (1768).
35 Dr Johnson, *Rasselas* (1759), ch. 19.
36 ibid., ch. 21.
37 *Sketches in Architecture* (6, 26), p. 2.
38 Mrs Radcliffe, *The Mysteries of Udolpho*, ch. 8.
39 Fanny Burney, *Camilla*, bk IV, ch. 2.
40 Sir Walter Scott, *Guy Mannering*, ch. 21.
41 *The Oxford Illustrated Jane Austen* (2, 78), pp. 176–8.
42 Jane Austen, *Sanditon*, chs 3, 4.

43   *Sense and Sensibility*, ch. 50.
44   ibid., ch. 36.
45   ibid.
46   ibid., ch. 37.
47   Jane Austen, *Persuasion*, ch. 14.
48   Letter to Cassandra, 5 May 1801.
49   Mary Crawford in *Mansfield Park*; Lady Susan in the epistolary novel, *Lady Susan*, written c. 1793–4, in *The Oxford Illustrated Jane Austen* (2, 78), pp. 245–6.
50   Jane Austen, *Northanger Abbey*, ch. 15.
51   *Mansfield Park*, ch. 38.
52   See p. 13.
53   Jane Austen, *Pride and Prejudice*, ch. 29.
54   *Little Dorrit*, part I, ch. 16.
55   Charles Dickens, *The Old Curiosity Shop*, ch. 22.
56   Charles Dickens, *Great Expectations*, ch. 25; see p. 23.
57   Charles Dickens, *Dombey and Son*, ch. 33; see pp. 178–9.
58   See pp. 206–8.
59   Charles Dickens, *Barnaby Rudge*, ch. 4.
60   E. M. Forster, *Howards End*, ch. 3.
61   Anthony Trollope, *Can You Forgive Her?*, ch. 14.
62   Anthony Trollope, *Orley Farm* (1862), ch. 2.
63   Anthony Trollope, *An Autobiography*, ch. 1.
64   *Orley Farm*, ch. 1.
65   ibid.
66   *An Autobiography*, ch. 20.
67   See pp. 27, 150.
68   John Ruskin, *The Stones of Venice* (1851–3), vol. II, ch. 6, section xlvi.
69   George Eliot, *Adam Bede*, ch. 17.
70   *Sense and Sensibility*, ch. 18.
71   William Lethaby, in *Arts and Crafts Essays* (1, 84), p. 307.
72   D. H. Lawrence, *The White Peacock*, part II, ch. 7.
73   ibid., part III, ch. 8.
74   ibid.
75   *Life in the English Country House* (2, 19), p. 303.
76   In Charles Kingsley, *Yeast*.
77   Quoted in P. N. Furbank, *E. M. Forster: a Life*, Cambridge, 1977, vol. I, p. 16.
78   *Howards End*, ch. 15.
79   ibid., ch. 1.
80   ibid., ch. 33.
81   Charlotte Brontë, *Jane Eyre*, ch. 28.
82   Quoted in *E. M. Foster: A Life* (6, 77), p. 16.
83   Quoted in *Disraeli* (6, 31), p. 410.
84   See p. 120.
85   See Marghanita Laski, *George Eliot and her World*, London, 1973, p. 109.
86   See p. 129.
87   Letter to M. de Cerjat, 7 July 1858.
88   *The World of Charles Dickens* (2, 5), p. 259.

89 Quoted in ibid., p. 257.
90 See ch. 23, 'The Perfect Plan', in *Elizabeth Gaskell* (4, 18),.
91 Letter to Frances Austin, 26 July 1809.
92 William Cobbett, *Rural Rides*, 30 September 1826.
93 *Lectures on Art and Industry* (1, 74), p. 261.
94 See Stefan Muthesius, *The English Terraced House*, New Haven, Conn., and London, 1982, Introduction, p. ix.

7   Immaterial walls

1   See pp. 13, 16–19.
2   See pp. 5–7.
3   Quoted in *Samuel Richardson: a Biography* (1, 5), p. 389.
4   ibid.
5   ibid., pp. 244, 103.
6   Letter to Aaron Hill, 1 February 1741.
7   *The History of Sir Charles Grandison* (1, 7), part III, pp. 114–15.
8   ibid., p. 269.
9   Anthony Trollope, *The Duke's Children*, chs 22, 25.
10 Anthony Trollope, *An Autobiography*, ch. 11. Descriptions of ancient houses form an exception to this rule.
11 *Samuel Richardson: a Biography* (1, 5), p. 498.
12 ibid., pp. 231, 449–50.
13 Letter from Samuel Richardson to John Duncombe, 24 August 1754.
14 Letter to Aaron Hill, 1 February 1741.
15 *Pamela* (1, 4), vol. II, p. 295.
16 See pp. 131–4.
17 Charlotte Brontë, *Jane Eyre*, ch. 11.
18 William Wycherley, *The Country Wife* (1695), IV, iii.
19 *Pamela* (1, 4), vol. I, p. 64.
20 Daniel Defoe, *A Journal of the Plague Year* (1722), Everyman, London, 1908, p. 59.
21 ibid., p. 126.
22 *Lectures on Architecture* (1, 10), p. 64.
23 Retrospective comment in William Lethaby, *Architecture, Nature and Magic*, 1956 edn, p. 15, on his theme in *Architecture, Mysticism and Myth*, 1891; quoted in the Architectural Press edition of the latter, London, 1974, p. 273.
24 Jane Austen, *Pride and Prejudice*, ch. 22.
25 Harriet Martineau, *Deerbrook*, ch. 14.
26 William Makepeace Thackeray, *Lovel the Widower*, ch. 2.
27 *Victorian Artists* (3, 135), p. 60.
28 Anthony Trollope, *Doctor Thorne*, ch. 21.
29 In Joseph Conrad, *Tales of Unrest* (1898).
30 Oscar Wilde, 'The Decay of Lying', in *Intentions* (1891).
31 Charles Dickens, *The Mystery of Edwin Drood*, ch. 22.
32 Henry James, *The Golden Bowl*, ch. 2.
33 ibid., ch. 7.
34 ibid.

35 ibid., ch. 10.
36 ibid.
37 Henry James, *The Tragic Muse*, ch. 32.
38 Charles Dickens, *Our Mutual Friend*, ch. 2.
39 See p. 151.
40 Charles Dickens, *Bleak House*, ch. 37.
41 Henry James, *The Portrait of a Lady*, ch. 19.
42 ibid., ch. 26.
43 E. M. Forster, *The Longest Journey*, ch. 17.
44 ibid., ch. 3.
45 ibid., ch. 6.
46 Sigmund Freud, *The Psychopathology of Everyday Life* (1901), ch. 9. The quotation from Sterne was inserted in 1920.
47 Laurence Sterne, *Tristram Shandy*, bk VI, ch. 5.
48 Sigmund Freud, *Introductory Lectures on Psychoanalysis* (1915–17), Lecture 10.
49 *Palladio* (1, 12), p. 54.
50 Quoted in *Life in the English Country House* (2, 19), p. 122.
51 *Introductory Lectures on Psychoanalysis*, Lecture 10.
52 E. M. Forster, *Howards End*, ch. 5.
53 See pp. 151–2.
54 Thomas Hardy, *Tess of the d'Urbevilles*, ch. 50.
55 ibid.
56 Quoted in *Samuel Richardson: a Biography* (1, 5), p. 449.
57 *The Gentleman's House* (2, 129), pp. 321–4.
58 John Ruskin, *Sesame and Lilies*, Lecture II, Section iii.
59 *Introductory Lectures on Psychoanalysis*, Lecture 10.
60 Sigmund Freud, *The Interpretation of Dreams* (1900), ch. 6, D.
61 Henry Fielding, *Tom Jones*, bk I, ch. 4.
62 *The Interpretation of Dreams*, ch. 6, D.
63 *Pamela* (1, 4), vol. I, pp. 131–3.
64 *Clarissa* (1, 1), vol. I, pp. 446–7, 484–5.
65 See p. 4.
66 *Pamela* (1, 4), vol. I, pp. 11–12.
67 ibid., p. 426.
68 ibid., p. 313.
69 Letter from Jane Austen to Cassandra, 2 December 1815.
70 *Pride and Prejudice*, ch. 43.
71 Jane Austen, *Mansfield Park*, ch. 10.
72 *The Elements of Architecture* (1, 9), part I, 'Of Doors and Windows'.
73 *Mansfield Park*, ch. 9.
74 *Introductory Lectures on Psychoanalysis*, Lecture 10.
75 *Clarissa* (1, 1), vol. III, p. 287.
76 ibid., pp. 210–11.
77 See p. 59.
78 Henry James, *The Other House*, ch. 28.
79 ibid., ch. 2.
80 *The Elements of Architecture* (1, 9), part I, 'Of Doors and Windows'.

81 *Clarissa* (1, 1), vol. III, p. 227.
82 Jane Austen, *Emma*, ch. 34.
83 *Mansfield Park*, ch. 11.
84 E. M. Forster, *A Room with a View*, ch. 15.
85 *Pride and Prejudice*, ch. 43.
86 *Mansfield Park*, ch. 9.
87 *Emma*, ch. 48.
88 ibid., ch. 49.
89 Jane Austen, *Northanger Abbey*, ch. 29.
90 Letter to J. Edward Austen, 9 July 1816.
91 See p. 13.
92 Emily Brontë, *Wuthering Heights*, ch. 6.
93 Sigmund Freud, *Case Histories I*, 'Little Hans' (1909), ch. 2.
94 *Our Mutual Friend*, bk II, ch. 7.
95 Charles Dickens, *Dombey and Son*, ch. 18.
96 In the volume of short stories of that name, published as a collection 1913.
97 *Dombey and Son*, ch. 53.
98 *Mansfield Park*, ch. 33.
99 Letter to Cassandra, 6 November 1813.
100 ibid.
101 *The World of Charles Dickens* (2, 5), p. 146.
102 F. R. Leavis, *The Great Tradition* (1948), Harmondsworth, 1966, p. 29.
103 Henry James, *The Wings of the Dove*, bk. I, ch. 2.
104 Ford Madox Ford, *The Good Soldier*, part I, ch. 2.
105 *Dombey and Son*, ch. 18.
106 *Architecture, Mysticism and Myth* (7, 23), p. 81.
107 Sir Isaac Ware, *A Complete Body of Architecture*, London, 1756, bk III, p. 328.
108 See Girouard's account of the 'axis of honour', in *Life in the English Country House* (2, 19), pp. 145–6.
109 *Pamela* (1, 4), vol. I, pp. 79, 259–62.
110 *Clarissa* (1, 1), pp. 68, 69.
111 ibid., vol. III, p. 269.
112 *The History of Sir Charles Grandison* (1, 7), part II, p. 66.
113 See p. 12.
114 *Mansfield Park*, ch. 7.
115 Jane Austen, *Sense and Sensibility*, ch. 39.
116 Given in R. W. Chapman (ed.), *The Oxford Illustrated Jane Austen*, London, 1923, vol. V, pp. 258–68.
117 See pp. 60–1.
118 See pp. 178–90.
119 *The Wings of the Dove*, bk II, ch. 2.
120 *The Interpretation of Dreams*, ch. 6, E, addition of 1909.
121 *A Complete Body of Architecture* (7, 107), bk III, p. 328.
122 Letter to Cassandra, 17 May 1799; letter to Cassandra, 24 January 1809.
123 *Pamela* (1, 4), vol. I, p. 64.
124 ibid., p. 47.
125 ibid., p. 68.

126 *The History of Sir Charles Grandison* (1, 7), part III, p. 271.
127 *Pamela* (1, 4), vol. I, pp. 173, 175.
128 ibid., p. 316.
129 ibid., p. 425.
130 *Clarissa* (1, 1), vol. II, p. 199.
131 ibid., vol. IV, p. 87.
132 *The History of Sir Charles Grandison* (1, 7), part II, p. 211.
133 *Clarissa* (1, 1), vol. II, pp. 245–6.
134 *The History of Sir Charles Grandison* (1, 7), part II, pp. 503–4.
135 ibid., pp. 500–1.
136 ibid., part III, p. 235.
137 ibid., p. 311.
138 ibid., p. 270.
139 *Pride and Prejudice*, ch. 48.
140 Anthony Trollope, *The Warden* (1855), ch. 8.
141 John Ruskin, *Arrows of the Chase*, 1880, vol. I, *Letters on Art*, part III, 'Pre-Raphaelitism'.
142 See pp. 179, 189–90.
143 George Eliot, *Daniel Deronda*, chs 3, 18.
144 *The Golden Bowl*, ch. 26; see also p. 27.
145 Mrs Gaskell, *Cousin Phillis*, part II.
146 ibid., part IV.
147 *Tess of the d'Urbervilles*, ch. 35.
148 Charles Dickens, *Barnaby Rudge*, ch. 42.
149 *Bleak House*, ch. 58.
150 Quoted in Leon Edel's Introduction to *The Spoils of Poynton*, London, 1967, p. 23.
151 Sir Walter Scott, *Guy Mannering*, ch. 13.
152 Charles Reade, *Hard Cash* (1863), ch. 37.
153 Thomas Hardy, *The Mayor of Casterbridge* (1886), ch. 18.
154 Joseph Conrad, *The Secret Agent*, ch. 5.
155 *Guy Mannering*, ch. 13.
156 D. H. Lawrence, *The Rainbow*, ch. 14.
157 D. H. Lawrence, *Women in Love*, ch. 27.
158 See p. 28.
159 D. H. Lawrence, *Kangaroo* (1923), ch. 4.
160 *Women in Love*, ch. 27.
161 See pp. 179, 189–90, 259.
162 Charles Dickens, *A Christmas Carol* (1843), Stave 3.
163 *Our Mutual Friend*, ch. 12.
164 *Dombey and Son*, ch. 9.
165 *Bleak House*, ch. 6.
166 Charles Dickens, *The Old Curiosity Shop*, ch. 22.
167 Charlotte Brontë, *Villette* (1853), ch. 41.
168 *Deerbrook*, ch. 15 (my italics).
169 Nikolaus Pevsner, *North Somerset and Bristol*, Harmondsworth, 1958, pp. 468–9.
170 Charles Dickens, *Great Expectations*, ch. 25.
171 *Victorian Architecture* (1, 55), p. 102.

172 *The Decoration of Houses* (5, 69), p. 3.
173 See N. H. H. Sitwell, *The World the Romans Knew*, London, 1984, pp. 6–7.
174 See p. 98.
175 See pp. 93–4.
176 See Arthur Raistrick, *Buildings in the Yorkshire Dales*, Clapham, 1976, p. 42.
177 Charles Dickens, *The Battle of Life* (1846), part II.

Index